PEOPLES OF THE WORLD

Asians and Pacific Islanders

PEOPLES OF THE WORLD

Asians and Pacific Islanders

Joyce Moss • George Wilson

The Culture, Geographical Setting, and Historical Background of 41 Asian and Pacific Island Peoples

FIRST EDITION

Gale Research Inc. • DETROIT • WASHINGTON, D.C. • LONDON

Joyce Moss
George Wilson

Gale Research Inc. staff

Coordinating Editors: Linda Metzger, Victoria Coughlin

Production Director: Mary Beth Trimper

Production Associate: Catherine Kemp

Art Director: Cindy Baldwin

Keyliners: Nicholas Jakubiak, C. J. Jonik

Camera Operator: Willie Mathis

The paper used in this publication meets the minimum requirements of American National Standard for Information Sciences—Permanence Paper for Printed Library Materials, ANSI Z39.48-1984. ♾™

ISBN: 0-8103-8866-9

Printed in the United States of America
Published in the United States by Gale Research Inc.
Published simultaneously in the United Kingdom
by Gale Research International Limited
(An affiliated company of Gale Research Inc.)

The trademark **ITP** is used under license.

10 9 8 7 6 5 4

Contents

Preface

A long cultural development, isolation from the West, and separation from each other over the largest of the world's continents has made Asian cultures diversified and different from those of the West. As the Asian societies restructure and increasingly participate in the world economy, there is a growing need to understand the background and current activity of this large group of peoples.

Perhaps 8,000 years ago Asia had begun to develop societies of farmers who settled in communities along the great rivers of this largest continent of the world—the Indus River in present-day India and its extension into the five-river region that gave the north its name, Punjab; the Yellow River in northern China, the Yangtse River in central China, and various large rivers of the southeast. The people there developed written scripts based on ancient languages such as Sanskrit. As the societies grew, they developed their own languages and began to create great literature to express the views of religious leaders. Poetry became an almost universal form of oral, then written, expression. The ancient Indian Vedas, and the Mahabharata set out belief patterns and moral codes that endure today, even though they were created before and during a golden age of Asian philosophy more than 500 years before the Common Era. In the 500s B.C., Buddha, Confucius, and Laozi defined other enduring religious and philosophic beliefs.

Isolated from the West except for occasional visitors such as Marco Polo, and later dominated in many regions by European colonists, the Asian people struggled for independence in the first half of the twentieth century. They succeeded with the aid of the large emerging forces of Communism. A stream of political changes has followed. Asian countries form and reform governments as they develop economies that will one day rank this area high among the world's economic powers. Already Japan, Korea, and Taiwan have taken their places as world leaders in manufacturing and marketing. Other countries, for example Laos with few resources of its own, are searching for a way to join in the world economy.

Asia is a part of the world little understood by the West. Although two main forces, India and China have helped to shape the face of Asia, time and distances have divided the people. Languages and religions vary greatly from those of Europe and America; art forms are unique; and customs and traditions set Asians apart from Europeans and from each other. This largest continent is a mosaic of differing economies, resources, and interests. The various pieces of the mosaic demand increasing attention as they grow in influence on world economics and world thought.

Acknowledgements

The authors are particularly indebted to Dr. Francesca Bray, Professor of Anthropology, University of California at Los Angeles, who read and added valuable information and accuracy to the manuscript. We are grateful to the following people who contributed to the research and writing of various sections of the book:

Shiva Rea Bailey
Colin Wells
Harbans S. Grover, AIA
Pany Sudick, PhD
David Young

A special acknowledgement is extended to Shiva Rea Bailey, Dr. W. Paul Fischer, Redlands University, Richard and Rebecca Harms, Wayne Mitchell, and David Tuch for allowing us to select photographs from their private collections. For additional illustrations, gratitude is extended to the Bishop Museum and the Smithsonian Institution. Finally, thank you to Dana Huebler for her careful proofreading.

Introduction

The year 1956 marked the 2,500th anniversary of the birth of Gautama Buddha, founder of one of Asia's great religions. This Gautama lived at about the same time as Confucius, whose teachings included what came to be known as the golden rule. At least 1,500 years before Buddha, great cities had arisen in western India and Pakistan as the capitals of established societies along the Indus River and north into the land of five rivers, Punjab. The capital cities Mokenjo Dara in the south and Harappa in the north had been laid out with straight streets, drainage systems, public baths, and private wells more than a thousand years before the building of Rome. In these ancient societies Hinduism grew to become the dominant religion of southern Asia. The Buddhist and Hindu religions along with the philosophical teachings of Confucius and Laozi (Lao tse) have guided most of the peoples of Asia to the present time.

In the east, along the great rivers of today's China, other societies arose (Yang Shao, Lung Shan). These were replaced before 1500 B.C. by the first dynasty of the Chinese, the Shang. As the Etruscan city-states were competing with Carthage in the West, the Shang Dynasty that had been in existence for 1,000 years finally gave way to contending Ch'in and Chou states. At the time that Rome was emerging as a dominant force in present-day Italy, the Ch'in Dynasty was reestablishing an Asian civilization and reorganizing it into a government by civil service.

As societies formed and reformed political entities in the south, large sections of present-day China were being organized into powerful dynasties. In 206 B.C., for example, a century before Rome began to become an organizing force in the West, the Han Dynasty organized much of China and established a rule that was to last for 400 years and lay the foundations of civil service and other policies that were to influence subsequent Chinese governments.

Far away, and practically unknown by the West, Asian societies merged, formed magnificent larger societies, and began to develop strong works of art and literature. Orderly cities and strong governments were established before Greeks and Romans began to change the face of Europe.

Asian societies, presided over by divine rulers, and governed by the powerful religious beliefs, were first jolted by the militaristic and aggressive expansions of the Western colonists of the 1600s to 1800s.

East and West. In the 1600s A.D., traders from the West began to challenge the structure of Asian empires that had been ruled by divine right and supported by the long-established religions. Portuguese, Dutch, British, French, and German invaders started to establish trade with the East and to make claims on the people of Asia. At first accepting of the Western visitors and later blocking them in a desire to continue its isolation and preserve the long-tested ways, the Asians eventually bent to the West. Great areas of the world's largest continent fell into the control of Western militant powers. In the 1700s and 1800s India became a British satellite, Hong Kong was wrested from China, and all of Indochina was being formed into a new colony by France. Meanwhile Dutch traders and military personnel had established colonies in Malaysia and Sri Lanka.

The nineteenth and twentieth centuries saw renewed efforts to throw off the yoke of European colonization. Western influences had revealed a different world, one of technology and exploitation of resources, along with new religions. Since World War II, Asians have been experimenting with patterns of government and economics that would explore the use of the abundant natural resources and, at the same time, reconcile the moral codes of the great Eastern religions with the relatively new influences of Islam and, much more recently, Christianity. Some Asian countries shaped their own forms of communism as the best hope of ridding their lands of European colonists. Now free, these countries are striving to build new and viable social structures and are revising their governments to suit the industrial world of the 1990s.

This book explores a number of distinct societies as they adjust to becoming part of a larger world economy.

Format and Arrangement of Entries

Reflecting the influences on today's Asian cultures, this book is divided into four sections—Asian Religions, Ancient Cultures, Cultures Today, and Countries Today. **The Ancient Cultures** provides a brief overview of Asia before the Common Era. This section is brief—many ancient Asian cultures have persisted so that they are included in Cultures Today. Ancient Cultures describes the societies that grew out of the great migrations to the fertile river valleys of Asia.

A single chapter attempts to describe the basic tenants of the major religions of the East—Hinduism, Buddhism, Shintoism,

Daoism and the more recent religious influences—Islam and Christianity. The mix of these religions illustrates the strength and flexibility of the early Asian beliefs. **Asian Religions** attempts to position the powerful influences of old and newer beliefs in that region today.

Organized alphabetically by people names, **Cultures Today** includes a sampling of the hundreds of societies giving color and variety to Asia. **Countries Today** provides a brief sketch of the geographic and political situation in each Asian country.

Each culture entry is arranged as follows:

- A dictionary-style definition introduces the entry, pronouncing the people's name, describing the group in brief, and furnishing the key facts of population, location, and language.
- Following this introduction are detailed descriptions under three main headings: Geographical Setting, Historical Background, and the category Culture (for the old societies) or Culture Today.
- For quick access to information, subheadings appear under main headings. The Culture Today section, for example, may include the following categories—Food, clothing, and shelter; Religion; Education; Business; Family life; and the arts. Due to the unique experience of each group, the subheadings vary somewhat across the entries. The entries in Cultures Today conclude with a section headed For More Information, which is a selective guide for readers wanting to conduct further research on the featured group.

Each entry includes a map showing the location of the society within the array of political states in Asia. Photographs illustrate the entries and assist the reader in understanding cultural differences.

In the **Countries Today** section, the country briefs include two maps, one to locate the country in Asia and another to show some geographical features and to indicate the country's relationship to some of the societies living there. The briefs contain information about population, languages, and cities as well as a description of the government of the nation and current events and issues within each country.

Other Helpful Features

A Bibliography of sources used to compile this work is included in the back matter. Although every effort is made to explain foreign or difficult terms within the text, a Glossary has been compiled to further aid the reader. A comprehensive Subject Index provides another point of access to the information contained in the entries.

The table on the following page illustrates the relationship of Asian countries to the societies described in this book.

Comments and Suggestions

Your comments on this work, as well as your suggestions for future *Peoples of the World* volumes, are welcome. Please write: Editors, *Peoples of the World*, Gale Research Inc., 835 Penobscot Bldg., Detroit, Michigan 48226-4094.

Asian Countries and Major Ethnic Groups

Country	Major Societies Within the Country
Australia	**Australians** (European), **Australian Aborigines**
Bangladesh	**Bengalis**, several hill tribes
Bhutan	Bhutanese, Lepchas, **Nepalese**, Paharias
Cambodia	**Chinese**, **Khmer**, **Malays**, **Vietnamese**
Fiji	**Fijians**, Indians
India	**Dravidians, Gonds, Gurkha, Indo-Aryans, Punjabis**, Sikhs
Indonesia	**Balinese**, Bataks, Dayaks, **Javanese, Madurese, Malays, Menangkabau**
Japan	**Ainu, Japanese**
Laos	**Laotians, Vietnamese**, various tribal groups
Malaysia	Bajaus, Bruneis, **Chinese**, Dusuns, **Iban**, Kedayans, **Malays**, Melanau, Murats, **Tamils**
Mongolia	Kazakhs, **Mongols**
Myanmar	**Burmans** (Bamars), Chin, **Chinese**, Kachin, **Karen**, Kayakhs, Nagas, **Shan**
Nepal	**Nepalese** (**Gurkhas**, Newars, Murmis, Gurungs, Magars, Kiratis, Lepchas)
New Zealand	**Maori, New Zealanders** (European), **Samoans**
North Korea	**Koreans, Chinese**
Pakistan	Baluchi, Pathans, **Punjabis**, Rajputs
Papua New Guinea	**Papua New Guineans**
People's Republic of China	**Chinese**, Chuang, **Koreans**, Miao, **Mongols**, **Tibetans**, Uigurs, Yi
Philippines	**Filipinos** (in history some 200 local groups)
South Korea	**Koreans**
Sri Lanka	Indians, Kandyans, **Sinhalese, Tamils**
Taiwan	**Chinese**
Thailand	Cambodians, **Hmong**, Lu, Puthai, **Shan, Thai**
Vietnam	**Cambodians (Khmer), Chinese**, Montagnards, Muong, Nung, Tay, **Vietnamese**
Western Samoa	**Samoans**

ANCIENT CULTURES

AINU

(eye′ noo)

Early inhabitants of the islands now forming Japan.

Population: Unknown, probably near zero. In the 1960s there were estimated to be about 300 pure-blooded Ainu still living. About that time the Ainu objected to being distinguished in the Japanese census and that procedure was stopped.
Location: Japan (the coastal area of the northernmost Japanese islands, mainly Hokkaido).
Languages: Ainu, a language most related to languages of the American Indians; Japanese.

Geographical Setting

The nation of Japan, the home of the past Ainu and a remaining few who have not been integrated into Japanese society, consists of four main islands and many smaller ones. From the south, the main islands are Kyüshü, Shikoku, Honshü, and Hokkaido. All are mountainous, volcanic islands subject to many earthquakes. The jagged coastlines provide bays and inlets that become excellent harbors. Short, rapid rivers flow from the mountains to the Japanese Sea and the Pacific Ocean.

The islands vary climatically with their distances from the equator and north pole. The southern islands and the eastern portion of Honshü are hot in the summer and cool in the winter, with heavy rainfall during the year of sixty to eighty inches. The temperatures and rainfall are more moderate on the Pacific Ocean coast of Honshü. The northernmost island, Hokkaido, is subject to even lower rainfall amounts, twenty to forty inches a year, and more extremes of temperature.

When the Japanese migrated from the mainland to the islands more than twenty-five hundred years ago, they found all the islands inhabited by a people called Ainu, a word that means "man." Establishing themselves on the more comfortable and arable southern islands, the Japanese forced the Ainu farther north, until the last Ainu settlements remained on the island of Hokkaido.

Historical Background

For centuries, a group of people lived in near isolation on the islands that are now Japan. As the Japanese moved into the islands from the mainland, these people were pushed to the northernmost islands. Although their ancient religious beliefs show some similarities with those of Japanese, the Ainu were thus isolated and largely ignored by the the newcomers. It was not until the northern islands began to be important to mainland hunters and fishers from Russia that the Japanese became interested. Then the Ainu were absorbed into the new society and, as a result, represent a disappearing culture today.

Origin. Little is known of the origin or early history of the Ainu. They have no written language, and no art objects have been found to reveal their history. Possibly part of a great Caucasian group who inhabited most of Northern Asia long ago, the Ainu may have come to their present homeland from the north, crossing the Tsugaru Strait from Hokkaido to the other islands. In what is now Japan, they established themselves among the earlier pit-dwellers and are thought to have inhabited most of the area of all the Japanese islands at one period of time.

As the Japanese moved into the area about A.D. 1000, the Ainu were driven north, back across the Tsugaru Strait, to their present location on the northern islands of Japan. There they were left nearly alone until the close of the eighteenth century, when Russian hunting and fishing drew the attention of the Japanese to the northern region. The Japanese shogun (chief military leader) then claimed the area but took a lenient attitude toward the new northern subjects. The Ainu, once reputed to have been fierce warriors, showed themselves to have become docile, indifferent citizens. In the nineteenth century, the Japanese colonized the Ainu island of Hokkaido. Japanese settlers moved onto the most fertile land, driving the Ainu into barren areas and at one point barring them from farming, wearing the traditional straw hats, or speaking Japanese. They survived on the coastal areas of the northern islands by hunting, fishing, gathering wild plants and carrying out minimal gardening.

Perhaps because of their relative anonymity, or their lack of Mongoloid characteristics, or a past policy of never shaving, myths have risen about the Ainu. They have been described as an exceptionally hairy people, for example. Yet in spite of some differences in appearance, habit, language, and earlier beliefs that they may have been related to the Australian aborigines, the Ainu are not unlike the Japanese immigrants to the area. The Ainu of the twentieth century have mixed freely with the Japanese so that now there may be as few as three hundred remaining full-blooded survivors.

Culture

Appearance. In the past, Ainu men and women could be seen in the traditional dress, a robe spun from the bark of the elm tree, or in winter cloaks, leggings, and boots of animal skin. Both men and women cut their thick, wavy hair shoulder length and were fond of earrings made first of grapevines, then of materials traded from the Japanese. Men typically had full beards and women wore blue moustache-like tattoos around their mouths. Recently, the younger Ainu have espoused Japanese ways. Tattoos are now rarely seen even on members of the oldest generation, and the ancient dress is giving way to Western clothing. Young Ainu have, for the last half of the 1900s, been eager to discard Ainu styles and adopt Japanese ways. The few remaining Ainu can be identified by their short, blocky stature and by a complexion that is more nearly like a tanned European than that of a Japanese.

Food, clothing, and shelter. The Ainu in the early twentieth century lived in reed-thatched houses with mats serving as the only flooring or furnishing. The single room was multipurpose, with a fireplace in the center on which the family cooked a meal consisting mostly of boiled meat or fish. A door faced toward the west and a window was placed so that it opened to the east. The house served as both residence and temple. To the east were the mountains of Japan and the beginnings of the great rivers. The east-facing window was therefore sacred. No one was allowed to look in through the window or to shadow the view of the sacred mountains and waterways.

Wild fruits, berries, nuts, seeds, leaves, shoots, roots, and bulbs were gathered by the Ainu women for food. To this, the men added wild game. But the most important food for the Ainu family was gathered from the sea. Fish, sea mammals, and shellfish were gathered

An Ainu family and their home. *Courtesy of the Smithsonian Institution.*

by damming streams, or fishing with hooks and lines or nets from stream edges or in ocean-going boats. Early in their existence on the islands, the Ainu had learned to carve boats from logs. The food gathered by either hunting, scavaging, or fishing was most often prepared for eating by boiling.

Robes resembling heavy bathrobes held at the waist by a belt were worn by men and women, and were sewn from a cloth made by weaving the inner bark of the mountain elm. The men's robes were calf length, while those of the women were nearly ankle length. Under these robes women wore a chemise and men a loincloth. Leggings of bark or bark cloth protected the legs, along with boots of leather or salmon skin. As the Ainu associated with their Japanese neighbors, these items gave way to clothing like that of the Japanese, such as girdles and embroidered cloth coats.

Family life. Within this house, the family organization was highly structured. Seating for meals was assigned, even for visitors. Men wielded the authority in the old Ainu house. Property was inherited by the sons, except for household articles passed from mother to daughter. Girls did not inherit property even if there was no son; in that case the man's property fell to the husband of his oldest daughter. Men hunted and fished while women planted crops, gathered fuel, searched for wild fruits and vegetables, prepared the food, tended the fires, drew water, and made barkcloth and woven clothing.

Bride and groom decided to marry, without arrangements by the parents. But the parents arranged the wedding. The two fathers would share drinks of saki and exchange old swords. The bride prepared millet cake which she shared with the groom, and the groom shared saki with the bride. After the wedding, bride and groom made gifts for each other, and the marriage was complete. A prosperous Ainu man could take more than one wife, with the first wife ruling over the later ones. Each couple hoped to have children, but infant mortality was great, and families remained small.

Oral literature. Until the Japanese established schools, the Ainu had no written history. They did, however, have a strong oral tradition. Over time, Ainu in different parts of the islands came to speak such different dialects that they were unable to communicate, except in an ancient version of the language used for storytelling. Stories were told and retold in Ainu families in this ancient language. Stories tell of many floating worlds, with the "Ainu world" resting on the back of a giant fish. The wiggling of the fish explains the earthquakes of this region. There was little evidence that the pre-Japanese Ainu had developed other arts. Few signs of artistic interest exist except for an ornate stick used as a moustache lifter to aid in eating.

Language. The Ainu language was not related to any other known language but might be most akin to some languages spoken by American Indians. The Ainus used some 14,000 words, which were arranged in a very fixed pattern to form sentences. Measurement among the Ainu was equally simple, using such measures as a step or a span, and not including measurement of weight or area. The Ainu language did provide for counting, using a system based on 20 that ended at 800.

Religion. A supreme deity was said to rule over this world assisted by moon, sun, water, and monster gods who travel on a river that is the Milky Way. But the services of worship most noted by visitors were paid to the bear, an animal believed to have descended from the sky to rescue the Ainu during a great famine. Despite its significance in worship, the animal was hunted and eaten by the Ainu.

The Ainu religion also differed from others in its lack of spiritual leaders, or priests. A village chief or even the senior male of a household could perform essential religious ceremonies. Such ceremonies center on *kamui*, spirits that inhabit all parts of the natural world.

Thus every object in the environment was thought to have its own divine owner. Kamui Fuchi was known as the Supreme Ancestress of the Ainu people. Aeoina, the first ancestor of the Ainu and the being who taught them to fish and hunt, was near to being the supreme god of these people. The Ainu were very religious and prayed often to these specific gods. In some places, the Ainu religion was shamanistic. The shaman was not in office by right of heredity. Rather each shaman was believed to have been called to the duty in his youth. The religion was also heavily reliant on fetishes. The *inao*, a partially whittled willow wand, was a particularly important fetish set up wherever the spirits were likely to gather.

Government. Now subject to Japanese law, the Ainu were once governed by hereditary chiefs. The whole Ainu land was loosely divided into three governing regions within which each village was ruled by three chiefs, although even these chiefs had little power. Day-to-day management was left to the father of each family except when questions involved the entire group. Later, government and judicial matters were separated. Village elders sat in panels to judge criminal acts and to mete out punishment, which most often took the form of beatings—even for crimes of murder.

Integration. Today integration between communities of Ainu and Japanese has been nearly completed. Less than one hundred Ainu villages remain and the old Ainu culture is largely maintained as a tourist attraction. The customary practices of the people are rapidly disappearing—giving way to Japanese traditions and Westernizing influences.

For More Information

Hilger, M. Inez. *Together with the Ainu: A Vanishing People.* Norman: University of Oklahoma Press, 1971.

Murdock, George Peter. *Our Primitive Contemporaries.* New York: Macmillan, 1934.

Tasker, Peter. *The Japanese.* New York: E. P. Dutton, 1987.

DRAVIDIANS

(dra vid′ ee uns)

Peoples of many groups who have lived for more than four thousand years in southern India and northern Sri Lanka (Ceylon).

Population: Unknown.
Location: The hill country and mountain areas of southern India and northern Sri Lanka.
Language: Dravidian, of which Tamil, Telugu, Tulu, Gondi, Oraon, and Malayalam are modern dialects that have evolved into distinct languages.

Geographical Setting

South of the Vindu Mountains and the Narbada River, the country of India narrows into a long peninsula dividing the Indian Ocean from the Bay of Bengal. Mountains and hills throughout this region are broken by many stream-cut valleys. A narrow coastline on the west rises to a range of low mountains, the Western Ghats. These are joined in the south by the Eastern Ghats, curving along the eastern side of the peninsula and separating a central hilly area from the flat and fertile coastline. The coastal flat land extends into northern Sri Lanka over a series of islands that nearly form a landbridge between that island country and the mainland.

Historical Background

When the Indo-Aryans moved into the region of present-day Pakistan and India and followed the rivers to the Indus River valley, the Ganges River valley, and then southward, they found the land occupied by tribes of darker-skinned and often shorter people. Whether these people were those sometimes called Dravidians (although this name is most often given to a group of similar languages of southern India), who were driven south by the Indo-Aryans, or whether they were longtime residents of southern India is not known. At any rate, the various groups known to speak the Dravidian dialects had been settled in the southern India hill country since before the Indo-Aryans arrived and had established agricultural and trade communities. The agricultural communities cleared from the extensive forests in the region and often were not permanent. Rather, many of the farming people cleared land of trees and bamboo, farmed it for a few years, and then move on to other land cleared from nearby forests.

Culture

As the Indo-Aryans worked their way south from the Indus and Ganges valleys, they found people organized into great kingdoms, divided by wealth, land features, and varied, but related, languages. Andhras, Cheras, Cholas, Pandyas, and others were highly civilized societies whose customs varied greatly from those of the invaders.

Religion. Each kingdom or set of villages had its own set of gods who protected and looked upon the citizens. One frequently venerated god, Murugan, was the god of the hills. Another, Shiva, was a violent god. The universally accepted gods were joined by local gods who were favored and prayed to at totem-like shrines built of logs or stone. Each person was thought to be a dual person with a *shade*, or spirit, associated with a body until death. Thereupon, the shade took up residence in the village area and was free to intercede in village affairs (see GONDS).

Economy. Early records of the people of the south indicated that they were agriculturists, but that large and attractive cities had been developed as trade centers. In some areas jewels, gold, and pearls were gathered and traded. In others, prosperous cotton-growing grew into cotton-processing and cloth-making enterprises. Some Dravidians constructed ships in which they traveled throughout the east in search of commerce.

Open society. The Indo-Aryan/Hindu tradition of castes did not exist among the Dravidians. Rulers and religious leaders were held in high esteem, but were spoken to as equals. Women enjoyed much personal freedom and independence as well.

Language. That the Dravidians easily adopted Indo-Aryan ways has tended to obscure their beginnings. The single most conspicuous symbol of their common origin is the language. The various people of the south spoke and wrote in various dialects of Dravidian, and this language does not seem to be related to Sanskrit or any other of the Asian languages. Later in their history, the various groups began to write in an alphabet called Vatteluattu. The language of the Tamil, Tulu and Telugu peoples are the most widely used versions of the Dravidian language today and the Tamils have an extensive ancient literature (see TAMILS).

Hinduism. The Indo-Aryans introduced the ideas of the Vedas and of Hinduism to the Dravidians by absorbing much of the old religion. Dravidian gods were accepted, renamed, and added to the array of Hindu gods. And since Hinduism was not a religion that prescribed a fixed lifestyle on its believers, it was easily adjusted to include local customs. As centuries of contact between the two groups continued, the foreign idea of castes was introduced to the southern tribes.

For More Information

Aijar, R. Swaminatha. *Dravidian Theories.* India: Southeast Asia Books, 1989.

Bright, William. *Language Variations in South Asia.* London: Oxford University Press, 1990.

Dasqupia, K. K., et al, editors. *Studies in Ancient Indian History.* India: Southeast Asia Books, 1988.

INDO-ARYANS

(in′ do air′ ee uns)

Early migrants from the regions of the Black and Caspian seas to India.

Population: Unknown.
Location: At first the valley of the Indus River, later the valley of the Ganges River and all of northern India.
Language: Sanskrit.

Geographical Setting

Long ago, the region that now includes Pakistan, India, Bangladesh, and part of Burma was a separate continent. The collision of this continent with the great land mass of Asia is marked by the highest mountain ranges in the world, the Himalayas. In the far north of India, these mountains become a swirl of twisted and torn ranges, the Hindu Kush. More mountains extend roughly southward from the Hindu Kush through Pakistan. Far to the south, as India narrows into a peninsula in the Indian Ocean, an east-west mountain range divides India and makes the southern tip of the country ruggedly hilly and mountainous. Waters from the Hindu Kush gather to form the Indus River, which flows through Pakistan, creating a wide and fertile valley before it empties into the Arabian Sea. Similarly, the waters of the Himalayas gather into many streams that form the Ganges River in another great valley. The Ganges stretches to the Bay of Bengal and forms part of the boundary between Bangladesh and India. It is in these river valleys that some of the earliest human societies developed.

Historical Background

As early as 3000 B.C., the Indus Valley was the dwelling place of people who farmed the land and lived in mud and thatch houses organized into villages. About 1500 B.C., Caucasian people, possibly migrating from the Russian steppes near the Black and Caspian seas, began to enter the Indian subcontinent. In a few hundred years, these "Aryans" had began to replace or assimilate the earlier residents of the Indus valley. Gradually, they expanded their land until they reached the Ganges River. Beyond the Ganges, mountains again blocked the path and the Aryans began to occupy all the land that is now Pakistan and India except for the southern end of the Indian peninsula.

Culture

Language and literature. As they expanded their area, the Aryans broke up into tribal units. At first they had no written language and no cities. A family counted its wealth only in the number of cattle it kept. The tribal head, often the one with the most cattle, was called rajah. As the Aryans spread across the north, they formed small kingdoms. Separated by land features and frequent wars between the petty kings, the peoples of the kingdoms developed different customs and languages.

Gradually, these languages borrowed from earlier Indian languages and the union was established as a formal written language, Sanskrit, before the fourth century B.C. Earlier poems in this language spoken and perpetuated by bards, were gathered into the *Vedas*, tales of early religion, philosophy, and magic. India's longest early poem, *Mahakhayavad,* tells of the struggles between the tribes and small kingdoms. A subsection of this poem called *Bahgavad-Gita* tells of the responsibilities of men of that time. These tales originated in what is called the Vedic Age (1500–800 B.C.). During this period, society was at first simply structured—divided only into nobility and commoners—but the principles laid out in the Vedas became common practice and formed the basis for Hinduism with its multitude of castes.

Castes. But even this early, Aryans were encountering earlier inhabitants of different physical appearance and becoming concerned with maintaining the purity of their race. The early distinction between nobles and peasants grew to separation between peoples of different appearances and educations. In the next historical period, written of as the Epic Age (900–500 B.C.), small kingdoms arose along the upper Ganges River. Warfare between states was common and the people had begun to protect themselves by living in cities surrounded by moats and walls. In this period, too, the caste system became established. Some claim that the original system for distinguishing people of different languages, customs, or positions included the five castes that remained until British efforts disrupted the caste system in the nineteenth century A.D. Other researchers claim that the five described were never really part of the array of two or three thousand castes that developed among the Indian people. At any rate, it appears that the early Indo-Aryans placed a warrior class at the top of their rankings, followed by priests, then traders, farm workers, and finally a group of outcasts. Shortly, however, the writings of the Vedas evolved into Hinduism and the dominant class became the Brahmans (Hindu priests) rather than the Kshatriyas (warriors).

Religion. The early Indo-Aryan tribes venerated an array of gods, each tribe with its own ranking of the gods and with its own special gods. These gods were celebrated in prayer and with sacrifices of animals. One popular god, India, was a rebel god who threw thunderbolts, ate bulls, and could drink vast quantities of wine. The ancient religion came to teach of a life after this earthly one in which each person was assigned by the gods to eternal punishment or bliss.

The idea of many gods carried over into Hinduism and allowed this religion to incorporate other local beliefs by adding more gods to the array. In Indo-Aryan Hinduism, there was an immaterial force permeating and uniting all things on earth, Brahman. Within this encompassing force, the god Atman stood as a supreme soul. The soul of every person was with Brahman. The religion taught that the material things of life tended to distract us from the force of Brahman and that distraction due to material things causes pain. Relief from pain could come only from awareness of the oneness of all things in Brahman, and that awareness grew through experience. Reincarnation was a means for adding to the earthly experience, and working to perfect oneself under an eternal moral law, karma. Thus the purpose of life was spiritual rather than physical, freeing the soul by becoming one with Brahman.

As Hinduism grew, Brahman was given creator status and was joined by other gods such as Vishnu, the preserver, and Shiva, the destroyer.

Food, clothing, shelter, and protection. The Indo-Aryans probably lived in houses built of mud, with clay floors and thatched roofs. In the great river valleys they divided their work between the earlier herding life and agriculture. Indo-Aryans in northern India grew grains along with vegetables and fruit and raised cattle. While they occasionally ate the meat of cattle and horses, mostly they lived on the milk of their animal along with barley cakes, fruits, and vegetables. Their clothing consisted of a shawl and a piece of cloth wrapped around the lower body to form a long skirt.

The early kingdoms fought often among themselves and with the people into whose land they were migrating. Indo-Aryan warriors fought with bows and arrows, spears, chariots, and protective armor. The people gathered in villages to share protection and land. Most often, the villages were clusters of houses shared by related families that divided their work and income. Women played important roles in the village, sometimes serving on the ruling village council. Some of these villages became walled fortresses, and by the Epic Age, some of them were carrying out a thriving trade with the people of Mesopotamia.

Continuity. Other great centers of civilization in Egypt and Mesopotamia experienced a decline and then an interruption before a new civilization developed, so that the societies in Iran, Iraq, and Egypt today have little in common with the ancient ones. Contrarily, the Indo-Aryan societies developed patterns that, while incorporating other societies such as the Dravidians of the south and east, continue today. Village life, the caste system, the flexible Hindu religion, and the joint family (extended families pooling their economic resources) formed the basis for the modern Indian society.

For More Information

Dattu, Amaresh. *Encyclopedia of Indian Literature*, India: Asia Book Corp., 1987.

Masica, Colin P. *The Indo-Aryan Languages*. London: Cambridge University Press, 1991.

NOTE: For information about other ancient cultures that have persisted until today, see MONGOLS, CHINESE, and KHMER in Cultures Today.

ASIAN RELIGIONS

RELIGIONS OF ASIA AND THE PACIFIC ISLANDS

Of the five major world religions (Hinduism, Judaism, Buddhism, Christianity and Islam, in order of age) two—Hinduism and Buddhism—originated and evolved in Asia. Judaism, Christianity and Islam, by contrast, originated from common roots in the Middle East, evolving largely in the Mediterranean area at first. Of these Middle Eastern religions, Islam spread most successfully to Asia, but most countries have significant Christian populations. Christianity has largely replaced traditional religions in the Pacific Islands. Small numbers of Jews are found in some countries, particularly Australia.

Other religions included in this entry are Sikhism, Jainism, Taoism, Confucianism, and Shintoism.

Geographical Setting

Generally, Hinduism is prevalent in India, Islam in Pakistan, Bangladesh, and parts of southeast Asia, and Buddhism in east Asia and parts of southeast Asia. (Despite Islam's Middle Eastern origins, it has more followers in Asia than in the Middle East; Indonesia has a greater Islamic population than any other country.) In China and Japan, a religious person most often combines Buddhism with aspects of native religions (Confucianism and Taoism in China, and Shintoism in Japan).

In Australia and New Zealand, descendants of white settlers practice Christianity, which has been adopted by various native peoples throughout the Pacific Islands. However, some of these peoples continue to practice animist religions, or blend such native traditions with elements of Christianity, Islam, or Buddhism.

In the following rough guide, countries in which each religion's adherents comprise a majority are given in italics. The numbers given are estimates only.

Asian Distribution of Major Religions

- Hinduism: *India* (650,000,000); *Nepal* (17,000,000).
- Buddhism: *China* (unknown, but perhaps 300–600,000,000 of China's 1,000,000,000 people observe elements of Buddhism and Taoism); *Thailand* (55,000,000); Japan (20–50,000,000); *Vietnam* (perhaps 20,000,000); *Cambodia* (6,000,000); *Laos* (3,500,000); *South Korea* (8,500,000); *Mongolia* (2,000,000).
- Islam: *Indonesia* (150,000,000); *Pakistan* (115,000,000); *Bangladesh* (100,000,000); *Malaysia* (11,000,000); large Muslim communities exist in Central Asia and China, with significant minorities in Sri Lanka, Myanmar (Burma), Thailand, and the Philippines.
- Christianity: *Philippines* (50,000,000); Indonesia (20,000,000); *Australia* (15,000,000); South Korea (8,500,000); *Pacific Islands* (6,000,000); China (6,000,000).

Hinduism

Historical Background. The religion of India, like the country itself, takes its English name from the Indus River in the northwest corner of the subcontinent. Around this river valley arose a sophisticated city culture, which flourished from about 2500 B.C. Sometime after 2000 B.C., this Dravidian culture was gradually overcome by invaders from the northwest, the lighter-skinned, taller Aryans. Hinduism and Indian culture subsequently emerged from the melding of the two ethnic groups. (For an overview of Indian history, see PUNJABIS, BENGALIS, and TAMILS.)

Aryan traditions, dating from before their arrival in India, survive in the *Vedas*, the Hindus' oldest religious texts. These ancient stories were probably compiled between 1500 and 800 B.C. The *Upanishads*, compiled between 800 and 300 B.C., comment on philosophical questions raised in the Vedas: the origins of man and the universe, the relationship between man and the divine, and the nature of death. The *Puranas,* or Epics, are the Hindus' third group of sacred texts, most important of which are the *Mahabharata*, or Great India Story, and the *Ramayana*, or Story of Rama. Best known is the *Bhagavad-Gita*, or Song of the Lord, a small section of the Ramayana that tells of the god Krishna. The Mahabharata and the Ramayana were composed by about 400 A.D., by which time Hinduism had spread from the north throughout all India. Other Puranas continued to be composed into the Middle Ages.

Hinduism has been reformed in modern times, especially in regard to its most controversial teaching, which divided society into castes, or levels. Thousands of castes (the names and numbers varying by region) developed over the centuries. However, there have been four basic ones. At the top of society are the *Brahmans* (priests), followed by the *Rajas* and *Kshatriyas* (rulers and warriors), the *Vaishya* (artisans and merchants), and the *Shudra* (servants). At the very bottom of society are the untouchables, who traditionally perform menial tasks. Separation between the castes has been rigid in the past. For example, members of the different castes in theory were prohibited from eating with each other. Such divisions have been discouraged and somewhat diminished under India's modern government. Much of society continues to observe them to some degree, however.

Belief and practice. Hindus believe that the soul is immortal, reappearing over and over again in human, animal, or vegetable form. Whether the soul is reincarnated in a higher or lower state depends on *karma* (good works); if one behaves well, one is reincarnated on a higher level, if badly, on a lower one. A Hindu's ultimate goal is *moksha*, or escape from the cycle of reincarnation. Karma entails respect for human and animal life, and many Hindus are vegetarians. None eat beef, as the cow is venerated in the Hindu society. This tradition and others are expressed in *dharma* (the way of life, or duty). Other aspects of dharma describe the children's duties towards their parents (obedience, respect) and the parents' towards their children (protection, feeding, education). The wealthy also have an obligation to help those less well off.

There are many types of Hindu holy men who practice *yoga* (discipline). *Hatha* (force) yoga consists of bodily discipline, such as breathing control and physical exercise, while *Raja* (royal) yoga develops mental concentration. Yoga masters claim mind-over-matter powers, such as levitation or the ability to walk on burning coals.

Hindus worship a large number of gods, but each is ideally viewed as a different aspect of a single god, *Brahman*. Thus, *Brahma* (the creator), *Vishnu* (the preserver), and *Shiva* (the destroyer) represent Brahman's various roles. Vishnu is widely worshipped and is thought to have appeared in ten forms or *avatars*, most important of which are *Rama* and *Krishna*. Each of these gods also has a wife, who is assigned a special province. Brahma's wife, *Saraswati*, is goddess of wisdom and learning; Vishnu's wife, *Laxmi*, is goddess of wealth and luck; Shiva's wife *Parvati* (also worshipped as *Kali*) is associated with destruction and rebirth.

There are many minor gods and goddesses; a Hindu is free to choose which god he or she likes best. Most, however, worship either Vishnu, Shiva, or Parvati. Worship takes place at home or in any of the thousands of temples scattered throughout the land. The temples are large, beautiful, and elaborate stone structures—often architectural masterpieces dating back hundreds of years. Most are dedicated to a single god. They are built on holy places, chief among which is the city of Varanasi, on the Ganges River, which is also considered holy. Hindus believe that washing in the Ganges will cleanse them spiritually; huge festivals are held regularly in which millions gather to wash in the Ganges.

Buddhism

Historical Background. Buddhism also arose in India, founded by an Indian named Siddhartha Gautama, who lived in the 500s B.C. Gautama was born to a wealthy Kshatriya family in northern India near the border of present-day Nepal. At the age of 29, he renounced his wealth, left his wife and young son, and wandered the countryside in search of spiritual enlightenment. After many trials and disappointments, he came to a tree—the Bodhi Tree, or Tree of Enlightenment—and decided to sit there, reflecting on the universe until he reached the deeper awareness he sought. Reach it he did, and from then on he was called the Buddha; he taught a growing number of followers, establishing communities of monks and nuns in northern India and southern Nepal.

In the 200s B.C., Buddhism was adopted by Asoka, ruler of the Mauryan Empire, the first state to encompass most of modern India, Pakistan and Bangladesh. With Mauryan support, Buddhist monks spread their message throughout India and Sri Lanka. In following centuries, the monks brought Buddhism to southeast Asia, China, and Japan, where it evolved and still prospers today. Though popular in India for over 1,000 years, Buddhism eventually waned there in the face of a Hindu revival and Muslim invasions.

Belief and practice. Like Hindus, Buddhists believe in karma, but they do not associate it with reincarnation. Instead of an immortal soul that reappears in different forms, Buddha taught that there is no soul but a universal one, no constant "I." Rather, every person is reborn from moment to moment, with karma shaping these constant rebirths. The sense of an "I" is created by our grasping desire, which is also the source of all suffering. Extinguish desire, and suffering ends as well. The extinction of all desire is called *nirvana* ("blowing out," as in blowing out a candle).

Buddhists similarly took the idea of *dharma* from the Hindus, changing it subtly also. For Buddhists, dharma denotes what is called the Middle Way, by which one avoids extremes of self-denial and self-indulgence. The Middle Way leads to the Eightfold Path, which in turn aids in attaining nirvana. The Eightfold Path consists of eight steps in self-discipline: Right View, Right Resolve, Right Speech, Right Action, Right Livelihood, Right Effort, Right Concentration, and Right Contemplation. The last and most advanced step involves meditation, central to a Buddhist's life, in which he or she achieves inner calm through quiet reflection.

Buddhism has evolved in two directions. In Burma, Thailand, Cambodia, and other parts of southeast Asia, Buddhists follow *Theravada*, the Way of the Elders, while in Nepal, Tibet, Vietnam, Korea, Japan, and China they follow *Mahayana*, the Great Way. Theravada Buddhists strive for nirvana, in emulation of the Buddha himself. Mahayana Buddhists hold a further goal, that of the *bodhisattva*, one who has reached nirvana but delays salvation in order to help others in their suffering. Such compassion for others is viewed as the greatest virtue. Out of Mahayana Buddhism grew Zen Buddhism, practiced in China and Japan. While many common people observe elements of Buddhism in their daily lives, it is the monks who pursue nirvana with the utmost devotion. They are highly visible in many countries, with distinctive orange or yellow (saffron) robes, and often rely on gifts of food in order to eat.

Islam

Historical Background. Founded in Arabia by Muhammad (A.D. 572–632), Islam spread rapidly following Muhammad's death. By the 700s, conquering Arab armies had established an empire extending from Spain to India. By about A.D. 1000, leadership of the Islamic world had passed to the Turks, originally a nomadic people from Central Asia. From around 1000 to 1250, Turkish armies conquered much of northern India. As a result, large Islamic populations live there today, particularly in Pakistan and Bangladesh, Islamic states which broke off from Hindu India in modern times. Over the following centuries, Islam spread to Southeast Asian countries such as Indonesia and Malaysia. It is also practiced by Turkish minorities in China and Mongolia.

Belief and practice. Muslims, as the followers of Islam are called, believe that Muhammad was the last of a line of prophets, viewing him as a successor to the Jewish prophets of the Old Testament and to Christ as well, whom they accept as a prophet but not as the son of God. There are basic beliefs of the Islamic faith:

1) There is but one God (Allah) and Muhammad is his prophet;
2) Prayer is to be said five times a day, with the prayer-sayer turned in the direction of the holy city of Mecca, in Saudi Arabia;
3) The faithful should be generous to the sick and poor;
4) Healthy adults should fast during daylight hours in the ninth month of the Muslim calendar, called *Ramadan*;
5) Every able Muslim should make a pilgrimage (*hajj*) to Mecca at least once.

Islam's sacred book, the Quran (Koran), is believed to be the word of God as revealed to Muhammad. Muhammad exhorted his followers to spread this word throughout the world and to gather together in holy war (*jihad*) against those who opposed them.

Christianity

Historical Background. Christianity spread rapidly after Christ's death, around A.D. 30, and eventually (by the 300s) became the official religion of the Roman Empire. In A.D. 1054 the Christian Church split into two halves: Roman Catholicism in Western Europe, and the Orthodox Churches in the Eastern Mediterranean. Then in the 1500s, the Protestant Churches split off from Roman Catholicism.

Christianity spread eastward throughout Asia in the first several centuries after the time of Christ. In southern India, communities of Syrian Orthodox Christians claiming to have been founded by the Apostle Thomas exist today, though the earliest surviving evidence for their existence dates from the 400s. Nestorian Christian missionaries reached China in the 600s. Christianity did not begin to spread significantly in Asia and the Pacific Islands, however, until the age of European expansion. Beginning in the 1500s, European missionaries established Catholic and Protestant missions throughout the East. In the 1700s and 1800s, these missions worked hand in hand with the colonial governments that ruled much of the region. The Philippines, under Spanish rule for over 300 years, is Asia's most predominantly Christian country, but significant minorities exist in most countries. While missions converted large numbers, especially in the islands, the influx of European settlers to Australia and New Zealand in the 1700s and 1800s also contributed to those countries' Christian majorities. The Aborigines in Australia and the Maori in New Zealand, as a result, are mostly Christian today.

Belief and practice. Christians believe that Jesus Christ, whose deeds are recounted in the New Testament, is the Son of God and that he came to earth to cleanse the sins of humankind. Catholic and Protestant churches alike believe in spreading this belief by sending "missions" aimed at converting non-Christian peoples. There are more Roman Catholics than Protestants in Asia, but that is because of the Philippines' majority of Catholics (45,000,000, to 5,000,000 Protestants). Outside of the Philippines, more of the Christians are Protestant. In the Pacific Islands, including Australia and New Zealand, there are about 14,000,000 Protestants as compared with 8,000,000 Roman Catholics.

Confucianism and Taoism (Daoism)

Historical Background. Confucianism has often been called more of a philosophy than a religion. Its founder, known in Western countries as Confucius (551–478 B.C.), was certainly more like Socrates than like Buddha or Muhammad. By asking questions of his students, he evolved a set of beliefs to guide social interactions. His beliefs, recorded in his writings such as the *Lun Yu* or *Analects*, did not become influential until the 100s B.C., when Chinese rulers began to incorporate them into the government. Eventually, Confucian ideas came to dominate the emperor's powerful civil service, and rigorous examinations on his writings remained the standard test for entry into the civil service until modern times. Confucian temples are devoted to the worship of a clan's ancestors.

Taoism was founded by Lao Zi, a mysterious figure believed to have lived about the same time as Confucius. He is supposed to have written the classic of Taoist thought, the *Daode jing* (The Way and Its Power). Taoism later became associated with a number of gods and with the practice of magic. Where Confucius analyzed interaction among men, Taoism emphasizes harmony between man and the universe. These two complementary movements both opposed Buddhism at first and then partly merged with it. Buddhism first gained a wide following in China in the A.D. 600s.

Belief and practice. Religion, but not the Confucian philosophy and the practice of ancestor worship, has traditionally been frowned on by the Chinese government. The officially atheist Communist regime that has ruled since 1949 extended its disapproval to Confucian beliefs and practices. Religion is officially viewed as an unscientific holdover from the past. Nonetheless, many continue to observe elements of traditional religion, particularly those to do with magic or the many Taoist gods. Zen Buddhism incorporates elements of Taoism, in that it seeks enlightenment through harmony with nature. This sort of religious mix characterizes Chinese religious practice, which tends to be inclusive rather than exclusive. Asian religions are flexible and can easily incorporate elements of other beliefs. Thus, many temples are dedicated to Confucius and Buddha as well as to a Taoist god.

Shintoism

Historical Background. Buddhist monks, arriving in Japan from China in the 500s, called the native religion *Shen-Tao*, the Way of the Gods, as opposed to the way of the Buddha. Shinto and Buddhism soon grew intertwined. Shinto had become the religious path through which the emperor derived the divine right to rule. Over the centuries this idea was viewed with varying intensity. When Emperor Meiji was restored to power in 1868, State Shinto, the worship of the emperor, was imposed by the government. In contrast, the popular form of the religion, called Sect Shinto, included the worship of the traditional gods, as well as the incorporation of Buddhist elements. State Shinto ended in 1946, when the emperor publicly denied his own divinity.

Belief and practice. Shinto deities are generally nature gods, chief among them being the sun goddess Amaterasu (from whom the emperor was believed to have descended). Others are connected with storms, mountains, the ocean, food, or fertility. Shinto shrines were at first simple wooden structures but were made more ornate after the arrival of Buddhism. State Shinto was associated with virulent nationalism; Sect Shinto has tended to focus more on the individual's spirituality. Faith healing has been a popular theme among the sects.

Sikhism

Historical Background. Sikhism arose in the Punjab, in northwest India, and was founded by the Guru (teacher) Nanak (1469–1539). Combining aspects of Hinduism and Islam, Nanak preached a strict moral code to groups of *sikhs,* or disciples. Nine gurus succeeded Guru Nanak, each adding new elements to the Sikh code. In the face of persecution by Islamic rulers, the last Guru, Gobind Singh (1675–1708), transformed the Sikhs into what amounted to a military brotherhood. During the 1700s, the Sikhs struggled against a weakening Islamic grip on power. In 1799, under the leadership of a warrior and statesman named Ranjit Singh, the Sikhs established a state that included the Punjab and surrounding areas. Today, about 14,000,000 Sikhs live in India.

Belief and practice. Sikhs proclaim one God, with Guru Nanak as his teacher. The *Adi Granth* (first book) is their sacred text and includes verse by Hindu and Muslim poets, as well as by Nanak and other Gurus. Taking ideas from both Hinduism and Islam, Nanak defined a religion with one basic tenet: that there is only one God, and He is our Father; therefore, we must all be brothers. The brotherhood of Sikhs, the Khalsa, is identified by the five K's followed by Sikh men: kesh (uncut hair), kanga (a comb worn in the hair), kirpan (a sword), kara (a steel bracelet), and kachk (shorts worn as underwear).

Sikhs believe they should always remember God and share what they earn with less fortunate ones. Sikh temples include a langar, or free kitchen, where needy people of all religions can find food and often free rooms in which to rest. The Sikh's most holy place is a golden temple at Amristar, set in a manmade lake. This temple was the subject of great concern in recent years as Indian militia invaded it in search of rebellious Sikhs.

Jains

Historical Background. The Jains, numbering about 4,000,000, follow an ancient religion that possibly predates Hinduism. They claim that their faith was laid down by 24 *jinas* (conquerors), the last of

The following chart compares beliefs of the major religions of Asia.

	Theravada Buddhism	Mahayana Buddhism
Human problem	suffering	suffering
Founder	Gautama	Gautama
Life's goals	attainment of nirvana	attainment of nirvana
Sin	external acts	external acts
Buddha	saint	savior
Jesus	teacher	possible possessor of Buddhahood
Muhammad	teacher	possible possessor of Buddhahood
Supreme being	existence irrelevant	concept of god is irrelevant
Salvation	man saves himself	faith in Buddha and personal effort in right thinking and good deeds
Life after death	none	pure land: heaven
Chief virtue	wisdom	compassion

Hinduism	Islam	Christianity
suffering	sin	sin
unknown	Muhammad	Jesus Christ
moksha—release from the cycle of rebirths	eventual entry into paradise	heaven, communion with God
violence, breaks with nature, deviation from caste behavior	failure to submit to God's will	internal disposition external acts
may be included among manifestations of god	world religious leader	world religious leader
teacher	an early prophet	unique manifestation of God, savior
teacher	last prophet of God	world religious leader
one God in various manifestations	God in one presence only	one God in a trinity of manifestations
performing according to one's own place in the universe	strict adherence to the laws of God	following the teachings of Jesus
rebirth at different levels until attainment of moksha	life in various degrees of heaven	eternal life with God or in exile
nonviolence, oneness with nature	charity	love

whom lived about the same time as the Buddha. Like the Buddha, Mahavira (Great Man) attained spiritual enlightenment and established a following of monks and nuns.

Belief and practice. Jains worship their 24 jinas rather than a God. Like the Buddhists, they believe that the individual can reach nirvana by renouncing desire. The best-known Jain belief is *ahimsa* (harmlessness), which holds that all life is sacred, and that one should take no life, even by accident. Jain monks sweep the ground before they walk to avoid walking on any insects and wear gauze masks to avoid inhaling them. Jain nonviolence has inspired non-Jain leaders such as Mahatma Gandhi.

Animism and Cargo Cults

In the Pacific Islands, as in China and Japan, new religions have often blended with older, traditional beliefs. Animism, in which natural objects are endowed with divine powers, is sometimes mixed with Christian, Muslim or Buddhist beliefs. Agama Java, observed on the Indonesian island of Java, is classified as Muslim but contains strands also from animism, Hinduism, and Buddhism. In Australia, the Aborigines, Christian in name, still use traditional ideas such as totems and supernatural entities. Priests and chiefs in Polynesia and New Zealand are still believed to possess *mana* (supernatural power). In Pacific Island cultures, "Cargo Cults" arose when Western commerce led charismatic leaders to preach that immeasurable cargoes would be delivered to them by supernatural means. Seventy such cults existed in New Guinea alone.

For More Information

Bunge, Frederick M. *Oceania: A Country Study*. Washington, DC: United States Government Printing Office, 1984.

Haskins, James. *Religions*. Philadelphia: J. B. Lipponcott Co., 1973.

Kanitkar, V. P. *Hinduism*. New York: Bookwright Press, 1986.

Snelling, John. *Buddhism*. New York: Bookwright Press, 1986.

The Far East and Australasia 1992. London: Europa Publications Ltd., 1991.

CULTURES TODAY

ABORIGINAL AUSTRALIANS

(ab uh ridg′ ih nul aw strayl′ eeuns)

Indigenous peoples of the subcontinent of Australia and nearby islands.

Population: 230,000 (1990 estimate).
Location: Australia.
Languages: English and 300–500 Aboriginal languages and dialects.

Geographical Setting

The Aboriginal Australians occupied the entire island continent of Australia before the arrival of white European settlers in the late 1700s and are today represented by at least 260 clans spread across the continent. Approximately as large as the continental United States, Australia lies in the southern hemisphere, with Southeast Asia to the north, the Indian Ocean to the west, the Pacific to the east, and the Antarctic to the south. Its western half consists of a desert plateau divided into the Great Victoria Desert in the south and the Great Sandy Desert in the north. Desert conditions continue farther east, in the Northern Territory and South Australia, where Aboriginal Australians occupy massive government reserves of land. Here, in the center of Australia, is Ayers Rock, Australia's most famous natural feature and an emblem of the Aboriginal Australians' religion and culture. To the north, east of Darwin, is Kakadu National Park, included on the World Heritage list for its ancient Aboriginal cave paintings. In eastern Australia, landscape ranges from patches of tropical rainforest in northern Queensland to scrubland and coastal mountain ranges.

While eighty percent of Australia's seventeen million whites live on the southeastern "Boomerang Coast"—the coastal string of major

cities from Brisbane to Adelaide—the Aboriginal population is more evenly distributed across Australia. In the past, many lived on government settlements and reserves, such as those in central Australia, considered undesirable by the whites. In recent years, the Aboriginal land rights movement has led to the reclaiming of some ancestral lands, where increasing numbers have resettled.

With the exceptions of some coastal areas, most of Australia is hot and dry. In over 70 percent of its area, annual evaporation exceeds annual rainfall.

Historical Background

Prehistorical arrival. Archaeologists believe that the Aboriginal Australians' ancestors migrated into Australia about thirty to fifty thousand years ago. During this time, the last Ice Age of the Pleistocene Era, much of the earth's water was locked up in polar ice caps. With sea levels thus about 400 feet lower than today, Australia and New Guinea were one large landmass. Many of the islands north of Australia were joined to the Asian mainland, or separated from each other by narrow channels. It is thought that the Aboriginal Australians' ancestors came south from Asia, island-hopping on primitive boats or bamboo rafts. From Timor or Indonesia, for example, they might easily have been blown to Australia's northwestern shores.

Unique isolation. In no other part of the world has such a large area been occupied continuously by culturally similar groups of peoples. In contrast to the wars and migrations of Africa, Europe, Asia and the Americas, Australia for tens of thousands of years developed in near total isolation. This isolation not only separated the Aboriginal Australians from other parts of the world, but also isolated various groups on the continent. The result was the development of a large number of clans, speaking their own languages and developing similar but varied cultures. Just as unique forms of animal life—most notably the marsupials–evolved out of this isolation, so did a unique human society. A third consequences arose: Australia possessed no native plants or animals suitable for domestication. Elsewhere in the world agriculture gave rise to pastoral nomadism or cities, but the Aboriginal Australians remained tribal hunters and gatherers. Their culture also remained non-literate. Without writing skills, the people developed a detailed, sophisticated mythology linking them to each other and—equally important—to the landscape.

European invasion. Dutch, Portuguese, and Spanish ships sighted Australia in the 1600s, and the Dutch made several landings in the 1600s and 1700s. In 1770, the British explorer and navigator Captain James Cook claimed the island continent for the British. In 1788, the British set up a penal colony at what is now Sydney, eventually settling over 160,000 convicts there. Other British, Irish, and European settlers followed, as Australia passed into British colonial rule and eventual white-ruled independence in the 1900s.

Population decline. The settlers viewed the Aboriginal Australians' land as unclaimed territory, open for their own use. They brought sheep and cattle, fencing off large tracts of land and disrupting the Aboriginal Australians' supplies of game. Some used the Aboriginal Australians as a cheap labor supply, as "stockmen" on the cattle or sheep ranches. Most often, however, the whites simply drove them away or killed them. When the Aboriginal Australians resisted, they were no match for the armed and mounted new settlers. Those who didn't resist were either exterminated outright—gunned down, hanged, and poisoned—or pushed into an aimless existence on the fringes of new settlements. Many thousands fell victim to diseases brought by the immigrants, such as smallpox, against which they had no natural defenses. From an estimated 750,000 in 1778, the number of Aboriginal Australians declined to perhaps 40,000 by 1900. The Aboriginal Australians of Tasmania, related to those of continental Australia, were wiped out completely.

The dying pillow. By the mid-1800s, the colonial government had adopted a plan to protect the Aboriginal Australians from the most brutal of the settlers. "Native homesteads" were established, at which Aboriginal Australians from a particular region were collected on reserves of about ten square miles. Christian missionaries set up stations to assist the Aboriginal Australians, attempting to convert them to Christianity as well. While small numbers managed to cling to their old ways, most became dependent on government-supplied food and clothing. Many whites believed that the Aboriginal Australians were becoming extinct. In talking about them, whites often used the phrase "smooth the dying pillow"—that is, make the Aboriginal Australians' "deathbed" a comfortable one.

Changing attitudes. Beginning in the 1920s and 1930s, white attitudes slowly began to shift. Anthropologists, in studying the Aboriginal Australians and writing about them, passed on a greater understanding of their culture to many other Australians. Improved health services led to stabilization and then increases in the numbers of Aboriginal Australians and part-Aboriginal Australians. In 1948, the Australian government abandoned the policy of segregation and protection. Instead, education, health, and employment programs were set up to assimilate the Aboriginal Australians into the general population. Yet the Aboriginal Australians' leaders objected to this well-meaning approach, pointing out that it would mean the end of their ancient culture.

Activism. In the 1960s and 1970s, a movement began among Aboriginal Australians to reclaim land rights and to reassert their cultural identity. The federal government returned thousands of square miles in the Northern Territory (which it administers directly) to the Aboriginal Australians who lived there. Such "inalienable" title to lands means that in designated areas the Aboriginal occupants control mineral and development rights to the land. In other areas, notably the states of Queensland (where over 25 percent of the Aboriginal Australians live) and Western Australia, state governments have prevented similar measures from being enacted. During the 1980s, powerful mining interests, allied with state governments, succeeded in stopping the federal government from further extending land rights. Yet Aborigine leaders, having come of age politically in recent decades, continue to press for greater rights for their people. Their culture, now the subject of popular books and television specials, has become more familiar to the white population. Most important, the Aboriginal Australians themselves have begun successfully to explore ways of coexisting with white culture without being absorbed by it.

Culture Today

The Dreamtime. The Aboriginal Australians' profound attachment to their ancestral lands can be traced to their cultures' ancient core: the concept of Dreamtime. In the far distant past, according to the traditional belief, spirit ancestors of all humans, animals, and natural objects inhabited the earth. During the Dreamtime, they stirred themselves and undertook great journeys across the landscape. On these journeys, the spirits created animals, waterholes, plants, rivers, mountains, rock formations—all the natural features of the land. Finally, they created the Aboriginal Australians to enjoy and respect the fruits of their efforts.

Songlines. Each ancestor's journey—his exact route, as well as all his actions along the way—is recounted in a special song and handed down through generations. There are thousands of such journeys, and they crisscross the landscape like a fine web—or like a roadmap. At each stop on the journey lies a sign—a rock, a cave, or some other geological feature—associated with an episode of the ancestor's battles or adventures. Nearly every natural feature of the landscape lies along one of these "songlines" or "dreaming tracks." Each feature has a verse or verses, which usually tell the story of how it was formed by the ancestor. A well-educated adult would be familiar with territory he or she had never visited through a wide knowledge of different songs. Because the songlines (also called "dreaming tracks") often wind from one side of the continent to the other, they cross many tribal and linguistic barriers. Though the words of the song change, each songline retains its own recognizable tune from beginning to end.

Many peoples, similar cultures. In the past, the songlines acted as a communication network linking different areas together through the common backdrop of the Dreamtime. Each area was occupied by a group usually called a clan, with its own distinctive language or dialect. The clan areas varied greatly in size, and boundaries between the clans were flexible. Often nearly adjacent groups did not immediately understand each other's language, but most adults learned to speak the languages of two or three neighboring clans. The Aboriginal Australians are still known for their linguistic skill.

Some well-known clans are the Aranda, Bidjandjara, Dieri, and Wailbri of Central Australia and the Gagadju and Tiwi of north Queensland. Once, there were probably 700 to 1,000 clans, averaging perhaps 1,000 members each. Members of each group were semi-nomadic within their area, moving in small family units to follow seasonal food supplies, traveling with little baggage and pitching temporary camps. Clans in harsh areas like the Western Desert needed large territories; in more lush areas such as the coasts or the forests of Queensland, food was more plentiful, clans more numerous, and their areas smaller. Today many clans have ceased to exist, their territory fully settled or claimed by other Australians. Even among those remaining, clan links have weakened as a settled lifestyle has almost entirely replaced the wandering of the past.

Religious links. Aside from family and tribal membership, each Aboriginal Australian has a totemic "Dreaming," a communication about the spirit ancestor from whom he or she is descended. The totem is often an animal—for example, the wallaby, which is like a small kangaroo. If asked about Dreamings, an Aboriginal man or woman might say that he or she has a Wallaby Dreaming. In most cases, he or she would not be allowed to eat wallabies, who are his brothers. They are descended from a common ancestor, the spirit Wallaby of the Dreamtime. The Aboriginal Australian would also be related with members of other clans who have the same dreaming or dreamings.

Food, clothing, and shelter. Traditional songs also acted as libraries of detailed knowledge about hunting and food-gathering techniques. The meat most commonly eaten has been kangaroo, wallaby, and emu, a large flightless bird. Dozens of smaller animals—birds, turtles, lizards, or possums, for example—are also caught and eaten. In coastal areas, fish and shellfish have enriched the Aboriginal Australians' diet.

An Aboriginal Australian family and their camp. *Courtesy of the Bishop Museum.*

Grass seeds are collected and pounded to make flat cakes; yams, nuts, berries, and fruits such as peaches, plums, and figs all grow wild in the bush. Meats are usually lightly cooked. Fruit can be eaten on the spot or dried. A well-known delicacy is the witchetty grub, a caterpillar larva said to be especially tasty when lightly toasted.

In the past, Aboriginal Australians wore little or no clothing, aside from a strong belt of braided hair, which was used to carry tools or weapons, with perhaps a loincloth of hide or treated bark. Men's gear included a spear with a wooden sling or spearthrower, a shield, a small "dilly bag" for bits of food and other items, and perhaps a stone ax or a wooden boomerang. (The boomerang, a wooden throwing weapon curved so that it returns to the thrower, is a traditional hunting tool.) Women's gear might comprise a larger dilly bag (for gathering seeds or fruit), a digging stick, a shallow wooden dish, and a sling for carrying babies or small children. Body decoration is traditionally important. Earrings, nose pegs, and decorative scars have been common. For religious rituals, mythological designs are smeared on the body in colored clay or ochre, and elaborate costumes incorporate feathers or leafy branches. While such costumes may still be used, most Aboriginal Australians today wear European-style clothing and are becoming integrated into the multicultural Australian mainstream. Shorts and a T-shirt are common, as are long pants and boots for stockmen.

Traditional shelters were simple, usually consisting of a few timbers lashed together and covered with branches, most often acting as a windbreak or sunshade. When more solid structures were built—huts of dried mud on timber frames in South Australia, or bark huts on stilts in wet, northern Arnhemland—they were used just for sleeping or storage. For the most part, life was lived outdoors. Today, housing is a major issue for Aboriginal Australians. Dispossessed of their old lands and lifestyle, many became squatters on derelict land, living in makeshift shelters built out of discarded materials. Though some government programs have provided modest homes, many still live in poverty-stricken conditions on rural "reserves" or in city slums.

Family life. Traditional family life stresses education, cooperation, and mutual support. Children spend most time with their parents, but are also cared for by a wide number of other relatives and family friends. Older children spend much time playing together. Education is traditionally informal and continuous, as the parents constantly increase the child's knowledge about society and the natural world. Women have generally been responsible for collecting small animals, shellfish, seeds, and fruit, while the men hunted larger animals and fish. For girls, adulthood is a gradual process, as a girl is progressively introduced to the women's social and religious duties. Men come of age more abruptly, undergoing harsh physical trials and periods of isolation. Aboriginal Australian families have been severely disrupted by the influence of the larger Australian culture. For decades, children in poor Aboriginal families were taken from their parents by force. Other families simply disintegrated with the cultural collapse that came with the loss of ancestral lands.

Religion. Rooted in the Dreamtime, Aboriginal religion pervades virtually every aspect of traditional daily life. It weaves totemism, myth, ritual, and magic into a sophisticated belief system, offering a guide for any situation likely to arise. The largest and most significant religious ceremonies are the male initiation rites. When a number of boys are ready to be initiated, several clans will gather at a sacred location. In the past, preparation for the ritual might last for weeks or even months, as might the ceremonies themselves. During them, members of various totemic clans would share their songs or enact various myths and legends. Finally, the boys would undergo physical trials such as circumcision, after which they would be sent into the wild on their own. When they returned, they would be accepted as men. Such rituals, now sometimes modified, remain important for Aboriginal Australians who live even partly within their ancient traditions.

Literature and the arts. Aboriginal Australians are reputedly fine storytellers, whether drawing on their own vast body of traditional myths and legends or relating events that happened to them or to others. Myths and songs often explain the origins of animals, of natural objects, of clans, or of social customs. They vary widely among different areas. Many have a moral, teaching proper behavior. Others tell of epic adventures in mythical lands or encounters with spirit creatures. One common theme is of battles with giant kangaroos or other animals, which archaeological evidence shows to have lived in Australia in the prehistoric past.

Aboriginal Australian art has gained wide recognition, commanding high prices in galleries around the world. The paintings are

Aboriginal Australian bark painters from an area near Darwin.
Courtesy of the Bishop Museum.

done on bark, using thick "paints" of colored ochre mixed with plant and animal materials. They use circles, dots, straight lines, and arcs to tell the story of an ancestral being's journey. They are visual interpretations of the songlines. Since the 1970s, Aboriginal painters in central Australia have continued this traditional style in the Desert Painting Movement. Centered in the area around Alice Springs, the movement has not only brought international recognition, but has also helped pass on the old traditions to children and others who had lost the old culture. For tens of thousands of years, Aboriginal Australians have also painted on cave walls and other rock surfaces. The Obiri rock paintings in Kakadu National Park, home of the Gagadju and Kunwinjku peoples, date back perhaps 30,000 years or more. Included in the World Heritage List, they have been called humanity's oldest surviving creative achievement.

Renaissance. It has been said that the Aboriginal Australians' traditional life is doomed to extinction. Apparently a small proportion have maintained old ways. A slightly larger proportion, who never gave them up entirely, have begun to rediscover their heritage after centuries of interaction with whites. The largest proportion, however,

Aboriginal Australian artists perform dances wearing traditional paint. *Courtesy of Rebecca and Richard Harms.*

manifest no cultural ties. They have, according to one Aborigine, no dreaming. Living on the fringes of towns, many turned to alcohol.

Today there is a a renaissance in the population. As Aboriginal Austalian artists have shown by their success, cultural continuity can exist despite the abandonment or modification of old ways. After 200 years of racism, oppression and discrimination, the Aboriginal Australians have only recently begun to salvage the possibility of such continuity. Much has been lost, but much remains of their heritage. Despite continued white racism, the 1980s brought hope to many Aboriginal Australians. Their official numbers increased from 160,000 in 1982 to 227,000 in 1987—reflecting not so much a higher birth rate as a greater willingness to declare Aboriginal ancestry. One important outlet for this newfound pride is the Outstation Movement of the Northern Territory. There, Aboriginal Australians have set up cattle stations on land won in the 1970s, where hundreds of people are able to support themselves. Like the Desert Painters, they follow elements of the traditional life, yet live successfully in the modern world.

For More Information

Chatwin, Bruce. *The Songlines.* New York: Penguin Books, 1987.

Isaacs, Jennifer. *Australian Aboriginal Paintings.* New York: Dutton Studio Books, 1992.

Pilger, John. *A Secret Country: The Hidden Australia.* New York: Alfred A. Knopf, 1991.

AUSTRALIANS

(aw strayl′ eeuns)

People, mostly of European ancestry, living in Australia.

Population: 16,806,730 (1989 official estimate).
Location: The continent of Australia and surrounding islands, the largest of which is Tasmania. Australia lies southeast of the Malay Peninsula and its related islands. The country also includes the Keeling (Cocos) Islands, 27 largely Malay-populated islands in the Indian Ocean that elected to join Australia in 1984, and islands lying in the strait that separates Australia from New Guinea.
Language: English.

Geographical Setting

Lying in the southern hemisphere about as far south of the equator as northern Mexico is north of it, the island continent of Australia forms a country about seven-eighths the size of the United States. For the most part the land is desert or bushland. In the north, the desert gives way to savannah (grasslands). Around the edges ranges of mountains rise in the east, west, and north. Mountains also dot the interior of the desert land. The mountains drop abruptly to the ocean in many places, helping to form a rugged coastline that is interrupted by fewer than a dozen harbors suitable for seagoing ships. There are few rivers and none of great length in Australia. In fact, one explorer walked 1,200 miles along Australia's south coast without crossing a single stream.

Most of the Australians live in the southeast and east, where the climate is moderate and rainfall suitable for growing a wide range of crops. In this area are the large port cities of Melbourne, Sydney, and Brisbane. A second population concentration is in the southwest,

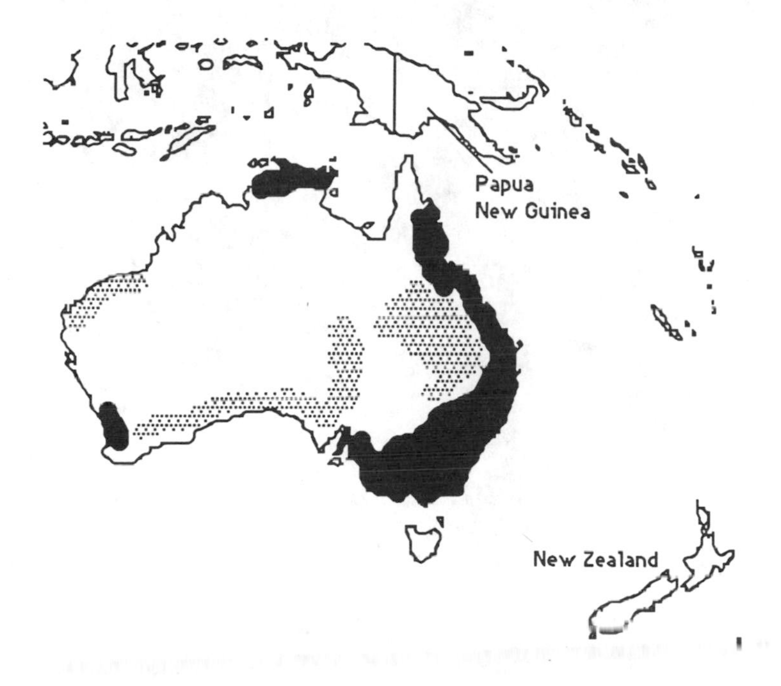

centered at Perth. In this area there is also a flat plain between mountains and sea and with moderate rainfall and temperature variations. A low and level area in the southeast is separated by the central peaks of the Petermann Ranges from a higher western land that is mostly desert. The northwest is a mostly uninhabitable sandy desert. In the southeast, Australia is separated by the Bass Strait from the island of Tasmania, once populated by the same aboriginal people as the main island. Between the Australian continent and the island country of Papua New Guinea lies the Torres Strait, named after an early explorer of the area. Many small islands dot this strait and are part of the country of Australia. About 27,000 people live on these islands and the nearby continental coast. Like the Australian Aborigines, the Torres Strait Islanders have their own unique culture.

Historical Background

Before Europeans. Fifty million years ago, Australia was connected to the Asian mainland through landbridges of which Malaysia and Indonesia are remaining parts. Animals that were common to southern Asia inhabited the Australian island-to-be. Gradually erosion

Some animals of Australia are unlike those on any other continent.
Courtesy of Rebecca and Richard Harms.

wore away the landbridge, isolating Australia at the foot of a series of stepping-stonelike islands. In their isolation, the animals and plants of Australia evolved into unique species. Where mammals developed to fill many niches in Asia and other parts of the world, marsupials filled these niches in Australia.

Across these islands about 40,000 to 60,000 years ago came people from Asia bringing the only animal they had succeeded in domesticating, the dog. They also brought skill with stone and wood tools and weapons, and in hunting and gathering food. These nomadic people had little knowledge of village structure or of agriculture. The early settlers formed into many small kin groups (clans) to roam the vast island continent, hunting insects and small marsupials and gathering wild plants for food. Over the years they refined their tools, perfecting the *boomerang* and another hunting weapon, the *woomera*. At the time the first Europeans reached Australia (Dutch sailors in 1606) there were about 300,000 of these nomadic hunters spread throughout the land.

Much of inland Australia is brush and desert, some of it dotted with termite mounds. *Courtesy of Rebecca and Richard Harms.*

First Europeans. On August 23, 1768, Captain James Cook landed at a bay near present-day Sydney that he called Stingray Bay and which later became Botany Bay. Although Captain Cook claimed the land for his native Great Britain, little was done with it until Joseph Banks, a representative of the British Royal Academy, proposed that Botany Bay be used as a penal colony. Britain sorely needed more space to house prisoners. British law of that time made it a major crime to steal as little as ten cents by force or one dollar by stealth, and the prisons were bulging with prisoners with little hope of release. By 1788, fifteen hundred prisoners and others had embarked on the trip to Australia under the supervision of a British navy captain, Arthur Phillip. Captain Phillip landed near Sydney and decided on Sydney Cove rather than Botany Bay for his penal colony. Seven hundred thirty-six convicts (188 of them women), 17 children, 211 marines, and 19 of their children established the first colony. Before the policy of exiling prisoners to Australia ceased in 1840, about 160,000 British prisoners were to be sent to penal colonies.

Penal colonies. Although Captain Phillip was a conscientious and considerate ruler in this first colony, he soon began to find trouble as convicts and marines squabbled over fishing and sealing rights, farmlands, and trade. Order was kept in this colony and the later ones with the aid of the lash. A disorderly convict could be sentenced to as many as 500 lashes for grumbling or for more serious crimes. Nevertheless, the British penal colonies prospered, and others, hearing of opportunity in the new land, also booked passage from England. By 1820 colonies were prospering along the southern and western coasts, and by 1830 German settlers had joined the British in new colonization, bringing along sheep.

In the 1840s, the use of Australia as a site for British penal colonies ceased. However, many of the Australians of the 1990s can claim ancestry to these early "criminals," exiled from Britain for violations ranging from stealing bread to armed robbery and rape. Almost universally these early settlers had reason to distrust and avoid the governing elements. A disdain for governmental authority endures in Australians of the twentieth century.

Gold. The 1850s brought a new incentive for migrants to the new land—gold. First found in the southeast of the colony near Sydney, the gold discovery expanded into New South Wales. In the more extreme southeast in the province of Victoria, gold brought settlers who by 1852 had expanded their base into nearby Tasmania (then known as Van Dieman's Land). New South Wales and Victoria began to organize under separate constitutions. Meanwhile, settlers had spread as squatters, claiming large portions of land throughout the southwest and west. By 1860, land claims were so muddled that the colonial governments had to intercede and arbitrarily reclaim some of the land from squatters—selling portions back to the same settlers.

Industrialization. With the gold rush over by 1870, Australians turned to industrialization, based largely on the wool of the millions of sheep that then inhabited the land. The demand for labor resulted in the immigration of 400,000 workers, many of them from Asia, between 1880 and 1890. By that time there were estimated to be 4,000,000 British immigrants to Australia. Great cities grew with industry and Australians became largely city dwellers. In 1890 almost two-thirds of all Australians lived in cities and towns. Sydney and Melbourne in the southeast both had populations of more than 500,000 by 1900.

Nationalism. Industrialization was just underway when a great depression struck Australians in the 1890s and brought the various colonies together. Common problems of stimulating growth and development began to encourage a sense of nationalism. By 1901 Aus-

Sydney is one of the large cities along Australia's eastern coastline.
Courtesy of Rebecca and Richard Harms.

The Territorial Composition of Australia

Six states—New South Wales, Queensland, South Australia, Western Australia, Tasmania, Victoria.

Three internal territories—Northern Territory, Australian Capital Territory, Jervis Bay Territory.

Seven external territories—Norfolk Islands, Coral Sea Islands, Cocos Islands, Christmas Island, Ashmore and Cartier Islands, Heard Island and McDonald Islands, Australian Antarctic.

tralians were prepared to organize into a federated nation. In that year they organized under a constitution that had been generally accepted in July 1900. Patterned after the British and American models, this constitution called for a bicameral legislation (Senate and House of Representatives) at the national level, but also provided for great responsibility for each of six "states" and three internal and seven external territories. As part of the British Commonwealth of Nations, Australians recognize Queen Elizabeth II as head of state, represented by a governor-general. However, the actual government of Australia is directed by a prime minister and a cabinet.

Economic reorganization. For much of its short history, Australia has been directed by a liberal government—until the 1970s by the

Liberal Party and then by a Labor Party. Both seemed to work on the widely held assumption that all Australians had the right to a reasonable standard of living, and that if the economy failed to provide this, the government must help. There has been much government involvement in business. Major parts of the economy—for example, the airlines—were controlled and operated by the the federal government. In the 1980s, Australians have begun to turn to private ownership of most industries.

Ethnic diversity. During the 1900s, Australia was viewed by many as a land of promise. Particularly after World War II, immigrants from Europe and Asia came to be a significant part of the population. By the 1970s, it was estimated that Australians of British ancestry accounted for only 70 percent of the population. An example that illustrates the wide cultural diversity of Australians is the population of the Keeling Islands, which was originally made up of Malay people, and later augmented by the importation of other laborers for the large plantations. These Australians live in the tropics, are mostly Muslims, and raise coconuts for export.

For much of their history, British Australians chose to hold power and to invest that power in Anglo males. Programs of equality excluded non-whites, and although women had voting rights early, they

Queenstown is on the smaller Australian island of Tasmania. *Courtesy of Rebecca and Richard Harms.*

were underserved by the government. In the past quarter century, Australians have come to recognize these inequalities and have initiated programs to integrate minorities and women into the mainstream of Australian society. An early move in this direction was the ban on sex discrimination in the work place that was enacted in 1973.

Until World War II, the population of Australia grew mostly through immigration from other British Commonwealth states. In 1945 the population was about 7,400,000. Between 1945 and 1991, the population grew rapidly to its present nearly 17,000,000. This growth includes about five million immigrants—1,790,000 from Britain and Ireland and the others from countries throughout the rest of the world. Germany, Greece, Italy, Lebanon, Malaysia, the Netherlands, New Zealand, the United States, and Vietnam have all contributed large numbers to the population of Australia. Today, Australians represent a wide diversity of heritages and cultures similar to the cultural diversity of the United States.

Culture Today

Australian qualities, real and imagined. Outside Australia, Australians are pictured mostly as the rugged, hard-pressed, and individualistic few who work the cattle and sheep ranches in the outback—the savannah and bushlands of the interior of Australia. Some of this image is justified. Australians generally believe in a society of equals, display a large measure of independence, and share a common wariness of authority. However, those workers on the large ranches of central Australia are few. A large majority of the population is made up of city people with much the same interests, ambitions, and desires as city dwellers in the Western world. Despite the desire for equality, there is a large middle class, and a substantial lower class made up mostly of non-white Australians. In other ways, Australia is a truly cosmopolitan society with roots in both Western and Eastern cultures.

One uniquely Australian custom of the past that is now waning was mateship, the formation of long-term bonds of friendship and mutual support among Australian men. Still today, men in Australia often form friendships that transcend social and economic stratifications.

Government and goals. Australians have never given up the independence of the original colonies. The six states that evolved from the colonial structure, plus three territories, enjoy considerable freedom to govern their own people under the constitution. Australia is a federation of independent states. Following the two world wars the national government saw strong growth as a step toward being a more active international power. One stumbling block not found in other Western nations was the lack of manpower. The Australian government perceived a need to increase the nation's population as quickly as possible and initiated a policy of inviting immigrants. Although this policy has been somewhat curtailed in the 1990s, about 100,000 new Australians are added each year by immigration.

The national government assumed as its responsibility "placing permanently within the reach of every one of us freedom from basic economic worries . . . " (Younger 1966, p. 663). A liberal government tried to ensure this goal by active government participation in business and industry and by an encompassing social security system. In recent years, Australians have experienced great changes as the government moved toward less government control of business and industry. Australians generally enjoy a high standard of living.

Workers shear sheep on a large station in southeastern Australia. *Courtesy of Rebecca and Richard Harms.*

Economy. World War II brought expanded industrialization to the country. Agriculture and rich mineral resources now support industries such as food processing, steel making, cement production, and chemical manufacture as well as cotton industries. Wool production and processing remains one of the most important industries (there are more than 125,000,000 sheep in Australia, 15 percent of the sheep of the world). These sheep provide about one-third of the world's supply of wool. More than half the Australian workers are employed in manufacturing (although the 1980s saw a 50 percent decline in this area), trade, and public services. Fewer than one in ten Australians work in agriculture. Larger numbers work in construction and transportation.

Food, clothing, and shelter. A large number of Australians live in single-family dwellings, built for a nuclear family of husband, wife, and children. These structures vary as widely as in other industrial nations of the West, from the frame brick homes of Sydney, which

A few of the large ranches, called stations in Australia, also serve as rest spots for tourists. *Courtesy of Rebecca and Richard Harms.*

resemble those of their ancestors in England, to the rectangular wood homes raised on pilings above the ground in tropical Darwin in the north, to homes with concrete block walls built inside caves and old mines in the mining regions.

Most Australians dress in Western-style clothing—suits, jeans, shirts, T-shirts, shorts, dresses, and gowns—that varies with the occasion and the weather.

One unique aspect of Australian life is their eating style. Australians are said to consume more calories daily than the average person in the United States. For some Australians the diet contains an average of more than 2,300 calories a day and is heavily laden with meat; the typical Australian consumes more than 210 pounds of meat a year. To eat these calories, the people generally consume three meals a day plus organized snacks. A typical breakfast might include steak and eggs. This is followed about 11:00 A.M. by tea and a pastry. A late lunch is the heaviest meal of the day: typically more meat, vegetables, and perhaps a pudding for dessert. An afternoon tea is also accompanied by pastry. The Australian's main meal is lighter than lunch but again includes meat and dessert. In addition, many Australians drink beer at various times. While the above description still holds in some areas and can be said to be an average of the past, with the post World War II encouragement of immigrants has come the introduction of many ethnic foods into the Australian diet, mostly foods of Asia. Today, a "typical" diet of the Australians cannot be described. As in other industrialized nations, Australians have become health conscious in the 1980s and 1990s and also diet conscious. This has resulted in widening the rich variety of foods that make up Australia's current food consumption.

Recreation. Australians work and play hard. Water sports such as swimming and surfing are enjoyed all along the coast. Australian interest in water is seen in the numerous life saving clubs formed for companionship and competition. Reflecting the British heritage, cricket, rugby, and soccer are popular activities as well as spectator sports. Perhaps involving an even greater number of players is tennis, which has produced international champions such as Margaret Court, Rod Laver, and the Aboriginal Australian ace, Yvonne Goolagong. One count in the 1970s listed more than 7,800 tennis clubs in Australia. Finally, nowhere in the most heavily inhabited parts of Australia is it a far distance to the bush, or wild country. Hiking in this wild area is a popular activity with many Australians.

Station homes can be large and comfortable. *Courtesy of Rebecca and Richard Harms.*

Australians also enjoy theater and opera. The opera house at Sydney stands as a symbol of the national interest in music, and is a world-famous symbol of Australian architecture.

Holidays. Australians are proud of their history and celebrate it in four national holidays. Captain Arthur Phillip landed at Sydney Cove with the first penal group from Great Britain on January 26, 1778. January 26 is celebrated as Australia Day much as July 4 is celebrated in the United States. During World War I, Australian soldiers joined New Zealanders and shipped to Europe to fight with the British. These Australian-New Zealanders were first involved in an attempted landing at Gallipoli in Turkey. Fighting against formidable odds, they established beach holds and fought bravely for several days before being forced to abandon the landing. This activity is celebrated on April 25 as ANZAC Day, the equivalent of the American Veteran's Day. From the beginning, Australia has been firmly united with Britain in the British Commonwealth of Nations. Australians recognize this tie by celebrating the birthday of the reigning British ruler. The birthday of Queen Elizabeth II is June 11.

Religion. Religion, too, reflects Australian history. Nearly one-third of the churchgoers of Australia claim membership in the Church of England. However, other immigrants to this country came from Ireland and from various countries of continental Europe. Thus, about one-fourth of the Australians are Catholic while smaller groups represent the Methodism and Presbyterianism of the European continent. Hindus, Buddhists, Jews, and Muslims add to the religious diversity of the country.

Language. The language of Australians is English, but it is an English that has evolved into its own unique dialect. It began with the cockney dialect of early settlers and has been modified by other English and other languages. Words once unknown elsewhere have been borrowed from the aboriginal natives and added to the language—for example, *boomerang, mulga*, and *kookaburra.* Other words have been abbreviated or distorted into new terms (*mosquito* has become *mozzie*, for example). Still other terms have created Australian terms for English meanings—a "smoke-oh" is an Australian work break; "strides" are trousers.

Australian English contains unique slang terms, and these terms are often in a sort of rhythm and rhyme. Thus, an earlier Australian might have referred to his wife as "me trouble and strife," or to his own suit of clothing as a "bag." However, such slang terms appear in nearly every language of the world and have been given exaggerated emphasis by such international motion picture figures as "Crocodile Dundee."

In addition to changes in standard English, Australian pronunciation has been varied so that *a* is often pronounced as *i*; *r* is sometimes not pronounced and at other times spoken when it does not appear in writing. In many places, Australians add to the distortion by abbreviating spoken words. One oft-quoted example of spoken words is "Hazzy garit non wither mare thorgan?" which elsewhere in conventional English would read, "How is he getting on with the mouth organ?" (Bone 1992, p. 105).

Literature. Early writing in novel and verse was inspired by newness of the country and its most peculiar ways of life. "The Song of a Sentimental Bloke" and "Ginger Mick," poetry of 1915 and 1916, recounted the romantic lives imagined for some Australians. These poems, written by C. J. Dennis, were read throughout Australia and replaced an older favorite, "The Bush," by Bernard O'Dowd. Following World War I, a few novelists began to write on Australian themes: Henry Handel Richardson wrote a trilogy, *The Fortunes of Richard Mahoney*, about the gold rush days; Katherine Susannah Prichard created *Black Opals* and *Working Bullocks.* The hard times of the 1930s depression fueled new styles in writing and established an Australian press. Leaders in this movement were Ion Idriess (*Last Ride*) and William Hatfield (*Sheepmates*). Stories of pioneer days and of life in the bush became popular themes, and more recently, Australian writers have begun to explore ethnic issues. Australian writing has been and is an attempt to define the unique interaction between European traditions and a new geography. Rex Ingamells defined the authors' issues:

> Inextricably interwoven with the transplanted European culture are our own experiences of Australian environment. How far we and this environment have changed and reacted through contact, we owe to self-honesty to understand, and such an understanding can arise properly only through cultural expression. (Younger 1969, p. 572)

For the most part, however, an Australian literature was born only after the various colonies agreed to form a federation in 1901 and there began to develop a sense of Australian nationalism. In this century Arthur Adams wrote *The Australians*, about life in Sydney; Sydney de Loughe wrote about Australians in the first World War; William G. Hay and Martin à Becket Boyd led the field of historical writers; and James Devaney and Dorothy Cottrell gained renown as fiction writers. More recently, Patrick White has been awarded the Nobel Prize for Literature, and the list of well-known Australian authors has grown to include:

Henry Handel Richardson
Hal Porter
Thea Astley
Peter Carey
Colleen McCullough
David Malouf
Kate Grenville
Patricia Wrightson
Louis Stone
Dame Mary Gilmore
Thomas Keneally
Morris West
Elizabeth Jolley
Beverley Farmer
Ivan Southall
Colin Thiele

Music and art. Australians enjoy a wide variety of music, from opera to rock. One performing arts center, the Sydney Entertainment

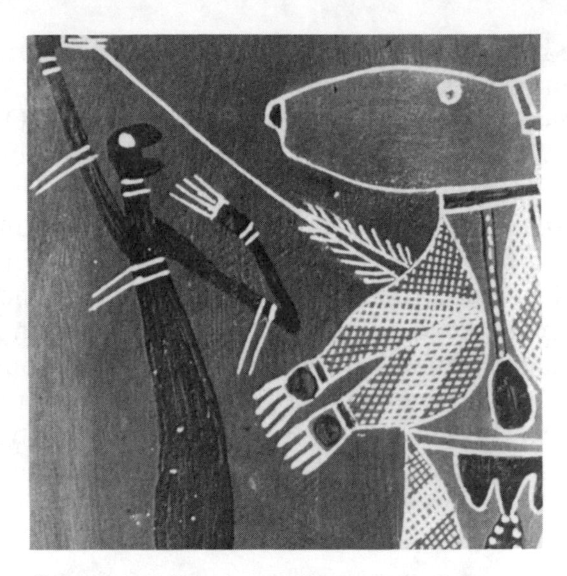

Some popular Australian art is drawn from the Aboriginal Australian designs.
Courtesy of Wayne Mitchell.

Centre, holds 12,000 people for rock concerts and other popular performances. The Sydney Opera House can accommodate an audience of 2,600. Australian tastes in music are not unlike that in other English-speaking countries, as is evidenced by the exchanges of artists. Liza Minelli and Frank Sinatra have performed at the Entertainment Centre, for example, and Australian singer Olivia Newton-John is popular in America. Perhaps the most uniquely Australian music is the bush ballad, a musical story of life in the pioneer areas of the continent. A typical ballad is the world-famous "Waltzing Matilda." Written in 1895 by "Banjo" Patterson, it is the story of a lone man who poaches an animal, is caught by the police, and commits suicide rather than face prison. This ballad so illustrates the independence and wariness of authority held by many Australians that it is sometimes proposed as Australia's national anthem.

Much of Australian art is devoted to picturing the unusual landscape of the continent and its coast, which is rimmed by a 1,200-mile-long barrier reef. Abraham Louis Buvelot, perhaps the best of the pioneer landscape artists, painted scenes in Victoria in the 1860s. Frederick Garling painted world-known marine scenes in the following decade.

As Australians became more conscious of ethnic diversity on the continent, aboriginal art began to be recognized. This art ranges from colorful cave paintings, to wood carvings, and the to most well-known items now produced for tourist attractions, bark paintings. Earlier aboriginal art includes some examples of a style termed x-ray art because of its detail of the internal structures of natural objects (see AUSTRALIAN ABORIGINES).

For More Information

Bone, Robert W. *Maverick Guide to Australia.* Gretna, Louisiana: Pelican Publishing, 1992.

Constable, George et al, editors. *Australia*, a Library of Nations edition. London: Time-Life, 1985.

Smith, Robin E., editor. *Australia.* Canberra: Australian Government Printing Service, 1992.

Younger, R. M. *Australia and the Australians.* Adelaide, Australia: Rigby Limited, 1970.

BALINESE

(ba li neez′)

People of the Indonesian Island of Bali.

Population: 2,043,119 (1990 census).
Location: Between the Indonesian islands Java and Lombok within Southeast Asia.
Languages: Balinese; Bahasa Indonesian.

Geographical Setting

Bali is one of 13,667 islands within the archipelago of the country of Indonesia located in Southeast Asia in the Indian and Pacific oceans. It is one of the smallest islands in Indonesia, with an area of 2,171 square miles. Recognized for its rich natural resources and unique cultural heritage, Bali lies east of Java, the main island of Indonesia, and west of the island of Lombok, with the Java Sea stretching to the north and the Indonesian Ocean to the south. Volcanic ranges dominate the landscape. According to Balinese mythology, the island was originally unstable. To stop it wobbling, the gods set down upon it the mountain Mahameru, the holy mountain of Hinduism. The Balinese called it *Gunung Agung* ("The Great Mountain"). It is 10,308 feet high and an active volcano which last erupted in 1963. Other mountainous volcanoes include Mount Batukau in the west and Mount Batur and Mount Abang in the central region.

The volcanic strip stretching from the east and west sides of the islands divides the island in half. The northern region of Buleleng, a narrow coastal strip, quickly merges into lush foothills and is the fertile soil that produces Bali's main exports: cattle and coffee. The rains carry fertile mountain soil down into the densely populated plains of central Bali where rice is harvested twice a year. The low

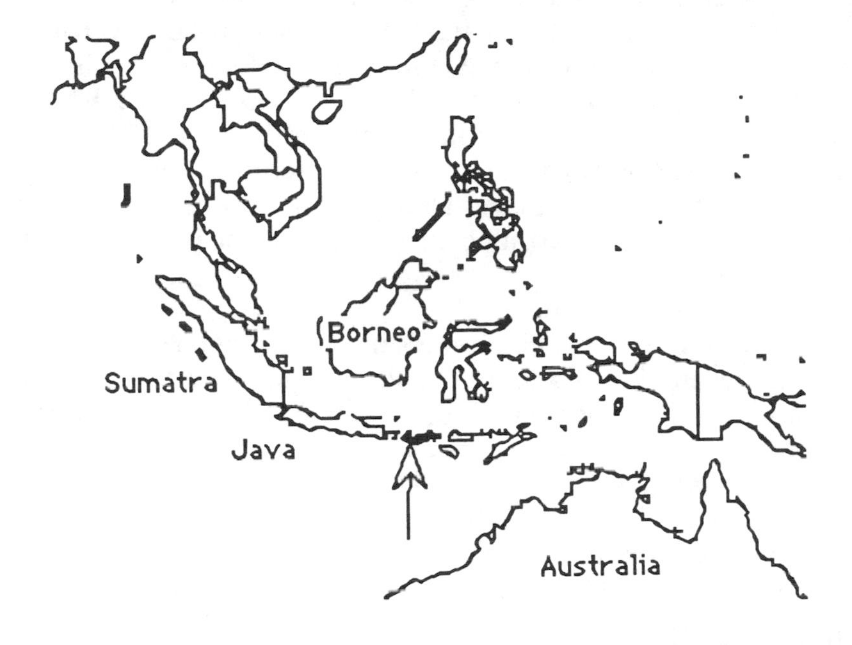

dusty brush of the uninhabited western region of Bali is known as Pulaki—the home of the invisible ones. In the south, the capital city of Denpasar lies along the coast across from the peninsula of Bukit. The eastern side of Bali is the site of Gunung Agung volcano.

Just eight degrees south of the equator, Bali has the even and warm climate of the tropics. The only noticeable change in weather is a wetter season between November and March and a drier season from June through October. The plentiful rains and rich volcanic soil provide Bali with the abundance of rice-growing terraces which dot the landscape throughout the island.

Historical Background

Early history. Archaeological records show that Indonesia was inhabited by Homo sapiens as long as ago 1,700,000 years, but these inhabitants were the ancestors of Australoid peoples such as those living in New Guinea today. The present population of Bali most likely descended from Mongolian immigrants who came to the region around 5000 B.C., pushing the original Australoid inhabitants further southeast. There is little archaeological record of the early history of

Bali until around 300 B.C., from which time the remains of burial pottery and bronze and iron implements have been unearthed. Of the present population in Bali, the oldest Balinese inhabitants are called the *Bali Aga* or "original Balinese," an isolated community of non-Hindu Balinese who live in the hills of East Bali. The primary Bali Aga village of Tenganan is shut off from the world by a solid wall that surrounds the village. These Bali Aga descendants who only marry within their village are considered to be the oldest inhabitants of the island.

Hindu penetration of Bali. Hinduism formally entered Java around A.D. 700, where there was already a long-standing trade network linking Indonesia to India and China. However, Bali did not become a vassal of the great Hindu empire until the eleventh century during the reign of King Airlangga (1019–1042) of eastern Java. Airlangga's mother, Queen Gunapriyadharmapatni, moved to Bali shortly after his birth and remarried a Balinese prince, Udayana. The two ruled Bali from about 1000–1019. They were succeeded by their two sons, Airlangga's half brothers, who formed a dynastic link between Java and Bali.

Semi-autonomy of Bali. When King Airlangga died in 1049, East Java was ruled by the Kediri dynasty. Bali, however, remained undisturbed and was governed by the descendants of Udayana. The island remained self-governing until the most powerful prince of the Javanese Singasari dynasty, Kertanagara, became king. In 1284, Kertanagara conquered Bali, but within eight years he died at the hands of a vassal. When his son later founded the dynasty of Majapahit amidst political dissension in Java, Bali temporarily gained independence. The last king of the Pejeng dynasty in South Bali, Dalem Bedalu, refused to recognize the rule of the Majapahit supremacy over Bali. In 1343, Bedalu was defeated by Javanese general Gajah Mada, who established a capital and palace for the appointed king of Bali.

The Gelgel dynasty. As the new faith of Islam lured the princes of Java to new loyalties, the Majapahit dynasty dissolved. The Gelgel dynasty arose and expanded under the leadership of its greatest ruler, Dalem Batur Enggong, who expanded into East Java and east towards the island of Lombok. With the rise of Islam, many Hindu-Javanese nobles, priests, and artisans came to Bali, the most important being

Danghynag Niratha, a Brahman priest. This religious leader became the court priest and had a profound influence on Balinese religion both at court and in the villages. The complex rituals for cremating the dead, creating offerings, and the religious language were most likely introduced at this time. The temples and palaces flourished with performances of plays, masked dances, and the melodies of the gamelon orchestra as Bali enjoyed a renaissance of Balinese culture.

The arrival of the Dutch. The Dutch arrived in Bali in 1597 and formed the Dutch East Indies Trading Company five years later to establish profitable trading relations with the islands of the Indonesian archipelago. In the beginning Bali was left to itself as it was not considered to have much economic value. Instead the Dutch concentrated their efforts on gaining control of Java and the spice island of Malukus. By the nineteenth century, the Netherlands government assumed full control of the disintegrating Dutch East Indies Company and began to colonize the islands of Indonesia. Later in that century, the Dutch government started to interfere directly into the affairs of the Balinese. In 1846, the ancient right of the Balinese to claim ship wrecked cargo that washed upon their shores brought the first Dutch military expedition to Bali. In 1882, the northern states of Buleleng and Jembrana were placed under direct administration of the Dutch government following a series of battles. A few years later, the Lombok War, in which the Balinese vassals of Lombok rebelled against the ruling princes, erupted.

Then in 1894, the Dutch sent an ultimatum to the king to pay a war fine of 1,000,000 guilders. The younger Balinese princes of Lombok rejected this plan and launched an attack on the Dutch encampments, forcing the Dutch to retreat to the sea with a loss of 100 men. When news of the defeat reached Holland, the Dutch government sent reinforcements with heavy artillery. A new Dutch offensive swept over the island, culminating in the capture of Cakra Negara, the last important city of the Balinese in Lombok. On September 20, 1906, the Dutch launched another attack on the Balinese from Sanur along the road to the present-day capital of Denpasar. Realizing that they were outnumbered in both size and strength of weapons, the three ruling kings of Denpasar sought the only honorable solution. Abiding by the warrior tradition, the kings of Denpasar led their priests, generals, and relatives, both men and women, into a *puputan*, a "fight unto death." Led into battle in a resplendent procession, one by one the Balinese warriors were gunned down by the enemy. At the end of the bloody day, the Dutch were horrified at a massacre of more than 3,600 Balinese. In 1914, the Dutch army was replaced by a police force and the government was reorganized to give rule to rajas until the political transformations brought independence.

World War II and the struggle for independence. When World War II struck Indonesia, the country was occupied by Japanese forces. Following Japan's abrupt occupation and final departure from the islands, the people refused to return to colonial rule. On August 17, 1945, on behalf of all Indonesians, national leader Sukarno proclaimed Indonesia's independence. However, it wasn't until four bloody years later that the Dutch government formally relinquished control of the islands that had been under their control for several centuries. It was during this time that the famous battle of Marga was fought in West Bali. Led by Lieutenant Colonel I Gusti Nugurah Rai, Bali's revolutionary forces refused to surrender until national independence was won. Just as the princes of early times, the Balinese commander and all of his soldiers were killed in a heroic battle, which included an air attack by the Dutch. When the Dutch officially recognized Indonesian independence at the Hague Round Table Conference in 1949, the nation was governed as a constitutional republic headed by president Sukarno.

Bali since independence. Bali has been part of the Indonesian government with its own governor and representation since that country's independence. The leadership of president Sukarno began to wane after the struggle for independence was won. In 1965, a coup involving the Indonesian Communist Party (PKI) led to a nationwide massacre of all Communists and later to Dr. Sukarno's downfall. On March 11, 1966, the Indonesian national army forced Sukarno to delegate extensive powers to his General Suharto and in 1968 he was appointed president of Indonesia. General Suharto has remained Indonesia's president into the present day. Due largely to the promotion of tourism under Suharto's leadership, Bali has become one of the most prosperous islands in Indonesia today.

Culture Today

Religion. Bali is the only Hindu island in the predominantly Muslim Indonesian archipelago. Although Hinduism originated in India, on Bali it developed its own unique form, becoming the largest Hindu outpost in the world outside of India. The Balinese worship the same gods as the Hindus of India—Brahma, Vishnu, and Shiva—although this Hindu trinity is alluded to and never seen in Bali. The basic tenet of the Balinese religion is the belief that the island belongs to the supreme god, *Sanghyang Widi,* and that the island has been handed down to the people in sacred trust. The Balinese religion divides most concepts into polarities: heaven and earth, sun and moon, day and night, gods and demons, men and women, hot and cold. The interaction of all of these pairs, working in harmony with each other, moves the world and determines one's fate. Balincse Hinduism is a form of the religion with a different caste system from that seen among Hindus in India.

To keep balance between the upper and lower worlds, and to show their gratitude to the gods, Balinese fill their lives with symbolic activities and worship. Veneration of life and the gods encompasses a wide range of art forms, from decorations on the utensils of everyday life to highly refined music and dance. Religious expression is at its height during temple festivals throughout the year. There are

Parades and processions are parts of most Balinese festivals.
Courtesy of Shiva Rea Bailey.

more than 20,000 temples on the island, each the focal point of more than 60 religious holidays a year. Every village has its own temple that is regulated by the *pemangkus* (family priests) and the high priest. Ritual and festivities regulate all aspects of life and provide a common basis within family, community, and the broader society.

Many of the temples and shrines are dedicated to deities of nature as the environment is considered the sacred manifestation of the supreme being. Abundant harvests are attributed to the benign effort of the goddess of rice and fertility, *Dewi Sri.* Divine spirits dwell in the lofty mountains; dark malevolent forces lurk in the seas. In the Balinese conception all of life is part of an ordered universe stretching from the heavens above the mountains to the depths of the sea.

The arts. It is said that in Bali everyone is an artist. Artistic knowledge, appreciation, and participation is part of the daily experience of all in the community. The artistic traditions within Bali have attracted visitors from around the world since the late nineteenth century. Central to Balinese culture, both traditional and within the present tourist industry, are both visual and performing arts. The visual arts and crafts include painting, wood carving and weaving. The performing arts include gamelon music, various dance styles, mask dance, theater, and puppetry.

Celebrations, religious holidays, festivals, private ceremonies, and large social gatherings are all occasions in which the performance of gamelon music and dance-drama is essential. The gamelon is a type of orchestra found throughout the islands of Indonesia, composed of bronze metallaphones, gongs, flutes, and drums, played by between five and forty people. Many Balinese dances are choreographed to complement the gamelon with expressive movements. Most dance forms are dramas, many based upon the Hindu epics, the *Ramayana* and the *Mahabharata.* Elaborate costumes, intricate hand and foot movement and facial expressions are characteristic of over fifty dances active on the island today. Some popular dances are: *Legong, Topeng, Wayang Wong, Cupak, Calon Arang, Arja, Kebyar, Kecak,* and *Sanghyang.* The latter is a trance dance performed by two young girls chosen from a village.

Family life. Family ties are strong and bind a person to family, community, and to the Balinese people in general. Marriage is expected of a young person as soon as that person comes of age, and children are considered to be the center of the family life. Family life in Bali is bonded by ritual ceremony that marks every aspect of a member's life. When a child is born, the umbilical cord and placenta are buried near their sleeping quarters and an altar is erected with offerings over the spot. Forty-two days after the birth, the child is blessed by a priest, and bracelets, anklets, and amulets are presented for the child to wear throughout the ceremonies of its first 210 days, one Balinese year.

By the time a child can walk, the young are left in the care of other children. Children are raised to be very independent and self-sufficiency is encouraged. At home, boys assist their fathers in the fields, in raising cattle, and in learning the father's trade. Young girls learn from their mothers how to cook, weave, thresh rice, and make offerings. An older custom that is still practiced today is the filing of teeth when boys and girls come of age. Marriage customs differ from caste to caste in Bali; however, most marriages observe the *ngrorod*, a prearranged kidnapping of the prospective bride. During the kidnapping, the couple make offerings to the gods to consecrate the marriage before the public ceremonies. A dowry of money is usually paid by the father of the bride to the groom at this time. *Masakapan* is the Balinese wedding festival which involves the whole community in its celebration. Other transitions in family life are occasions for rituals and ceremonies—the cremation following the death of a family member, for example.

Food. The staple of the Balinese diet is *nasi*, steamed rice that is served at every major meal. As the center of a meal, rice can be accompanied with vegetables, meat, dried fish or poultry, salted eggs, and *sambal*, a hot sauce made from peppers, fish paste and lime juice. Small food vendors are favorite sources of food at markets or at festivals, where they sell snacks like fried, boiled, or steamed bananas, small pieces of cake served with grated coconut, sweet rice steamed in banana leaves, sunflower seeds, and peanuts boiled in palm sugar to make a candylike peanut brittle. In Bali, fruits are plentiful: oranges ranging from the dark red to dark green, ten varieties of mangoes, several kinds of bananas, coconuts, pineapple, melons, pomelos, and mandarins. In addition there is breadfruit, rambutan, and *salak*, a pear-shaped fruit tasting like an apple.

Shelter. The typical Balinese home (*kuren*) consists of an extended family, several related families living within one enclosure, praying at a common family temple, and utilizing one gate and one kitchen. The entire plot of land of the homestead is surrounded by a wall and the entrance gate is the location of two small shrines (*apit lawang*) for offerings to keep away malevolent spirits. The house itself is constructed with the family shrine facing northeast, the direction towards the sacred mountain, Gunung Agung. The sleeping quarters are also built toward the mountain side of the house. Well-to-do family homes have elaborate pavilions called *bale* built on carved posts with thatch roof coverings. The bale is used either as a sleeping quarter or a social hall for entertainment. The houses of a village together are formed around the temple and local royalty house with the former again being located at the northeast of the village.

Clothing. The ordinary dress of both men and women is called the *kamben*, a long wrap of Javanese batik or domestic hand-woven material that is wrapped around the waist. The women wear this skirt wrapped tight around the hips reaching down to the feet and held at the waist by a *bulang*, or brightly colored sash. A long scarf (*kamben tjerik*) is worn over one shoulder or wound around the head to keep the hair in place. Men also wear the kamben but tie the cloth in the front in a manner that it can be pulled up and tied into a type of shorts when working in the fields. The men's head-cloth is worn as a turban and can be arranged into a variety of styles. Priests dress in all white and can be recognized by their staffs (*danda*). Ceremonial dress for the Balinese involves more elaborate silk cloth for the kamben and headdress. Women wear elaborate headdresses of flower petals and jewelry, ranging from simple arrangements to more complex representations of the sacred mountain Gunung Agung.

Language. While every Indonesian citizen is taught the national language of Bahasa Indonesian, Balinese people have their own language. Balinese has both a high and low form, which have separate roots, words, and pronunciation. The low language is spoken in the market, to equals at home, and at work. It is the native language of Bali and belongs to the Malayo-Polynesian family of languages. The high language is similar to Javanese, is of Sanskrit-Javanese origins, and is used to speak to people of high nobility such as elders, members of the priestly caste, and landowners. Kawi is a language that is used on ritual occasions. It is primarily Sanskrit combined with some old Javanese and is studied by priests and Balinese scholars.

Until the twentieth century, Balinese wrote mostly using Javanese characters. In this century, however, many Balinese write using a Roman script.

A Balinese family in traditional dress. *Courtesy of Shiva Rea Bailey.*

Social organization. The Balinese adopted the Hindu caste system. Each family belongs to a certain class of nobility or a general common class known as the *Shudras.* The Hindu-Balinese nobility is divided into three well-known groups: the priests, *Brahmanas,* the ruling royalty, *Satrias,* and the military class, *Wesias*—all of which are said to be descendants of divinities. The *Shudras* make up the majority of Balinese. The caste system dictates the vocation of a person and the language of interaction between the members. Among the *desa* (all the people of a village), the *banjar* is one of the most important forms of social organization. A banjar is a cooperative society, a section of a village, bound together to assist its members with marriages, home festivals, and especially during the expensive cremations. Every adult belongs to both his banjar and his desa, where he carries out most of his responsibilities to the village. The banjar own the community's orchestra and dance properties and have a kitchen for preparing banquets, an alarm drum tower to call meetings, and a little communal temple. Every banjar has a meeting hall or clubhouse called the *bale banjar* where men gather for leisure hours or for council meetings.

The Balinese village may consist of one hundred to several thousand people. Each village has a central street crossing. At this intersection there is usually a village temple, a wall-less pavilion for meetings and for the cock-fighting ring, a large drum, and a coffee shop. Here, too, is the home of a prominent founder of the village. Temples abound everywhere. There are small family temples, community temples, and separate temples for the many religious cults.

Education. In Bali, educational opportunities are available from preschool until university. Denpasar is the location of a nationally known Institute for Performing Arts. In addition to formal schooling, children are educated by their families and the local banjar. The arts are taught at an early age. Children are involved in dance performances for temple festivals as early as five years of age and are welcome at the rehearsals and performances of adult art forms. In dance training, the teacher instructs the pupil through hand-held guidance, leading the movements from behind with very little verbal instruction. From infancy, children are encouraged to participate in the arts through play and performance.

Festivals. The Balinese have their own calendar system, which regulates holy festival days and other days that are auspicious for planting, harvesting, and planning any ceremonial event. In the Balinese system, there are two calendars, the *saka* and the *wuku.* The saka calendar is the lunar cycle and resembles the Western calendar. In the saka calendar, the new moon and full moon are days for temple festivals. The *wuku* calendar is a complex system of time used to determine festival dates. The calendar consists of ten weeks, ranging from a one-day week to a ten-day week. A Balinese year is made up of 210 days or thirty-seven-day weeks or *wukus.* Every 210 days the Balinese hold a great feast, *odalan*, in the major temples. The odalan is a day of prayer, feasting, and religious entertainment that lasts into the night. Beautiful offerings are brought to the temples and the priests conduct special ceremonies. Cockfights between two full-grown roosters are also a part of temple festivals. The Galungan festival happens islandwide once every 210 days and extends over a ten-day period during which the villages and towns are filled with dance-drama performances and processions through the village.

For More Information

Mabbett, Hugh. *The Balinese.* New Zealand: January Books, 1985.

Ramseyer, Urs. *The Art and Culture of Bali.* Oxford: Oxford University Press, 1977.

BENGALIS

(ben gah′ leez)

Bengali-speakers of mixed Dravidian, Aryan, Tibetan and Burmese ancestry.

Population: 176,000,000 (1991 estimate).
Location: Bangladesh and the Indian state of West Bengal.
Languages: Bengali (Bangla); English.

Geographical Setting

Nearly two-thirds of Bengalis (about 108,000,000) live in Bangladesh ("land of the Bengalis"), with most of the rest in West Bengal, the Indian state bordering Bangladesh to the west. Tucked into the northeast corner of the Indian subcontinent, the two areas have been politically united in the past, and are geographically similar. In West Bengal is centered the plain of the lower Ganges, one of the world's great rivers, which flows eastward across northern India. Soon after the Ganges enters Bangladesh (where it is called the Padma), it joins two other large rivers, the Brahmaputra (Jamuna in Bangladesh) and the Meghna. Both the Ganges and the Brahmaputra rise in the Himalayas, the highest mountains in the world, which run across northern India, Nepal, and Tibet. Although these towering mountains are close to Bangladesh, rising just to the north, Bangladesh itself is almost all flat lowland, comprising the delta formed by the rivers that flow through it to the Bay of Bengal. Most of the land is alluvial soil deposited by the rivers over the centuries, and yearly floods replenish the soil. The floods also disrupt farming, however, covering as much as half the land in a typical year. The yearly floods are caused by melting snow in the Himalayas; in recent years, deforestation in the mountains has caused flooding to become more severe than in the past.

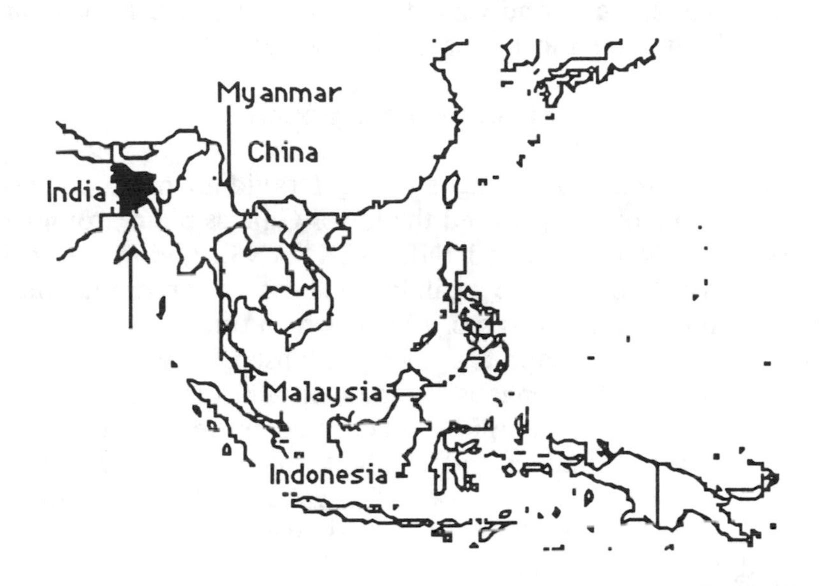

Frequent cyclones tear into crowded coastal areas from the Bay of Bengal, adding to the problems of flooding. Bangladesh has the highest population density of any country on earth, aside from city-states such as Hong Kong. Though only about the size of Wisconsin, it is home to nearly half as many people as the United States. (For the United States to be as crowded, the entire population of the world would have to live within its borders.) The overcrowding has forced many to live in the low-lying coastal areas and islands. When the cyclones strike, therefore, loss of life and property can be extreme. The worst such disaster came in 1970, when winds, flooding, and tidal waves killed possibly one-half million people and left millions more injured and homeless. Nearly as severe was a three-week period of cyclones in April 1991, which killed perhaps 150,000 and also left many more without homes. As with the floods, less severe but still devastating cyclones regularly take their toll of human life, property, crops, and livestock. On average, the tropical storms hit Bangladesh about 16 times every decade.

The climate of West Bengal and Bangladesh is tropical and subtropical, with warm, humid weather and extremely high rainfall. Three-quarters of the rain falls during the monsoon, which lasts from mid-June to October. Most Bengalis (about 90 percent in Bangladesh) live in rural areas. Largest cities are Dhaka (also spelled Dacca), capital of Bangladesh, and Calcutta, in West Bengal, India's largest city and the world's most congested urban center.

Historical Background

Ancient empires. It is thought that a Dravidian or Aryan people called the Bang or Vang settled the lower Ganges plain around 1000 B.C. (see DRAVIDIANS and INDO-ARYANS), giving rise to later names such as Bangla and Bengal. Bengal became part of the Mauryan empire of India in the 300s B.C., during which time Buddhism spread through the region. Mauryan power collapsed about 100 B.C., and little is known of the Bengalis for the next 800 years. At times, they became part of Hindu empires which held power in India, and at other times they remained independent. In the A.D. 700s, the Buddhist empire of the Padlas arose in Bengal and expanded into other areas of India. The last Padla ruler was overthrown in 1150 by the Hindu dynasty of the Senas.

Islam. Bengalis had never fully embraced Hinduism, disliking its rigid caste system, and the Senas did not enjoy wide support. They ruled for only about 50 years before new conquerors arrived, this time in the name of Islam (see ASIAN RELIGIONS). The Muslims conquered Bengal in the early 1200s, and over the next 550 years the Bengalis were part of several Islamic empires that ruled over most of India. Under Islamic rulers they also enjoyed periods of independence in the 1300s and 1400s. In 1576, Bengal was conquered by the Mughals, Muslim rulers of India. Over the entire period of Islamic rule (1202–1757), Bengalis abandoned Buddhism in favor of a casteless faith. Buddhism virtually died out in the region.

British rule. Europeans, beginning with the Portuguese, had established trade and missionary outposts in India from the early 1500s. The first such stations were at Chittagong, in the part of Bengal that now borders Burma. Dutch and French traders followed, along with the British, who founded Calcutta as a trading post in 1686. Soon the British became the dominant European power in India, with Bengal—particularly Calcutta—as the center of their influence. In 1757, the British East India Company took control of Bengal by defeating Sirajuddaulah, a local ruler, at the battle of Plassey (Pilasi).

British power eventually extended over all of India. In 1858, after Muslim Bengali soldiers of the British Indian Army led a year-long revolt against the British, the East India Company was dissolved and administration of India taken over by the British monarch.

British economic policy. The British viewed their colonies as sources of raw materials for British industry. Finished products, such as textiles woven from imported materials, could then be sold back to the colonies. This dumping of machine-made goods undermined local craft industries. Dhaka, once the major Bengali city, had earlier prospered by selling cloth such as muslin and silk. Under the British, Dhaka's trade and commerce collapsed, largely because of the growth of Calcutta as an import-export center. British rule also gave rise to new social divisions within Bengali society, as colonial policy favored the Hindu upper classes, often Calcutta merchants or landlords, over Muslim peasants in east Bengal (later Bangladesh). As a general rule, the Hindus tended to cooperate more fully with British interests and to adapt to British culture more easily, while the Muslims took less of a share in the spoils of empire.

Struggle for self-rule. In the late 1800s and early 1900s, movements for Indian independence arose among both Hindus and Muslims. The Indian National Congress, founded in 1885, advocated Hindu interests, and was supported by educated, upper-class Bengali Hindus in Calcutta. The Muslim League, founded in Dhaka in 1906, promoted the interests of Indian Muslims. In the 1930s, as the Indian independence movement gained momentum, the Muslim League began to call for the establishment of two Indian states, one Muslim and one Hindu. In 1947, in an atmosphere of growing violence between members of the two faiths, Britain declared India independent. Two such states became reality: India, largely Hindu, and Pakistan, almost entirely Muslim. Throughout the region, millions of people were displaced, as Hindus in the new Muslim state fled to India, and Muslims moved into Pakistan. Violent riots, in which perhaps one million were killed, pitted Hindus against Muslims in both countries.

Pakistan, East and West. Though the old India had been mostly Hindu, two areas had had Muslim majorities: east Bengal, in the far east, and three provinces in the far west. These two areas became Pakistan—a single nation, but in two parts separated by 1,000 miles of potentially hostile territory. Adding to the problems of geography, equally stark cultural and social divisions remained between the light-skinned Urdu-speaking West Pakistanis, more Middle Eastern in outlook, and the darker-skinned Asian-oriented Bengalis. The West Pakistanis monopolized the new nation's government, declaring that Urdu alone would be the official language. Yet the Bengalis outnumbered the West Pakistanis and contributed the lion's share of the nation's foreign earnings, which came from the export of jute (used in burlap). Though the jute was grown and processed in Bengal, its manufacture was mostly owned and controlled by West Pakistanis.

Bangladesh. Language soon became the focal point of Bengali nationalism. At Dhaka University in 1952, Pakistani police fired on students demonstrating for the right to use Bengali in public life, killing twenty-six and wounding 400. The killings left a deep scar on the Bengalis' memory, and are today commemorated by a monument to the dead in Dhaka. During the 1960s, a leader emerged for the Bengalis, the popular and charismatic speaker Sheik Mujibur Rahman (Mujib). In 1971, Mujib won a majority of the popular vote in a nationwide election, which, according to the new constitution, would make him the Pakistani prime minister. However, the West-Pakistani-dominated government refused to relinquish power. Instead, the West Pakistanis sent troops into east Bengal. For two days, beginning on March 25, 1971, Bengalis by the thousands were killed, raped and beaten, in a time of terror known as the "Crackdown." Millions of Bengalis fled to India as others formed an army. A brutal nine-month war ensued, in which the slaughter and rape of Bengalis continued as outnumbered Bengali fighters struggled against the occupiers. Eventually, India sent troops to help the Bengalis. The aid was decisive. Pakistan surrendered in December 1971, and the former East Pakistan became Bangladesh—land of the Bengalis.

Culture Today

Common ground. Bengalis may be from widely different religious or economic backgrounds. They may be Hindu or Muslim, Bangladeshi or Indian, sophisticated elites or slum-dwellers in Khaka or Calcutta, or rural peasants barely able to survive on what they grow. Yet these differences fade to unimportance compared to the common culture they share. The Bengali language, associated with an uncommonly rich literary and oral tradition, is the most important such commonality. Dress, food, music, folk art, and even holidays are also shared between Muslim and Hindu alike, and celebrated equally by rich and poor.

Language. Bengali (Bangla) is the easternmost language of the Indo-European family, from which most of the languages of India and Europe are derived. It is thus distantly related to English. Like Hindi (India's major language), to which it is closely related, Bengali comes from Sanskrit, India's ancient literary tongue. Bengalis are a poetic people, and their language often reflects an inventive use of imagery—*vyamer chata*, for example, means "frog's umbrella," or mushroom. The English words "pajamas" and "veranda" may have come from Bengali. There are a number of Bengali dialects, some of which have been influenced by Arabic and Persian elements (part of the Islamic heritage). In Bangladesh, Arabic phrases have entered the language, such as the common greeting *asalaam alaikhum* (peace be with you).

Literature. Bengali children grow up hearing ancient tales of maharajahs (kings) who are outsmarted by wily jesters, of heroes, kidnapped maidens, and evil demons. Often the stories make a humorous moral point. Both Hindus and Muslims enjoy stories about the many Hindu gods and goddesses. In the coastal wetlands called the Sundarbans (shared between West Bengal and Bangladesh) lives the Bengal tiger, one of the world's most majestic and feared animals. Children in the Sundarbans are told stories about Dakshin Rai, a ruler who was killed by a tiger and became the Tiger God.

In the 1800s, Western-educated Hindu Bengalis initiated a literary and cultural movement known as the Bengali Renaissance. Among the many writers who adapted Western forms such as the novel to Bengali culture, foremost was the Nobel Prize-winner Rabindranath Tagore (1861–1941). In his poems and stories, Tagore celebrated Bengal's beauty and explored the lives of common people. He used the everyday language rather than the formal one of traditional poetry, and also showed women outside of the idealized settings of the old poetry. Tagore is recognized as one of the world's great poets. One of his poems, *Sonar Bangla* ("Golden Bengal"), became Bangladesh's national anthem; another is India's. The Muslim poet Nazrul Islam (1899–1976) wrote poems advocating revolution against the British occupation, inspiring Bengalis to press for self-rule. His poetry reflects another deep love of the Bengalis, politics.

The arts. Bengali folk-arts are colorful and accomplished. Bengal cloth was once world-famous for its delicate texture. Woven for thousands of years, muslin and other fine cloths made pre-British Bengal one of India's most prosperous areas. Bengalis still weave silk into a delicate cloth called *jamdani*, which features geometric designs. Village women make bright quilts out of old scraps of cloth. Called *kanthas*, the quilts depict scenes of village life or episodes from well-known stories. Music and dance are also important and are combined in a number of ways. *Jatra* is a form of folk-opera, performed during local festivals in a large, brightly colored tent. *Manipuri* is the classical equivalent of ballet, requiring long and rigorous study. Bengali painters have depicted traditional scenes, as well as more disturbing renditions of human suffering—never far away in troubled Bangladesh.

Food, clothing, and shelter. The Bengalis' hot, spicy cuisine is similar to India's. Fish, often fried, is the most common meat, but heavily seasoned chicken, beef, or mutton dishes, served with rice, are popular when available. Chopped vegetables are cooked with *masala*, a fried curry paste, and flavored also with garlic and onion. Meals are accompanied by tea and *chappatis*, or flat, round bread. Tropical fruits such as mangoes and bananas are common. *Litchis* are the size of plums, with a tough reddish shell and sweet white insides; jackfruit (called *bel*) is eaten raw or included in cooked dishes.

Dress is also similar to that of India. Women wear the *sari*, a long rectangle of cotton or silk wrapped around the body. Hindu

A Bengali village near Calcutta, India. *Courtesy of the Smithsonian Institution.*

village men wear the *dhoti*, a long piece of cotton (often white), folded into leggings; Muslim men wear pants or a *lungi*, a length of colored cloth wrapped around the waist and extending to the ankle. The lungi is often worn with a T-shirt or Western-style shirt, and is now commonly replaced with shorts.

Ninety percent of Bengalis live in rural villages, where homes are simple huts made of straw and dried mud. The interiors are dark, because the glassless windows must be small enough to prevent the frequent rains from getting in. Furniture generally consists of a few *charpoys,* or woven-rope mats, on which the family sleeps and sits. While some urban Bengalis live in comfortable, middle-class apartments, or even opulent Calcutta residences, the vast majority of city-dwellers occupy crowded and filthy slums, where a family is lucky to have even the most squalid living space. Conditions in Calcutta shock visitors, even those who have lived in India all their lives. In both city and country, diseases such as cholera stalk the people, becoming especially virulent in times of flooding. (Many diseases are water-borne.)

Family life. Bengali families, including the poorest, are hospitable and welcoming to visitors. All Bengalis value good manners and use terms of respect when addressing each other: "brother," "sister," "honored mother," for example, are common ways to address strangers. Manners are instilled in children, who receive constant and loving attention. In villages, children receive little formal education, however. Instead, by the age of eight or nine they must spend a large part of each day working to help the family. Girls help their mothers with food or with younger children; boys help prepare jute plants for sale, help in the rice paddies, thresh grain, catch fish or care for cattle. Middle-class children in the cities, by contrast, go to school and often have outside tutoring in such subjects as Bengali dance or music. Relations between boys and girls are strictly regulated by the family. Marriages are usually arranged, even in families that are otherwise Western in outlook. Today, though, the prospective partners are allowed to meet and spend time together before the wedding—with older relatives keeping close watch—and are not forced to marry if they object strongly. Servants are common in upper-class homes.

Religion. About 83 percent of Bengalis in Bangladesh are Muslim, and about 13 percent Hindu. The remainder of Bangladesh Bengalis are Buddhist or Christian. In West Bengal (India), the religious preferences are reversed, with about 20 percent Muslim and the dominant group Hindu. Bengali Muslims are heavily influenced by the branch of Islam called *Sufism*, which originated in the 700s. Sufis emphasize self-knowledge and meditation. Sufism's mystical aspects have a deep appeal for the Bengalis and were instrumental in the conversions from Buddhism that began in the 1200s (see RELIGIONS OF ASIA).

Women. Traditionally, women occupy a subordinate role in Bengali society. This is still widely the case. Women bear the brunt of burdens such as high rates of childbirth, low access to health care, and diminished access to education. During the war with Pakistan, women suffered especially, being targeted for what appeared to be a conscious policy of rape by the Pakistani soldiers. The aim, apparently, was both to change the Bengali's racial makeup and to make the women outcasts in society. Today, among the more educated middle-class women, several groups have organized in order to improve the lot of Bengali women.

No easy solutions. Bengalis in Bangladesh face an immediate future in which starvation, disease, and poverty are unavoidable, even given the best of all possible outcomes. In good years, the people cannot grow enough food to feed themselves and good years are few and far between. Foreign aid remains crucial. The ravages of weather, deforestation, overpopulation, and (probably) Greenhouse warming will continue to impose harsh conditions on the Bengalis. Bengali historians look back on the prosperous nation that once existed, in hopes that it will regain its footing.

For More Information

Baxter, Craig and Rahman, Syedur. *Historical Dictionary of Bangladesh.* Metuchen: Scarecrow Press, 1989.

Brata, Sasthi. *India: Labyrinths in the Lotus Land.* New York: William Morrow & Co., 1985.

Heitzman, James and Worden, Robert L. *Bangladesh: A Country Study.* Washington, DC: Dept. of the Army, 1989.

McClure, Vimala. *Bangladesh: Rivers in Crowded Land.* Minneapolis: Dillon Press, Inc., 1989.

BURMANS

(bur′ muns)

The people of Myanmar are here called Burmese; Burmans are the dominant subgroup of the Burmese.

Population: 25,600,000 (1990 estimate).
Location: The Union of Myanmar, a country of Asia east of India on the Bay of Bengal.
Language: Burmese, a Sino-Tibetan language.

Geographical Setting

The country of Myanmar (Burma) and the lives of the people who reside there have been molded by the path and power of the Irrawaddy River and by interactions with foreign traders such as the British. To the north and east, the land of Burma is mountainous, with high mountains giving way southward to a region of steep hills and valleys. This region helps to isolate the area from India, of which it was a part from 1875 until 1937. Hills and valleys demand descents and assents of 4,000 feet or more even before reaching the mountains. Most Burmans (or Bamars), the largest group in the country, live along the Irrawaddy River.

The climate in the Irrawaddy River, along which most of the Burmans live, is tropical. Temperatures average eighty degrees Fahrenheit, and heavy rains fall from May to October. This "monsoon" season is a liability and an asset to the Burmans. While the river itself during this season may grow from its average one-and-one-half miles across to ten miles or more, covering much agricultural land, it causes heavy river flow that brings new soil to rebuild the valley's crop land.

Historical Background

Settlers from China. The present country of Myanmar was inhabited by a group known as the Mon when other peoples, seeking to escape Chinese domination, migrated to the area from the Tibetan highlands. The migrants became the Burmans. By the tenth century they had established two small kingdoms that kept an uneasy peace with the Mon for nearly a century. Then King Anawratha of Pagan succeeded in uniting the Burmans and Mon into one kingdom with Pagan as its capital. He imprisoned 3,000 Mon people, but is said to have been deeply influenced by a Mon monk who brought Buddhism to the country. This king espoused a form of Buddhism known as Theravada, a form that recognizes only the first Buddha, Gautama, who lived in the sixth century B.C. Anawratha's successor, Kyansitta, expanded the realm and solidified the adoption of Buddhism by building the Ananda Pagoda. At its peak, Pagan was the site of more than a thousand Buddhist shrines. Since the union, the Burmans have been the most significant ethnic group in the political history of the country that was, until 1990, called Burma.

Mongols. The Pagan dynasty lasted until 1287, when Mongol invaders led by Kublai Khan conquered the region. The old kingdom was split and the people who spoke the Burmese language were driven south, migrating as far as Siam and Cambodia.

The second Burma. When the Mongols left, another group of Burmese, the Shan, developed a strong government that ruled much of the Irrawaddy basin from the early 1300s to the 1500s. The region was further divided when European settlers declared the formation of "kingdoms" along the coast in the Irrawaddy Delta area. In the 1500s the Burmans regained power and unified the peoples of the country again under the Toungoo dynasty, which ruled until the Burmans were defeated in a war with Siam in the seventeenth century.

The third Burma. King Alaungpaya reunited the Burmans for a third time in 1760 under a government based at Pegu, and extended his territory by the conquest of other people as far away as Siam. The new border overlapped into India on land controlled by the British and resulted in three wars with Britain between 1824 and 1885. General Bandula, now a Burmese folk hero, resisted British domination, but to no avail.

India and independence. In 1885, the peaceful King Mendon, whose capital was Mandalay, yielded to the British, and Myanmar became part of India. Although the Burmans resented the association with India, that relationship continued until 1936 when Myanmar became an independent state in the British Commonwealth. During its relationship with the British, the Burmans and particularly their Buddhist monks were often at odds with the structure that created a caste system with British at the top, followed by Indian and Chinese government workers and merchants, and finally the natives of Myanmar. One aggravation was the refusal of British military people to remove their shoes when entering a Buddhist Pagoda platform, an issue that became known as the "shoe issue." These aggravations turned some Burmans toward Japan in spite of Japan's brutal actions in China.

During World War II, British control was lost to the Japanese, and, following this war, Myanmar, with political power in the hands of the Burmans, became an independent socialist nation. Since then there has been continuing unrest, yet the Burmans, who form sixty-five percent of the population, have managed to hold an uneasy power over the other peoples of the nation.

Interaction with Mons. Throughout its history the Burmans have contended with and been influenced by the Mons to whose land they migrated. The Mons were an Indian-speaking people whose language merged with the Chinese/Tibetan language of immigrants to create the Burmese language. In religion, the Burmans became followers of the Buddhist religion, which the Mons had adopted earlier.

Uneasy politics. Burmans and Mons are not all the people of Myanmar. Several other groups, such as the Shan, Karen, and Kachin, occupy large areas in the hills. This diversity, along with the philosophical strain of the competition of communism, socialism, and capitalism, have made the short history of Myanmar a hectic political one. Before its independence, the people of this country were united in agitation first to become an independent British crown colony apart from India, and then for complete independence. That independence came in 1948 under the leadership of Thakin Nu, who then took the name U Nu. ("Thakin" is a Burmese term for master, a title first given the British out of respect, and later demanded by them.) Burmese agitators for independence adopted the term as a symbol that the Burmese should become their own masters. That accomplished, the leaders of Myanmar dropped the title in favor of U meaning simply "uncle" or "mister."

By 1958 various political parties had made it difficult for U Nu to rule and the country gave way to a military takeover. New elections were scheduled and U Nu was elected president again in 1960. But that government was again replaced by the military in 1962. General Ne Win then formed a political party, the Myanmar Socialist Programme Party (BSPP) and succeeded in outlawing all other political parties. A constitution prepared in 1973 described the country as democratic and socialist. Under this document, new elections were held in 1978 and U Ne Win was elected president. Under much pressure for more rapid economic improvement, U Ne Win resigned in 1988 and was replaced by U Sien Lwin, who, after just 17 days, also resigned to be replaced by Dr. Maung Maung. Under him, members of the military were barred from the dominant BSPP.

The military leadership responded by again taking control of Myanmar. While once again preparing for popular elections for seats in the country's legislative body (Pyithu Hluttaw, or People's Assembly) and opening this election to other political parties, the military suppressed student and worker uprisings violently. In 1989 a peaceful march of protest by more than 100 political factions led by Aung San

Sou Kyi. This woman had planned to use the march to commemorate her father, Aung San, who had been assassinated in 1947. When elections finally selected the 499 members of the Pyithu Hluttaw, the military government declared that this body had been elected only to prepare a new constitution to be enacted by popular vote. To decrease the potential for protest, Aung San Sou Kyi was placed under house arrest. Still, by 1991 some of the newly elected representatives had broken off and formed a mostly symbolic separate government in a city near the Thai border. Meanwhile, in June 1989, the military government attempted to enlist support among other-than-Burman groups by changing the name of the country from Burma to a more inclusive Union of Myanmar (*myanmah* literally means "fast" or strong").

Culture Today

Village people. Mandalay and Yangon (Rangoon) are now large industrial cities that operate as centers of trade, manufacturing, and oil distribution, but these Westernized cities house only about fifteen percent of the Burman people. Villages of a few hundred houses still predominate in the country. The Burman villages are communal. The people live in one- or two-room homes clustered together and share the work in nearby fields or forests. Rice is the principal crop of Myanmar, but the village people also grow tea in some areas and harvest teak wood from the abundant forests. In some areas, villagers also mine and prepare jade for market.

Religion. Life in the village centers on religion. Almost every village has a temple and there is often a monastery just outside the village. Religion is very important to the Burmans, most of whom are Buddhists, having brought the Buddhist teachings from India. The temples are ornate, sometimes decorated with gold. Music, dance, and art often have religious inspiration. One is the famous Golden Pagoda in Yangon.

Since 1983, Buddhism has not been given official status as the state religion of Myanmar. However, the Burmans still revere the more than twenty thousand priests to whom they look for education and leadership. A goal of Buddhism is to practice self-denial in an effort to wean one's self away from earthly objects. Eating sparingly, avoiding sexual relationships, or, in fact, avoiding emotional or embarrassing incidents is desirable. Buddhists believe that they gain

The Burman village of Tounquine. *Courtesy of the Smithsonian Institution.*

merits by demonstrating their good intentions through giving to Buddhism. This mark for giving does not expand to include earthly charities, only the support of the religion and the priest who symbolize its purpose. Yellow-cloaked priests are those who have demonstrated an advanced step toward *nirvana* by strict adherence to 227 rules that divorce them from earthly objects.

Language. The Burmese language is a monosyllabic language that depends for its meaning on the inflection with which the word is pronounced. Thus a single word using the same alphabetical symbols may mean different things depending on how it is spoken. Burmese is a language related to Tibetan and Chinese.

The names of Burman people often carry descriptive terms: U for mister, or uncle; Dau for madam or aunt; Ma for sister or Miss; Maung for young boy (used by even elderly men such as Maung Maung); Ko for brother; Bo for officer. In addition, the single Myanmar name, if it is a common one, may sometimes be defined by adding the name of the city in which the person was born or resides.

A Burman Buddhist Pagoda at Yangon. *Courtesy of the Smithsonian Institution.*

Literature and arts. Burman music is unusual in that it uses only five notes and is played on large sets of drums and gongs. The music forms the background for the popular plays, *pwes*, that are a major attraction for Burmans. These plays re-enact ancient stories and may last four or five hours.

Burmans have a long literary tradition. The earliest written efforts yet discovered are inscriptions on stone that date back to about A.D. 1113. From the fourteenth to the nineteenth centuries works of poetry and prose were scribed on palm leaves or folds of paper by Buddhist monks. A large body of Myanmar literature, the *Pyo* (written in an ancient Indian language, Paoi), is based on religious stories of Buddha that have been reset in Myanmar and embellished with lively details. The earliest of these, Birth Story 543 by Ra-hta-tha-ra, was written in 1484. The achievements of their ancestors are recounted in a rich body of historical ballads and other poems. Since most early literature was religious, printed words are held in high respect in Myanmar. Many Burmans are dismayed to find a work of writing lying on a floor.

Food, clothing, and shelter. Even at celebrations, the Burmans might be seen in everyday dress. The village grain farmers wear a sarong-like *longiji* under a loose shirt, and women wear a wraparound skirt called a *khtamen* and a blouse. Women augment their dress with jewelry and with hair styled and set with oil.

The Myanmar farmers raise cattle and buffalo, but use them as beasts of burden rather than for food. Most Burmans eat two meals daily. The staple food at each meal is boiled rice, often supplemented by vegetables and fish curry. In addition to growing rice, vegetables, and millet for their own food needs, the Myanmar farmers raise tobacco, cotton, and onions as cash crops. Burmans eat this fare from bowls, using their fingers to collect balls of rice and vegetables.

Women. In Burmese society, and therefore among the Burmans, men are permitted to marry only one woman at a time, but may keep as many mistresses as they can afford. Economic issues hold the keeping of mistresses and female servants to a limited number. Women are otherwise free in Burmese society to move about independently and to carry on business with men and other women.

A Myanmar woman may own property, enter into politics, or practice any of the professions, although there are few Myanmar female monks. In public Myanmar women are usually cheerful and self-confident. They defer to their husbands by walking behind them, a custom further explained by the saying, "Let the men go first, for that is where the snakes are." In every way other than symbolism, Myanmar women have long been the equals of the men (see reference to Aung San Sou Kyi above). A book written in the 1940s described women as "Myanmar's Greatest Asset."

Education. In Myanmar, education is free wherever it is available, but is not required. Still, more than sixty percent of the students between five and fifteen attend the primary schools (ages five to ten) or secondary schools. In 1988 student riots resulted in the government closing of all schools. In 1989 they reopened the primary and secondary schools. About one-fifth of the adults of Myanmar are illiterate.

Economy. Lumber (teak and hardwood) and other goods are brought to and from the cities by boat, a main means of transportation for Burmans who live along the Irrawaddy River. However, the chief occupation of Burmans has been the cultivation of rice. Through the centuries, Myanmar has been a rich agricultural culture. Agriculture, fishing, and forestry produce nearly half of the income of Myanmar.

In the last half of the nineteenth century, oil was discovered in Myanmar. This energy resource was a major attraction for the Japanese in World War II. Another attraction was the Myanmar Road, which led along the Irrawaddy River and gave the Japanese access to China. After the war, oil overshadowed the mining of jade, rubies, and other precious stones.

Government. Burmans control the government of Myanmar, although there is tension with other groups, such as the Shan of northeast Myanmar. The Burmans are generally reputed to be easygoing people. Their government is loosely held; often, other peoples maintain nearly independent states inside Myanmar. Within the country east of the territory of the Burmans, small groups of people are influenced by China and Thailand. With a tradition of escape from Chinese domination, the Burmans have little in common with these groups and are influenced more by the ways of the early Indian inhabitants of Myanmar.

In 1992 the peoples of Myanmar were locked in a brutal civil war, determined to throw off the yoke of a military dictatorship that has proven willing to use any force and violate any laws and elections to preserve its own existence.

For More Information

Bunge, Frederica M., editor. *Burma, A Country Study.* Washington, DC: American University, 1983.

Mya Maung, *The Burma Road to Poverty.* New York: Frederick A. Praeger, 1991.

Scott, Sir J. George. *Burma and Beyond.* London: Grayson and Grayson, 1982.

Trager, Helen G. *We the Burmese: Voices from Burma,* New York: Frederick A. Praeger, 1969.

CHINESE MINORITIES

(chi neez′ mih nohr′ ih tees)

Peoples of China who are not members of the ethnic Han majority.

Population: 70,000,000 (1990 estimate).
Location: The People's Republic of China, mostly in northern and southwestern border regions.
Languages: Most peoples speak their own languages along with Mandarin Chinese.

Geographical Setting

The Chinese government recognizes fifty-six "nationalities" within its borders—the majority, Han Chinese, numbering just over 1,000,000,000—and fifty-five minority peoples, who number about 70,000,000 and make up roughly eight percent of the overall population. Until recent times, this smaller minority population occupied about sixty percent of China's territory. Most were scattered through the vast reaches of desert and mountain ranges on China's northern and southwestern borders. They still occupy the same areas, but during the 1970s and 1980s large numbers of Han Chinese moved into these areas as well.

The minorities can be divided into five main groups, each with its distinctive geographic distribution. Clockwise from the southwest, the first group is the Tai, including the Zhuang, at over 13,000,000 China's largest minority. The Tai peoples occupy the "autonomous region" of Guangzi, bordering Vietnam. To Guangzi's north lies the province of Buangzhou, in and around which are centered the Miao and related peoples (about 8,000,000 to 10,000,000). Next, the Tibeto-Burman group (about 15,000,000) includes over fifteen nationalities,

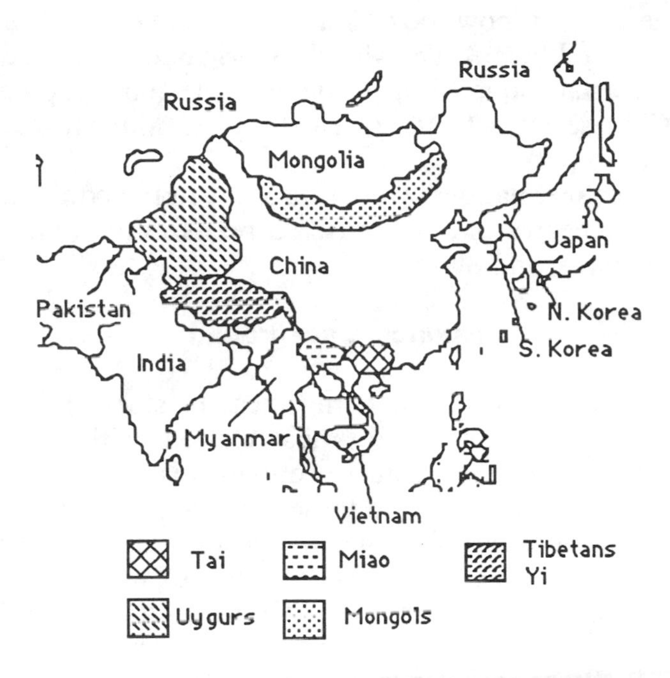

most numerous being the Tibetans and the Yi. The Yi live mostly in Guizhou and the neighboring provinces of Yunnan and Sichuan, while the related Tibetans occupy the autonomous region of Tibet (see TIBETANS). North of Tibet, along the ancient trading routes to the west, the Turkic peoples dominate the autonomous region of Zinjiang. Descended from the same nomads as the Turks who founded Turkey, they number about 6,000,000 to 9,000,000. Most numerous are the Uygurs, Kazakhs and Kyrgyz. Finally, various Mongolian peoples also have their own autonomous region, Inner Mongolia, to the east of Xinjiang. The largest group is the Mongols themselves, about 4,000,000 people.

These large groups of border peoples most often spread over the Chinese border into other countries. The Tais are closely related to the Thai people of Thailand and share the name except for the difference in spelling, which the Thailanders adopted to distinguish their society. The Miao extend into Southeast Asia, where they are called the Hmong (see HMONG). Ethnic Mongols and Turks both occupy huge regions outside of China. In addition, some minorities are scattered throughout China. For example, the Hui, numbering about 7,000,000, are Islamic descendants of Arab traders who intermarried with Chinese. They now look Chinese and have adopted Chinese ways (except for religion). The Manchus, originally a nomadic people of the northeast, conquered the Chinese in the 1600s and have since adopted Chinese ways to the extent that old Manchu culture has largely disappeared.

Various smaller national groups also live in the borderland areas near their respective homelands: Koreans, Vietnamese, Mon-Khmers, Iranians, and Slavs.

Historical Background

Chinese sources. Through modern times, the story of China's border peoples is largely the story of their relations with the Han. The oldest records come from Chinese sources, historical works which date back nearly 3,000 years. In these early centuries, what became Han Chinese culture occupied a relatively small area in north China, centered around the Yellow River. The rest of what is now China was controlled by peoples whom the Chinese historians referred to as early as 1000 B.C., while the Miao appear in records from the 200s B.C. In the 1940s, one scholar found over 8,000 various peoples mentioned in 3,000 years of Chinese history. As Chinese power and culture expanded, many peoples were assimilated, both adopting and helping to shape Chinese ways.

Great Wall. Conflicts arose regularly, at first especially between the Han and their nomadic, warlike neighbors to the north. During the 200s B.C., the Chinese built the first version of the Great Wall, stretched along the northern border and designed to keep out the marauding nomads. At the same time, Chinese rulers began the first systematic absorption of non-Han peoples, through conquest and cultural expansion.

Spread of Chinese culture. The Han extended their rule both north and south. A common pattern involved the installation of armed, walled fortress-cities in remote areas, followed by an influx of Han settlers into the surrounding countryside. The settlers' farming techniques—utilizing irrigation, iron tools, and manure fertilization—generally proved superior to that of the local people, who would then take them up. Agriculture thus often proved to be the spearhead of Chinese ways. However, Han military power did not always prevail, especially in the north. From the A.D. 300s until the 1900s, various northern peoples established dynasties over all or part of Han territory, often for centuries at a time. Usually, the conquerors adopted Chinese governmental institutions and were assimilated into the Han population. They themselves thus became Chinese. A notable exception was the Yuan Dynasty (1260–1368), founded by Mongol conquerors who incorporated China into the vast Mongol Empire.

Rebellions. Like the Mongols, a number of peoples resisted Han cultural and political influence. Throughout Chinese history, the border minorities participated in some fifteen major rebellions, mostly in the southwest. The Miao group of peoples resisted especially strongly. The Yao subgroup pursued a revolt against the Ming Dynasty for nearly 250 years (from 1375–1627) before being overcome. The Miao, Tai, and Tibeto-Burman groups all warred sporadically against Han domination. Yet Chinese power continued to grow, as Han settlers populated the south.

Manchu Dynasty. In 1644, invading Manchus overthrew the Ming Dynasty and began nearly 300 years of rule in China. These northern nomads at first kept themselves apart from their Han subjects, although they quickly adopted Han administrative institutions. Under the Manchu Qing Dynasty, Chinese territorial expansion surged westward, taking in Tibet and Zinjiang in the 1700s. The Tibetans and Turkic Muslims who occupied these areas rebelled repeatedly in the 1800s, as did the Zhuang, Yao, and other southern peoples. Many of the Miao fled to Southeast Asia, where they live today (see HMONG). In particular, the southern peoples supported the Taiping Rebellion, China's most widespread peasant revolt, which lasted from 1850–1864 (see MAINLAND CHINESE).

Chinese Republic. The Qing Dynasty was overthrown in 1911, and for nearly forty years the Guomindang (Republican) government struggled to maintain its shaky grip on power. During this time, parts of Tibet, Xinjiang, and Mongolia claimed independence. British aid (from India) helped the Tibetans retain effective independence until the 1950s. Independence proved shorter-lived for the Xinjaing Turks. Their leader, a Han Chinese called Sheng Shicai, submitted to the Guomindang in 1942. The Mongolians, with Soviet assistance, achieved more lasting success. The Mongolian People's Republic, also called Outer Mongolia, remains independent to this day, while China rules Inner Mongolia.

Communist rule. In 1949, Chinese Communists defeated the Guomindang, driving them from the mainland to the island of Taiwan (see TAIWANESE). Since the 1930s, the Communists had made attempts to win the minorities over. Once in power, the Communists offered the minorities limited rights, short of full independence but allowing more freedom than under previous regimes. Yet, since Communist authority has been stronger than that of past governments, Han influence has in effect been further reaching.

The darkest time for the minorities came during the Cultural Revolution (1966–70), when leftist radicals came to power. They thought China had strayed from Communist principles, and wished to uproot all remnants of old, "feudal" ways. While the Cultural Revolution wreaked havoc throughout Chinese society, it brought serious violence to many minority areas, as the leftists tried to wipe out the minority cultures. The leftists fell from power in the 1970s, and their ideas have been rejected. Since the 1980s, official policy has recognized the value of the minorities' contribution to China's cultural life.

Minority Cultures Today

Government. Communist policy in China outlines a system that allows different levels of autonomy (self-rule) to areas with high concentrations of minorities. The highest level is the "autonomous region," which is equivalent to a province. China has five autonomous regions, most of which were set up in the 1950s and 1960s: Guangxi Zhuang, Xizang (Tibet), Xinjiang Uygur, Ningxia Hui, and Inner Mongolia. Under this system, the minorities in an area must each be represented in the local government. Autonomy, however, does not equal freedom. No political parties are allowed, aside from the Communist Party, which is controlled from Beijing, China's capital. Local decisions may not go against those of the central government. Instead, autonomy supposedly preserves the right for the minorities to use their own languages, traditions, and religious practices. Conflict between local people and the central government has arisen most notably in Tibet, where agitation for independence led to severe and violent repression in the late 1980s. China has drawn much criticism for its policy in Tibet, which many observers see as an attempt to eradicate Tibetan culture (see TIBETANS).

Religion. With most minority nationalities, religion remains a strong marker of cultural identity. Islam in particular has served to set its followers apart from the Han majority. Islam is followed by the Turkic peoples (Uygurs, Kazakhs, Kyrgyz, Tatars, and Uzbecks), the Iranian Tajiks, and the Hui. Islamic practices sometimes conflict with Chinese law, and in such cases are usually overruled. For example, Muslims allow each man as many as four wives, a tradition that the government has disallowed. Other practices—diet and clothing, for example—differ merely from Chinese custom. Muslims may not eat pork, for instance, which is the favorite Chinese meat. Most Muslim women also wear the veil, which Han women do not.

Buddhism, the religion of the Tibetans and Mongolians, also has many followers among the Han. Like the Han, the Tibetans and Mongolians follow Mahayana (Great Path) Buddhism. Unlike the Han, however, Tibetans and Mongolians adhere to a type of Mahayana Buddhism called Lamaism, which honors religious leaders called lamas. Some lamas, such as Tibet's traditional ruler, the Dalai Lama, also wield political power. The Dalai Lama, who fled to India from Chinese troops in 1959, has become a symbol of Tibetan resistance. Hinayana (Lesser Path) Buddhism is followed by some Tai and Tibeto-Burman peoples of the southwest.

Many Miao and Tibeto-Burman peoples worship various traditional nature gods. Shamanistic beliefs are also common among these tribal villagers, and exist also among some peoples of Xinjiang and the far northeast. Some Miao and others have been converted by Christian missionaries, and most of the nearly 3,000 Russians in northwest Xinjiang still worship in the Eastern Orthodox Church.

Family life. In general, the small, nuclear family has predominated among the minorities. Whether in the agricultural villages of the southwest, the traditionally nomadic communities of the Turks and Mongols, or the hunting and fishing villages of the northeast, the closely knit families share the burden of survival. Often, both parents take part in child-raising, the usual exception being Turkic Muslim families, in which the father spends less time with family and more in the company of male friends. Among the Miao and other peoples of the southwest, children are treated especially warmly. Still, they begin doing their share of work while young. Courtship and sexual play among southwestern nationalities tends to be much less supervised than among other peoples, particularly the Muslims and the Han. Most nationalities have their own holidays, featuring contests, songs, and dancing, which provide an important opportunity for courtship. Marriage, in turn, itself offers another chance for public festivity.

Food, clothing, and shelter. Rice is the primary staple grain of the south, wheat of the north. Most nationalities raise livestock such as pigs (except Muslims), goats, and chickens, along with fruits and vegetables. Fishing is common in the mountain streams of the southwest and northeast. Dairy products such as goat's-milk yogurt are popular among Turkic Muslim herders and nomads.

Traditional clothing tends to be very distinctive, with each nationality having its own styles and colorful patterns. The Miao are specially known for the fineness of their embroidery and silver jewelry. In most cultures, both sexes tend to dress more brightly for special occasions. As a general rule, men's work clothing may be simpler and more drab, while the women at work may wear less elaborate versions of their festive costumes. Different styles of headgear—often turbans for the Turks and Mongols, hats and caps for the rest—also set the various peoples apart. Peoples who are highly integrated with the Han, like the Zhuang and Hui, are more likely to wear clothing similar to those of the majority. Most common are the simple blue or gray cotton shirts and "Mao jackets" identified with the Communist leader. Traditional costumes are seen more among less integrated peoples.

Traditional homes vary widely by region. In the southwest, houses are often made of wooden or bamboo frames with thatched roofs. Sedentary farming Turks (such as the Uygurs) sometimes build simple stone structures, while nomadic Turks and Mongols live in round, goat's-hair tents called yurts.

Language. The Hui (Chinese Muslims) and the Manchus now use Chinese; all other nationalities have their own languages. The main language families are Sino-Tibetan, spoken by most of the southwestern peoples, and Altaic, spoken by the Turkic and Mongolian peoples. While Mandarin Chinese is essential for an ambitious young urbanite, minority languages show no sign of dying out in public use. In Mongolia, for example, one of the two radio stations broadcasts in Mongolian, the other in Chinese. Education is carried out in the dominant local language—or dialect, for most of the larger nationalities have splintered into various dialect groups. Some, like Miao, had no written language at all until an alphabet was created after the Communist victory. The Zhuang, the largest nationality and the one best integrated with the Han, gave up their own script for Chinese over the centuries, only to have a new one created in 1955.

Literature and the arts. Of the nationalities with written languages, the Tibetans, Mongolians, Uygurs, and Manchus have produced the most literature. In the past, the first three cultures have written mostly religious works, while the early Manchu literature consists largely of historical texts. After the Manchu conquest (1644), Manchu literature merged with Chinese. These four nationalities, and most others as well, also possess rich traditions of oral, epic poetry, which is unknown in the Han culture. China's "three great epics" are the Tibetan

One of the largest groups among the Chinese minorities is the Miao. *Courtesy of the Smithsonian Institution.*

Gesar, the Mongolian *Jangghar*, and the Kyrgyz *Manas*. The ancient poems tell the stories of heroes, soldiers, kings, demons, and battles. Some, like the *Manas*, also give a vibrant snapshot of daily life in times past. They pass on traditions bordering on history, dealing with the nationality's origins, migrations, and conflicts with other peoples.

Traditional art forms include sculpture, architecture, and painting. Much is religious in nature, such as the famous Potala Palace in Lhasa, capital of Tibet, or the Buddhist sculptures of the Yungang Caves in northern China's Shanxi province. In non-religious daily life, crafts and performing arts, especially music and dance, hold a central place. Embroidery, weaving, and metalwork provide venues for traditional patterns and motifs. Often the patterns distinguish subgroups within a nationality, as they also mark the nationality itself. In many cultures, from those in the southwest (e.g., Miao) to the Turkic or Mongolian peoples of the north, music and dance provide the most important avenue for courtship. Love and wooing are the themes of traditional songs and dances performed at public festivals in which the whole community takes part. Such dances are especially common among the peoples of the southwest. Among the Dong, Miao, Yi, and Hani (all in the southwest) the dancers accompany themselves on a reed pipe. Courting lovers are partners in the dance, and may sneak off together while the dance continues.

For More Information

Gill, Lunda Hoy. *Portraits of China.* Honolulu: University of Hawaii Press, 1990.

Gladney, Dru, C. *Muslim Chinese.* Cambridge: Harvard University Press, 1991.

Rau, Margaret. *The Minority Peoples of China.* New York: Julian Messner, 1982.

FIJIANS

(fee′ jee uns)

Native peoples of the Fiji Islands.

Population: 360,100 (1990 estimate).
Location: 80 of more than 800 islands or islets that make up the Fijian group; 1,100 miles north of New Zealand and 1,700 miles northeast of Sydney, Australia. (More than half the population lives on one island, Viti Levu.)
Languages: English; Fijian.

Geographical Background

Of volcanic origin and enhanced by coral growths, the Fiji Islands lie in the belt of islands known as Melanesia. Although there are

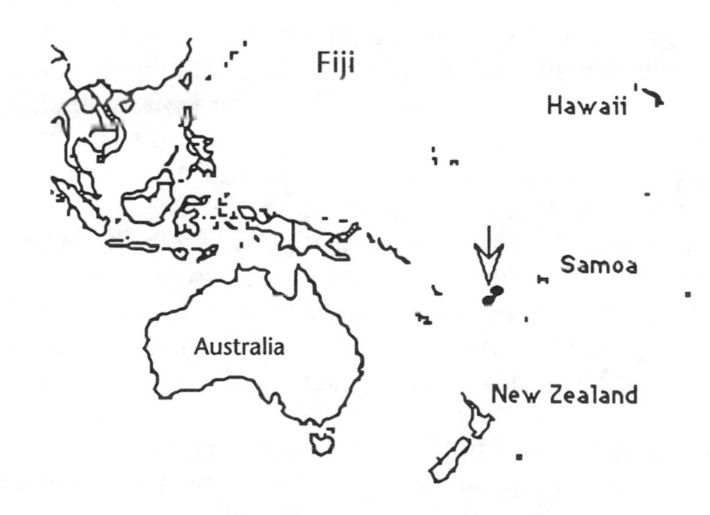

more than 250 islands of sufficient size to have once been claimed by the British, two islands make up more than 80 percent of the total land area—Viti Levu and Vanua Levu. Stretching for nearly 250 miles east to west, the entire island group lies south of the equator and is tropical in climate. Typical of tropical islands, each Fijian island has a wet side and a dry side. Moisture sweeps in from the windward and falls as rain as it rises over the central island hills. More than 100 inches of rain fall in many parts of the islands, helping a dense brush to grow over areas once covered by forests of sandalwood. The extinct volcanos spread ash over the islands making a fertile, but thin layer of topsoil. In this soil, plants such as palms, tree ferns, bamboo, and tree-sized orchids similar to those of the East Indies thrive. Animals found on the islands are mostly imported; the only native mammals are bats and rodents. There are, however, more than 80 species of birds of which more than 20 are unique to Fiji. The volcanic action has uncovered some mineral wealth on the large islands—gold, copper, and iron.

The climate of the islands is tropical, seldom varying more than between 60 degrees and 90 degrees Fahrenheit. However, the islands lie in a region where heavy winds and rains occur mostly in the months of April and November.

Historical Background

Early history. Sailors from mainland Asia reached the Fiji Islands more than 3,500 years ago. There they settled and developed a kind of pottery (Lapita) that has served to date and distinguish them. For centuries the Fijians lived and fought with one another on the various islands—ruled by an array of chiefs, each claiming jurisdiction over a small part of the land. Master sailors, the Fijians made boats of hollowed logs and sailed without navigation tools unerringly from one island to another across vast expanses of water.

These early settlers established an active trade with inhabitants on the other islands. The first navigators to reach the islands of the Pacific Ocean, these seamen then continued to settle Samoa, Tonga, and other islands in the regions now known as Melanesia and Polynesia. Thus the Fijians blended the distinct Polynesian characteristics with the languages of Melanesia.

Europeans. It was not until 1643 that the islands were sighted by sailors from European lands led by Abel Tasman. Captain James

Cook visited Fiji in 1773. A Frenchman, Dumont d'Urville, came in 1827, and the European interest in the Fijis began to grow. The various European interests encouraged the Fijian tradition of fighting among themselves. Local chiefs increased their warring over control of the islands until, in 1850, Ratu (Chief) Cakobau had gained authority over all the western islands. Almost immediately Cakobau began to differ with some United States' interests in the islands. To counter American disfavor, he turned to the British for support. He was at first unsuccessful in his request for help, but in 1874 the British agreed to adopt Fiji as a crown colony.

The British governors were careful to preserve the land for the original owners, but over time the Fijians themselves leased great portions of the most tillable land to British plantation builders. Sugar cane and coconut became prominent agricultural products for export. However, the first British governor, Sir Arthur Gordon, believed he would be protecting Fiji society by not hiring Fijians as plantation workers. Therefore, while 80 percent of the land remained in Fijian ownership, 90 percent of these valuable agricultural products were grown by foreigners. Later, epidemics of measles and influenza killed nearly half of the Fijians, and accelerated the importation of foreign workers. These came mostly from India, with some from China. (The popular name for an imported Chinese laborer, *coolie,* may have come from the Fijian word for dog, *koli.*) Indian indentured workers increased after World War II and the foreign population soon outnumbered the native Fijians. In the late 1800s and early 1900s, Fijians owned the land, had their own system of government, and made up the greatest portion of the army but were a minority to the Indians in the country.

Independence. In 1970 the people of Fiji became an independent nation within the British Commonwealth under their own constitution. For seventeen years, leadership of the government fell to a Fijian, Ratu Sir Kamisese Mara. However, a 1977 election brought victory to the Alliance Party. (The National Federation party actually won the election but failed to form a government due to internal friction.) The Indians feared Fijian reprisals and did not follow up the election by forming a government. Their fear proved to be well founded as in 1982 Fijians joined with a Nationalist Party that had been founded in 1970 dedicated to the motto "Fiji for Fijians." It was not until April of 1987 that the Indian majority was able to form a government. In May of the same year, the Indian-dominated Fijian

Fiji is a land of beautiful beaches and resorts. *Courtesy of Rebecca and Richard Harms.*

government was overthrown by a military coup led by Major General Sitiveni Rabuka. Rabuka governed with the aid of an Advisory Council drawing heavily on the Great Council of Chiefs, a long-standing body of the hereditary ratus of the Fijians.

Fijian majority. Throughout the major areas of Fiji, racial violence erupted along with demonstrations against the military regime. Many Indian people fled from the islands for fear of persecution. One result was that by 1989 Fijians, aided by a falling birthrate among Indians, were again the largest ethnic group on the islands, with 48 percent of the total population. The elected Indian officials pressed their claims in the Fiji Supreme Court and the Rabuka-appointed prime minister, Ratu Sir Penaia Garilau, pressed for a coalition government to ease the racial tensions. A compromise plan was developed, but before it could be put into action, Rabuka staged a second coup and announced that he would form a republic. The constitution was revoked and Queen Elizabeth II deposed as Head of State. By October 1987, the British-appointed governor had resigned and not been replaced. Fiji was no longer considered to be part of the British Commonwealth. A new constitution was devised and approved by the Great Council of Chiefs. Finally, in 1991, Rabuka eased fear of another military coup by resigning from military duty to become a member of the new Cabinet. Labor problems and disputes between the government and the Fijian Trades Union Conference have continued since the settling of the new government.

The new Fijian constitution provides for a house of representatives of 70 members elected so as to represent the ethnic diversity of Fiji: 37 native Fijians, 27 Indians, 5 who are neither Indian, Fijian, or Rotuman, and 1 Rotuman. (Rotuma is the largest of a group of small islands 230 miles north northwest of the larger islands of Fiji. It has been part of Fiji since 1881.) The Senate is appointed: 24 Fijians appointed by the Great Council of chiefs, 1 Rotuman, and 9 members, not Fijian or Rotuman, appointed by the president.

Culture Today

Social structure. Through all the turmoil over a national government, the old structure of Fijian society persisted. The basic unit of government of the Fijians is a patrilineal extended family, the *takatoka*, directed by a senior male. Several related takatoka come together in a *mataqali*, a clan. These clans are led by hereditary chiefs, the *Ratus*. Several mataqali, who trace their ancestry to a common god-ancestor, come together in a tribe, the *yavusa*, headed by a tribal chief. While these social organizations still exert much influence among the Fijians, they are no longer as powerful as in the past since the Fiji population now includes many people from other countries, particularly India. Thus the roles of the mataqali are changing from their earlier and adventurous traditions.

In earlier Fiji history, warfare among the clans and tribes, and rumors of cannibalism were common. (Cannibalism is said to have existed as recently as 1867 when one missionary, Reverend Thomas Baker, is reported to have been a victim of this practice.) Also almost vanished are the boats built for clan and tribal adventures to other island kingdoms. In earlier days, Fijians were master sailors (having originally come to the islands from Micronesia and then from Polynesia). They built great canoes of dug out or spliced-together logs with a second solid log as the outrigger. *Drua*, long boats of more than 100 feet decorated with shells, and moved by matted sails rigged on 60-foot-tall masts, carried warring parties throughout the island complex. The earlier Fijians were proud to be warriors. In fact, it was necessary for a young man to kill an enemy before being given full manhood status.

Also nearly vanished are the pre-Christian taboos and rituals, although *yagona*, a grog, is still used as a ceremonial drink. The

Events in Recent Fiji Political History

October 10, 1874	Fiji, ceded to Britain, becomes British Colony.
October 10, 1970	Fiji becomes independent under Ratu Sir Kanaisese Mara, the first prime minister of Fiji.
April 1977	Fiji's first general election. Although the National Federation Party gains most votes, it is unable to form a government. The Governor General invites Mara and his alliance party to form a caretaker government.
September 1977	General elections. Alliance Party gains the majority and returns as the governing body.
April 1987	General elections are won by a coalition of the Fiji Labour Party and the National Federation Party under the leadership of Dr. Mimou Bavadra.
May 14, 1987	A military coup led by Lieutenant Colonel Sitiveni Rabuka establishes an interim government directed by a Council of Ministers.
September 1987	The Denba Accord brings contending parties into a "government of national unity" until new elections can be held.
September 26, 1987	Military coup led by Mr. Rabuka. 1970 constitution is set aside and Rabuka declares himself Head of State.
October 7, 1987	Mr. Rabuka declares Fiji a republic.
October 16, 1987	Governor General Ratu Sir Penaia Gamilan resigns.
October 18, 1987	Fiji's membership in the British Commonwealth lapses.
December 5, 1987	Ratu Sir Penaia Gamilan is appointed Head of State and Ratu Sir Kamisese Mora becomes Prime Minister. Rabuka become Minister for Home Affairs in this interim government.
July 1990	A new constitution is adopted calling for a parliament of the President, a House of Representatives, and a Senate. The president is to be chosen by the Great Council of Chiefs for a term of five years.
June 1992	General elections led by Prime Minister Mr. Sitivens Rabuka.

presentation of the *tabua*, giving a sperm whale's tooth as a symbol of respect, is still sometimes used.

In the 1990s, Fijians are agriculturalists. Land cleared by the ear-

Fiji villagers are often relatives. This gathering is from Lami village.
Courtesy of Wayne Mitchell.

lier brisk trade in sandalwood has been transformed into sugar and coconut plantations, where Fijians join with Indians and Chinese to grow cash crops while growing maize and raising cattle and pigs for their own food. They are also traders and emerging industrialists; tourism is a large industry. The principal city, Suva, reflects tradition and change. In one section is the established trading and shipping center established under British rule. In another, modern high-rise hotels and offices cater to the growing tourist trade and other industries.

Village life. Suva is, however, not a large city, having a population of fewer than 200,000 including its suburban areas. Fijians are villagers. A clan or part of the clan selects a site, usually near the water, to build a village. A common "green" is developed and around it are placed the chief's house and consultation room, one of the *bures* and, once, a *bure kalori* (spirit house) but now a church. Another bure on the green is a visiting place for the village men and perhaps a place to house visitors to the village. Lesser dignitaries of the village locate their houses around the green, and other villagers build homes at greater distances from it. The distance from the green is indicative of the owner's social status. Also indicative of status is the height of the mound on which the house is erected. Thus a chief may build his house on a mound several feet high and ringed with a sort of stone fence. Lesser dignitaries build their homes on lower mounds and with lower retaining walls. Finally, the villagers with the lowest status live in homes raised only a few inches above normal ground level and with only a token row of stones marking the limits. In the past, houses were made of wood frames over which palm fronds and other large leaves formed a roof estending in a continuous line to form the house walls. Buildings in the village could be distinguished by their roofs. Homes had roofs supported by ridge poles and were rectangular, while the chief's consulting room had a pyramidal roof covering a square structure.

As exposure to other cultures grew, the Fijian home has changed. Clapboard became the material for walls, and tin roofs replaced the fronds. Homes became objects of Fijian art, with walls often decorated in bright colors. Wooden shutters or glass windows were added. In the 1990s, concrete has replaced the clapboard, particularly along the immediate coasts, as a better protection against the heavy winds and rains.

Food and clothing. The Fijian house is furnished simply. Mats for sitting and other mats piled on a sleeping mound make up the furniture. Meals are served on a tablecloth placed on the matted floor. Place settings of Western-style silverware may be laid on the cloth along with finger bowls should someone want to eat with fingers alone. A typical meal includes rice and yams in great quantity along with fish. On special occasions beef or pork may be added to these dishes. Small game such as birds are sometimes part of the diet. By the 1990s tinned goods, particularly meats, had been added to the menu.

Fijians were slow to change their old styles of dress. The loincloth and a simple skirt of leaves or barkcloth were sufficient dress in the tropical climate. Dress is still relaxed in Fiji although Western-style clothing is finding its way to all but the most remote villages. Loose-fitting shirts and trousers are customary in the larger towns as are simply designed dresses for the women.

Family life. Men still dominate the Fijian family, although women today do not eat separately from the men. They are still expected to prepare and serve the food. Men fish and tend the fields. Women take care of the home, which now is built for a lifetime. (In the past the wood and thatch houses lasted a maximum of 20 years and were then abandoned, to be replaced by new homes built near the site of

Open markets are common sights in Fiji. *Courtesy of Wayne Mitchell.*

the old decaying ones. Today, the old homes are rennovated and kept in use.)

Religion. According to legend, the first Fijians came to the island from a distant place in a very large boat, Kuamitoni, carrying settlers and the materials they would need to reestablish their lives in the islands. They brought plants to sow, as well as domesticated animals. They also brought a religion that included veneration of several gods, chief of which was Degai, the creator god who made the world and Fijians. The 1800s brought Christian missionaries to the islands and Christianity was soon the religion of the majority. The Fijians blended Christian teachings with their old beliefs to create their unique brand of Christianity. In this new religion, for example, Degai was transformed into a heathen devil. Fijians have been introduced to Hinduism and Islam. Still, 53 percent of the islands' inhabitants and nearly all the native Fijians claim Christianity as their religion. Christianity today is practiced nearly as it is in the Western world, with Catholic practices sanctioned by the Vatican and Methodism practiced as preached by John Wesley.

Chinese immigrants to Fiji have brought their Confucian philosophy to the Fijians, who readily adopted these thoughts and integrated them into their old as well as the new Christian religions. Balance in a world of opposites, blending with or becoming part of the rhythms of nature, and accepting one's duty to society and reflecting it in rules of decorum and etiquette are parts of the Fijian culture. This sense of etiquette is illustrated by the custom of lowering one's head at the sight of a chief so as always to be below that person.

Language and literature. English is the official language of Fiji. However, Fijian is widely used. This is an ancient oral language to which a Roman alphabet was fitted by David Cargill in the 1830s. However, even though Fijian words can now be written in Roman letters, some of these letters carry different sounds than in English. For example the letter *b* is pronounced in Fijian *mb*, *d* is *nd*, *c* is *th*, and *g* is *ng*. Some words spelled identically take on different meanings according to the accented part; *kaka* has different meanings according to the pronunciation of the final *a*.

Since English was in common usage before there was a written Fijian language, most of the Fijian literary heritage is oral. A vehicle for this oral history, the *meke,* is still a popular recreation among Fijians. In the meke, historical events, epics, and legends are told, sung, and danced. One popular dance, the spear dance, reflects the days of intertribal warfare.

Education. While there are no such examples as the queen of the Fijians' distant relatives, the Hawaiians, who is said to have learned to read in five days, Fijians are avid learners. Elementary education, which includes elementary school from ages six to twelve and an additional two-year program, is offered by the state. Even though this schooling is not compulsory, more than 94 percent of the young people attend school. Students may choose to advance to the University of the South Pacific located in the only sizeable town (population 70,000) in the nation and its capital, Suva. The result of this educational opportunity and the Fijian interest in learning has been a large reduction in illiteracy. In 1976, 21 percent of the Fijian population was illiterate. By 1986 that number had been reduced to 15 percent.

Outside influences. The impact on contact with Western nations is illustrated by the change in materials for home construction, in the development of light industries and exploitation of forests and minerals, but most visibly in the numbers of radio and television sets in the country. In a total country population of 588,000 there are 410,000 radio receivers and 55,000 television receivers. China has also had much influence in Fiji and in 1991 supported the construction of two television transmitters—one in Suva and the other in Monsavu, a town of fewer than 20,000 inhabitants.

For More Information

Deane, W. *Fijian Society*. New York: AMS Press, 1977.

Geraghty, Paul. *The History of Fijian Languages*. Honolulu: University of Hawaii Press, 1983.

Sahlins, Marshall D. *Islands of History*. Chicago: University of Chicago Press, 1985.

Thomas, Nicholas. *Planets Around the Sun: Dynamics and Contradictions of the Fijian Matanitu*. Sydney, Australia: University of Sydney, 1986.

Wright, Ronald. *On Fiji Islands*. New York: Viking-Penguin, 1986.

FILIPINOS

(fihl ih pee′ nohs)

People of Malay, Chinese, Spanish, and American heritage who live in the Philippines.

Population: 60,685,000 (1991 estimate).
Location: About 7,100 islands that extend 1,200 miles north to south and separate the South China Sea from the Pacific Ocean.
Languages: English, Pilipino (a Tagalog dialect), and more than seventy languages of native groups.

Geographical Setting

The Philippine Islands are of volcanic origin and remain mountainous except for narrow coastal plains and inland valleys on the larger islands, such as the central plateau of Luzon, the Cagayan Valley of Luzon's largest river in the north east of that island, and the basin of the Agusan River on Mindanao. Luzon in the north and Mindanao in the south anchor the array of islands. These two islands make up nearly two-thirds of the land mass of the Philippines.

The region is one of tropical climate and active volcanoes. The temperature hovers around 80 degrees Fahrenheit in most parts of the islands. There are two seasons, a wet (monsoon) season and a dry one. Except for the extreme southwest, rainfall is more than eighty inches a year throughout the islands. Once covered with tropical forests, about half the land of the Philippines remains hardwood forests, where the most well-known tree is the *narra*, or Philippine mahogany. However, as with most tropical forests, the number of plant species is great; more than 2,000 tree varieties grow in these forests.

The volcanic soil is rich, allowing farmers in places such as the Cagayan Valley to produce rice and other crops for the islands and

for the world. At higher elevations, the volcanic rock contains many important minerals.

Historical Background

Early settlers. Perhaps as long ago as 30,000 years, Negrito people from the Asian continent migrated to the Philippines over landbridges that joined the regions at that time. Through many centuries, after the landbridges disappeared, Malay explorers settled along the coasts and in the river valleys of the islands. The multitude of islands and their rugged terrain resulted in these settlers separating into separate groups that developed their own languages. Over the years, these groups established a common lifestyle based on a small village or part of a village made up of people who were kin or were dependent upon one another. This barrio life (in the Philippines a barrio is called a *barangay*) is the basis of Philippine life today, except in the largest cities.

The Filipinos established rice farming and fishing and carried on an active trade with their old homelands in Malaysia. By the tenth century, they had extended their trade activities to China, and by the fifteenth century to Japan. But shortly, Spanish intervention turned Filipino attention toward the west.

Spanish rule. In the A.D. 1500s, Malayans brought the Muslim religion to the southern island of Mindanao. However, in that same century Ferdinand Magellan landed in the Philippines and claimed them for Spain, naming the region after the Spanish king Phillip II. Although Magellan was killed by a local Filipino chief, the Spanish were soon to control the islands. By 1565, Miguel Lopez de Legazpi had founded a settlement at Cebu on a central island and had begun to drive the Muslim ruler from Manila. (Muslims were eventually restricted to the southwest of the archipelago.) From that time until 1868, except for two years (1762–1764) when British seamen captured Manila, the Philippines were claimed by Spain, although often with such little interest that the real government of the territory came from Spanish Mexico.

In real practice, the Philippines became dominated by representatives of the Roman Catholic church. Franciscans, Augustinians, and Recollect friars settled in each barangay, establishing small churches as headquarters and taking on such tasks as educating the Filipinos, providing health services, taking the census, collecting taxes, and reporting the activities of villagers to the Spanish governors. Most of these friars were from Mexico or Spain, and few Filipinos could aspire to positions of responsibility. The friars and government appointees established restrictions on the Filipinos. They were sometimes forced into corvée labor (labor for the government or church with little or no pay, called *polo*) and *vandela* (forced sale of their produce through government channels).

Over the years of Spanish rule, resentment grew over polo and vandela, but particularly over the lack of opportunity for Filipinos in the church orders. While Catholicism grew and Islam was restricted to the southwestern area, there were numerous signs of unrest, most of them readily suppressed by the Spanish governors. By 1744, one dissenter, Francisco Dagoboy, had gathered an army and established a separate "kingdom" in Bohol. This group managed to remain relatively independent until 1929.

Another dissenter, Apolinario de la Cruz, a Tagalog of Luzon, became disenchanted when he was not able to become a friar and organized the Contradia de San José. Many Tagalog people joined him in rebellion, but in 1841, de la Cruz was captured and executed. His followers fled into the mountains.

Rebellions of these sorts resulted in some action by the Spanish. In 1863, government schools were organized, diminishing some of the strength of the friars. Then in 1868, Carlos Maria de la Torre became the Spanish governor and established a much more understanding government. Filipinos could now aspire to become *gobernadorillos*, pueblo magistrates. Still, in the early 1870s, only 181 of 973 Catholic parishes were served by Filipino friars. Yet it was the actions of Catholic leaders that led to the final expulsion of Spanish rule.

In 1872, a year after the rule of de la Torre, 200 dock workers in Manila rebelled against their working conditions. As the incident was suppressed, three Catholic priests were accused of encouraging the rebellion. Over the protests of the bishop of Manila, Bishop Martinez, the three were tried and executed in a public park. Bishop Martinez responded by calling for church bells throughout the Philippines to toll in honor of the priests. This was the stimulus for renewed and more vigorous rebellion. By this time, strong leadership was emerging from *ilustrados*, children of prosperous Filipinos with advanced educations. A Filipino lawyer, José Rizal, established the Liga Filipino to press for independence. Andres Bonifacio established a secret order, Katipunan, to work for the same purpose. Although Rizal was arrested and exiled, and Bonifacio was paid hundreds of millions of pesos to move to Hong Kong, the spirit of nationalism and pressure for independence continued.

Freedom from Spain. However, it was another island in another ocean that finally brought the downfall of the Spanish rule in the Philippines. Concerned over the Spanish stronghold in the Americas, Cuba, the United States involved itself in war with Spain over Cuban independence. As part of this war, Commodore George Dewey sailed into Manila Bay in 1898 with the idea of destroying the Spanish ships there. That accomplished, Dewey made an alliance with rebel Filipinos to take Manila. This partnership was soon dissolved, as Dewey was instructed to severe his connection with the rebels and therefore refused their help in taking the city. Anticipating Filipino independence, Bonifacio returned to Manila but was persuaded to stand for government by the United States until such time as the Filipinos were prepared for self-government. The Treaty of Paris, signed in December 1898, gave rule of the Philippines to the United States. As the "invasion" of Manila was prearranged between Spanish and Americans, this treaty was unusual in that the two governments exchanged "gifts"—in exchange for $20,000,000, Spain gave the Philippines to the United States. But, anticipating their own freedom, Filipinos had organized for self-government. Emilio Aguinaldo, mayor of the town of Cavite, had organized a provisional government and an assembly. When it was clear that the United States had no intention of immediately relinquishing the islands, a two-year war between the Filipinos and Americans demanded the involvement of 126,000 American troops. Twenty thousand soldiers from both sides were killed before Aguinaldo settled for a promise of future independence. His followers continued the rebellion through 1903.

A presidential commission appointed in 1899 declared the Filipinos not ready for independence. A series of American congressional acts were put in place to prepare for this eventual self-government: an act of 1902 that provided for some Filipino participation in government; the Jones Act (1916), which established a popularly elected Senate and House of Representatives for the Philippines; and an act of 1934 that established commonwealth status for this area. Full independence was to come in 1945. (In reality the Philippines were restored to full commonwealth status again in this year as World War II ended.) Through all these changes, the Moros (southwestern Muslims) objected to independence, feeling that their small minority was better served if protected from the Christian majority by an outside government.

Independence. A major deterrent to independence was the rapid growth of the population. This resulted in some agricultural failure and some restructuring of the old and very close bonds between landlords and tenants. A greater deterrent was World War II, during which Japan successfully invaded and took control of the Philippines. Fighting for their freedom from the Japanese, 1,000,000 Filipinos lost their lives. Full independence came in 1946. Ramon Magsaysay became the first president of the Republic of the Philippines.

Since that time, the Philippines have been in almost constant turmoil, with a government thought to represent only the elite being opposed in civil war by communist groups who occupy the inland parts of the islands, and by the Moros who feel that their only safety is in complete independence from the Christian majority.

Marcos. The most dynamic, and controversial, leader in recent years was Ferdinand Marcos, who became president in a popular election in 1963 and was re-elected through 1986, although he had declared martial law in 1972 and become a virtual dictator over the islands. Accused of conducting false elections and of exploiting government monies for his own uses, Marcos was forced to withdraw after an election he claimed to have won in 1986. He was replaced by Corazon Aquino, wife of Benigno Aquino, a Marcos opponent who had been assassinated in 1983.

Aquino. The presidency of Corazon Aquino has been marked by civil war with communist groups and the Moros, by accusations of her own governments misdealings, and by re-emergence of the longstanding resentment of a United States presence in the Philippines. Remembering past oppressions, many Filipinos pressed for dissolution of the two large naval and air bases leased by the United States, Subic Bay and Clark Air Base. These bases became less desirable after nearby volcanic action in 1983, but were the subject of discussion and negotiation resulting in an offer of more than $480,000,000 annually in payment by the United States and a counter demand of nearly $1,000,000,000 annually by the Aquino government. Under these circumstances, the United States has agreed to withdraw from the Philippines. Since these dealings Corazon Aquino has been replaced in a new presidential election by Fidel Ramos.

Culture Today

Villagers. The major division among Filipinos today is not religion nor politics, but a division between city-dwellers and rural inhabitants. While 8,000,000 Filipinos live in cities larger than 100,000 citizens (more than 5,000,000 live in Manila and its suburbs), seven of ten Filipinos live in small towns and villages. Here life centers on the church and on values that focus on unity of the local barangay.

The structure of these villages is changing as the Philippines search for ways to participate in the world market. Some villages, especially those nearer the large metropolises, contain homes of wood frame or stucco homes not unlike those in the United States and Europe. The homes in more distant villages are often made almost exclusively of bamboo, with palm leaf roofs. Often these homes are built on stilts to protect against floods. A typical barangay, or village, contains 150 to 200 houses and a chapel. There is most often a village elementary school. Within the barangay, which is the smallest unit of government, related families cluster their homes into a *sitio*, a group in which the people are interdependent.

In the past, each barangay was ruled by a local chief, a *datu*, who was chosen for his ability to settle local disputes and his strength in battle with other barangay. The power of these chiefs has given way to local rule by nationally appointed agents in the 1980s and 1990s, but the datu are still powerful among inland mountain people and among the Moros, southern Muslims.

Family life. The sitios of each barangay are often groups of related families. Thus the family is the center of Filipino life. The related families in the sitio share work in the fields or help with preparations for special events. Once landowners and tenants lived close together in the barangay, but in the 1990s landlords have distanced themselves more from their tenants, often living in the major cities instead of the barangay.

The typical family is one of a single husband and wife and their children. In the home, the mother is responsible for the care of the home and the children. She watches the family finances, and helps decide on investments. The Filipino woman has long been a behind-the-scenes power in family decisions and in decisions between families. Still, many Filipino women work outside the home, helping support the family with a second income. In these jobs, women are accepted and can become leaders in their professions. Imelda Marcos, wife of Ferdinand Marcos, Corazon Aquino, the former Philippine president, and Eva Estrada Kalaw are examples of women in government who have risen to positions of power outside their own families.

Food and clothing. Rice is the staple food of the Filipinos and is often accompanied by the abundant fish from nearby waters. The ocean area south of Mindanao is one of the richest fisheries in the world, and the largest fish in the world have been found in Manila Bay. Fishing fleets of bamboo rafts rigged with nets comb the rivers and streams for fish.

The soil of the Philippines is rich and produces a wide variety of fruits and vegetables for the Filipino table. Centuries ago, the mountain people known as Ifugao carved terraces in the mountains for growing rice. In other places, banana plantations, pineapple farms, and sites for growing many kinds of tropical fruits have been cleared.

Most often, because of their long exposure to Europe and the Americas, Filipinos wear Western-style clothing. But some rural people still dress in the pajama-like costumes of earlier times. Farmers in the Philippines often go barefoot. Hats are seldom worn on the islands. During fiestas, of which there are many, Filipino men don shoes and the national costume, the *barang tagalong*, which is a long-tailed shirt with a starched collar and embroidered panels worn over conventional trousers. The cloth for the barang tagalong is made from pineapple fiber and is silklike and light.

Women wear a *balintawak*, a two-piece dress consisting of a *camisa* and *saya* (skirt). The camisa is made of hemp fiber dyed vivid colors and ruffled into fanlike pieces over the shoulders. The saya is a colored cotton skirt reaching to the ankles. A scarf and wooden shoes (*bakya*) or slippers (*zapatilla*) complete the woman's fiesta costume.

Values. The people of the barangay are held together largely by the emphasis on esteem for self and others. Called *amor proprio*, this esteem is reflected in the ways the members of the barangay address each other and behave toward one another. Filipino villagers live under *hiya*, a fear that they will bring disgrace to their families or themselves by improper behavior to another. Those who do not manifest the proper esteem for others are said to be "*walang haya*" (without shame), and therefore not to be respected themselves. Filipino village life is based on *tiwala*, trust.

Strong bonds with one another arise from tiwala. Filipinos value above all good relationships and firm bonds among kin. They extend these relationships to include *compadrazgo* (ritual kins developed from baptism, confirmation, or marriage) and *barkada* (friends). Another bonding link among Filipinos is based on *utang na loob*, repayment of debt. Saving a life, providing an educational opportunity, and providing employment are the bases for lifetime loyalties. Filipinos also form buyer-seller bonds, in which a seller provides the best goods for a good price, and the buyer restricts purchases to that seller.

Religion. Ninety percent of the Filipinos are Roman Catholic, five percent are Muslim, and four percent belong to other faiths. Muslims in the Philippines adhere to much that is held important in other Muslim groups. They take pride in making the hajj, the pilgrimage to Mecca, and in returning home wearing the symbolic white turban. Muslims attend to the muezzin call to prayer several times a day and enter the mosque shoeless to prostrate themselves toward Mecca to pray. However, Philippine Muslims take a more relaxed view of other practices—for example, women are not required to wear veils.

Both Muslims and Roman Catholics in the Philippines blend that basic religion with religious concepts of local importance or historical importance, such as the belief in the intervention of spirits. Still, Roman Catholicism is holding strong in the face of spin-off religions that have their bases in the Filipino revolution. Cults such as the Iglesia Filipina Independiente grew through confiscation of Catholic property and conversion of Catholic priests early in this century. The Iglesia ni Kristo began in 1914 and has grown as an anchor for fading values. Its members must attend church twice a week and pay specified membership dues based on ability to pay. Members cannot belong to a labor union, must be clean and well-groomed, and must not overindulge in alcohol or gambling. In the past, this church instructed its members on how to vote.

Education. Filipinos place strong emphasis on education. Each barangay has an elementary school open to all children and patterned after the schools of the United States. In 1990, about 10,000,000 students attended the more than 30,000 elementary schools. Most of these were public schools supported by the government. However, there were also about 1,200 schools operated by the Catholic church, more than 120 schools run by the Chinese minority, and about 1,000 madrasahs (Muslim schools). The public schools offer six years of elementary school and four years of high school. However, some barangays can afford only four years of elementary school, and only one-sixth of the elementary students attend high school. In the elementary schools, students often begin learning in their local language or in Pilipino, then change to English after three years. So, many Filipinos are bilingual or even trilingual at an early age. Nearly ninety percent of Filipinos are literate.

Although high school students are required to pay a fee to attend school, nearly half the high school age children attend school. The importance of education in the Philippines can be seen in the number of university and college students. More than 1,000,000 students attend 810 institutions of higher learning.

The importance of university education has been borne out in the history of the Filipinos. Leaders of the movement for independence, which reached its strength in the 1890s, were *ilustrados*, children of wealthy families who were sent to high schools even when there were few schools for non-Spaniards. Many of these leaders of the revolution attended the University of Santo Tomás in Manila or were sent overseas for a university education.

Arts. In the history of the Philippines, as many as 200 different groups have separated themselves from others and established tribal languages. Then for more than 300 years, Spanish was the language of the lowlands, except in the south where the Arabic language was used by the Moros. A large minority of Chinese, mostly merchants, used their own language. A result has been the development of literature in a half-dozen languages, each having been expressed in more than 100 books. With Spanish overlords, most of the writing and speech was Spanish, but that language has nearly disappeared from usage in the Philippines now. Today, books and newspapers are printed in English, while Pilipino, a Tagalog dialect, is required to be taught in the schools.

Perhaps greater than the fragmented tradition in literature, Filipinos are known for their music and dance. One Filipino dance that has become well known elsewhere is performed to the music of a guitar and the rhythmic beating of two bamboo poles held at each end and clapped together just above ground level. Dancers in their colorful traditional costumes skip and hop in and out between the poles as these are clapped. The dance is named after the sound of the poles striking each other, the *tinikling*. Other dances reflect local influences. For example, dances of the Moros in the south are slow and rhythmic like the dances in Malaysia. Dances are performed at fiestas, of which there are many, to the music of *musikong bumbong* (bands with bamboo instruments) or *rondella* (guitar players). Singing is also part of each fiesta. The most popular old song is the *Kundeman* (a great love song). But exposure to Western influences has brought all forms of music to the Filipinos. Their country is among the most Westernized of all Asian countries.

Gold is one of the minerals mined in the Philippines and gold jewelry is made by artisans there. Artists in other tribal groups are skilled potters. Some Ifugao, the ancient rice growers who developed the mountainous rice terraces, have become skilled wood carvers who produce animal figures, human figures, and other sculptures from the hardwoods of the Philippine forests.

Economy. In the 1990s, educators have been concerned about the weakening of financing for education as the national government has struggled with reorganization and recovery from the excesses of the

Marcos government. With the weak economy, twenty percent of the workers are unemployed. About half the 23,000,000 Filipino laborers are farmers, fishers, or lumber people. The farmers raise rice for local use and for export. On Luzon, hemp is a strong market product, and on Mindanao, tobacco. Still, Filipinos are dependent on imported food to supplement their own farm produce. In many places, farming is still done with unsophisticated tools such as plows drawn by water buffalo.

A major obstacle to modernization of farming, besides the rugged terrain, which requires terracing of rice cultivation in some areas, there is a lack of energy. Petroleum was discovered in the Philippines in the 1970s and the industry is still growing toward its maximum potential. The problem of energy supply is seen in the frequent blackouts and brownouts in Manila and other places on the island of Luzon.

The land of the Filipinos is rich in mineral resources; copper and aluminum are major items of export. However, about one-fourth of the potential mineral wealth of the country has not been tapped. Filipinos hold a rich land, but one that has long been less than fully developed.

Holidays. Filipinos celebrate many holidays related to their struggles for independence in addition to the traditional Christian holidays. February 25 is Freedom Day, the day in 1986 when the Filipinos ousted the Marcos government. May 6 is Araw ng kagitingan. June 12 is the Filipino Independence, the day of the declaration of freedom from Spain in 1898. July 4, 1946, was the day on which the Philippine Islands became independent of the United States and is celebrated each year as Philippine-American Friendship Day. August 27 is National Heroes' Day. November 30 is Bonifacio Day and December 30 is Rizal Day, celebrations honoring the two major champions of Filipino independence.

Beyond the national holidays, each barangay in the Philippines has its own patron saint. This saint is celebrated with a fiesta—there are so many fiestas that one can be attended nearly every day of the year. To celebrate, a fairground is set up near the church, and villagers come to dance, sing, and ride carnival rides. Cockfights are popular events at the fiestas as is the enacting of the drama, Moro-moro, an old and violent play about the battles between Christians and Muslims.

Two popular fiestas occur in May. The Flores de May features girls dancing and the crowning of the Queen of the Flowers. Santa-

Prosperous Filipinos enjoy a decorated jeep, but this one is used as a taxi. *Courtesy of Dr. W. Paul Fischer.*

cruzan commemorates the recovery of the Holy Cross, although today it has almost lost its religious meaning. Boys and girls parade with lighted candles behind a girl who portrays Reina Helena and a boy who plays Emperor Constantine. These two represent the ancient champion of Christianity, Emperor Constantine, and his mother, Helena.

For More Information

Bunge, Frederica M., ed. *Philippines: A Country Study*. Washington, DC: American University, 1983.

Mossman, Jennifer, ed. *Holidays and Anniversaries of the World.* Detroit: Gale Research, 1990.

Nelson, Raymond. *The Philippines.* New York: Walker and Company, 1968.

The Europa World Yearbook, 1991. London: Europa Publications Ltd, 1991.

GONDS

(gaunds)

Animistic people of central India.

Population: 4,000,000 (1990 estimate).
Location: Central India.
Language: Gondi, a Dravidian language.

Geographical Setting

The land of the Gonds is a region known as the Central Provinces of India, particularly Orissa. It is a mountainous, tree-covered plateau marked by large rivers on three sides—the Pain Ganga, Pranhita, and Godavari on the west, the Indravati on the east, and the Nerbudda on the north.

The Gonds were early associated with a large region in India known as Gondwana. While so varied in landscape that some parts serve as watersheds for the many streams, the land is almost universally hilly. The Gond villages lie in the valleys or plateaus at altitudes of 2,000 to 4,000 feet. The numerous streams coursing northward and southward through the hills provide sufficient water for some Gonds to practice agriculture with irrigation.

Gondwana was central to a subcontinent of India that once was a separate continent. Scientists developing the idea of plate tectonics, borrowed the name of the old kingdom and its people to name the prehistoric separate continent of Gondwanaland.

Historical Background

Origins. The people known collectively as Gonds make up several related tribes, each arriving at their own place and developing dif-

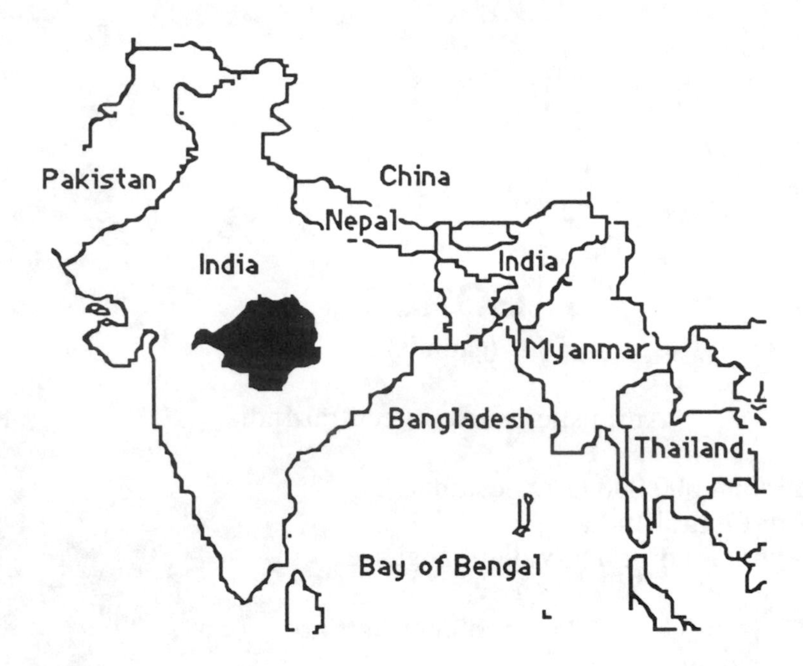

fering but similar cultures at different times. They were probably very early settlers in the mountains, having arrived in central India before the Dravidians settled there and later moved to the south. Folktales of the Gond people who inhabit mountain areas in central India tell of a single female ancestor from whom all Gonds can trace their heritage. Other stories tell of a great council called by the gods, at which no gods of Gond appeared. Thereupon, Karta Subal, the heir of Shiva, who had created the Gonds, fasted and begged for the gods of the Gonds to be represented in the Divine Council. Thus began the recognition of the Gond people.

The scarce factual accounts of the people place them in the central mountains of India, where they were living in small feudal organizations before the thirteenth century. Possibly the name Gond is associated with a word for hill and may have been given the people by early Hindu or Muslim visitors more as a description of the place where the Gonds live. Most Gonds called themselves Koitors until the Indian government began to use the new name.

Mongols and Maranthas. By A.D. 1240, clans of the Gonds had formed a loosely held empire that included a number of kingdoms with a central capital at Sirpur. These Gond kings paid tribute to Mogul emperors when they conquered the area and so remained in power. They built capitals in large walled cities and accumulated great wealth. However failing to unite and with little hold on the Gond peasants, the kingdoms were overrun by nearby Maratha kings in the 1700s and absorbed into the Maratha Empire. Many Gonds retreated to the mountains and there continued their own traditions in small villages.

Britain. In the 1800s, Great Britain took control of the area, and the Gonds became British subjects until independence was granted to India in 1947. Today, the Gonds live in forested areas of central India separated from other groups by their tendency to cling to animistic religions along with Hinduism.

The Indian government has considered the tribal nature of some of its citizens to be a problem. The national government has therefore assigned leaders of local governments, managers of the forest in Gond lands, and have endeavored to draw the Gonds into the mainstream of Indian society.

Over the years, Gonds have grown more and more to be a part of the major body of Indians, adopting the English language and sometimes, Western-style dress. But they have continued to hold to a culture that is based on tranquility and kindliness, with a distinct religion that is a blend of old animism and Hindu ideas.

Culture Today

Politics and economics. Organized into clans, the dark-skinned, round-faced Gond people live today much as they have for centuries, sometimes with one clan occupying a single village, but sharing the village with other people who are allowed to do the more undesirable tasks. There are many different Gond groups (e.g., Raj Gonds, Murias, Dhakar), so there are many different kinds of village patterns. While some villages consist of tightly grouped homes, others are more widely spread communities with sections that house vocational specialties. The residents in each section are identified with one particular way of earning a living—there are sections for blacksmiths, artists, farmers, cattle raisers, fishermen, and so on. Some of the farming groups continue to plow the fields with wooden, ox-drawn plows and are still migratory, shifting from one place to another so the soil can replenish itself. They clear forest land to farm, then after a year leave the land to reforest itself and clear other lands. In earlier times, rajas presided over each Gond group. The Gonds were loosely bound into one group by kinship among the rajas. Today a headman and priests settle issues in the village; they in turn are managed by a government-appointed manager or managers.

Villages. In 1980, one researcher, Kidar Nath Thusu, described one Gond village, Kamalapur, in the south of the Gond kingdom of Chanda. A village of more than 300 Gonds, Kamalapur is a place where several unpaved streets intersect, connecting this village with others and with parts of itself that are separated from the main village by a half mile or more. Houses are scattered along these dirt roads sometimes closely, sometimes seemingly randomly. The houses have thatched or tiled roofs that slope either two or four ways. Three of the houses in the village serve also as shops, but a row of newer buildings facing the main street are also shops, marking Kamalapur as a shopping center. There is a small area in the village where a weekly market is held. Ten wells provide water for the houses, although there is a reservoir nearby that holds water for animals and agricultural use as well as for bathing and washing clothes.

The village of Kamalapur, like most other Gond villages, has well-identified shrines which are visited by the villagers at appropriate

A parade in the Hindu holy city of Hardwar, India. *Courtesy of Dr. W. Paul Fischer.*

times to plead causes with the gods of the village. Kamalapur has six such shrines, ranging from uncarved wooden posts to stone images, some roofed over with palm fronds, and sometimes left open to the elements.

The village and its two suburban settlements were carved from forest land. About 500 acres have been cleared for farming and for housing, leaving more than one million acres of forest land adjacent to the village.

As in other Gond villages, a large percentage of the residents are not Gonds, but Hindus, Muslims, and peoples of other religions. These residents do not own land around the village but do tasks other than farming, which are less appealing to the Gonds. In Kalamapura, for example, two of these people operate grocery stores, several make leather products, and one is a teacher in the village school.

Villages are further classified or described according to how many local deities are claimed. A village of six shrines holds a different ranking than one of, for example, four shrines.

Social structure. The social patterns of the Gonds have grown more complex through the years of association and rule by Mughals, Maratha, British, and the Indian government. A ruling class, known as Raj Gonds, separates itself from the others by refusing to take food or drink from the hands of people of lesser caste. These include other Gonds (Naik-Gonds, Dadwe Gonds, Gaita Gonds, etc.). Some of the Raj Gonds form an elite aristocratic section called Srimants—those believed to hold political power. The former feudal chiefs, Jagirdars, although now supposedly without power, are still respected and cared for by other villagers. In addition, some families of former landholders from the time when land could be gained through service to the ruling Raja, the Zemindar, hold special rank within the society. In recent years, these classifications have tended to break down as the government of India appoints officers to manage the cities and the forests. Thus some of the old rulers become paid government employees while some lose their authority.

Many Gond legends have arisen about the origins of some Gond clans. One story tells how a poorer clan was created:

> A monkey married a human girl, and the marriage was not successful, and yet the clan has descended from the couple.
>
> (Mehta 1984, p. 406)

Food, clothing, and shelter. Villages such as Kamalapur are made up of small homes that typically include a living room, kitchen, loft or attic, and a veranda. Built of timber and bamboo with thatched roofs, homes are lightly furnished since it is not the custom to acquire many worldly goods. Furnishing may consist only of mats and necessary cooking pots and pans.

Men dress in a loincloth, often with a Western-style shirt or coat. Women usually wear cotton blouses and saris, long cloth strips with one end wrapped around the waist as a skirt and the other draped over the shoulder. Accessories include heavy beaded or aluminum jewelry—necklaces and anklets—worn by both men and women. An important part of a woman's costume among some Gonds is a white bamboo comb.

The clans of the Gonds each demonstrate some unique qualities. For example, the members of the Moria clan tattoo their faces and shave their heads.

Growing up. Boys and girls among the Muria Gonds live in village dormitories known as *ghotuls*. Girls accept combs from boys they find attractive and may end up wearing as many as six combs in a row. Then when they marry, each girl limits the wearing of combs to just the one selected by her husband. The forming of romantic relationships is encouraged and the young people are trained in the civic duties of adult members of the group. Women and men share chores and responsibilities equally in the Gond community.

Once young men and women were united in marriage by agreement of their families before the age of twenty. But as Gond communities were brought into the manufacturing and industrial complex of India, the marriageable age has tended to increase. Marriage may or may not involve a special marriage ceremony. One account tells of a couple who married by living together and by the wife cooking for her husband. They were subsequently called to task by the village council for not having a wedding ceremony. The penalty for this action was a fine assessed to the husband and used to buy drink with which to celebrate the occasion—accompanied by an admonition by the elders to respect the marital union in which the couple had united.

When a couple does have a formal marriage ceremony, the bride is escorted to the groom's house and a marriage ceremony is performed in the groom's family's cattle shed.

Bearing many children is encouraged in the Gond family. Most often the birth is attended by a village midwife, who is paid according to the sex of the baby. Boys are considered more desirable than girls and demand a higher pay to the midwife.

Religion. The Gonds pay tribute to many gods, both of Hindu beliefs and of their own animistic faith, and have a system of worship that includes animal sacrifice and ancestor worship. A person is thought to have a *shade* that joins its ancestors after death and a soul that joins a supreme god Bhagwan and may then be reincarnated in the same family on earth. To the Gonds, Shiva is the creator god (who became the destroyer god of the Hindus). Another universally held god, Lingo, is said in some villages to be the creator of the youth

This Stupa is in the region of the Gonds in central India. *Courtesy of Shiva Rea Bailey.*

halls, in others as a playful companion to the village girls, and in others to be a ruthless and cruel punisher of his own wives.

Gond religious beliefs also ascribe spirits and powers to the living things and even to inanimate objects. One story tells of an evil man who set out to destroy a village by breaking a dam above it. Succeeding, Kana Pen also emptied the water in which the bod fish lived. A bod fish vowed to eat out one of Kana Pen's eyes and succeeded in doing so.

> Since that day we worship him and with him we worship the bod fish in order to stop it eating his other eye.
>
> (Mehta 1984, p. 407)

In accordance with tradition, families erect monuments to departed relatives. In some communities these practices and other old ways of life are yielding to the new India as the land in which the Gonds have traditionally moved about freely becomes more populated and Gond communities become more permanent.

Festivals. Throughout the year, Gond villagers arrange festivals in honor of their gods and to celebrate planting and harvesting. One festival, Pola, is noted with decorations of the horns of cattle and with special food, singing, and dancing. The festival of Deepavali also includes special foods, song, and dance (mostly performed by young people of the village and visitors from nearby villages). The celebration begins with decorating houses with geometric patterns painted with rice flour and arranging special lamps in the yards of many of the houses. There is a religious ceremony at one or more of the shrines. Other celebrations include ritual eating of the new rice harvest or the picking of the mahua flowers that are sold in markets. Some Gond festivals require sacrifices of goats to the gods.

For More Information

Kidar Nath Thusu. *Gond Kingdom of Chanda.* Calcutta, India: Anthropological Survey of India, 1980.

Mehta, B. H. *Gonds of the Central Indian Highlands.* New Delhi, India: Concept Publishing Company, 1984.

GURKHA

(ghor ka′)

A group claiming descent from the powerful Hindu rulers of northern India, who settled in Nepal and are noted for their service in British and Indian armies.

Population: 600,000 (1990 estimate).
Location: Nepal.
Language: English.

Geographical Setting

While the southern part of the country of Nepal flattens into a great valley below Mount Katmandu, the northern part contains some of the highest mountains in the world. The Nepal Valley, a plateau at least a mile high, spreads between the Himalayas in the north and a more central mountain range, the Mahabharat. Toward the southern end of this valley is the capital of Nepal, Katmandu, at an elevation of 4,700 feet. About seventy miles northeast of Katmandu lies the old city of Gurkha. It is in the foothills of the Himalayas near this ancient capital that the Gurkha people live in the style of most Nepalese, except that the Gurkha culture has been greatly influenced by their contacts with the British, first as foes and then as members of the British and Indian armies.

The Nepal Valley rises from 4,000 feet in the south to altitudes of 11,000 feet in the north, and the climate varies accordingly. Most of the region in which the Gurkha live has a rainy season that begins in June and lasts through October. It is followed by a cold season that lasts until April, when warming begins and temperatures rise to nearly ninety degrees Fahrenheit before being cooled by the new rainy season. Annual rainfall averages about sixty inches. There is a thick snow during most of the long winter.

Historical Background

Origin. The present-day Gurkha form a cultural unit among the Nepalese that has grown to be unique in its dependence on the British Indian economy and more recently on Indian military service.

Nepalese. Driven from their homeland in India by Muslim invaders, the ancestors of the Gurkha joined residents of the central valley of the country that is now Nepal but which, until 1768, was a land broken into many small kingdoms and clan groups. One of these kingdoms, located around the city of Gorkha, expanded under the leadership of Prithwi Narayama until it included most of the Katmandu Valley and the slopes near Katmandu Peak. Raja Prithwi Narayama was ambitious to expand the territory but resistant to any interaction with foreign peoples. His kingdom was successful and is still the ruling force in Nepal. Prithwi Narayama's policy of isolation allowed the Nepalese to build a distinct culture. However, within this culture a smaller group drawn from seven clans became attached to and virtually dependent on the British and Indian armies, establishing a new culture based on soldiering. This is the group known as the Gurkha, given that name by the British.

Wars with the British. The people around Gurkha in the late 1700s and early 1800s took advantage of weak border management by the British in India. Frequent raids across the ill-defined border eventually resulted in a British declaration of war against Nepal. Twenty-two thousand troops were sent into Nepal under the leadership of three generals in 1814. The generals encountered defenders of small stature but of great strength and determination. One fort was defended by 600 Nepalese and held for so long that the British failed in their campaign against it. As a result, British troops gained much respect for these Nepalese fighters from the Gurkha area, the Gurkhas. (The word *Gurkha* probably comes from *gorkha*, which actually means "protector.") One legend about this fort's defense tells of a wounded Gurkha soldier who walked through the lines under a flag of truce, asking for medical aid. Once he had recovered, the Gurkha requested permission to return to the besieged fort so that he might continue fighting. Actions such as this convinced the British to make a special request when they finally defeated General Amar Sing and his Nepalese soldiers in 1816. As part of the peace agreement made in the Treaty of Segauli, the British requested the right to recruit Gurkha men for the British and Indian armies. Since then, the Gurkha people have built a cultural pattern based on ambitions for service in these armies. Thus, the original organizers of Nepal originally settled near Gurkha and now number among the fourteen million Nepalese. The small subgroup of Nepalese known as Gurkhas numbers about 600,000.

In 1947, India ceased employing the Gurkhas for their army, but the British still kept battalions of Gurkhas in the British Army. Soon after the Indian ban on Gurkha soldiers, the area near the border was closed to the British. So great was the Gurkha dependency on employment in the British army, that the government of Nepal arranged for a British recruiting station at the border with India.

In the 1960s and 1970s, relations with India declined until it was necessary in 1983 and 1984 to negotiate new trade agreements between the two countries. Meanwhile, Communist parties had arisen in Nepal, one of them the Gurkha Liberation Front. This militant organization was accused of conducting raids into India and in 1988, India retaliated by crossing the Nepal border and burning some houses. New negotiations were necessary to ensure the safety and free traffic of goods between the two states. Meanwhile, Nepal, one of the poorest nations of the world, has been given a great deal of support from Communist China. Still, the average income of the Nepalese, including the Gurkhas, is about 160 dollars a year.

Culture Today

Rice farmers and cattle herders. The seven clans that make up the Gurkha people are the Thapa, Pun, Ale, Rana, and Gurung of the western Katmandu Valley along with the Limbus and Rais of the east. All of these people are short and muscular. They lived as rice farmers and cattle-herders and had little contact with the world outside their valley until 1951 except for their occasional raids into Indian land. In this isolation, they were part of the greater group of Nepalese. There were no roads, railroads, or airlines through the valley and the hills. All materials needed in the valley were carried on the backs of the Gurkhas, held partly by a *doko*, a band around the load to be carried, and the carrier's forehead.

Rice farming is slowly becoming mechanized in Gurkha territory. However, the rice fields are still sown by hand by the men and harvested and flailed, again by hand, by the Gurkha women. Children help with these chores since schooling is not considered to be compulsory (although the government of Nepal has declared it so) among the Nepalese, and not highly respected among the Gurkha.

Many Gurkhas, accustomed to carrying exceptionally heavy loads through the mountain trails, supplement their farming income by serving as guides in the high mountains. Others still supplement their income by spending time in the British army.

Homes. In spite of their isolation, the people of Nepal built a great palace, Hanumann Dokha, in the capital city of Katmandu on the slopes of the Himalayas, and also built many temples in the city and in nearby towns. Katmandu is now a resort city of one-half million people. Still, most Gurkhas live along the central valley in wood or bamboo houses with thatched roofs. The western Gurkha gather together in village clusters. The homes of the eastern Gurkha are widely scattered with farmlands in between.

Military influence. Many Gurkha men were soldiers in the British army and, later, the Indian army. Gurkha no longer serve in the Indian army but are recruited in India to serve in the British army.

Gurkha life is often divided between their homes in Nepal and homes in India.

At home, Gurkha families often dress in discarded military clothes. Men may wear a military coat over a skirt. Women wear long dresses with a "shawl" draped around the waist and over one shoulder to be used for carrying. Walking and backpacking are still the dominant means of transportation.

Not until 1951 did the king of Nepal recognize the need to strengthen communications with people outside Nepal. The first road through Gurkha country was built in 1955.

Education. There is no written history of the clans that make up the Gurkha people. Education was not considered important, so the illiteracy rate was high. Nepal schools were initiated by the British during their period of control of India and its surrounding countries. Modeled after English schools, elementary education begins at age six and lasts until age eleven. Secondary schools extend this free schooling for an additional five years. In 1975, the language of instruction began to change from English to Nepali. However, this education is offered in government schools which are not always accessible to the Gurkhas. Even now, nearly eighty percent of the Gurkha people cannot read or write. (This compares with an illiteracy rate of seventy-four percent throughout Nepal.)

Divided society. Today most Gurkha men hope to find jobs in the British army. There are eleven Gurkha infantry regiments in these services. At home, Gurkha people live in the traditional style as planters and herders. There, in spite of their long military record, the Gurkhas are classed among the Nepalese as Vassiya, the class of traders, herders, and cultivators. Gurkha men not serving in the army add to the family income by becoming porters and guides for those visitors to Nepal who wish to hike the high mountains that border the Ghurkas' homes.

Religion. Originally Buddhists, the Gurkhas have been converted to a form of Hinduism through their long associations in India. However, Hinduism is loosely defined among the Gurkhas and includes many Buddhist ideas. The mix of religions sometimes results in taboos such as the refusal to eat eggs or to touch goats.

For More Information

Farwell, Byron. *Gurkhas.* New York: Norton, 1990.

Northey, William B. *The Land of the Gurkhas.* New York: AMS Press, 1937.

HAWAIIANS

(huh wye′ uns)

The people of the Hawaiian Islands; descendants of the original Polynesian inhabitants and more recent immigrants and their descendants.

Population: 1,100,000 (1990 estimate).
Location: The Hawaiian Islands, principally eight islands stretching for 390 miles in the Pacific Ocean about 2,100 miles southwest of San Francisco.
Languages: English, Hawaiian, Samoan, and Asian languages.

Geographical Setting

The Hawaiian Islands form a long archipelago—like a string of beads—across the northern Pacific Ocean. Eight islands make up most of the land area in the archipelago but are extended in small islands and sand banks as far as the Marshall Islands, 1,300 miles away. The chain runs northwest to southeast, from remote Kure Island to the close-set group of larger islands on the southerly tip. These eight islands—Niihau, Kauai, Oahu, Molokai, Lanai, Maui, Kahoolawe, and Hawaii itself—are generally considered to be the Hawaiian Islands. The big island of Hawaii contains two-thirds of the land mass of the group. Nearly all of the islands' population, as well as the 6,000,000 tourists who visit Hawaii each year, is concentrated on the four largest islands—Kauai, Oahu, Maui, and Hawaii. Oahu is the most highly developed. The state capital and largest city, Honolulu, sits on the southern shore between the huge U.S. military base of Pearl Harbor and the resort area of Waikiki.

The islands are among the world's youngest land masses, volcanic action having begun their formation only about 70,000,000 years ago.

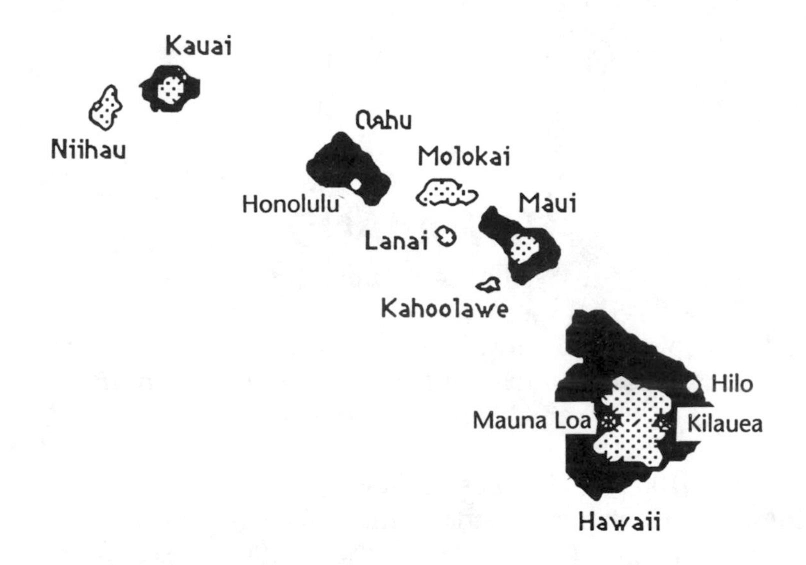

This volcanism results from a "hot spot" deep in the earth's mantle, over which the Pacific plate—that is, the ocean floor—has drifted steadily northwestward. Molten rock, or magma, has forced itself through the plate at intervals, creating the island sequence. As each island formed, the plate continued its northwestward course, leaving the stationary hot spot to create a new island. Kure is thus the oldest of the islands. On the youngest, the big island of Hawaii, active volcanoes such as Kilauea and Mauna Loa continue to expel massive streams of lava.

All the main islands contain volcanic mountains, though most are inactive. In fact, the islands are mountains, huge "shield" volcanoes jutting up from the ocean floor. Majestic Mauna Kea's famous snow-capped peak towers 13,796 feet above sea level—but nearly 30,000 feet above the ocean floor. Its overall height, from base to summit, thus outreaches Mount Everest's 29,108-foot altitude above sea level.

Hawaii's even, temperate climate is moderated by the famous trade winds, which blow steadily from the northeast. Despite Hawaii's tropical latitude, the trade winds—so called because sailing ships relied on their consistent flow in trips across the Pacific—keep humidity low and temperatures in the 70 and 80 degrees Fahrenheit year-round. Rainfall is heaviest from October to April. Heavy rains can come any time, however, especially in the higher elevations on the northern, windward coasts of the islands.

Historical Background

Polynesian discoverers. For millions of years, the Hawaiian Islands remained without human inhabitants. Then, beginning about 1100 B.C., seafaring peoples began settling the South Pacific islands. Europeans would later call these southern islands Polynesia (Greek for "many islands"). Probably sometime between A.D. 300 and 500, navigating by sun and stars and following the northward migrations of birds, the Polynesians reached the remote northern islands of Hawaii. They called the largest island *Havaiki* after one of the major islands of their former home. With them, these migrants brought the plants and animals important to their way of life. Dogs, pigs, chickens, the staple tuber called taro, coconuts, bananas, breadfruit, yams, and sugar cane comprised much of the traditional Polynesian diet. The mulberry plant called *wauke* was pounded and bleached to make kapa or bark-cloth. *Tl*, a lily, provided leaves for the *hula* skirts and roots to weave into matting or brew into a liquor called *okolehao*. Such material goods, transported to the new environment, helped the settlers maintain their Polynesian ways.

Europeans. More than 1,000 years of isolation ended for the Hawaiians in 1778, when Captain James Cook, the British navigator and explorer, "discovered" the islands for a second time. The white men brought two things that began almost immediately to change the islanders' lives: disease and technology. Like the American Indians, the Hawaiians had no immunity to diseases such as mumps, measles, and syphilis. Within forty years, their population would decline from about 300,000 to 60–70,000. At the same time, European and American traders, who soon began using the islands as a stopover on their ocean voyages, introduced the islanders to European technology.

Kamehameha. A dynamic and ambitious Hawaiian chief called Kamehameha wasted no time in mastering such advantages as firearms and new sailing techniques. As a young man, Kamehameha had impressed Cook with his intelligence, curiosity, and presence. By the

1780s, Kamehameha had schooner-rigged a double canoe, arming the vessel with two cannons. Skillfully consolidating both his political base and his military power (swelled by European arms), Kamehameha had ruthlessly conquered seven islands by 1810. (The eighth and last, Kauai, agreed to come into the kingdom without a battle.) Hawaiian chiefs had traditionally waged war among themselves, but never before had a single chief combined drive, power, and luck to triumph over all of them. Kamehameha, Hawaii's first king, died in 1819.

Sandalwood, whaling, and missionaries. While Kamehameha ruled, fur traders bound for China continued to interrupt their voyages with stops in the islands—many taking on cargoes of the fragrant sandalwood that was prized by the Chinese. By the 1830s, the fur trade had fallen off and the sandalwood forests had been depleted. From the 1830s through the 1860s, however, British and American whaling fleets, like the earlier fur traders, found the islands a pleasant and convenient rest and resupply point. Missionaries also began to arrive during this period, mostly from New England. They wished to convert the Hawaiians to Christianity and to suppress traditional ways that conflicted with their own beliefs. During this colorful period, many Hawaiians found work on whaling ships, or otherwise joined the rowdy, rough-and-tumble maritime life. Others, such as Kamehameha's powerful wife, Kaahumanu, took up the missionaries' Christian values. Under such outside influences, and under the continuing ravages of disease, Hawaiian culture suffered violent and disruptive changes.

Sugar cane and new arrivals. In the 1850s and 1860s, a new industry began to replace the now-declining whaling industry as the islands' economic mainstay. American businessmen had started the first sugar cane plantation on Kauai in 1835. By the late 1800s, sugar was Hawaii's main export; by 1910, more than fifty plantations employed almost 50,000 workers. Sugar, and to a lesser degree pineapples, dominated the islands' economy. They were controlled by a relatively small group of wealthy, white Americans. At first, the planters used Hawaiians as field laborers. In the 1850s, however, they began hiring contract laborers from Asian and European countries. Immigrants from Asia came to Hawaii in successive waves that were controlled by white planters. As each population grew—Chinese, Japanese, and Filipino in turn—the owners, fearing that the laborers might organize into unions, turned to a new source. The Asians came in the tens of thousands. Smaller numbers of European workers came from Portugal, Germany, Norway, and other countries. Some worked out their contracts, then returned home with the money they had saved. Many others stayed, making Hawaii the uniquely multiethnic society that it is today.

Plantation politics. The wealthy white planters wielded immense power in the islands. In 1893, with American military backing, white businessmen overthrew Queen Liliuokalani and established a "provisional government" under Sanford B. Dole. In 1898, the United States government annexed the islands and created the Territory of Hawaii.

Military importance. During the early 1900s, Hawaii became the major center of expanding American military power in the Pacific. By 1920, about 6,000 military personnel were stationed there, mostly on the island of Oahu. The Japanese attack on Pearl Harbor and other military sites, on December 7, 1941, resulted in America's entering World War II. Hawaii retains its military role, with over 50,000 soldiers, sailors, and pilots stationed there, still primarily on Oahu.

Statehood and tourism. In 1959, the year that Hawaii became the fiftieth state of the United States, the first jetliners arrived in Honolulu. Over the next few decades, tourism outstripped both the military and the sugar industry (now a poor third) as Hawaii's major revenue source. One of the world's most popular vacation destinations, the islands offer a wide range of exotic pleasures, from the glamour and hustle of sophisticated Waikiki to self-contained resort complexes on the "neighbor islands." Alongside the Hawaii of travel posters, however, exists the unique mix of cultures bequeathed to the islands by history.

Culture Today

East meets West. Hawaii may be the most racially mixed society in the world. Of its 1,100,000 people twenty-three percent describe themselves as white, twenty-two percent as Japanese, twenty percent as part Hawaiian, eleven percent as Filipino, four percent as Chinese, two percent as black, and about one percent each as Korean and pure Hawaiian. Such clear-cut terms blur when faced by another statistic, however: about half of all Hawaiian marriages now occur between men and women of different races. In describing this interracial culture, this entry will highlight its ethnic Hawaiian elements, focusing also on contributions from Asian and other Pacific Island peoples.

Hawaii comeback. In the first century of contact between Hawaiians and *haole* (the Hawaiian word for whites), white-born diseases killed nearly all the Hawaiians. In the following century, cultural discrimination nearly finished the job of eradicating Hawaiian ways. Missionaries taught that "heathen" Hawaiian culture was inferior to European-based, white American culture. In recent years, however, Hawaiians have begun to stage a comeback, both numerically and culturally. Only about 10,000 "pure" Hawaiians remain, while many have married into other racial groups in past decades. Their descendants, the part-Hawaiians, number about 220,000 and are the fastest-growing population group in the islands. As a rule, they consider themselves Hawaiian, and have fought for "Hawaiian rights" in the islands, as well as to revive traditions such as hula dancing. Part-Hawaiians of the present era have included major landowners (such as the late Richard Smart, who owned America's largest ranch), politicians (such as Congressman Daniel Akaka and Governor John Waihee), and other public figures (for example, entertainer Don Ho).

Asians and others. The Japanese came to Hawaii in the largest numbers and over the longest time, only recently being outnumbered by the haole. After World War II, in which many Japanese-Americans served with great distinction, the Japanese vote broke the political power of the planter elite. Despite the current haole numerical edge, the Japanese-Americans continue to dominate local politics. The islands' many Zen and Shinto shrines and temples, the popularity of foods like *sashimi*, and Japanese-language television and radio stations and newspapers also make the more than 1,000,000 Japanese tourists who visit Hawaii each year feel at home in this state. In the last decade, Japanese investors have spent more than ten billion dollars buying Hawaiian hotels, homes, and condominiums. Between them, Japanese tourists and investors contribute to an estimated twenty-five percent of Hawaii's economy.

Filipinos broke new ground in attempting to organize the sugar laborers in the early 1900s. Today, they play an important role in the state legislature. Chinese represent the islands' oldest Asian immigrant group. Like the Japanese, most started as contract workers who saved their wages to open small businesses. The Chinese community in Hawaii is part of an extensive network of Chinese immigrants in Asia and the Pacific. It was in Honolulu that Dr. Sun Yat Sen, leader of the 1911 Chinese Revolution, founded his political party in 1895. He had come to study there, joining his older brother, who had emigrated earlier. Smaller groups in Hawaii include Samoans, Koreans, and Thais.

Food, clothing, and shelter. Hawaii's patchwork past is most apparent in its varied cuisine. Japanese *manju* (sweet black bean pastry), Portuguese sweet bread, Chinese noodles or crispy duck, and spicy Korean *kim chee* are as easy to find as Hawaiian *poi*, a thick paste of mashed taro which is served as the traditional island staple. Hawaiians eat about twice as much fish as residents of any other state, as well as more fresh fruit. Mangoes, papayas, bananas, pineapples, oranges, and avocados are locally grown. Different areas are famed for speciality crops: open-air markets on Oahu overflow with Kahuku watermelons, Maui onions, Waimanalo corn, Manoa lettuce, and

Hawaiian women sorting tubers. *Courtesy of Wayne Mitchell.*

Puna papayas. The traditional Hawaiian feast is the *luau*, in which a pig is roasted in a pit lined with wood, lava rocks, and banana stumps. The pig is stuffed with hot rocks, wrapped in leaves, and buried along with pieces of fish, taro, yams, and breadfruit. A festive banquet for friends and extended family, the luau has absorbed non-Hawaiian elements. In the 1800s, missionaries brought cakes, Chinese brought chicken, and Norwegian whalers brought salmon marinated with onion and tomato (lomi salmon). All are now standard luau dishes.

Hawaii's climate meant that in past times usually no more than a strip or two of barkcloth (*kapa*) was used as clothing. Many Hawaiians also covered much of their bodies with tattoos. Warriors ornamented themselves with spectacular scarlet and gold capes and helmets of woven feathers. (Some believe that the style of the helmets, unknown elsewere in Polynesian culture, might have come from the helmets of Spanish soldiers who may have visited the islands before Cook's arrival. No other evidence for such a theory exists, though Hawaii lay on the Spanish trade route between Mexico and the Philippines.) Today, Hawaiians still dress casually, often simply in shorts and sandals, with perhaps a T-shirt or tank top. In the multiethnic Hawaiian society, Western-style dress, lightened for the warm weather, is the most usual costume. However, women still wear the *muumuu*, a voluminous dress originally designed by modest missionaries for Hawaiian women. Now the muumuus are printed in bright colorful cotton or silk. The "Hawaiian shirt," with its bold floral prints, has become a cliché of the tourist age. More firmly grounded in Hawaiian culture, if now equally developed for tourism, is the *lei*, a colorful wreath of fresh flowers or other decorative objects worn around the neck. Originally an artful offering to the gods, leis have become an emblem of Hawaiian hospitality and warmth. A lei will be offered with a kiss to arriving friends and strangers alike, or worn by all at island celebrations.

Traditional homes were built of wooden poles and grass thatching. The dirt floor was covered with woven grass mats to keep out moisture and insects. A single low doorway acted as entrance and window. Tapa hangings, spears, fishing equipment, and ceremonial gourds hung on the walls. Easily built and maintained, the homes were simple but cozy. Today houses are built in a variety of modern styles, often designed to take advantage of the cooling trade winds and the plentiful views of mountains or sea.

Family life. In traditional Hawaiian society, child-rearing fell to the grandparents. Boys were taken over by the father's parents, girls by the mother's. Some Hawaiian families continue this practice, called *hanai*. Even in those that do not, grandparents usually enjoy a special closeness with grandchildren, showering them with gifts and following their education and social lives in detail. Traditionally, a boy's training would come according to his grandfather's occupation. Such occupations include fishing, religious or priestly work, or making tools. Men and women were forbidden from eating together. Such prohibitions, called *kapu* ("tabu" in Polynesian, which became *taboo* in English), were an integral part of Hawaiian Polynesian heritage. Other kapu acts included letting one's shadow fall on any part of a king's body. Breaking a kapu was usually punished by death.

Asian immigrants to the islands, finding themselves in a new and often hostile cultural environment, relied heavily on family support. A general pattern was for a father or older brother to arrive first, to be joined later by dependent family members. Among Filipino immigrants, who continue to come in significant numbers, men have outnumbered women and the traditional family has tended to be smaller than in the Philippines. Thus, the Filipinos evolved a system called *compadrazgo*, in which a child is given as many as thirty godparents when baptized. As well as providing future support for the child, compadrazgo strengthens the connections among friends who share the role.

Language. Polynesian-based Hawaiian is dying out as a spoken language. Today, it survives mostly on the island of Niihau, in some religious services, and in words and phrases used by English-speakers (the predominant group of Hawaiians), rather than as a language of everyday use. Traditionally unwritten, Hawaiian had no alphabet until the arrival of the haole. In general, vowels are pronounced separately, except for diphthongs such as *ai* (eye), *au* (ow), and *ei* (ay). Thus, Kamehameha is pronounced *kah may hah MAY hah*. Fewer than 2,500 people speak Hawaiian as their mother tongue, most being older people who rarely speak it to their children. It is estimated that within thirty years, Hawaiian will survive only in isolated phrases and in place names throughout the islands. Out of the immigrant past arose a dialect of English called *pidgin*, which has a number of local variations. Today, pidgin marks the "local"—whatever his racial background—as opposed to the newcomer or educated haole.

High school students at a performance of Hawaiian dance. *Courtesy of Wayne Mitchell.*

Religion. The Hawaiians' ancient religion, incorporating hundreds of deities as well as magical and animist beliefs, disappeared completely in the early 1800s. Hawaiians worshipped both in their homes and in open-air temples called *heiau.* Ruins of the heiau are still visible on all the islands. The largest were the heiau waikaua or war temples, at which sacrifices occurred. Chief gods were *Ku*, god of war and male fertility; *Kane*, the creator and chief god; *Lono*, god of thunder and agriculture; and *Kanaloa*, god of the ocean and winds. The old gods died with the arrival of haole missionaries, and today Hawaiians are no more or less religious, and have no less religious diversity, than Americans in other states. Immigrants, as elsewhere, tend to drop old religions by the third generation, though Chinese and Japanese Buddhist and Shinto temples are maintained. Filipinos, with their Spanish colonial background, are heavily Roman Catholic.

Literature and the arts. The Hawaiians' unwritten language was the vessel for centuries of orally transmitted poems, songs, genealogies,

The rhythmic hula dance and the welcoming necklace of blossoms are part of the Hawaiian heritage. *Courtesy of Wayne Mitchell.*

histories, and myths. These traditions show strong powers of observation and analysis of both natural and human ways. For example, the *Kumulipo* chant, created about 1700, tells of the universe's origins, and is sequentially arranged to include accounts of weather elements, plants, animals, and humans. Religious sculpture achieved particular sophistication, as did the weaving of supple and colorful feather capes and helmets. Today, traditional Hawaiian arts are preserved in such tourist attractions as the Polynesian Cultural Center.

Music and dance have proved the most vital survivors of the old arts. Hawaiian music has influenced musicians and composers worldwide. Using guitars brought by haole, Hawaiians loosened the strings and developed the unique "slack key" sound. This technique remains a "Hawaiian" instrumental signature. The ukelele, a small guitar originally brought by Portuguese laborers, also soon became recognized as "Hawaiian." The islands' music captivated European and American audiences beginning in the late 1800s, giving rise to a number of popular songs. The songs (known as "hapa-haole" or half-haole) were featured in many Hollywood movies, and were sung by artists as diverse as Bing Crosby and Elvis Presley. The best-known Hawaiian song, "Aloha 'Oe," however, was written by Queen Liliuokalani.

Holidays and recreation. Aside from sharing all United States holidays, Hawaiians observe "Aloha Friday" each week, marked by shirts of especially bright colors and (for women) a flower tucked behind one ear and perhaps a lei around the neck. The weekly occasion is marked by a celebratory attitude and a sense of fun, standard gear among a people who gave the world the sport of surfing. This fast-moving and now-popular sport was invented by the Polynesians and popularized by Hawaiians in the 1900s.

Surfing, music, the lei, and the hula—of the Hawaiians' many contributions to world culture, perhaps none is more immediately recognized than the word "aloha." Now used for both greeting and saying goodbye, the word originally denoted love or affection. It included a sense of giving in order that you might receive, a reciprocal hospitality that became perhaps the islanders' most valuable resource in their dealings with the outside world.

For More Information

Anderson, Robert N. *Filipinos in Hawaii.* Honolulu: University of Hawaii Press, 1984.

Fodor's 91 Hawaii. New York: Fodor's Travel Publications, 1991.

Graham, Judith. *Hawaii Voices.* Honolulu: Bess Press, 1982.

Lueras, Leonard. *Insight Guides: Hawaii.* Singapore: APA Publications, 1992.

Tabrah, Ruth. *Hawaii: A History.* New York: W. W. Norton and Company, 1980.

HMONG

(hmong)

People who live in the mountains of northeast Thailand and northern Laos but are rapidly being displaced.

Population: 53,000 in Thailand (1991 estimate). The Hmong are a branch of the larger body of people with similar customs called the Lao/Meo in Vietnam and Laos (233,000 and 150,000) and the Miao in China (2,680,000).
Location: The mountains of northeastern Thailand.
Languages: Hmong, a Miao language related to languages of China, Laos, and Vietnam; Thai.

Geographical Setting

The country of Thailand is separated from its neighbor, Laos, on the east by the Mekong River, and on the north and west by low mountains from Myanmar (Burma). Except for a basin in the east and the west central valley through which the country's major rivers (Ping, Chao Phraya) flow, most of the country is hilly. This is particularly true of the northeast, where the hills are more rugged as they rise to the low mountains separating Thailand from China. Here much of the land was once heavily forested, and some dense forests remain.

The low but rugged mountains of northeastern Thailand and northern Laos are not subject to as severe rainstorms as the monsoon areas of the lowlands and Myanmar. Some regions receive as little as six inches of rain annually. However, much of Thailand receives as much as forty to sixty inches of rain a year. It is in the forest regions of the northeast that the Hmong have long established themselves.

Historical Background

Chinese origin. The ancestors of most of the people of the region including Thailand, Laos, Cambodia, and Vietnam once lived in south China. At one time, the Thai people were part of a powerful kingdom there—Nan-Chao. However, increasing pressure from other Chinese populations resulted in a migration south. Here some people who are related to the present-day Miao of southern China divided—some traveling across the mountains into the region of Thailand, others following the Mekong River into Laos and Vietnam. All were part of a family of peoples known in their new residences as Lao. Shortly after their arrival, the people of Thailand established kingdoms along the rivers. Those entering the Chao Phraya River valley drove out the Khmer who lived there, united into a single kingdom, and began to call themselves Thais to distinguish themselves from the Lao of Laos and Vietnam. Some of these migrants from China chose to live in the forest areas of the northeast, where the rugged hills and mountains isolated them from the mainstream of the lowland Thai. Over the centuries, the languages of Indo-China became regional.

Thailand. The lowland Thai kingdom (Siam) grew in power to include parts of Laos, Burma, and Cambodia by the fourteenth century, and had trade agreements with Europeans by the sixteenth century. A feudal state run by powerful nobles, the country emerged from feudalism only during the reigns of two forward-looking monarchs of the nineteenth century: Mongkut (1851–1868) and Chulalongkorn (1868–1910). From that time on, Thailand was involved in disputes, first over boundaries with neighboring Cambodia and Laos, and then over ideology as the Chinese introduced Communism into the, by then, constitutional monarchy. By the 1950s, Siam was torn with internal conflict from which emerged a military government led by Marshal Sharit Thanarat. For most of the years since 1958, Siam, renamed Thailand, has been under military rule. In recent years, this government has been struggling to improve the Thai economy while the country has been subjected to rebellion and revolution brutally held in check by the ruling militia.

Hmong settlements. Meanwhile, the people known as Hmong preferred to live in isolation in the mountain forest, clearing the land for rice farming and moving to another part of the virgin forest when the soil became too poor to sustain the rice crop, as they have done for about 150 years. Frequent droughts have brought the Hmong to seek a dry farming crop that could be raised in conjunction with the water-dependent rice. Maize was introduced as one such crop. But as the population grew beyond the ability of the maize and rice growers to supply food, the Hmong looked for a cash crop that could be converted on the lowland markets to money with which to buy needed materials. The scarcity of land required that this crop be sown and harvested at a time of year that would not interfere with rice-growing. The opium poppy proved to be the most profitable crop.

Vietnam War. During the war over Vietnam many Hmong seized the opportunity to change their lives by serving as soldiers aiding the United States. In recent years, spurred by the country's need for trade goods, the Thai government has established offices in many Hmong villages and, at the same time, has begun to compete with the Hmong for forest land by encouraging a large lumber trade in such woods as teak. Two factors, international pressure and the growing addiction of the Thai youth to opium, have resulted in government opposition to growing the opium poppy. The isolation of Hmong villages and the lack of an alternate crop have caused the government regulations to be only superficially carried out. Hmong leaders have repeatedly asked the government for help in identifying an equally profitable and rice-compatible cash crop, but have received little assistance. Opium continues to be grown in the region known as the Golden Triangle of the Indo-Chinese mountains. However, the combination of opposition to opium, government claims to forest land, and the development of forestry has resulted in forced migrations of Hmong to lowlands, where they often live under very poor conditions.

The Hmong in the Laotian mountains sided with the French against the Communists and then with the United States. As Communism emerged victorious in the long war, and both France and the United States withdrew, the Laos government showed its disapproval of the Hmong in a determined effort to eliminate them from Laos. Hmong villages, already decimated of manpower by their heavy losses in the war, were bombed and gassed. Whole villages were forced to flee across the Mekong River into Thailand. Here they were often welcomed with fines and beatings and sent to live in refugee camps such as Ban Vinai. In Thailand, the Hmong resumed their lifestyle of strong families and family clans. A Hmong saying reflects the importance of this organization even in the face of flight and refuge:

> To be with family is to be happy.
> To be without family is to be lost.
> (Goldfarb 1982, p. 14)

Culture today

Hmong village. A typical Hmong village is accessible from large towns below only by trails. Traders walk up narrow mountain trails, sometimes for many hours, to return to their homes from a trading trip to the nearest town. The village consists of twenty to forty or more homes and some local shops. Today's village also frequently has some former homes converted to offices for the government officials who now regulate the village and help with problems such as building dams for irrigation. A village is established by a group of relatives who seek new land on which to farm. The villagers all claim a common ancestor, even though the residents may represent two or three clans (*xeem*)—organizations of several closer family units. Until recently, these villages were directed by a head man chosen by the villagers, and were temporary. An old village might have been twenty-five years old. Villagers came together to clear a section of forest land and divided it among themselves for rice growing. In a short time, the cleared land would be unsuitable for rice growing, and the villagers would choose another part of the forest, preferring old forest land, on which to build a new village and system of farms.

As the Thai government has attempted to regulate Hmong life and to build a forest industry, some of the responsibilities of the head man have been taken over by government-appointed officers. These officers encourage a more stable pattern of reclaiming the same land, varying crops, and building local dams for water storage. Hmong villages are becoming more stable as a result. At the same time, the competition for land has driven some Hmong out of the area.

In some villages, Hmong people still resist Thai control and the intrusion of the more settled Karen people into their forests. Fighting among Hmong, Karen, and Thai is not uncommon, even though many Hmong villages allow itinerant farm workers to live in the village. Karen known as nowhere men hire themselves to the more prosperous landowners for harvesting or sowing crops.

Wars have reduced the number of Hmong men. As a result, refugee camps such as Ban Vinai find polygamy to be common. A man might have as many wives as he can support. In this way, a large family is assembled to live in the cramped quarters of the refugee camp. In one example, twenty-four family members lived in a concrete, metal-roofed apartment of one large room and three tiny bedrooms.

Houses. Hmong village houses are made of wood or bamboo built on the ground and walled with shingle that was lashed together with hemp or notched to interconnect. Roofs are thatched with teak leaves or cogon grass. Some are shingled with split bamboo. A few of the more wealthy residents may roof their homes with zinc or plastic. Water is brought to the village from a nearby stream or dam through pipes of split bamboo. Near the houses, raised wooden granaries protect the stored grain from water damage and forest animals.

Inside furnishings are few and simple, benches for sleeping and sitting, cooking utensils, and equipment for such activities as embroidering (at which nearly all Hmong women spend much time).

Pots, pans, and house and farm tools hang from the rafters.

Economy. Each village family has its own section of farm land while sharing some farm duties among other villagers. If this farm land is some distance from the village, a farmer may build a rough field house in which to live during the busiest seasons. From here or from home in the village, men and their children do the farm work, while the women guard the village home and care for the younger children along with performing chores such as making clothes for the family. In the fields, men and children grow rice in season, then sow maize, and, at another time, opium poppies. There is a growing interest in sugar cane as a cash crop and pumpkins. The poppies are picked and carried to a larger town to be traded for cash or for needed household goods. When farm chores ease, the men go into the forests to trap birds to augment the diet. In the village, Hmong farmers keep pigs and chickens for food. There are also some cattle and horses raised by these farmers.

In the refugee camps, men still work as farmers. There are shops, markets, and tea houses as in the old village. Girls and women still draw water from community wells and carry it home for cooking. A stew of boiled vegetables, chicken, or fish is served with rice. This food is delivered to the camp by Thai overseers and supplied by the United Nations. Some Hmong women produce beautiful tapestries which they hope to sell to earn money for necessities within camp and to save for a future life outside of the camp.

Food. Rice is the staple food of the Hmong. It is supplemented with maize (really grown as a cash crop), home-grown fruits and vegetables, chicken, occasionally pork, and wild birds that are sometimes trapped by the farmers.

Clothing. T-shirts and loose-fitting trousers held at the waist by a sash make up the common apparel in Hmong villages. Sometimes the weather or the occasion demand covering this costume with a robe. Sandals are common footwear at home or in the field. More wealthy Hmong, and those who carry on trade with larger towns, have been exposed to Western-style clothing.

Women weave rough cloth from hemp. Some of this cloth is used to make a sort of carrying strap. The women can be seen in the villages carrying young children on their backs supported by this strap, or carrying wood in the same manner.

Boys and girls. When they are young, Hmong boys and girls play together. A popular game is to capture dung beetles and set a pair of them to fighting. As young people grow into adolescence, they tend to separate, the boys helping their fathers in the field and the girls learning from their mothers. Early marriage is encouraged, and young men and women court each other in the dark of the evening by disappearing as couples into the forest. Although most marriages are accepted by the respective families and are expected by the relatives, symbolic marriage by capture, with the young man carrying off the woman is typical among the Hmong.

Language and literature. The Hmong language is a Miao language brought with them from China. It is a language predominated by eight tones that sound something like the English sounds of *b, j, v, s, g, m,* and *d.* For most of Hmong history, there was no written Hmong language. What writing was done used Chinese script. The first Hmong script is less than a century old and was devised by a visitor among them, Sam Pollard. Still, the Hmong have an oral language influenced by their religions, shamanism supplemented by Buddhism and a little Christianity. Their oral tradition also shows some modern wit. About government officers, for example, Hmongs might say that to see a tiger is to die; to see an official is to become destitute. In recent years, Hmong scholars have written in other languages, particularly Thai, French, or English. An example is *I Am a Shaman* by Paja Thao.

Religion. Buddhism came to Thailand from China with the migration south. Later, Christian missionaries found some interest among the Hmong. However, the Hmong treat these religions lightly, blending them with a form of shamanism. Shamans foretell the future, heal the sick, and suggest ways to ward off evil spirits. In religion, Hmong are not sexually biased. Both men and women practice as shamans among them.

Much of the religious responsibility of the village falls to the head man. He presides over important rituals; for example, making an offering to the gods of the first new rice at harvest time. The head man also gives a ritual blessing to the village at the new year celebration—perhaps the most important celebration among the Hmong. All villagers and neighbors from other villages assemble on this day to receive the blessing in a ceremony of unity that involves circling under cords strung for the occasion.

The strong Hmong belief in spirits related to almost everything about them has been carried over to their refugee camp situation. As in their old village, Hmong refugees place markers of various kinds around their living quarters and throughout the community to lure the spirits of their ancestors and to repel evil spirits.

Education. The Thai government has brought formal education to the Hmong as to the other peoples of Thailand. Partly, in the Hmong view, to disseminate Thai propaganda, education has been made free and compulsory for six years. However, to protect local cultures, these schools can either be government schools or schools founded by the people of the villages, sometimes supported by the government. Almost every Hmong village, therefore, has a primary school within the village limits. Throughout Thailand, new primary schools have been built in towns and villages at the rate of 100 a year in the late 1980s and early 1990s. Frequently among the Hmong, the teachers in these schools are drawn from other cultures. Equally frequently, the Hmong do not honor mandatory school attendance. Hmong children still do not attend school if farm or other family duties interfere.

Dislocation. Scarce land, exhausted land, and government pressure have made the lives of Hmong people more difficult in recent years. Thousands of them have abandoned their village life in the face of these problems and fled to refugee camps set up by the Thai and Cambodian governments. There the Hmong live under minimally acceptable conditions and face rapid cultural change. Many have abandoned hope of continuing their old lifestyles and have opted for an even greater cultural leap as they move to other countries such as the United States.

For More Information

Goldfarb, Mace, M.D. *Fighters, Refugees, Immigrants: A Story of the Hmong.* Minneapolis: Carolrhoda Books Inc., 1982.

Thao, Paja. *I Am a Shaman: Hmong Life Story.* Boston: Southeast Asia Refugee Studies Project, University of Massachusetts, 1989.

Trapp, Nicholas. *Sovereignty and Rebellion: The White Hmong of North Thailand.* New York: Oxford University Press, 1989.

HONG KONG CHINESE

(hong kong chi neez')

Chinese who live in the British crown colony of Hong Kong.

Population: 5,800,000 (1990 estimate).
Location: Southern China.
Languages: Cantonese Chinese; Mandarin Chinese; English.

Geographical Setting

The British colony of Hong Kong, comprising both island and mainland territory, lies on the south China coast, about midway between the island of Taiwan to the east and the Gulf of Tongking to the west. Its nearly 400 square miles can be divided into four areas: Hong Kong Island (about thirty square miles); Kowloon peninsula (about three square miles), the point of land across Victoria Harbor from the main island; the New Territories, stretching north from Kowloon; and the over 200 Outlying Islands, together making up over 365 square miles. Hong Kong's busy city life is centered on the two cities of Victoria, on Hong Kong Island, and Kowloon, just across the harbor, on the peninsula's southern tip. With their suburbs the two cities hold over ninety percent of the population. They are generally considered a single city. Linked by numerous ferries and an underwater tunnel, they are what most people—tourists and inhabitants alike—think of as Hong Kong. Parts of this central area are the most crowded places on earth, where a few minute's walk can take one from glittering skyscrapers to densely packed shantytowns.

The rocky hills of the New Territories and the Outlying Islands have discouraged agriculture and settlement, though some farms and fishing villages manage to survive. Fishing especially has declined in recent years, because Hong Kong's freewheeling, capitalist economy,

Pleasant gardens mark the New Territory of Hong Kong. *Courtesy of David Tuch.*

largely unregulated, has brought severe pollution problems. The colony has no natural resources, save for its magnificent natural harbor, its strategic trade position, and the energy and enterprise of its people, ninety-eight percent of whom are Chinese.

Hong Kong's climate is semitropical, with very hot, humid summers (sometimes over 100 degrees Fahrenheit) and cool winters (with low temperatures brought by cold northern winds). Typhoons, the Pacific Ocean's version of hurricanes, may hit between June and October. The violent storms bring life to a standstill, sometimes interrupting electric power and other services. Since many people in Hong Kong live on boats that are moored in the harbor, the typhoons also frequently bring death and destruction. The worst typhoon hit in 1937, when over 1,000 boats sank and approximately 2,500 people drowned.

Historical Background

Before the British. Archaeological evidence reveals settlements in the Hong Kong area from as early as 4,000 years ago. The earliest inhabitants are thought to have been not Chinese, but Malayan in origin. Not until the 200s B.C. did the area come under Chinese control, and Chinese did not arrive there in significant numbers until the Song Dynasty (A.D. 960–1279) and later. Most of the early Chinese arrivals were the Cantonese Punti ("local people"); the Tankas ("egg people"); and, beginning mostly in the 1600s, growing numbers of Hakka ("strangers"), a northern Chinese people fleeing southward to escape persecution.

Opium trade. By the early 1800s, Britain had come to dominate European trade with Asia, displacing the Dutch and the Portuguese. Trade with the West was based in the Chinese city of Canton, northwest of Hong Kong, at the mouth of the Pearl River. The Western merchants brought home tea and silk, but there was little of value aside from cash that they could offer the Chinese. Fearful of depleting their cash reserves, British merchants in 1773 brought 1,000 chests of opium, each weighing 150 pounds, to China from British-controlled Bengal in India. The drug, which the Chinese called "foreign mud," proved popular among the Chinese, although the Chinese government protested and attempted to curtail the British-controlled drug trade.

Spoils of the Opium War. In 1839, when a staggering 40,000 chests of opium were imported, the Chinese emperor appointed Lin Tse-hsu as trade commissioner with orders to eradicate the opium trade. Lin commanded the British to surrender all the opium in their warehouses; after six weeks, the British commander, a Captain Elliot, ordered the merchants to hand over the opium, which Lin then destroyed. However, fighting soon broke out between the British and the Chinese, which the authorities in Britain seized as an opportunity to attack Chinese ports. China was forced to negotiate, and on his own authority Captain Elliot secured British possession of the tiny island of Hong Kong. The British, who thought their victory should have brought a greater reward than the barren islet, sent Elliot home in disgrace. He was later assigned to Texas and is almost forgotten in Hong Kong.

Kowloon and the New Territories. When Britain took possession of the island in 1841, about 5,000 Chinese lived there in small farming and fishing villages. Soon Chinese laborers, attracted by job prospects, began arriving, and by 1845 the population had reached 20,000. Further British military victories and Chinese concessions brought Kowloon (1860) and the New Territories (1898) under British control. However, the Hong Kong Island and the Kowloon peninsula had become British possessions outright; the New Territories were leased for a limited term of ninety-nine years. During this period of expansion, the colony's population continued to grow, with waves of immigration resulting from disturbances on the mainland. The first large wave came during the Taiping Rebellion (1851–1864) and brought Chinese of all classes and occupations. By 1864 the Chinese population had reached nearly 120,000, with about 4,000 Westerners (mostly British) also living in the colony.

Gateway to China. By the end of the 1800s, the opium trade had been suppressed, and the wealthy and powerful British merchant houses had turned to other goods. Rice, sugar, and textiles came through Hong Kong's ideally situated harbor, on their way to and from Europe, Japan, Korea, Southeast Asia, and the western Pacific. In addition, Hong Kong became (with Shanghai to the north) one of China's main ports, handling about thirty percent of her foreign trade. With growth in shipping, banking, and insurance came increased urbanization. Pressed for space by hills behind Victoria and Kowloon and by water in front, the British (with Chinese labor) cut into the rocks and reclaimed land from the sea. Development proceeded apace—yet the colony's great wealth was not generally shared by its Chinese inhabitants but controlled by the British merchants and colonial administrators. Some Chinese did become rich and powerful businessmen, agents, shipowners, and the *compradors*—a Portuguese word referring to the translators who served as middlemen between the European traders and the Chinese. Most of the rest lived in crowded, unsanitary conditions. In the mid-1890s, nearly 3,000 Chinese died in an outbreak of bubonic plague.

Growth in the 1900s. Throughout the 1900s—from the Boxer Rebellion of 1900 to the massacre in Tiananmen Square in 1989—successive disturbances in China have brought waves of Chinese to Hong Kong. Some have fled to preserve their wealth, others to escape their poverty. Many came to Hong Kong after the revolution in 1911, during the Japanese invasion and occupation of the 1930s, or after the Chinese civil war and Communist victory in 1949; many hundreds of thousands fled and continue to flee the Communist regime (see MAINLAND CHINESE). Except for a brief but harsh period of Japanese occupation (1941–1945), Hong Kong's economy has kept up its growth, booming in the 1960s, '70s and '80s. As British power faded after 1945, Hong Kong's Chinese have taken a larger and larger share in her economic growth. Emphasis has shifted from trade to manufacturing, with raw materials being imported and finished products exported. In 1984, China and British agreed that the colony would be handed back to China in 1997; even this agreement has done little to disrupt one of the world's smallest but most productive economic centers.

Culture Today

Borrowed land, borrowed time. Today, less than five years remains until the expiration of Britain's ninety-nine-year lease of the New Territories. On July 1, 1997, the Territories will revert to China. Without them, where Kowloon's suburbs now spread and where one-third of the people live, Hong Kong would not long survive. In 1984, China and Britain signed a treaty agreeing that, with the New Territories, the rest of the colony will be returned to China as well. China, which has come to rely on Hong Kong's economic might, has agreed not to interfere unduly in the former colony's capitalist ways. With the decline of Shanghai in the 1900s, Hong Kong is China's major port, its trade and industry contributing billions of dollars annually to the Chinese economy. Still, both Chinese and other residents share a growing nervousness about Communist rule. They live, in the words of Chinese writer Han Su-yin, "on borrowed time in a borrowed place." Some, especially the wealthy, have made plans to move abroad. In the meantime, wealthy and struggling alike carry on with Hong Kong's principal occupation and pastime: making money.

Cantonese ways. Most Hong Kong Chinese are Cantonese, the predominant ethnic group of southern China. They have their origins in Guangdong (Canton in the old English spelling) Province. About two-thirds were born in Hong Kong, and the rest—many of them now elderly—immigrated. Descendants of the early Tankas and Hakkas remain, and comprise many of the surviving fishers and farmers. From the earliest days, however, the Cantonese dominated these other groups, and the Five Great Clans (the pre-British landowning families) were all Punti Cantonese.

Hong Kong harbor is a busy trading center. *Courtesy of Dr. W. Paul Fischer.*

While Chinese from all parts of China have come to Hong Kong in modern times, the Cantonese and their ways remain the culture's main influence. Much of Hong Kong's economic success can perhaps be traced to its Cantonese origins. In the past, Chinese emperors (whose power was concentrated in the north) wished to keep the Western traders as far away as possible. They viewed trade as an occupation unfit for civilized people, thinking of the Westerners as barbarians. Thus, it was the southern region of Guangdong that was earliest exposed to Western commercialism. In modern Communist China, Guangdong remains the most economically productive area, with special rules that allow it a higher degree of free enterprise than in the north.

Food, clothing, and shelter. Chinese cuisine is often called the world's most developed and flavorful. Of its many regional variations, the popular Cantonese version has become what most Westerners know as "Chinese food." The usual Cantonese greeting, *Sik tzo fan mei?*—literally, "Have you eaten?"—shows the importance of food in Cantonese society. Meals are long and elaborate exercises in pleasure, always taken in company rather than alone. They offer contrasting shades of taste and texture: sweet and sour, crunchy and soft, hot and cool, spicy and bland. Many dishes are served with rice, and accompanied by sauces. All sauces are meant to enhance the food's natural flavor, never to alter or conceal it. Flavor is also preserved by cooking foods, especially vegetables, lightly, so that they are crisp and tasty. Vegetables and meat (often pork or chicken) are stir-fried in a *wok* (a bowl-shaped pan now popular in the West); vegetables and fish are also frequently steamed, also lightly.

Popular dishes include shark's fin soup, *laap cheong* (smoked pork sausage) served with rice, various versions of shrimp and crab with black bean sauce, and an endless array of barbecued meats. The Cantonese have also traditionally enjoyed a number of exotic delicacies, including bear paws, deer tails, and monkey brains. More palatable to Western tastes is the savory selection of small, bite-sized morsels called *dim-sum.* Featuring meats, often ground and spiced, combined with rice or flour to form a variety of dumpling-like treats, dim-sum has become as fashionable in the West as in Hong Kong. Some famous northern dishes, such as Peking Duck, are also popular in Hong Kong as elsewhere. Tea, believed to have health-giving properties, has long been China's favorite drink, and was its earliest contribution to world cuisine.

Most Hong Kong Chinese have adopted Western-style clothing, especially when it comes to doing business. A number of fashionable tailoring houses have existed since the heyday of British power, though nowadays their expensive suits are made for wealthy Chinese businessmen. Casual wear for the older people often includes slacks and a collared shirt; in the summer many wear shorts. Sandals are popular, though it is considered rude to wear flip-flops in public. Young people relax in jeans, sneakers, and T-shirts. In small villages in the New Territories one may still see Hakka women wearing their traditional black pajama-like costumes and broad black-rimmed hats. The agricultural Hakkas are a matriarchal society, and the women are known for doing work elsewhere performed by men.

In crowded Hong Kong, money buys space. Over half the population—almost 3,000,000 people—live in the small urban centers of Hong Kong Island and Kowloon. There, on average, each person has less than nine square feet of living space. Shamshuipo, a district of Kowloon, has the highest population density in the history of the world. Most urban families live in high-rise apartment buildings, often occupying a small, single room with a common bathroom in the hall. Extremes of comfort range from the millionaires' homes on Victoria Peak to the sprawling and unsanitary shantytowns on the city's outskirts. There, families live in small, makeshift dwellings of discarded wood and other materials. About fifteen percent of the city-

For many Chinese of Hong Kong, their boat is their home. *Courtesy of David Tuch.*

dwellers live in such houses, where long lines form for public water and washroom facilities. Often they are working families who are not poor but simply cannot afford the relatively expensive private apartments, yet do not qualify for limited public housing. The shantytowns are dangerous, subject to destruction by typhoons or fire. The worst fire, in 1953, left 60,000 homeless.

Around 100,000 people also live on boats called junks or sampans, which raft onto one another to form floating cities. The largest such city is in Aberdeen, on the south side of Hong Kong Island. Many of the boat families are Tanka fisherfolk, whose numbers are decreasing as fishing declines because of pollution and overfishing. Boat life is cramped and difficult. Because of typhoons, it is—like life in the shantytowns—also dangerous.

Family life. With so much of the people's energy devoted to the pursuit of the Hong Kong dollar, much of family life is geared toward generating income. Most small business are run by families. While child labor in factories has been outlawed, many young children still work long hours in the home or on the street, manufacturing or selling the family wares. They make cheap toys such as dolls or stuffed animals, clothing, and firecrackers, or cook and sell food from family stalls. The pressure of freewheeling city life has eroded traditionally strong Chinese family values to some extent. Street crime and drug use, often controlled by powerful gangs, add to the problems families face.

Education is now compulsory and free through the third year of junior high school. Generally, only the children of wealthier Chinese go on to further education.

Literature and the arts. Arising as they do from people with little time for reflection, the arts have not been a highly significant part of Hong Kong culture. Those that do exist have largely been imported, and survive only if they are sure-fire money-makers. Examples are filmmaking and jewelry; exceptions are some traditional theater arts, which are performed by amateur as well as professional companies. Chinese opera and puppet theater are both popular. The Cantonese version of Chinese opera includes modern and foreign references and themes. The least traditional of three opera forms performed in Hong Kong, it is the favorite. Hong Kong boasts one of the world's largest film industries, producing about 130 movies per year. Older filmmakers such as Sir Run Run Shaw turned out money-making action movies, and in the 1970s Hong Kong produced many hugely popular Kung Fu movies. More recently, directors such as Ann Hui have produced a "new wave" of more socially conscious films. Hui's 1983 movie *Boat People* described the misery of families forced to flee post-war Vietnam, many of whom sought shelter in Hong Kong.

Religion. Chinese religions are less exclusive than Western ones, and often incorporate elements of what the West would consider philosophy. Of the three main faiths, two (Buddhism and Taoism) have strong philosophical overtones, while Confucianism is really a highly influential philosophy that has taken on religious aspects. Most Hong Kong Chinese observe aspects of all three religions, while also keeping plenty of room for folk religion or superstition. The Chinese worship a number of gods and goddesses. Most popular in Hong Kong are Tin Hau, goddess of seafarers, and Kuanyin, goddess of mercy. Luck, or *joss,* is considered highly important in making money and can even itself be bought as a kind of investment. Numbers have especially strong significance, and the government regularly auctions off lucky numbers for license plates. The luckiest number, three, which signifies "living or giving birth," once was auctioned for $132,000 (U.S.).

Language. Most Hong Kong Chinese speak Cantonese, a complex language related to the Mandarin Chinese spoken in the north. However, the two are mutually unintelligible, being about as different as English and French. They share a written form, which uses characters or pictographs rather than letters. Each character represents an idea, and most words consist of two or three characters that combine ideas to form a new concept. English is necessary both for higher education and for success in the business world, and most people can speak it conversationally, if not write it.

Holidays. The people of Hong Kong enjoy a double dose of holidays: one set (including New Year, Christmas, and Easter) dictated by the Western solar calendar and the other by the Chinese lunar calendar. The lunar holidays fall on a different solar day each year. For example, Chinese New Year, the biggest holiday, may fall anytime between late January and mid-February. Traditionally the celebration continues for fifteen days, but the pressures of modern life have shortened its observance for most Chinese to three days. The New Year is a time to pay old debts (or risk bad joss), clean the house, and generally put one's affairs in order. People wish each other prosperity in the coming year, and fill the streets in noisy, crowded celebrations. Other important holidays include Ching Ming ("clear and bright"), in early spring, which is the time to tend to the graves of family ancestors so that they will bring the family good luck; the Dragon Boat Festival, in June, featuring races among boats paddled by teams of up to eighty men; and Mid-Autumn Lantern Festival, originally a harvest celebration. A host of minor holidays ensures that the hard-working Hong Kong Chinese enjoy a chance to play hard as well.

Sports and leisure. Other favorite pastimes include nightlife (Hong Kong offers a glittering array of night clubs and less reputable establishments) and shopping. Horse racing, a preoccupation of the British, caught on among the Chinese as well, and is now a multimillion dollar industry. Gambling in all forms fascinates the Chinese. A popular form is the complex game of mahjong, traditionally not understandable by Westerners, but involving tiles similar to dominoes. Mahjong invokes lots of betting, and lots of shouting. It is played anywhere, from the beach to fancy dinner parties.

Rickshaws still provide transportation to the Star Ferry Port. *Courtesy of Dr. W. Paul Fischer.*

For More Information

Lueras, Leonard, et al., editors. *Insight Guides: Hong Kong*. Singapore: APA Publications, Inc., 1990.

Morris, Jan. *Hong Kong*. New York: Random House, 1988.

Storey, Robert. *Hong Kong, Macau & Canton: A Travel Survival Kit*. Melbourne, Australia: Lonely Planet Publications, 1992.

IBAN

(ee ban′)

Native peoples of Sarawak.

Population: 514,000 (1990 estimate).
Location: Sarawak, a Malaysian state, which is located in the northwest section of the island of Borneo. Bordered on the east by the Upper Kapuas and Iran Mountains, which form the border between Malaysia (Sarawak) and Indonesia (Kalimantan)
Languages: Iban; Malaysian; English.

Geographical Setting

Sarawak is a mountainous state in Malaysia. Several large rivers and many tributaries rush from the mountains that separate Indonesian and Malaysian sections of Borneo and empty into the South China Sea. Heavy rainfall and its location just north of the equator make this a tropical forest land—warm and damp. Except for a small region in the north near Brunei, an old British colony turned independent country, almost all the land is hilly or mountainous, with mountains rising to 7,000 feet. Three hundred fifty miles of coastline is jaggedly broken by the streams. It is along these streams that the people known as Iban have long been established.

Historical Background

The Malay Peninsula and the islands offshore were the scenes of Chinese influence and trade as early as the second century B.C. By A.D. 631 this Chinese interest had grown so that Chinese settlers, expanding their area beyond the natural harbor of Brunei, established an iron smelting plant in the Sarawak mountains. However, from the

seventh to the thirteenth century, the people of Sarawak were ruled from Sumatra under the Hindu kingdom of Sri Vijaija. In the fourteenth and fifteenth centuries, the region fell to the Hindu-Javanese kingdom of Majapchit and, with Borneo, formed the region of Tanjory Pulo.

The next century again brought change as the island was invaded by Islamic settlers who established a system of sultanates. Then, later in the sixteenth century, Portuguese and Spanish merchants and seamen arrived on the island. With such pressure from India, Muslim areas, and Europe, the Iban, who had formed a large part of the population of the entire Borneo-Sarawak-Sabah-Brunei island made a mass migration to the mountains and streams of what is now Sarawak.

James Brooke. In 1839, disturbed by pirating in the South China Sea, a veteran of South Pacific wars, James Brooke, set out in a purchased British royal yacht to rid the South China Sea of pirates. Brooke arrived in Sarawak to find the ruling rajah there engulfed in a rebellion involving the Sea Dayaks, Iban sailor-pirates. In return for his help, Rajah Muda of Sarawak promised to make Brooke his successor. This promise was kept by the king of Borneo two years after Rajah Muda relinquished the title. James Brooke set himself up as the "White Rajah" and proceeded to unite Sarawak while pursuing his design to fight the coastal "pirates," many of whom were Iban sailors. To do this, he outlawed piracy and established a strict code of behavior guaranteeing Sea Dayaks equal treatment with others in Sarawak. In 1849, Brooke engaged many of these pirates in battle at sea, which ended with the deaths of 500 to 800 native seamen and with Brooke carrying off a large bounty. The White Rajah used this bounty to strengthen his hold on Sarawak, building forts at the mouths of many of the rivers and thus shutting the Iban off from their pirating. Though opposed to the British and Malaysian settlers, the Iban, some of whom were hunters, settled into an agricultural way of life.

Charles Brooke. In 1917, James Brooke's holdings were inherited by his grandson, Charles Vyner Brooke. Except for the period of World War II (1941–1945) when the Japanese held the region, Charles Vyner Brooke ruled over the Malaysians and Iban in Sarawak. However, after the war, and after the country had been returned to Brooke, he wearied of controlling the Iban and others there and deeded Sarawak to Britain. For a short time, the British seemed to favor the Iban over the Malaysians and Chinese who had become the port operators and merchants of Sarawak. Then, in 1948, falling to great pressure for Malay independence, the British abandoned their claims on the region around the South China Sea. Malaysia became an independent nation and included Sarawak.

Malaysia. The Malaysian government has continuously pursued a policy of opposition to Communism and of developing economic security through the free enterprise system that is heavily influenced by the national government's intervention. The whole country is rich in resources, including petroleum in the South China Sea, hardwood forests in Sarawak and on the mainland, and many mineral resources. Using these resources to develop international trade, Malaysia has increased its gross national product by nearly ten percent each year. Except for a three-year period in the 1960s when Indonesia made a strong but failed attempt to claim Sarawak, this region has grown along with the rest of Malaysia.

However, the Iban, long at odds with the Malaysians, have not gained economically as rapidly as the country's other citizens, most of whom are of either Chinese or Malaysian ancestry and live in the four major seaports. Little touched by British and Malaysian development of large rubber plantations, the Iban continue to be subsistence rice farmers along the Sarawak rivers. This continues despite the organization of Iban and Sarawak political parties to protect their interests as early as the 1960s.

Culture Today

The longhouse. Along the streams of Sarawak, amid the tropical rain forest, the Iban people build their one-building communities. Finding a place where some forest land can be cut and burned to make way for rice farming and where a good stream for fishing is nearby, an Iban leader gathers related families to build a village. This village consists of a single long building, perched on stilts ten-to-thirty feet high on the banks of a stream, and twenty-to-fifty yards long. This longhouse will become a home apartment building for related families. The original founder will have an apartment (*bilik*) in the middle of the building, and others will build next to that apartment under one roof. The longhouse is built under strict conditions guided by Iban beliefs. For example, evil is believed to be the fate of a longhouse built over a stream or its tributary.

Apartments for the families of the longhouse are built along one side. They are joined on their inside wall by a long, covered but open area, the *rudi*. Beyond the rudi, there is a raised area used for sleeping (young men do not sleep with their families in the family apartment), and beyond that an unroofed porch, the *tanju*.

In this longhouse, parents, grandparents, and the families of children, including some "adopted" into the family, live separately under one roof. Families live in their individual biliks and share the rudi and tanju with other longhouse residents. A headman with little authority other than a strong personality rules over the longhouse and settles disputes there. He is sometimes aided by an *augur*, a leader of the rituals who is charged with bringing favorable omens to the house. Other than this loose arrangement of government, each family in the longhouse is independent, owning its own farm land and settling its own disputes.

Family life. The roles of family members are strictly regulated by Iban custom. Women of the family slash undergrowth to clear land for planting, sow the rice and other garden produce, reap the harvest,

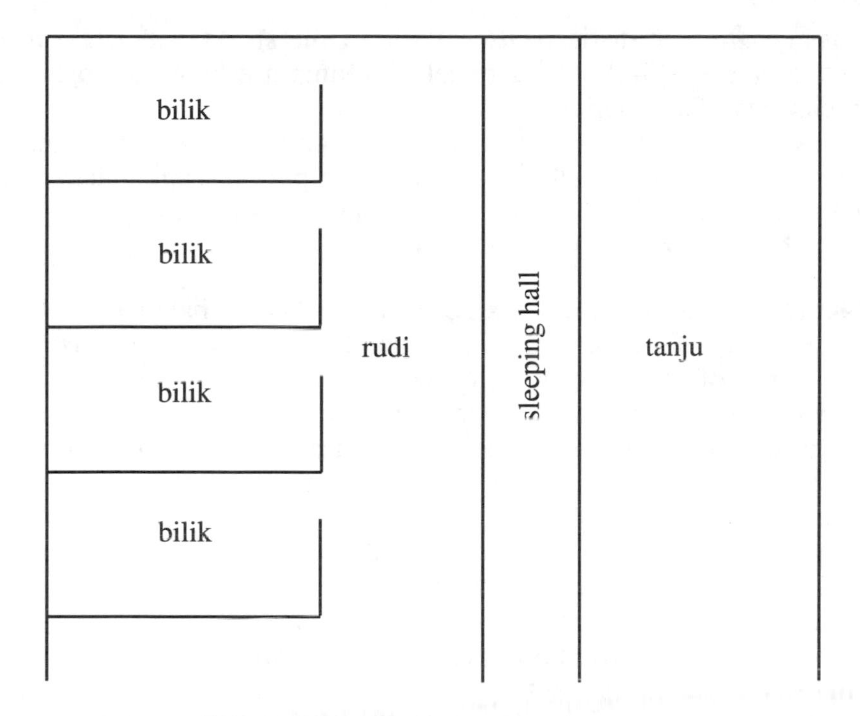

Portion of an Iban longhouse.

winnow the rice, prepare sacred seeds for rituals, and engage in some magic. Men clear the trees, help with slashing and and burning the undergrowth, hunt for food animals in the forest, collect rattan for weaving, and carry on some marketing. Some of the men are traders of Iban-made goods for Chinese jars, brass gongs, and ceramic items. By the age of twelve, children are helping with the chores.

The forests of Sarawak are filled with a variety of animal life. The most famous Sarawak forest resident is the orang-utang, but there is an abundance of monkeys, particularly the langur monkey. These animals are hunted by the men and boys and provide important supplements to the rice diet of the family.

Since 1910, Sarawak has been involved in production of rubber, along with pepper and palm oil as cash crops. Until recently, longhouse residents jointly owned and cared for these cash crops. Today, much of the land of Sarawak is being formed into large plantations and some Iban find jobs in these larger agricultural units.

Evenings are frequently spent in the rudi or on the tanju talking about the day's events with other longhouse families or listening to songs (*poutur*) or stories (*ansera*). Often the storytellers draw from their dreams to find stories to tell. Dreams are believed to be the revelations of wandering souls.

As they mature, young men of the family leave their sleeping quarters in the family bilik to sleep on the porch sleeping area. This gives them more freedom to court the girls of the longhouse and to meet them at forest edge at nightfall.

Religion. Ibans hold that it is necessary to keep a balance of all life forms. To do this, the souls of humans interact with gods (*petera*) and spirits of other living things (*antra*). There are several gods in the Iban religion. Benevolent gods include a god of the heavens, of treetops, and of wind. However, the paramount gods are Selampandai, a female god who creates humans from clay; Pulang Gana, god of the padi culture who oversees rice production; and Sungalang Burung, god of war, who also introduced the first Iban to rice. In the world of humans, there is a need for balance among the *antu* (spirits of the dead), *tubuk* (body), and *Sunangat* (soul).

Since rice cultivation is of primary importance, there are religious rituals involved in its planting and harvest—and there are taboos, for some actions result in poor harvests. Planting rituals begin with *maggol*, a ritual of sacrifice before clearing the land. One special tree is selected and omens laid on either side. A hen is then sacrificed for the blessing of the field. Then during planting, Iban are forbidden to:

> Cut hair (it will bring on an invasion of locusts).
> Pluck eyebrows (encourages an invasion of birds).
> Forge iron (results in solar burning of the crop).
> Clear creepers from the land.
> Bind or tie hair while weaving.
> Debark trees.
>
> (Freeman 1981, p. 134)

Arts. The Iban have no written language of their own. Their literature includes the dream-inspired songs and stories previously mentioned. Iban men forge some iron products, and the Iban are expert wood carvers, carving animals and other forms to sell. Iban weavers create materials which are dyed in bright reds and yellows, and decorate these for market. Among these items are baskets into which are woven designs of symbolic importance. These baskets are greatly sought after by international collectors.

Clothing. The older costume of the Iban man consisted of a wide sash from which a loincloth was hung front and back and a weapon carried on one side. Shell, stone, and brass necklaces and armbands were used as decorations. The costume was completed with a turban made from a length of cloth wrapped around the skull. Girls of the old Sea Dayak groups wore richly dyed skirts of cloth, sometimes with fringe decoration. Over this, a girl might wear a sort of corset made of rattan hoops with red stripes and heavily bedecked with silver or bronze bracelets and decorations hung from the rattan. An ornately filigreed and tinseled comb held the hair in place. Metal and shell belts and necklaces completed the costume.

As the Iban come into greater contact with Chinese and Malay settlers, this costume has given way to trousers, skirts, and shirts.

Moving. A longhouse shelters family and friends for as long as the cleared forest will support a rice crop. Since there are two monsoon seasons in Sarawak—heavy rains from the northeast from October to January and lighter ones from April through July—the cleared land is soon depleted. As some families find the rice crop waning, they might decide to establish a new longhouse. Men of the family search the virgin forest for a suitable place where some land can be cleared for rice and where a longhouse can be built alongside a stream without bridging over even the smallest tributary. Here the ritual of land clearing is performed, land is cleared, and a new longhouse community built.

As the Malay government presses for development of forest resources and mining, and explores for new petroleum resources, this freedom of movement has become restricted for the Iban. Some of them have settled into more permanent residential styles, and some have joined the Malay and Chinese work forces to develop Malaysia's fast-growing industrial base.

Politics. Although they are the dominant ethnic group in Sarawak, the Iban are a minority in the Malay-controlled country of Malaysia. As a result, Iban people have from time to time pressed for independence. They are assured of representation in the legislature of Malaysia through the dedication of twenty-seven seats in that body to represent the people of Sarawak.

For More Information

Cramb, R. A. *The Evolution of Iban Land Tenure.* Bulletin of the Centre of South East Asia Studies, #39. Clayton, Australia: Monash University, 1986.

Freeman, Derek. *Some Reflections on the Nature of Iban Society*. Canberra, Australia: Australian National University, 1981.

Kidit, Pelu Mulok. *Modernization Among the Iban of Sarawak*. Kuala Lampur, Malaysia: Dewan Banusa Dan Pustaka, 1980.

JAPANESE

(jap uh neez′)

The people of the island country of Japan.

Population: 124,000,000 (1991 estimate).
Location: Japan.
Language: Japanese, a language unrelated to nearby Asian languages.

Geographical Setting

The Japanese people occupy four large islands and many lesser ones arching along the coast of the Asian mainland about a hundred miles from the mainland country of Korea. The four islands—from south to north, Kyosho, Shikoku, Honsu, and Hokaido—provide a land area that is about one-and-one-half times that of Great Britain. However, Japan is a mountainous country of rugged mountains and hills spotted by the higher peaks of volcanoes. The result is that the Japanese live along the coast or scattered in the fertile valleys of the hills and mountains. Less than one-fifth of the land is suitable for agriculture, and much of that is in the valleys carved through the volcanic hills by the many streams. Fertile valleys are divided by tree-covered mountains. The total ecology has contributed to the Japanese love of beauty and association of beauty with the environment.

The largest near-level region is the 120-mile-long Kanto Plain around Tokyo. Packed into an area in which no land is more than seventy miles from the ocean, the Japanese people mostly live in large towns and great cities.

Short hot summers and cold winters leave most of the year pleasant. The hot summers are the rainy season, which means that crops can be grown almost anywhere in Japan for more than 200 days a year. Other than its scarce agricultural land, Japan has few natural

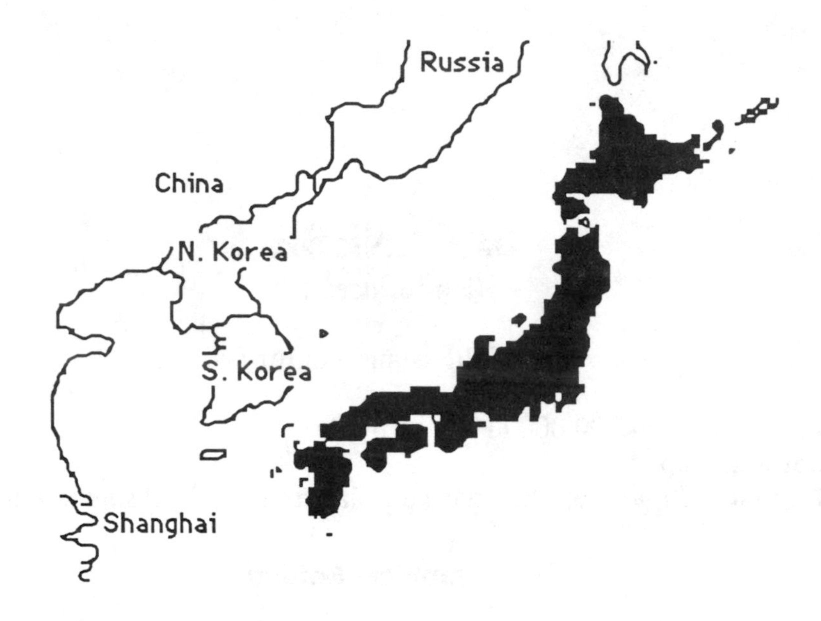

resources except for abundant hydro-electric energy for its growing industries.

The broken nature of the land has in the past made for a fragmented government by local groups. But high-speed trains and modern highways have helped to unify the country. Bridges and tunnels now join the islands.

Historical Background

Origin. The origins of the Japanese people are uncertain but their ancestors are thought to have migrated from mainland Asia to Japan by 1500 B.C. For centuries after that the Japanese remained relatively isolated, a posture encouraged by their island abode and by the leaders who ruled them. The first written records of the early Japanese are Chinese reports in the third century A.D. However, once contact was made with outside peoples, the Japanese demonstrated an aptitude for adopting the progressive ways of others and shaping these ways to their own particular liking.

Jomon era. Immigrant ancestors of the Japanese lived in small groups, each developing separate lifestyles as nomadic hunters, agricultural people, and seafarers. The early Japanese culture became known as the Jomon period because of the pots the people created by twisting clay into a rope pattern called jomon. During this period, in 660 B.C., the first emperor, Jimmu Tenno, is said to have united the people and assumed the throne claiming to be a descendant of the sun goddess. The emperors who succeeded him maintained this hereditary claim of divine right to rule. Still, Japan remained settled predominantly by various independent tribal groups.

China. Relations with China were established possibly as early as the first century B.C. Chinese language, painting, sculpture, and the religion of Buddhism were brought to Japan, and immigrants from China and Korea contributed to subsequent development of the Japanese culture. As the years passed, the Japanese showed themselves to be a practical people by adopting the advancements made by China but shaping them into a distinctive Japanese culture. By the 700s the Chinese written language had been changed to a more simple script that suited a Japanese spoken language not related to Chinese. The new language helped to unify the various groups of Japanese. In China, Buddhist monks were isolated from public life but in Japan they took an active part in society and government. Later, the governmental structure borrowed from the Chinese would be altered to include a hereditary base for rule.

Heian Age. Artistic achievement and military rule marked the period from 794 to 1185. This "Heian Age" was directed by the Fujiwara family, which controlled power even though the imperial family held the throne. Eventually, the Fujiwara family became part of the imperial family by marriage, and Fujiwara sons became emperors.

During this period, women of the court were not taken seriously, and thought of mainly as attractive accouterments. With little to do, many of them took to keeping diaries. The world's first novel, *The Tale of Gengi*, written by a Japanese woman named Murasaki Shikibu at the beginning of the eleventh century, grew from this diary-keeping.

Ruling families. Power-wielding families in Japan have, throughout history, shown a pattern for gaining power and then losing it to underlings, while rulers remained comfortable in their background roles as figureheads. Eventually, the Fujiwara family lost real power to govern to the Taira clan. Then, in 1185 A.D., the Minammoto clan leader, Yoritomo, upset the Taira clan and established a military government in an area near Tokyo. The emperor was forced to appoint Yorimoto to the position of Seii Tai Shogun (leading general). He was the first of many shoguns who were the real rulers of Japan until 1867. The rule of the shoguns was interrupted intermittently from the thirteenth century by Mongol invasions and by frequent disputes between the great families. Mounting the largest fleet ever assembled up to that time, the Mongols invaded Japan. They were repelled by a comparatively few Japanese nobles until unusually strong storms resulted in the loss of the Mongol fleet. Again, Japan fell into its ancient tribal patterns.

Tokugawa Era. Finally, in the seventeenth century, peace was restored under the leadership of Shogun Tokugawa Ieyasu. He succeeded in replacing or demanding allegiance of other lords of Japan and organized a four-tier structure for Japanese society that, even though long disbanded, has strong effects on the Japanese today. Shogun Tokugawa defined a ruling military class, the samurai, and below this class, rankings of farmers, craftsmen, and merchants. The samurai were all-powerful as indicated by this decree of Tokugawa Ieyasu:

> Farmers, craftsmen, and merchants may not behave in a rude manner towards samurai. The word for a rude man is "other-than-expected-fellow," and a samurai is not to be interfered with in cutting down a fellow who has behaved to him in a manner other than is expected.
>
> (Tasker 1987, p. 53)

Reacting to rumors of a Christian invasion, Shogun Ieyasu closed Japan to all outsiders. Christianity was outlawed and missionaries who refused to leave were massacred. The feudal society that had developed earlier became centralized under the shogun, his samurai warriors, and rich lords in the upper class. The lower classes were formed by peasants, artisans, and merchants. Japan was once again a unified nation, but with strongly feudalistic patterns. The feudal Tokugawa pattern was to dominate Japan until the late 1800s.

Commodore Perry. The arrival of Commodore Matthew C. Perry from America in 1853 brought an end to feudal Japan. Perry forced the shogun to sign a treaty establishing trade relations with the west, thereby demonstrating the weakness of the shogun. His enemies exploited the weakness and restored power to the emperor who assumed control along with a small group of powerful lords. The office of shogun was formally abolished in 1871. Following these changes, contact with outsiders brought a period of rapid growth as the practical Japanese again adapted the advancements of others to their own society. Public schools, libraries, newspapers, steamships, and factories were developed, and Japan took steps toward becoming a world industrial giant.

In 1889, a new constitution initiated what has become known as the Meiji period of constitutional government ruled by a Diet. The role of emperor, long a symbolic position, was given renewed emphasis as the emperor was declared sacred and inviolable. But while revered as a symbol of Japanese unity, the role of the emperor was weakened by the constitutional demand that his actions be approved by the legislature, the Diet.

Wars. The Japanese began to expand their territory through military conquest with three surprise attacks. The attacks led to victory in the Sino-Japanese War (1894–1895) and in the Russo-Japanese War (1904–1905), then to defeat in World War II (1941–1945). Damage to Japan in World War II was great. The cities of Hiroshima and Nagasaki had been destroyed by the atomic bomb and major damage had been done by conventional bombs to sixty other cities. In keeping with tradition, the Japanese reaction to defeat was a practical one. The people cooperated with the Allied forces that occupied the country after the war and began modernizing Japan by adopting and modifying their ways as demanded by the victorious Allies. A new constitution was passed in 1946, establishing a democratic government. While Emperor Hirohito remained the symbolic head of state, he renounced having any divine right to rule and a prime minister became the actual head of state. Occupation by the Allied forces ended in 1952, at which time the people officially became independent again. A period of astonishing material success began that has resulted in an exceptionally high standard of living for the present-day Japanese. Without a dependable internal energy source, Japan has become a leading manufacturer of many kinds of world trade goods from automobiles to electronics. In 1987 the Tokyo stock market was larger than either the New York or London exchanges.

Culture Today

Group or individual? Throughout its history and particularly during the time of the shoguns, Japanese people were led to a strong belief in group activities and acquiescence to the group. Individual Japanese often felt a need to satisfy the group and gain recognition through it. The group identity was so strong that suicide came to be recognized as an honorable way to atone for affronts to an individual's group.

Economy. The economic success of the Japanese has in part been attributed to the way the people are organized into company groups. The company provides workers with a salary that includes a built-in family allowance, and bonuses are awarded to the workers based on company profits. Trade unions are organized around individual businesses and are actively involved in the housing, recreation, and welfare of employees as well as in work-related issues. Companies

It is possible to buy almost anything on Black Mountain Alley in Naha. *Courtesy of Dr. W. Paul Fischer.*

rather than individuals tend to compete with one another. Employment is for life and workers are encouraged to commit themselves to the common goal of the company. In manufacturing, the Japanese have become the world's major producers of ships and passenger cars.

Extreme pollution problems have accompanied the rapid growth of industry, and have contributed to the rise in disease among the people. Methods to control the problems have met with some success so that life expectancy is still higher for the Japanese than for any other people in the world. Japanese men generally live to the age of seventy-four while life expectancy for women is seventy-nine.

Only fifteen percent of Japanese land is suitable for cultivation, so the majority of agricultural workers have combined farming with industry. Rice is the major crop grown and is supplemented by sweet potatoes, soybeans, mandarin oranges and persimmons. In addition, the Japanese fishing industry has captured fourteen percent of the world market.

Food, clothing, and shelter. In Japan fish is an important part of the daily diet of the people, eaten raw, dried, broiled or boiled in a clear soup. Fresh fruit or a bowl of rice with hot tea poured over it

Bamboo is a popular building material in Japan. This collection, to be used for scaffolding, was in Tachikawa. *Courtesy of Dr. W. Paul Fischer.*

Tokyo residents flock to this street of exclusive shops in the Ginza area. *Courtesy of Dr. W. Paul Fischer.*

are typical deserts. Thick tea *(koicha)* and thin tea (*usuicha*) with a light green froth at the top are artfully prepared beverages. Contact with Westerners has brought bread, meat, and dairy products into the Japanese diet.

Japanese homes are a combination of traditional and Westernized lifestyles. The traditional house is roofed with dark gray tile or rust-proof tin and may be surrounded by a small garden and outer walls. At the front of the house is an entranceway where shoes are exchanged for slippers. Inside are all-purpose rooms for eating, sleeping, and receiving guests, a kitchen, and a restroom. Rooms of the house are floored with *tatami* (woven straw mats) and used for occasions such as the customary tea ceremony. Some rooms in the traditional home are expandable because many interior walls are sliding doors made of wood, heavy paper or glass. Furniture consists mainly of low tables, cushions, and mats known as futons instead of beds. Modern apartments have become more common forms of housing in the cities and these are furnished with carpets, tables, and chairs. Still, regardless of the new comforts, old customs such as removing shoes before entering a home and sitting on the floor are still popular among the Japanese. Conveniences such as color television sets and refrigerators are common items in virtually all homes, whether modern or traditional.

Art, literature, and recreation. Although sports and art have expanded because of contact with the West, many traditional practices have been maintained. The seventeen-syllable haiku continues to be a popular form of Japanese poetry. A popular form of literature in the 1980s was the cartoon. Books of cartoons and newspapers, heavy with cartoon drawings, are abundant in modern Japan.

The Kabuki drama, in which elaborately costumed actors speak and sing of real events in stylized ways, is part of modern-day theater.

Japanese art often finds subjects in the beautiful landscapes of Japan, which are frequently developed on a small scale. Small gardens, dwarfed and carefully shaped plants, and home centers of paintings and flower arrangements are common in Japan. Color prints that picture a floating world of courtesans of earlier times or of common people such as fish peddlers and sailors still hang on Japanese walls.

The popularity of the marital arts (sumo, judo, karate) continues but today is shared with baseball, golf, and other sports from the west.

Japan is a land of many small, well-tended gardens such as this one near the American School at Tambochina. *Courtesy of Dr. W. Paul Fischer.*

Teahouses cared for by women in traditional Japanese dress are popular places of relaxation in Japan. This is one serves tourists near the Meiji Shrine. *Courtesy of Dr. W. Paul Fischer.*

Women. Women can occasionally be seen wearing the traditional *kimono*, a long loose-sleeved robe belted with a wide sash. But this traditional dress is mostly reserved for holidays and special events. At other times Japanese women are clad in Western-style dress. Not only the dress but also the position of Japanese women in society has undergone change. They now have the right to vote and work as professionals in Japan, but there is still evidence of their traditional subservience. In some families, the husband walks a few paces before the wife, enters a room before her, and is served before she is.

The Burakunin. Another persistent tradition is segregation of the *burakunin*, or lowest class of Japanese, from the rest of society. The burakunin are members of families who earn their living by performing services such as making shoes, tanning hides, and killing animals—occupations forbidden to Buddhists. Today they live in clearly defined areas of Japan and are often passed over for job and educational opportunities.

Religion. The ancient religion of the Japanese was Shinto, an animistic belief with many dieties (*kami*) drawn from natural things and from illustrious ancestors. Shrines to these kami were erected throughout Japan. Throughout much of its history, the emperor of

The Meiji Shrine in Tokyo. *Courtesy of Dr. W. Paul Fischer.*

Japan was required to be a follower of this religion. Shinto practicers call on or provide offerings to specific kami for assistance in daily life. Shintoism is not concerned with an afterlife. The most venerated religious symbol in Japan is the Shinto Shrine at Ise, which houses the imperial sword, mirror, and Jewel. Erected nearly 2,000 years ago, this shrine is torn down and identically replaced each twenty years. Even so, most Japanese do not give their total religious loyalty to Shintoism.

Early in their association with China, Buddhism was brought to the Japanese people. Originating in India and spread through China, Buddhism brought magic formulas, rituals, and art, taught salvation through faith, and self-reliance in seeking salvation through meditation. Many versions of Buddhism arose, with Zen being the most well-known one outside of Japan.

At first the two religions complemented one another, then Buddhism began to overshadow Shintoism, even though the emperor was required to be Shinto. In the late 1800s, a resurgence of Shintoism arose. Buddhism and Shintoism were completely separated and an attempt was made to relate Shintoism with national loyalty.

Today, many Japanese are comfortable following both religions and sometimes also follow another, Confucianism. Buddhist temples and Shinto shrines are scattered throughout Japan.

Education. Japanese education is modeled after that of the United States, and there is fierce competition for schooling at every level.

Tourists make frequent visits to one of the largest Buddha temples. *Courtesy of Dr. W. Paul Fischer.*

There are many Shinto temples in Japan; this one is in Kamakura. *Courtesy of Dr. W. Paul Fischer.*

Entrance into universities is based on examinations. The difficulty of these examinations has resulted in establishing a separate preparatory education and has created much debate even among leading government officials in the Diet, the lawmaking body of Japan.

Government. The Diet is made up of a House of Representatives and a House of Councillors with members elected by the people. Although the emperor is the official head of state, the role is mostly ceremonial and an elected prime minister is the day-to-day leader of the government. In accordance with the San Fransisco Treaty, the United States maintains forces in Japan for defense against outside attack. As dictated by the United States and its allies after World War II, Article 9 of the Japanese constitution renounces forever the use of war as a means of settling international disputes.

The election of a Diet and a prime minister follows most nearly the English pattern, with new elections taking place when the Diet does not show support for the actions of the prime minister and his aids. In this pattern of government, policies are more likely to be decided among the leaders of the ruling party than by the Diet as a whole.

Samurai. As the old Tokugawa regime aged, the military rulers found it increasingly necessary to look to the despised merchant class to finance the government. As a result, some merchants grew powerful, and some samurai families turned successfully to business and industry. The influence of the samurai, while officially disbanded in 1889, resulted in the location of major portions of the Japanese industry and business with powerful samurai families. An example is the Mitsubishi family, the second most influential industrial family in Japan, and once an equally powerful samurai family.

Seppuku. Another relic of the Tokugawa Era is the Japanese tradition of atoning for affronts to one's family or group by committing suicide (in Japanese, *seppuku*). Once, suicide by a ritualistic cutting of one's own stomach was an honorable vindication of such an affront. This ritual, popularly called *hara-kiri* outside of Japan, has long disappeared from the Japanese society. But suicide is still accepted as an honorable way to pay for a person's misdealings—actions which are still viewed as embarrassments to a person's family or group.

For More Information

Reischauer, Edwin O. *The Japanese Today.* Cambridge: Belknap Press of Harvard University Press, 1988.

Tasker, Peter. *The Japanese.* New York: Truman Talley Books/E. P. Dutton, 1987.

JAVANESE

(jav uh neez')

The largest native population of the island of Java.

Location: Island of the Indonesian archipelago in Southeast Asia.
Population: 120,000,000 (1992 estimate).
Languages: Javanese (a Malaya-Polynesian language); Bahasa Indonesian.

Geographical Setting

Java is a fertile, volcanic island located in the center of the Indonesia archipelago, an arc of some 13,667 islands stretching east-west across the Indian and Pacific oceans in Southeast Asia. More than 100 million people live on Java, an island the size of England with an area

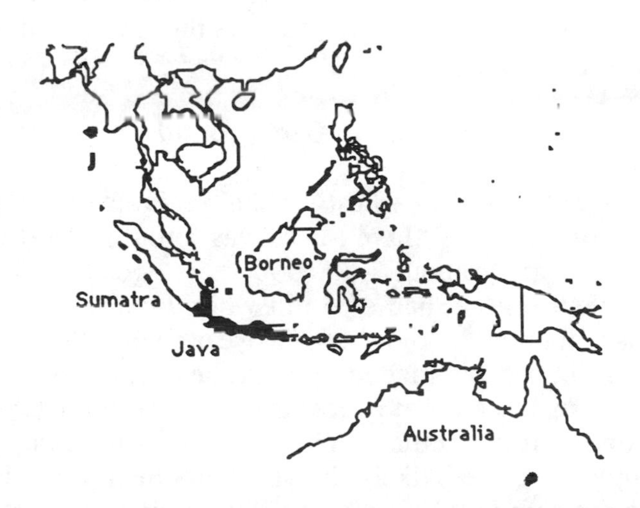

of 133,000 square kilometers. Physically, Java is distinguished by its many volcanoes—more than 121 cones in all—that can be seen rising above the landscape from almost any point on the island. Thirty of the volcanoes are still active. While eruptions have wiped out entire villages, the nutrient-rich ash spewed from the volcanoes and into the atmosphere over surrounding villages contributes to the natural fertilization of the rich farm land of this agriculturally prosperous land.

Wet-rice cultivation has formed the basis of the Javanese livelihood for centuries. Today, about sixty-three percent of Java's land area is cultivated, including the mountain peaks and urban concentrations. About one-third of the area is irrigated, both along the flat plains and terraces of the mountain regions. Other farm land receives the rains of the wet season. The climate of Java is tropical, with alternating wet and dry seasons. The dry season occurs between May and September and the wet season is between October and April. Relative humidity for Java averages a high of seventy-five percent.

There are three provinces of Java. Central Java is the center of Javanese culture, history, and language and an area of intensive farming amongst the rural populations. East Java is also inhabited by primarily Javanese, includes the industrial city of Surabaya, and emphasizes plantation agriculture. West Java is the land of a different people, the Sundanese, who are related to the Javanese in language and culture. In addition to the provinces, there are two different and special districts, Jakarta and Yogyakarta. Jakarta is the capital city and the most western of all of the Indonesian cities. Yogyakarta is still ruled by a sultan (Muslim king) and is the stronghold of Javanese culture and tradition.

Historical Background

Early origins. One of the earliest skeletal remains of a hominid (pre Homo sapien) known as "Java Man" was found in 1891 at Trinil in Central Java. Dating about 1,500,000 years ago, this skeleton represented a life form that had died out when Java was still connected to the Asian mainland. About 20,000 years ago, after the waters of the last great ice age had melted to form the present island formation of Indonesia, small bands of people migrated from the Chinese province of Yunnan into Vietnam, Thailand, and the Malay Peninsula. These people were most likely the ancestors of present-day Indonesians. The remains of "Wajak Man," found along the Brantas River in East Java and dating around 10,000 years old, is one of the oldest historical links between the migrating bands from China and the Javanese of today. Thus before recorded history, the Javanese were agriculturalists who had begun to settle in villages around seaports, which were the major points of contact with the Asian continent.

Influence along the trade routes. The history of Java is an important part of the history of Indonesia, since Java was an important part of the trade routes through Southeast Asia. As an agriculturally rich island, Java has always been able to support large populations and has often been led by powerful rulers. In 2,000 years, Java has never relinquished its role as the political and trading center of the Indonesian archipelago. The earliest written reference to Java occurs in the Chinese records of the Han dynasty—an account of the visit of an embassy from "Yavadvipa." A little later, around A.D. 160, the Roman geographer, Ptolemy, mentions the East Indian islands, a note that supports the possibility that Roman beads found on the island of Borneo near Java were evidence of early trade.

India was an early influence on Java. Under the northern Gupta dynasty (A.D. 300–600), India enjoyed a golden age of wide-ranged prosperity and influence as both traders and religious pilgrims (Buddhist and Hindu) reached Java. Great monuments and their inscriptions are still evidence of these influences. The oldest inscription in Java, found near Bogor and dating from the fifth century, records the name of King Purnavarman of Taruma, ruler of a kingdom about which little else is known. Around the eighth century, a kingdom rose in central Java under the Sailendras, "Lords of the Mountains," Buddhist rulers who were related to the Srivijaya Buddhist kingdom on the island of Sumatra near Java. They were powerful enough to erect a stupa in Borobudur, one of the most beautiful monuments in Java. For reasons unknown, the Sailendras moved their center of power to Srivijaya, and the leadership in Central Java passed to a short-lived dynasty, the Mataram. The change in the rulers also meant a change in the religion as the Mataram dynasty were followers of Hinduism and erected the outstanding Loro Jonggrang temples in Prambanan in honor of the Hindu god, Shiva. Dozens of temples were erected on the plains, plateaus, and hills of Central Java between 700–900—evidence of the economic, cultural, and artistic vitality of these kingdoms.

The rule of the kings of East Java. By the year 1000, the kingdom of Mataram was waning and new kingdoms were arising in East Java.

The best known of the East Java kings is King Airlangga, who ruled south of Surabaya from 1019 to 1049. Before claiming the throne and uniting East Java, King Airlangga spent many years as a hermit fasting, meditating, and cultivating wisdom and magical powers. Airlangga was followed by the Kediri dynasty (1049–1222) during which the Hindu epic, the Mahabharata, was translated to become an integral part of Java's cultural tradition. The fall of the Kediri brought seventy years of rule by the Singosari, during which time seven kings and princes in succession died by the sword. The last Singosari ruler, Kertonegoro, refused to pay tribute to the Great Kublai Khan of China, causing a military expedition of 20,000 Chinese/Mongol soldiers into Java. The Chinese troops left after the death of Kertonegoro, and a new king of the Majaphit dynasty was enthroned.

The Majaphit era. In 1289, after the Mongol invasion of Kublai Khan's military, Kertarajasa, son-in-law to Kertonegoro, established a capital city. However, it was not until 1310 that the Majaphit authority was established. During this time, Kertonegoro's daughter ruled and spread the Javanese culture and political control to Bali, Sumatra, and Borneo.

In 1350, Hayam Wuruk became king under the name of Rajasanagara. Hayam Wuruk's reign (1350–89) is remembered as the golden period of Javanese history. A poem called "Nagarakertagama," written by Parapanca in 1365, provides a rare glimpse into the life in the kingdom of Hayam Wuruk. The poem praises the king as a royal divinity purifying the land. Hayam Wuruk traveled extensively throughout the Indonesian islands, and with the help of his general, Gajah Mada, was able to spread his influence, unify Indonesia and collect tribute from across the land. He visited many of the Buddhist, Hindu, and ancient Javanese holy spots, crossing lines of religion. Hayam Wuruk required the heads of princely families to live in the capital city of Majaphit in order to consolidate his power at the center. The wealth of the Majaphit kingdom was based upon the successful cultivation of rice, which was traded in abundance within the islands of Indonesia and foreign traders. Hayam Wuruk died in 1389 without leaving a worthy successor to his throne. The Majaphit rule was the last of the great Hindu-Javanese kingdoms, for Islam slowly became established throughout Java from the north coast of Java.

The rise of Islam. Shortly after the Majaphit fall from power, Malacca, a powerful port-city under the leadership of Iskandar Shah, a

Muslim, became a major trading post and remained so for centuries. The establishment of the first Islamic centers in Java and other parts of Indonesia such as Sumatra was probably the result of trade from Malacca and other seaports whose rulers had most likely accepted Islam in order to attract Muslim and Javanese traders. The Islamic centers along the coast quickly rose to power. By 1500, every major port, from Aceh through Palembang and from Malacca on the north coast to the spice Islands of Indonesia, was in Muslim hands. Power at sea became the important key to success.

The Portuguese came to Java in 1522 and established a trading center in Sunda Kelapa (present-day capital of Jakarta). While the Portuguese were thrown out of Sunda Kelapa shortly after in 1527, they virtually monopolized the spice trade until the Dutch captured Malacca in 1641.

The growth of the Dutch empire. The first Dutch exploratory ships came to Java in 1596, where the enticing profits (high as 1,000 per cent) spurred greater trade. In 1602, the United East India Company, better known as the VOC (Vereenigde Oostindische Compagnie), was formed; it controlled Dutch trading fortunes until its demise in 1799. While the Dutch control of the trade in Indonesia developed gradually, the VOC laid the foundation for the Dutch imperial domination over Indonesia into the twentieth century. In 1755, the Dutch took advantage of infighting amongst the Javanese to gain control of one of the ruling inland powers, the kingdom of Mataram headed by the Sultan Agung. The Dutch intrusion divided the kingdom into two principalities, Yogyjakarta and Surakarta. The erosion of power by the princes and landowners increased in the eighteenth century as the Dutch government began to assume government of the entire island using a land-rent system called the Culture System. The system eventually led to the uprising by aristocratic landowners and farmers that is known as the Java War (1825–1830). The failed uprising only strengthened the Dutch's administration of the islands for the production of exports. Their system was so successful that between 1840 and 1880 the Dutch government reaped one-third of the Dutch annual budget from Indonesian exports. With the expansion of colonialists in other parts of the world in the nineteenth century, the Dutch began to establish schools for Western education, build roads, and construct government offices. During this time, as urbanization began to increase and some money reached Javanese villages, the traditional patterns of Javanese life began to loosen. As unrest spread throughout the colonial territories of Asia and Africa, Indonesian nationalism, a movement for independence from Dutch rule, began to rise.

The rise of nationalism. In 1815 the population of Java was a little more than 4,000,000. By 1920 it had reached 35,000,000 and was climbing steadily. Pressure was mounting for social, educational, and economic reforms, led by prominent Indonesians and some progressive Dutch reformers in Holland. In 1918, Indonesian representatives were admitted to the People's Council (Volksraad), while political parties rose and fell all over the archipelago. However, while the parties differed on many issues, they all agreed on the need for Indonesian independence. World War II provided a catalyst for change as the Dutch relinquished control of Indonesia for a brief period of Japanese occupation (1942–1945). When the Dutch returned to Java, they found that the Indonesian Declaration of Independence had been written. They also found that, as in other countries of Southeast Asia, people had looked to Communism as one of the more promising ways to rid themselves of colonialism. A Communist party, the PKI, had grown as an active supporter of nationalism. This group and others engaged in four years of struggle and international pressure before Queen Julianna of the Netherlands officially transferred all rights to the Republic of Indonesia on December 27, 1949. In the years of dispute and until about 1958, the economy of the Javanese, which had been based on the plantation development of the Dutch, fell into a long decline.

Indonesia since independence. The leader of Indonesian independence, Sukarno, was elected president of the new republic, but his power soon began to wane as the parliamentary system brought struggles for power amongst the different parties. In 1957, Sukarno announced a policy of rule referred to as a Guided Democracy, a militant nationalism aimed at decreasing dependence on foreign aid and power. In 1965, an attempted coup strongly involving the PKI led to the nationwide massacre of all Communists and Communist sympathizers–in all an estimated 2,000,000 to 3,000,000 people. On March 11, 1966, the Indonesian national army forced Sukarno to delegate extensive powers to General Suharto and, in 1968, Suharto was appointed president of Indonesia. General Suharto has remained Indonesia's president into the present day, and his political party as the single government-authorized party has strongly controlled Indonesia through military and economic policies. While many Javanese still depended on rice farming for subsistence, General Suharto began, with United States aid, to build a manufacturing economy. For many Javanese, rice farming became a secondary occupation, supplemented by work in low-paying assembly and manufacturing operations. A major difficulty with the development of a new industrial society and world trade has been Javanese inexperience and fear that the Chinese among them, who have long been the merchants in Indochina, would dominate the Javanese. This fear has resulted in preferential treatment to Javanese business people by the government of Indonesia.

The seat of Indonesia's government, Java has remained the central force in Indonesia's development and has braced itself to face the challenges of overpopulation and the resulting failure to produce adequate food. At the same time, the Javanese have found increasing prosperity in exports and from tourism.

Culture Today

Religion. Before the arrival of Buddhism, Hinduism, and finally Islam and Christianity to Java, the Javanese people practiced religious beliefs that were strongly connected to nature, the spirit world, and the veneration of the ancestors. Today more than ninety percent of the Javanese are Muslim, although the form of Islam practiced is not the orthodox style of the Middle East. In Java, some Muslims do not shy away from eating pork, some do not celebrate Ramadan, and others incorporate belief in ancestral spirits and in magic with their Islamic beliefs. Javanese Islam incorporates elements of the older Javanese religions. Before harvesting rice, the Javanese still provide offerings for the Hindu goddess Dewi Sri, who presides over the rice fields, and perform dances in the villages that are remnants of pre-Islamic Java. In Java, only about one-third of the Muslims follow orthodox practices. These orthodox Muslims are referred to as the *santri.* Members of the more Hinduized Muslim are called *priayi.* A third tradition, called *abangan,* is strongly influenced by belief in spirits and ancestor veneration and is closely associated with the peasants. Remarkably, these three groups are not in conflict with one another but rather are seen as belonging to the same origins. All groups recognize communal ceremonial feasting, called *selamatans,* held on special occasions.

Language. While the national language of Indonesia, Bahasa Indonesian, is spoken throughout Java, the Javanese people do have their own language. Bahasa Indonesian is derived from Malay, which was the primary language throughout Southeast Asia for centuries and was adopted in 1929 as the Indonesian national language. High Javanese is a complex language. Nine different styles of speech help distinguish one's social position, rank within the society, age, and degree of acquaintance with the person being spoken to. Other formalized references assign significance to possessions, name body parts, and are applied with consideration of the actions of the addressee. While Javanese is spoken within the courts and homes of the Javanese, Bahasa Indonesian is the language of school instruction, communications, and government.

Shelter. Housing in Java is greatly challenged by the demands from overpopulation. In Jakarta, the capital city, about 40,000 new households are added each year. However, few are approved as permanent structures. The majority of the urban dwellings lack a dependable supply of electricity, gas, water, and waste disposal. The rural areas employ primarily traditional construction—floors of pounded earth or cement, with wooden frame supporting walls of woven bamboo matting, and roofs of dried-palm fiber tiles. The shape of the home identifies the ancestors of the inhabitants. Three hundred to 3,000 people live in a cluster of these small homes, which make up a village. However, as the Javanese slowly move from subsistence farming to industrialization, the houses have changed. Today, brick-walled houses with tile roofs can be seen in the villages, and government officials working with the villagers live in more sumptuous homes that include pavilions.

The royal palace, or *kraton,* in Yogyakarta is the finest example of Javanese architecture. A walled-in structure, the kraton is a small village with artists, aristocrats, and attendants living within the palace. Central to the kraton is the *pendopo,* an open-air structure with a roof supported by slender poles under which performances are held.

Food. Centuries of contact with different cultures has left its mark on Javanese food. The basis for the Javanese meal is rice, or *nasi,* which is eaten with every meal. Spices and coconut are plentiful and are used in cooking vegetables, poultry, meat, and fish to accompany the rice. A sidedish, *sambal,* is made with red chilies grounded with shrimp paste and other seasonings. *Gado-Gado,* a vegetable salad with a rich peanut sauce, and *sate* (grilled meat) are national favorites enjoyed by the Javanese. Central Javanese delicacies include *gudeg*, fruit cooled in coconut milk, and *ayam goren*, fried chicken. In Jakarta, Indian stuffed pancakes called *martabak* and *gulai kambing* (mutton curry) are specialties. Tropical fruits are plentiful and include pineapples, bananas, papayas, mangoes, and unusual fruits like rambutans (hairy red-skinned fruit) and mangosteens (black-skinned fruit with juicy white meat inside).

Clothing. The ordinary dress of both men and women is called the *kamben*. It is a long wrap of Javanese *batik* or domestic hand-woven material that is wrapped around the waist and also used as a headcloth. The women wear this skirt wrapped tightly around the hips, reaching down to the feet and held at the waist by a *bulang*, a brightly colored sash. A long scarf (*kamben tjerik*) is worn over one shoulder or wound around the head to keep the hair in place. Once worn without a top, today a blouse or shirt is worn atop the kamben. Only in the most remote Javanese villages is the old costume worn without Western influences.

Men also wear the kamben but tie the cloth in the front in a manner that can be pulled up into a type of shorts when working in the fields. The type of Batik design is very important in making social distinctions. The brown and cream colored batiks printed on fine cotton or linen are worn within the courts of Java. Faded floral patterns are more common in the rice fields or for school uniforms. Whatever the style, the Javanese batik is worn throughout the island and is now becoming popular as a foreign export.

However, as elsewhere throughout the world, trade influences in the large cities have brought trousers, shirts, Western-style dresses to the bigger cities and towns of the Javanese. In these cities, new and old styles can be seen just as Western influences have brought a mix of automobiles, bicycles, and the older, three-wheeled pedaled taxi, the *betjak*.

Education. Since independence, Indonesia has placed a great emphasis on mass education. In Java, education is available from primary school through the university. Literacy rate averages around forty percent for the population over age ten. The greatest challenge to the educational system is a lack of adequate facilities and equipment. Materials and supplies are also limited as the demands of overpopulation increase. Since the 1970s, higher educational centers have been developed. The major universities in Java are the Universitas Indonesia in Jakarta, the Institut Teknologi Bandung, and Gadjah Mada University in Yogyakarta.

The arts. Javanese cultural arts are rich in form and variety, ranging from the refined sophistication of the Javanese court arts to village ceremonial performances. The two strong cultural influences in Java's history have been the great Hindu epics, the *Ramayana* and the *Mahabharata,* which established ethical and aesthetic codes that are still followed. The stories form the basis for the *wayang* or theatrical performance. There are many types of performances. The *wayang kulit* is the theater of the flat, leather, shadow puppets that are shown against a white screen under the expertise of a puppeteer, the *dalang.* These all-night performances are social gatherings which bring villages together to hear and see the *Ramayana* and *Mahabharata* epics. *Wayang golek* performances follow a similar pattern except that 3-dimensional puppets are used without the use of a screen. *Wayang wong* is a dramatization by live actors who move with highly stylized movements similar to the puppets. *Wayang topeng* is a masked dance version of the epic dance dramas. Beautifully carved masks are embued with the spirit of each of the individual characters of the epics, transforming the dancers into their persona.

Until the early part of this century, Javanese classical dance was not seen outside of the courts, where it had been developed over the centuries into a highly stylized and precise form. Originally of ritualistic and religious significance, Javanese dance has become the most highly regarded and refined of the arts. Today the dance is performed outside the palace, although the palace dance masters still instruct their students inside the palace. Gamelon music of Javanese dance dramas is instrumental—played by five to forty musicians using bronze metallaphones, gongs, flutes, and drums. From the high tones to the low tones, the orchestra weaves together interlocking parts to form a rich melodic sound.

Family life. Family life in Java is close-knit and bonded to the values and customs of village life. The harmony and welfare of the community is based around the observance of *adat* or customary law. Problems and disputes within the family and in the village are resolved through discussion (*musyawarah*) and a consensus of opinion (*mufakat*). The issue at hand is debated and analyzed until a unanimous agreement on a fair and just decision is reached. Each special family occasion such as a birth, marriage, death, religious observance, holiday, or opening a new business is marked by a communal meal known as a *selamatan.* The name of the ceremony comes from the word *selamat,* which means happy, welfare, prosperity, or good luck. The selamatan is an occasion of feasting and performance of masked dance or puppet plays celebrated to bring about *keadann selamat,* the "state of selamat" or collective welfare.

Industrialization's effect on the family has eroded past habits, but some marriages are still arranged among the two families under strict customs. Marriage within a nuclear family, with second cousins or with a relative of a deceased spouse is forbidden; marriage between people of two different generations is discouraged. The marriage procedure is established according to Muslim rule. The ritual begins with the groom's family bringing gifts to that of the bride. There is a large gathering of the bride's kin for a wedding party. A Muslim marriage contract is agreed to, and finally bride and groom meet one another. As is Islamic tradition, the man can ask for a divorce, which is granted easily. Young children involved remain with their mother, and she is entitled to one-third of the estate.

Inheritance among the Javanese does not follow male or female lines. A married daughter living at home inherits the family home, which then becomes the property of her husband. However, land and other possessions are distributed equally among both male and female children.

Many Javanese add to their income through home industries—including metal working, producing batik, hand weaving, and cigarette making. Women from several nearby villages unite in a single market to trade their goods.

Rice farming and cooperation. Rice farming is still a dominant form of work for the Javanese. It is a form of labor demanding cooperation among the inhabitants of the small villages surrounded by rice fields. Men plow the fields, build dams to retain water, and remove trees and weeds. Women sow the rice plants and harvest the crops. Harvesting is done with a small cutting tool that allows the women to harvest each head of rice separately and leave most of the plant for fertilizing the soil. This practice requires a great number of laborers to harvest even the smallest plots. Women of a farm village hire themselves to their neighbors and, in return, hire the neighbors to accomplish the harvest.

In the 1980s, well-meaning foreign influences attempted to change agriculture among the Javanese and other societies of Southeast Asia through a "green revolution." This revolution introduced new varieties of rice, crops, and agricultural practices to the Javanese. The "revolution" accomplished little, and Javanese rice farming moved slowly toward consolidation of landholdings. By 1990 six percent of the landowners owned more than half the rice farming land and employed the landless as hired hands in the fields. Forty percent of the rice farmers came to own less land than was needed to support their families. One result was that rice farming became a part-time occupation as family members sought jobs in light industries in order to earn a livelihood. The Javanese-controlled country of Indonesia is thus becoming a world-trade oriented economy.

Festivals. Festivals and celebrations in Java, both religious and secular, reflect the varied influences upon Java's cultural ceremonies. *Sekaten* is a week-long festival before *Grebeg Mulud*, the day commemorating the birth of the Prophet Muhammad. Big fairs are held near the kraton (palace) in Yogyakarta while continuous prayer sessions and sacred gamelon performances are played for the entire week. On *Waicek Day* at Borobudur, one of the world's greatest Buddhist shrines, the Buddha's birthday and death are commemorated in a celebration marked by a procession of thousands of yellow- and white-robed Buddhist priest and followers. Carrying candles, the procession slowly circles the temple, climbing to the top of the main stupa. *Labuhan,* which means offering, is a ritual to please *Nyai Loro Kidul*, the legendary goddess of the Indian Ocean. Taking place after the Sultan's birthday, a procession to the sea on the south coast takes the Sultan's old clothes out on a raft as an offering to the South Seas. *Kasada* is a spectacular midnight ceremony on the rim of the active volcano Mount Bromo in the Tengger region of eastern Java. At dawn, after the priest conducts a purification ceremony, a long procession slowly winds up the mountain to the volcano's rim, where the people cast their offerings into the crater for blessings by *Betoro*, the god of Bromo.

The festival *Tumplaik Wajik* occurs in the summer, when the preparation of *gunungan* (rice mounds with vegetables) takes place in the Yogyakarta kraton. The making of the rice mounds is accompanied by rhythmic pounding blocks and chanting to ward off evil spirits.

Change. As the Indonesian government presses to increased industrialization in Java, Javanese people are leaving their subsistence rice farms to find jobs in industry. As part of the change, farms are becoming larger and are not managed by individual farmers. The landless farmers of Java are moving to the cities to find jobs in the new industries. Also, while business in Java was once largely a Chinese domain, a new social class of Javanesc, *wong andajar*, now compete with the Chinese merchants.

For More Information

Hefner, Robert W. *Hindu Javanese Tengger Tradition and Islam.* Princeton: Princeton University Press, 1990.

Koentjaranigrat, R. M. *Javanese Culture.* London: Oxford University Prcss, 1989.

Lindsay, Jennifer. *Javanese Ganelau.* London: Oxford University Press, 1986.

KAREN

(ka′ ren)

People of various mountain tribes of Myanmar (formerly Burma) and Thailand.

Population: 3,300,000 (1990 estimate).
Location: Thailand, Myanmar.
Language: Various dialects of Karen, a language related to Chinese.

Geographical Setting

The country of Myanmar (Burma) is separated from India and Bangladesh by the Arakan Yoma, a rugged mountain range, and rises in the east to a high plateau in the north and to more rugged mountains along the boundary with Thailand. The center of the country is the plain carved by the Irrawaddy River. Many streams and short rivers flow from the eastern mountains to the Irrawaddy, carving valleys in the mountains in which the Karen people find fertile soil and solitude. Here, the mountains are covered with jungle and the climate is hot and humid. It is in the valleys of the mountains that the Karen people have settled to be rice farmers or to work the rich teak forests for lumber.

Historical Background

Origin. The name *Karen* is given to a number of peoples whose origins are uncertain but who speak separate languages, all of which suggest Chinese or pre-Chinese origin. They probably migrated from southern China about the sixth or seventh century A.D.

Karen sub-groups. Groups who became the Karen founded a homeland in a narrow mountainous strip on the west edge of Thailand

and in what is now Myanmar, although some have since migrated to lower land and taken up rice growing in the wetlands. The Karen are loosely divided between Whites, those living in the lowlands of Myanmar and Thailand, and Reds, those living in the mountains. About a million Karen people live in Myanmar, most of them outside the state along the Thai border, which is designated the Karen State. In Myanmar the "Sgaw" group of Karen is third in population after the Myanmars and Shan. Another nearly two million Karen live in the mountains of Thailand. Here the largest group is known as "Pwo" Karen.

Isolation. Having settled in isolated, rugged upland, the Karen had little contact with other people. Along with this physical isolation, their lack of a written language has helped to obscure the Karen history, which was maintained only by oral tradition until 1830.

Written language. At that time an American missionary is said to have invented such an effective written script for the Karen language that by 1900 many Karen could read and write. Some attended the Burmese universities and became leaders in the British colony. Before that, in 1841, the first Karen language newspaper was published in Tavoy.

National Karen Association. In 1881, groups of Karen-speaking people came together to form the National Karen Association for the purpose of protecting Karen interests against the more numerous Myanmars. This objective was reflected by the Karen in the ensuing years in several ways. At first Karen soldiers joined with British forces to solidify the Crown Colony. The Karen strongly supported remaining within the British Empire. As that proved difficult because of Myanmar opposition, the Karen pressed for a separate Karen nation. Meanwhile, many Karen took advantage of the schools of Rangoon to gain educations and take places in the British government of the country. These government workers found useful places as intermediaries between the British and the Burmese opposition party who called themselves Thaikins (masters). These actions resulted in widespread distrust of the Karens as Japan took command of the country during World War II. Karen were accused of spying for the British and many of them were executed. Meanwhile, other Karen were signifying their interest in Japan by having the rising sun tattooed on their backs.

Myanmars vs. Karen. Self-government in Myanmar came gradually, with the Myanmars taking an increasing role in the British government structure. In 1941, when a group know as the Thirty Comrades left Myanmar to be trained by the Japanese and through the period when many Burmese fought with the Japanese, the Karen sided with Britain. The Burmese eventually gained independence for the country amid much internal battling, some of it by the Karen, who, under the Karen National Union, rebelled against the new government in 1949, joining with the Mons to take possession of Mandalay and Basein. Although this rebellion was suppressed, Karen resistance to the the country's socialist government has continued. In this effort, the Karen have united with the Shan, Mon, Pa-O, Padaung, Wa, Arkanese, and Labu people to form the National Democratic Front, a strong political party.

Self-government. A self-governing Karen state within Myanmar has developed in recent years in spite of the difficulty of uniting a people with so many different dialects. The seat of government of the Karen state is Yangon (formerly Rangoon).

Culture Today

Village life. Most of the Karen people live scattered through the hills of Myanmar and Thailand in small villages of fifteen to thirty houses surrounded by a protective wall. The windowless houses are made of bamboo and covered with thatched roofs. A central fireplace serves to heat the home, and mats are the major furnishings.

The villagers are mostly rice farmers. They slash planting space from the dense forest, burn the land clear, and build elaborate irrigation systems for the wet rice crops, which are the Karen staple food. Most of the villages are along trails leading to larger towns, where the Karen supplement their income in many different ways such as weaving cotton cloth for trade or training elephants and then leasing them for heavy work. In Thailand the Karen raise animals and trade meat for rice and salt.

Karen families. Rice farming the Karen way is labor intensive, so a couple may have many children to help with the crops. The family is bound together by work, religion, and a tradition of monogamy that frowns on divorce and even discourages widows from remarrying.

Clothing. There is some variation in styles of dress among the different groups of Karen. One subgroup of Karen makes cotton clothing for trade with other Karen. A familiar dress style for White Karen women is a shirt (*hse*) that reaches below the knees. Unmarried girls wear these *hse* in white while married women wear long skirts and blouses with red trimmings. Red-Karen women in the mountain villages wear an unadorned smock sometimes with petticoats and more often with a knee-length skirt. Hair wrapped around a handkerchief and rolled into a knot and leg coverings of black cord or rattan complete the appearance of many Karen women. In other areas, Karen women wear a skirt with a black strip of cloth stretching from the back across one shoulder and held in place by a belt at the waist.

Common clothing for men includes long shirts and baggy trousers with a bright headband over long hair. Particularly among the Pwo Karen, men knot their hair to one side. Many Karen in Thailand, until recently, carried weapons as standard apparel. Men as well as women ornament themselves with beads and earrings.

In cold weather, both men and women add a red-and-white striped blanket.

Religion. A chief governs the village and leads the people in the many rites that mark agricultural cycles. Among some Karen groups, the chief also orders marriages, selecting the two participants and wedding them, by force if necessary. Villagers look to their shaman, a spiritual leader, to foretell the future, to diagnose illness, and to preside over healing rituals. Most Karen are Buddhists, while some were converted to Christianity by missionaries who visited early in their history in Myanmar and Thailand. As with many people of Asia, however, the Karen are not attached to these religions as the single religion. Rather, the new religions are blended with the older animism. Karen animism holds that all earthly objects have spirits, which, if not contained or appeased, are inclined to mischief. At a spring festival known as Kuto-bo, residents of the mountain villages erect a thirty-to-forty foot monument to the village spirits, or *nats.* Sometimes this is a bamboo pole, sometimes a heavy tree. The pole is adorned with a suitable symbol and erected at the entrance to the village. A dance celebrates the positioning of the pole, which is thereafter used as a site for sacrifices. In addition, each household has its own corner shrine.

But in many mountain villages, the Karen depend on their ability to divine considerations by consulting chicken bones. These bones are kept in each household and help to determine the best times for such events as planting, when to move, and marrying.

Spirits. Every object has a counterpart, a spirit, in Karen tradition. These spirits are not kindly but are rather often mean and vindictive. The isolated mountain Karen go to great length to appease or distract the spirits. Sacrifices of food are given in times that the spirits are thought to be restless. One good example of the interaction of Karen and spirits is the funeral. Among some Karen, a dead person cannot be buried unless the person's spirit is present. The body is held in state until a bell mounted over it tinkles that the spirit is present. Then the body is buried in a grave that is reached by a zig-zag trail designed so that the spirit will not find its way back to the village. Then the dead body to which the spirit is related is buried with clothing, tools, and other possessions to further appease the spirit.

Arts. Mountain Karen (the White or plains Karen have come in closer contact with other people and are more likely to be indistinguishable from them in dress or actions) are not given to much art. Music accompanies many of their celebrations. Two major celebrations of music and dance are the Kuto-bo held about April, and the E Dü held about August, both celebrations related to the rice harvest. (Months of celebration are approximated since the Karen do not have a fixed calendar, but rather indicate periods roughly by the phases of the moon. In fact the word for month and moon in Karen is the same, *le.*) Art objects are confined to silver work, sometimes lacquered pots, and the seed and bead jewelry that is worn by both men and women.

For More Information

Bunge, Fredcrica, M. ed. *Burma, A Country Study*. Washington, DC: American University, 1983.

Keyes, Charles, F. *Ethnic Adaptation and Identity: The Karen on the Thai Frontier with Myanmar*. Philadelphia: Institute for the Study of Human Issues, 1979.

Scott, Sir J. George. *Myanmar and Beyond.* London: Grayson and Grayson, 1982.

KHMER

(kmur)

One of the peoples of Cambodia that reached their height as a civilization in the Middle Ages.

Population: 8,000,000 (1990 estimate).
Location: Cambodia, Thailand, Vietnam.
Language: Khmer, a Mon-Khmer language.

Geographical Setting

Much of the land of the Khmer people is the great basin formed by the Mekong River. A mountain range, Phanom Dong Pak, lines the northern boundary, and there are mountain peaks dotting the coastline. However, most of Cambodia is level basin land. In the west, the farmland of the bottomland gives way to tropical jungle. Cambodia is tropical—warm and damp. Average temperatures hover around 80 degrees Fahrenheit, and annual rainfall is heavy, most of it falling during a rainy season from June through November.

Historical Background

Funan. Before the sixth century A.D., a great empire bordered the Gulf of Siam, inhabited by people known as the Funan. They worshipped Buddha and wrote in a Sanskrit language. About the sixth century, a great flood destroyed much of the writing and architecture of the Funan people.

Invasion. The disruption caused by the flood allowed another people to move from the north and blend with the Funan residents. The immigrants brought with them another language, Khmer, that was

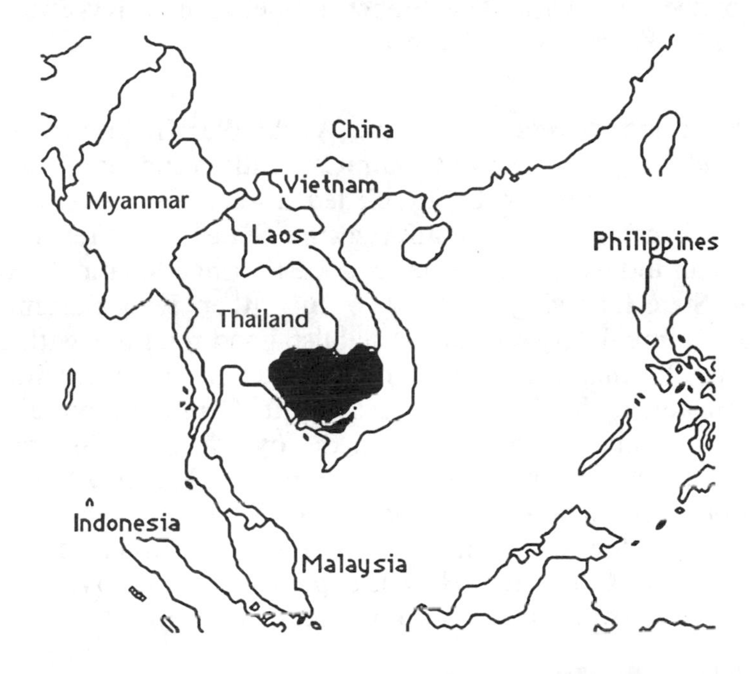

fused with the Sanskrit already used in the area. The Khmer-speaking people began a new empire called Kambujadesa in the region that is now part of Thailand and Cambodia, or Kampuchea.

Kambujadesa. The empire grew and flourished from the 600s to the mid-1400s. One of the cities of the empire, Angkor Wat, still stands as a symbol of the splendor of Kambujadesa. By 1200, this empire reached from the China Sea to the Malay Peninsula. With its capital at Angkor Thom, the Khmer were frequently at odds with the Thais and with the Annamese of Vietnam. In fact they were sometimes ruled by the Thais and at other times by the Annamese.

Thai, Vietnamese, and French. However, by 1400, the pressure of Thai people who had begun to move into the region from the west, to be joined later by Vietnamese from the south threatened the Khmer empire so that in 1864 France was asked to intercede on behalf of the Khmer. The influence of the French was great. They stabilized the government, persuaded the Khmer to abandon their use of slaves, and built modern schools. Vietnamese laborers were imported for much of the new work. The French influence had a Westernizing effect on the Khmer.

Cambodian independence. During World War II, French interest waned and there was a drive to gain Cambodian independence. The Khmer prince Norodom Sihanouk led a guerrilla movement and succeeded in establishing first an Associate State of the French Union and then an independent nation (in 1953). Prince Sihanouk became Head of State following the death of his father, King Suramarit in 1960. He immediately set out to establish good relations with China and North Vietnam, decrying United States involvement in Indochina. However, the different forces within Cambodia remained in constant turmoil, which resulted in the overthrow of Sihanouk in 1970 and his replacement with Lon Nol. Lon Nol proclaimed the formation of the Khmer Republic. Prince Sihanouk went into exile and formed a new government, the Royal Government of the National Union of Cambodia. He was supported in this government in exile by a pro-Communist group, the Khmer Rouge.

Khmer Rouge. For five years, Lon Nol attempted to reconcile the Cambodian people, but was eventually overthrown by the Khmer Rouge, a Communist group. For a time Prince Sihanouk was again Head of State (1975). The new government began a "cultural reform." Cities were virtually evacuated as the people were led into the countryside and put to work there. As many as 3,000,000 people vanished in this reform, but the action has not succeeded in bringing tranquility to Kampuchea. January 1976 saw a new constitution and the election of a People's Representative Assembly. In April Prince Sihanouk resigned, and the assembly elected Khien Sanipan as the first president and Pol Pot (secretary of the central committee of the Communist Party) as prime minister. The assembly also changed the country name to Democratic Kampuchea. The Communist government has had costly struggles with the Communist regime of Vietnam. In 1978, in retaliation for Khmer Rouge intrusions into their country, Vietnam invaded Kampuchea–in three days capturing Phnom-Penh—and the People's Republic of Kampuchea was declared. Kampuchea was subjected to annual invasions by the Vietnamese during the dry seasons. By 1982 Prince Sihanouk had again become leader of the Kampucheans as their president. The situation in the country was aggravated by Khmer fleeing to Vietnam to avoid the Khmer

Rouge, and after the 1984–85 invasion by Vietnam, by as many as 230,000 refugees who fled to Thailand.

In 1987, Prince Sihanouk took a one-year leave of absence to protest human rights violations and attacks by the Khmer Rouge. There remained two Kampuchean governments, Sihanouk's in exile, and the at-home government led by Heng Samrin. After long negotiations, Vietnam agreed to withdraw some of its troops in 1988. By now there were several groups squabbling over rights to rule Kampuchea, including Sihanouk's on-again-off-again government in exile and the Khmer Rouge.

Following further negotiations, the government of Heng Samrin succeeded in satisfying Vietnam's demands, and that country began to withdraw its troops from Kampuchea. The work was completed in 1990. Again Prince Sihanouk appeared as a Kampuchean leader. This time he announced the formation of the National Army of Independent Cambodia. Since then Prince Sihanouk has ruled as head of a fourteen-member council. However, the China-supported Khmer Rouge continues to wage wars along the borders, and a United Nations intervention did little to stabilize the country of Cambodia.

Culture Today

Religion. Before the adoption of communism, the Khmer were Buddhists. Their land held about 3,000 monasteries and was served by 70,000 monks, the Bikkus. The Buddhist monasteries were centers for education as well as religion, so the great number of monks included some with lifetime commitments. However, there were also many who served for only a short time in order to gain an education. Buddhist leaders were instrumental in extending the Khmer language and led resistance movements against the French. Throughout history, Buddhist monks have contributed to the independence movements of the Khmer. The monks held a dominant position in the hierarchical Khmer society.

Khmer Buddhists are of the Theravada (Way of the Elders) school. This facet of Buddhism emphasizes the conservative Buddhist beliefs—working to gain wisdom and earning one's own salvation through meditation and study in a monastery. Following the original teachings of Buddha, Theravada Buddhists follow doctrine set down in the common language of the day rather than the ancient Hindu of other sects. They celebrate holy days at each quarter of the moon,

New Years (in April), and a Hindu-influenced "fortnight of the departed," in which balls of rice are offered to their ancestors.

Social structure. The king of Cambodia owned both land and people but the Cambodians were influenced in many aspects of daily life by the French. The royal family was the government and held the highest place in a society that was layered by rankings of priests, Buddhist monks, government officials, commoners, then slaves. It was this ranking that the new government set out to abolish in 1975 when a reported 3,000,000 city workers were relocated in the country to live as farmers. In the 1970s and 1980s, Cambodia (Kampuchea) was virtually closed to the West, so little is known about how much of the old stratified structure of royal family, Brahman priests, Buddhist monks, officials, commoners, and slaves remains. It is known that while still under French rule, the Khmer people were persuaded to abolish slavery. In this and other aspects of life, the Westernizing influence of the French remains.

Clothing and shelter. Western-style clothing is common in Cambodian cities. In the countryside people still wear the traditional *sampot*, a ten-foot-long, three-foot-wide strip of cotton or silk wrapped around the waist and reaching below the knees. Women add a blouse and shawl, while men wear a shirt or tunic over the sampot.

New homes are of wood, tile, and masonry. The older ones are often small (one-room) rectangular structures of wood built on wood or concrete pilings with thatched-roof protection from the heavy rains. Wood floors support mats, cushions, and chests, which comprise the few furnishings of the Khmer home. In this home, the wife rules over matters of finance and of raising the children.

Family life. Khmer families consist of one husband, one wife, and their children. When these children marry, they may for a time live with the parents of the bride. The wife makes decisions about the upbringing of the children and about family finances. She is also influential in arranging marriages.

Weddings are arranged by the two sets of parents and are often elaborate ceremonies lasting up to three days. The ritual involves forming the families into a circle around which a metal, leaf-shaped object is passed along with a candle. The two symbols stand for female and male.

Farm life. Khmer farms, once owned by the king and worked by peasants, are now under Communist control and have been turned into collective farms. Each worker has an interest in the farm so that the average Khmer farmer now "owns" a farm plot of less than twelve acres. The land is "cooperative," technically owned by the government as the representative of all the people. The collective farmers raise food crops such as rice. Fish and fresh vegetables are plentiful in the country and common in the daily diet. Rice, lumber, and sugar palms are produced by the collective farms for market. The destruction of a palm sugar factory in the ongoing military conflict with Vietnam has seriously damaged sugar production in the country. Such incidents have led to close supervision of the people, and near isolation from other countries have made recent changes in Khmer life obscure.

Economy. The French established rubber plantations in Cambodia, and these produced nearly half the exported products of the entire country in 1991. Raw rubber was also changed in the few factories into bicycle tires and rubber footwear for export. However, two-thirds of the Khmer work force labors in agriculture, producing mostly rice, but also other vegetables, cattle, and pigs. Cambodia is heavily forested; the forestry industry provides hardwoods, logs for railway beds, veneers, and wood for fuel. When the Communist government began in 1976, all industry as well as all agriculture became the property of the government. That government established quotas for production and supervised each industry. This included about 1,500 rice mills and eighty state-owned factories. However, the Khmer government soon realized that collectivization reduced productivity by reducing the worker's incentives. By 1986, the government had authorized establishing some privately owned enterprises. Progress was slow, mostly because development required help from other countries, and many of these countries boycotted the Khmer because of their unstable government. In 1991, the Khmer government still found it necessary to import some necessary goods—an amount that far exceeded the value of Cambodian exports.

Education. Once the realm of the priests and monks, education is now encouraged and provided by the government. A Khmer student can attend primary school where such practical subjects as agriculture are emphasized. Some may attend secondary school. The total education provided by the government is ten years. Nearly 2,000,000

Khmer children attend primary school, but in 1991 only 20,000 of these went on to attend secondary or higher education.

Holidays. Beside the Buddhist celebrations (see Religion, above), the Khmer celebrate few national holidays. Liberation Day, January 7, celebrates the fall of Phnom-Penh to the Vietnamese. April 17 is Victory over American Imperialism Day. As in other Communist countries, May 1 is Labor Day. Other national holidays are religious fetes or celebrations of a new beginning—a day in April for New Year, and September 22, celebrated with much feasting and called the Feast of the Ancestors.

For More Information

Chandler, David P. *The Land and People of Cambodia.* New York, HarperCollins, 1991.

Ross, Russell R. *Cambodia: A Country Study.* Washington, DC: United States Government Printing Office, 1990.

KOREANS

(kuh ree′ ans)

People of North and South Korea.

Population: 64,500,000 (1990 estimate for both North and South Korea–North Korea, 22,000,000; South Korea, 42,500,000).
Location: North and South Korea (the Democratic People's Republic of Korea and the Republic of Korea, respectively).
Language: Korean, a language containing many Chinese terms.

Geographical Setting

The land of the Koreans is currently divided into two governmental units: a slightly larger and much less densely populated northern section and the smaller, heavily populated southern country. The whole region is mountainous. Eight- and nine-thousand-foot peaks dot the north, where a mountain range runs from China along the southern and eastern side of the Korean peninsula. A short distance into South Korea, a second range breaks off from this coastal range and makes its way diagonally across the bottom of the country. The result is a northern and eastern area of mountains and hills, which in the west and particularly the southwest, slope into a wide, fertile coastal plain. East of the mountains, the coastal plain is narrow. Only about five percent of the land, limited to the coastal plains and inland mountain valleys, is suitable for growing crops.

The climate varies from north to south and east to west, but is mostly pleasant, with twenty to forty inches of rain annually. Summers are warm and humid; winters, especially in the north, are cold. For many centuries, Koreans farmed the plains and mountain valleys and lived in thatched huts warmed by beneath-the-floor flumes of warm air.

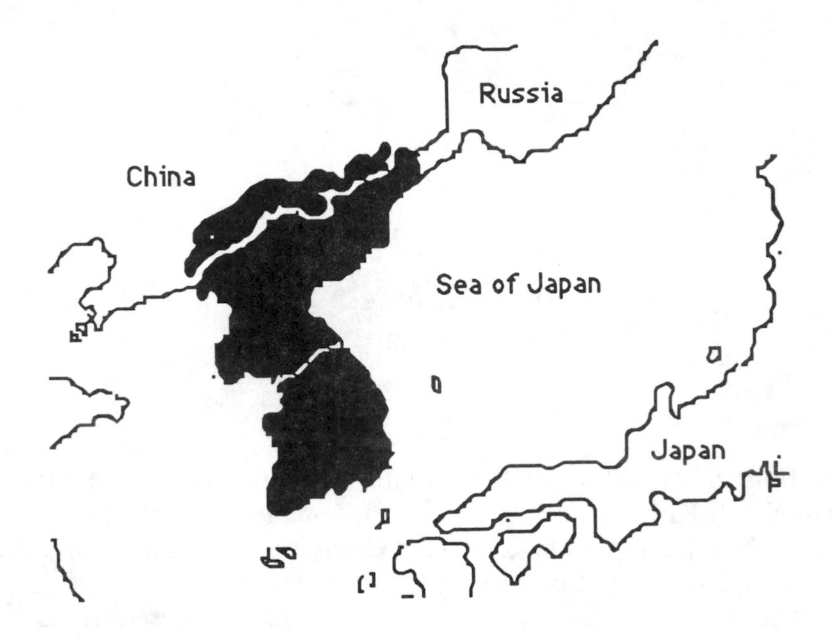

Historical Background

Beginnings. The history of the Korean people begins before 1000 B.C.—perhaps as early as 5,000 years ago. According to the Korean legends, Hwanung, the son of the creator of the earth, saw a bear turn into a beautiful woman. Hwanung's breath upon the woman resulted in the birth of Tan-gun, the first king of Korea.

Tan-gun is said to have been an actual king of a people who occupied the land that is now Korea beginning about 2300 B.C. However, the real beginnings of the Korean people might be traced to the migration of Kija, a Chinese scholar, and 5,000 of his followers into Korea about 1122 B.C. Kija and his followers, through assimilation into the groups that already lived there, became ancestors of the present population. The blending of Chinese- and Korean-based groups accelerated when China claimed command of the land in 108 B.C.

The Kingdom of Silla. Soon after the Chinese claim, the land was divided among three kingdoms—Silla, Packche, and Koguryo. Although they frequently quarreled among themselves, these three kingdoms flourished between 57 B.C. and A.D. 300. Silla defeated and assumed control over Packche in A.D. 660 and over Koguryo in 668, uniting most of Korea under one government. The kingdom of Silla survived until the year 935.

In 918, General Wangun of the Silla army led a revolt and formed an independent government with its base in Han Yung, a city near present-day Seoul. By 935 this government had replaced the Silla monarchy and the new country had been named Koryo. In 1392 General Yi Song-gye overthrew the existing Koryo dynasty and established Seoul as the capital.

Foreign intervention. In spite of its long history of self-government, the Korean people have often been subjected to foreign intervention in their affairs. During the Yi period, Korea became subject to the policies of China and adopted the philosophy of Confucius. When the Manchu forces threatened to invade Korea and China in the fifteenth century, China separated itself from Korea by laying waste to a strip of land between them and forcing the 300,000 residents there to move elsewhere. From 1592 to 1599 the Koreans were under Japanese domination. In 1627, after a short period of freedom from the Japanese, the Manchu government of China took control and directed Korean affairs until 1644. In 1653, Dutch traders and sailors visited Korea and began spreading a Western influence there. However, this Western influence remained small until 1882, when the United States made the first Korean-Western power trade treaty. In 1905 Japan was given Korea as protectorate in the Treaty of Portsmouth and then made it a colony of Japan in 1910.

Post World War II. After World War II, Japan lost its domination over Korea. The land was divided at the thirty-eighth parallel, with Soviet occupation in the Northern Korean state and the United States continuing firm relationships with South Korea. By 1950, China had become a strong supporter of the Communist government in the north. The boundary between the two Korean groups has been the setting of many skirmishes and violent actions that sometimes involved the former Soviet Union and the United States in dangerous confrontations. The Korean War, which was fought between the two sides from 1950 to 1953, ended inconclusively. A cease-fire line was drawn by the thirty-eighth parallel and a strip between the two Koreas designated a neutral zone, further dividing the Korean people. Beginning in 1972, discussions have been carried on over unification of the two Koreas. In 1985, it was agreed that annual discussions would consider this topic. However, various issues of mutual distrust have interfered with these meetings; for example, South Korea's sponsorship of the 1988 Olympics and its rejection of North Korea's bid to cosponsor the games. Another sensitive issue has been the management of the Han River, which flows from North Korea through the South Korean capital of Seoul. North Korea began construction of a large dam on this river, which was seen as a possible threat to the city of Seoul. South Korea protested to no avail and then decided to build a safeguard in the form of a second dam farther down the Han.

Meanwhile, North Korea has been ruled strongly by a Communist dictator; democratic South Korea has passed through periods of public control and military dictatorships. The year 1991 saw South Korea's first popular elections at the local levels.

Today, Russian and western influences have drastically changed the traditions of the Korean people in all areas, from dress to their means of livelihood to religious practices. There is little trace of traditional Korean religion in North and South Korea. In fact, in South Korea the YMCA, once a western Christian association, is one of the fastest-growing organizations.

Culture Today

Agriculture. Korea is a mountainous country in which only one fourth of the land is suitable for growing crops. Still, in spite of the growth of great cities like Seoul, the lives of most Koreans is dominated by agriculture. Korean farmers grow rice on flat lands or on hillside terraces. Almost always, they raise two crops on the land—rice in one season, and barley or soya beans in another. In addition, a Korean farmer might raise potatoes, maize, and sweet potatoes along with a few pigs or chickens. Three-fifths of the crop raised by the typical farmer is for home use; two-fifths might be used for trade when crops are good. Goods are carried to market in the towns and cities. Traditionally, the marketplace is moved to a new location every five days.

The farms are small, with the average farmer working only one hectare (about two-and-one-half acres) of land. With such small plots of farm land to work, there is little need for sophisticated tools. Most planting and harvesting is done with animal-drawn plows and wagons or with human hands.

Homes. Villages in the farm community are clusters of small houses with wood walls, often built on stone foundations. The floor is earthen and covered with layers of oiled paper. As the workers become more affluent, other rooms are added to the single living room. The first addition is a separate room for the male leader of the house, then perhaps a wood-floored room for visitors or, if the man has clan leadership responsibilities, a room for clan affairs. The single-room dwelling grows with wealth into an L shape, then a U, then a home with a central courtyard. Foot or bicycle trails connect the village with other villages and towns. Bicycles are the dominant way of travel among Koreans.

Earlier styles of housing, rarely seen except in remote rural places, were low rectangular structures with tile roofs. They were small—one room, a kitchen, and a separate toilet. The earlier styles of homes had cooking holes on one side of the house and systems of spaces between the stone floors that allowed warm air to pass under the house and emerge at chimneys on the other side. This arrangement allowed the same fuel used for cooking to heat the home. In the 1990s, nearly half the people of South Korea and a smaller number of North Koreans now live in large towns or cities. Here the old wood structure has given way to concrete. In furnishing them, the Koreans stay with traditional styles. There is little furniture, the families prefer to sit on mats on the floor, shoes removed. Often there is little distinction between living and sleeping quarters. Koreans prefer to sleep on mats that can be easily rolled out of the way during the day.

Family life. Throughout Korea, monuments to loyal subjects, loyal sons, and faithful women reflect the values of the family. A traditional family might have included several generations living under one roof, and with the eldest male ruling the household. Industrialization, with its resulting migration to the cities, has changed this pattern so that the family today is more likely to be only a husband and wife and their children.

Still, cooperation and respect for elders are major Korean values. Young Koreans are expected in words and actions to demonstrate this respect, both within and outside of the family. Furthermore, cooperation is a key to Korean life. The people, whether villagers or city-dwellers, form *kye* (cooperative relationships) for many activities that might prove a burden on a single family. Kyes bind people to share the care for the aged, for the arrangements of funerals and weddings, and for divination. Diviners are important to the family life. Koreans consider it important to build a home on a desirable site, and the diviner can help make that decision.

A birth of a baby and that baby's survival for its first six or seven months of life is hailed with celebration. On the two-hundredth day a ritual using red bean soup recognizes the passage of this early critical stage of life. Another large celebration in the Korean family is *hwan-gap*, honoring a person's sixtieth birthday.

Old-style dress. The village women still dress in the traditional clothes of quilted jackets and baggy trousers bound at the ankle. Whether or not they are married is evident by their hairstyles. In the past both unmarried men and women wore their hair braided to hang down the back. After marriage, men combed their hair up in a knot on the top of the head, then covered it with hats. Married women wore a knot through which they inserted a large hairpin. In the cities, the old and new blend, people in Western dress mingling with those in the traditional clothes. A meeting in the city might be attended

Seoul, Korea, has expanded greatly beyond its original walled confines. This is the South Gate of the old city. *Courtesy of Dr. W. Paul Fischer.*

by people in coats and ties, or in Western-style sports clothes. There might also be elderly gentlemen in the quilted jacket and black, lacquered, horsehair high hat that once symbolized the upper classes of Koreans.

Food. A visitor to a home or meeting place would be served meals that had been prepared and placed on individual tables in the kitchen area. Rice, millet, or barley cooked in boiling water are main dishes and may be accompanied by meat, fish, or vegetables. *Kimch'i*, or pickled cabbage and radish, is a popular side dish. The table and food are then brought out and placed for each person separately. The food might be served with a favorite Korean drink, *sungnyung*, prepared by boiling water in a pot that was used for cooking rice. The scorching from the rice adds a flavor to the water that is appealing to many Koreans.

Religion. Buddhism, once the dominant religion among Koreans, was blamed for many problems in the thirteenth and fourteenth centuries. A form of Confucianism then gained popularity among Koreans. In recent years, the people of North Korea have been encouraged by their government to abandon religion, while in South Korea, Christianity has become the second religion to Confucianism. Throughout these changes, the Koreans have held to their traditional values of venerating elders while giving much attention to the religious and educational welfare of the young.

Government. The Korean people have long regarded government as something outside of the major concerns in their own lives. As a result, the individual places little value on government and much importance on the cultural mores that regulate interaction among people. Their traditional belief in the value of work is now being applied to their production of goods, which compete in world trade. As a result, life in Korea is changing rapidly. New industries in clothing, electronics, and automobile manufacturing are attracting workers to the cities. As a result, there are new congestion and housing problems in the cities, while population problems in the farm areas have been alleviated. One related change is that the small farmer may no longer have members of an extended family to help with the labor-intensive farming methods of the past.

Arts. The artistic folk heritage of the people is maintained in drama, music, dance, and crafts. During the Yi dynasty artisans developed

Open markets in Seoul, Korea, are popular tourist attractions.
Courtesy of Dr. W. Paul Fischer.

a mother-of-pearl inlaying technique, which is used today on items such as wooden trays. Traditional dance includes religious (Shaman Dance, Buddhist Dance), court (sword dance, crane dance), and folk (Circle Dance, Farmers Dance) categories and is often associated with history. The circle dance, for example, was developed during the Japanese invasion of the sixteenth century. Young girls of coastal villages dance around bonfires as if they are soldiers on guard against boatloads of invading troops.

These dances are accompanied by music from uniquely Korean instruments. The *taigum* is a sort of flute; a *keyegun*, a form of twelve-string zither. There is a *haigum* (a two stringed fiddle); *wilgum* (the Korean guitar); and *chwago* (a suspended drum). Music of all kinds is enjoyed by Koreans. They have added Western styles to the melodic and slowly rhythmic traditional music. Korean opera is an example of the blending of the two musical styles. In addition to ten purely Korean operas, the people enjoy many of the European creations.

The same is true of drama. Modern film themes are popular in Korea, along with Shakespearean and other older dramas and the famous puppet show, the Khoktukakshi, a long production in eight acts. Earlier Korean plays dramatized the victories of the past or expressed Korean oneness with nature. The modern dramas are as likely to be searches for meaning or dramas based on everyday life issues.

Koreans have a long history of quality in the arts. Beautiful pottery is seen in many homes. Highly intricate wooden temples built as early as the twelfth and thirteenth centuries have been carefully maintained so as to be still useful today. They have been supplemented by chapels of modern design—spiring and gracefully rounded brick and concrete monuments to the skill of Korean architects.

These temples house examples of Korean sculpture—images of Buddha in stone and metal, and impressions of ancient gods. Early paintings, some on walls, reveal historic changes in Korean thought. Once representations of shamanistic ideas and, later, depictions of Buddhist philosophies, paintings have evolved into expressions of the beauty of nature through landscapes enhanced by calligraphy.

Literature. Closely tied to painting, Koreans have a long but mixed literary heritage. Much of the very old literature was written in Chinese; the Koreans had no symbols to express their spoken language. Gradually, Chinese symbols came to stand for Korean sounds in a mix of Chinese writing and Korean talk called Idu. Then in 1446, a turning point in Korean literature, King Sejon introduced a distinctly Korean alphabet.

The result is that Korean literature has a base in oral mythical stories in verse—verse developed from art and music. Koreans can point to *Hwanjoga* (Song of the Nightingale, by King Yuri) and *Haega*, an old Shilla sea song, as examples of this early time. Then came an age of deep admiration for the Chinese that resulted in peasant poems in Chinese, *sogga*. Following the development of the Korean alphabet, an experimental poem was written, *Yongbioch'on-ga*, the Song of the Dragon Flying to Heaven. Interested in the preciseness of the language, Korean writers developed the *shijo*, a three-lined verse. This eventually gave way to the *kara*, or longer verse. Outstanding early writers of Kara were Chong Ch'ol and Pak In-ro. From the kara, Korean writers expanded their interests to novels and short stories. For example, Yi Kwang-su was a novelist at the beginning of the twentieth century. Recognized as the most outstanding modern writers are Kal Kyong-ri, who wrote *Toji* ("The Earth"), and Hwang Sok-Yong, whose story *Chang Kil-San* tells of a legendary rebel. Twentieth-century subjects have expanded with the medium, and now deal with a wide range of human problems, including the anguish of missing loved ones.

Government services. Schooling is free and compulsory from the ages of five to fifteen in North Korea and from six to twelve in South Korea. Medical care, while not as extensively available as in the south, is free in North Korea. In South Korea about one-fourth the medical costs are borne by the government. Both governments provide services in sanitation and care of the needy.

Since their separation into two nations in 1945, most Koreans have cherished the hope that some day the people will be again united. However, over the years serious differences of ideology and economics have separated the two lands. Keeping the hope alive, however, the two governments agree to meet annually to discuss their differences and the possibilities of reunion.

For More Information

An Tai Sung. *North Korea in Transition: From Dictatorship to Dynasty*. Contributions in Political Science #95. Westport: Greenwood Press, 1983.

Carles, W. R. *Life in Korea*. New York: Macmillan, 1984.

Korean Overseas Information Service. *A Handbook of Korea*, Sixth Edition. Seoul: Seoul International Publishing House, 1987.

Macdonald, Donald Stone. *The Koreans: Contemporary Politics and Society*. Boulder: Westview Press, 1988.

LAO

(lou)

People of various groups who are related to the Thai people of Thailand and live in the country of Laos.

Population: 3,700,000 (1990 estimate).
Location: Southeast Asia, bordered by China, Vietnam, Cambodia, Myanmar, and Thailand.
Languages: Laotian; French; Mao; other tribal dialects.

Geographical Setting

Many people of Vietnam, Laos, and Thailand are of a common Tai origin. Over the years, the Tai have broken into various groups, including the Thai of Thailand, who changed the original name to distinguish themselves from the Tai groups of Laos, Vietnam, and China.

The various groups of Tai people, who make up most of the population of the Lao People's Democratic Republic, inhabit a landlocked country. The country is flower-shaped, with the head of the flower surrounded by Myanmar, China, and Vietnam to the north and the stem of the country trailing along the Mekong River toward the southeast. The country is mountainous except for a middle section that becomes part of the Mekong River basin, where that river forms the boundary of Laos and Thailand. In the north the mountains rise to many ridges and peaks more than 9,000-feet high. The southern mountains are less extreme, rising to 5,000 feet.

Laos is a tropical country. Monsoon rains fall from May to October, bringing more than sixty inches of rain to most areas. Temperatures are generally warm and are moderated by the variations in altitude. Much of this warm, wet land is covered with tropical forest.

The large exception is the central Mekong Valley region, which is mostly tropical savannah.

Historical Background

Origins. Lao were among the Tai people of southern China who migrated southward toward the Malay Peninsula and settled in Myanmar, Thailand, and Vietnam. While they recognize this common origin, the Tai have divided to become the Thai of Thailand, the Shan ruled by Burmans, and the Lao of present-day Laos and Vietnam. Lao is a political name given by the kingdoms of Thailand to further distinguish the non-Thai people who once were governed by them. These people are believed to have originally migrated from the Yunnan region of China. Moving southward, they encountered a well-established kingdom of the Khmer (today's Cambodians). The Lao merged with the northernmost of the Khmer to form the people of present-day Laos.

Early history. The people who settled in the mountains of present-day Laos organized into kingdoms sufficiently small to govern lightly and with few taxes. In the early 1300s, a prince named Fa Ngum ruled in the area of Luang Prabang. His son disgraced the family and was banished from the kingdom, migrating south to join the Khmer ruler at Angkor. There he gathered a Khmer army and set out to conquer his old homeland. By 1353, Fa Ngum had proclaimed himself king of the first Laotian empire, Lan Xang, with its capital at Luang Prabang. He bolstered his claim to rule by espousing Theravada Buddhism.

Unification of the Lao. Fa Ngum was able to unite most of the surrounding people into a single kingdom that was to endure for 200 years. In 1563 Thai and Burmese invasions had so unsettled the region around Luang Prabang that the seat of government was moved farther south to the town of Vientiane (also known as Viangchan). Still, the country was essentially a loose organization of independent states (*muong*) ruled by princes, and Luang Prabang remained a powerful base for the northern Lao.

Divided kingdom. After the 1694 death of King Soulingna Vongea, the country was divided. The king's nephew was able to raise an army and capture Vientiane, while his cousin took Luang Prabang and announced an independent kingdom. Four years later, the prince of Champassak also announced the formation of an independent kingdom. Thus were three weakened kingdoms of Lao created.

Burma and Thailand in Laos. In 1753 and 1771, Burmese armies sacked Luang Prabang. Thai armies invaded the Laotian kingdom again in 1778, capturing the capital city, Vientiane. The Thai took sacred Buddhist symbols (including the Emerald Buddha) to Bangkok. When the kingdom at Vientiane attacked Luang Prabang thirteen years later, the Thai again interfered in Laotian affairs. The king of Vientiane was deposed and replaced by Chou Anou, a puppet king paying homage to the king of Siam. However, Chou Anou rebelled against Thai rule and sought to reunite the Lao. Thai armies again took the capital and in 1827 Vientiane was destroyed. Meanwhile, a base of Laotian influence had been restored to Luang Prabang and this government sent 3,000 troops to aid the Thai in the destruction of Vientiane. The friction between north and south allowed Thai and Vietnamese to divide Laos.

France. In the middle of the nineteenth century, France began to take an interest in Laos as it expanded its holdings in the Indochina area. The French took advantage of a new Thai intrusion to claim those parts of Laos that had been controlled by Vietnam. By 1899 France had replaced Thailand and had taken Laos as its protectorate, intending to merge it with Vietnam and Cambodia into a single French Indochina. Vientiane was again made the Laotian capital. Dissent continued among the mountain peoples of the north and south. As early as 1899, revolts over French-imposed taxes and corvée (unpaid) labor resulted in major conflicts. (The French needed Laotian labor to build roads.) In the north, Lao joined with marauding Chinese to fight French rule up to 1917.

After World War I, the French concentrated their interest in Vietnam and left Laos in relative peace. French control was interrupted during World War II when Japanese forces seized power. Although the crown prince of Laos at first resisted he was finally forced to give up ties with the French and become an independent Laos under Japanese influence. As the end of the war neared and French troops reached Luang Prabang, the king residing there reversed his decision and a Provisional People's Assembly was formed at Vientiane. This assembly established a free Laotian government known as the Lao Issara. However, the French claimed their old territories, and the Lao Issara fled to Thailand and set up a government-in-exile.

Viet Minh and the Pathet Lao. By this time, a Communist movement, the Viet Minh, had become strong in northern Vietnam and had begun to take an active role in the rebellions in northern Laos. By 1949 pressure for independence from France had grown throughout Indochina, and the French agreed to the formation of an independent Laotian army and government. The old government-in-exile was disbanded in favor of this new arrangement. However, one of the old rulers in exile, Souphanouvong, withdrew in anger over the developments that still left France in control. Making his way to Vietnam, Souphanouvong met with the Viet Minh and, with that organization's support, organized a Laotian Communist wing, the Pathet Lao. The Pathet Lao organized a new government under a 19-member Central Committee. By 1951 this organization had joined Vietnamese and Cambodians in resistance to the French. Vietnamese troops entered Laos, particularly in the north where it was important to keep a supply line to China (the Ho Chi Minh Trail). Fighting drew international attention.

A new Laos. Under an International Control Commission, a new Laotian government was formed and the Royal Laotian Army reaffirmed. However, the Pathet Lao continued to control some provinces in northern Laos. By 1954 Laos had gained total independence even though a Communist Lao People's Party continued its resistance. In 1956 the Pathet Lao was reunited with the rest of Laos. Souphanouvong became Minister of Planning and Reconstruction in the new government. New elections were scheduled in which the Pathet Lao sought to increase its influcnce through the organization of a political party, the Lao Patriotic Front. However, with support from the United States, the anti-Communist leaders replaced the members of government.

United States Intervention. Communists and anti-Communists struggle for power continued through the 1960s, as did pressure from the United States to rid Laos of Communist influence and to involve Laos in the growing war in Vietnam. By 1973 the two Laotian factions, the Royal Lao Army and the Pathet Lao, had agreed to form a coalition government. By 1975 the United States had agreed to withdraw even its international aid offices from Laos. Souphanouvong and the Pathet Lao persuaded King Savang Vatthana to abdicate. The Lao People's Democratic Republic replaced the monarchy that had stood for six centuries.

Recent issues. The new government faced economic issues of great dimensions. In 1982 these issues caused dissension among the governing bodies, resulting in the formation of a Royal Lao Democratic Government. Between 1975 and 1985 persecution of those who opposed the Communist government was widespread—particularly of the Hmong tribesmen who had fought alongside the American forces. In those ten years, nearly a third of a million Laos fled the country, most of them through Thailand. Meanwhile, the Communist government strengthened its position. A 1984–85 purge eliminated those who were most outspoken about the failures of the government. A new anti-Communist organization, the United Lao National Liberation Front, was organized in 1989 and claimed control of one-third of Laos. A leader in this movement was General Vang Pao, who had been a Hmong secret army leader cooperating with the United States Central Intelligence Agency.

Movement for democracy continues, but since proponents of individual ownership of property were purged in 1990, the resistance movement has been operating from Thailand.

Culture Today

Who are the Lao? Laotian government statements describe the Lao as including 68 nationalities, not counting a large Chinese population and smaller contingents from other countries. Although there is no list of the 68 ethnic groups, there are a considerable number of former tribal units living within Laos who arrived at different times in history and speak their own unique dialects. The Lao have been broadly differentiated on the basis of their choice of living area—the Lao Theung prefer the mountain slopes in the south, the Lao Soung, including the Hmong (see HMONG), live near the mountain summits, and the Lao Loum settle in the lowland hills and valleys of the Mekong River and its tributaries.

Lao Theung. Living in the plateau region of the south and on northern mountain slopes, this group was the first of the Tai people to arrive in Laos, where they found a thriving society of Mon-Khmer people with a kingdom based at Angkor. Merging with the Mon, the Lao Theung came to speak a Mon-Khmer language akin to that of Cambodians. Some distance from the great Laotian bases at Luang Prabang and Vientiane, these people have held to the most primitive ways of Laos and are called Kha by the others—a name that means "slaves."

As with other Lao, Lao Theung build houses of timber and woven bamboo, often on pilings raising them above the floodwaters. They group their houses in village clusters around a large men's house where the men of the village can gather to talk, make sacrifices, or decide on village issues. Although ruled by the central Laotian government, the most important governor of the Lao Thueng is a local chieftan, chosen from a hereditary line to be a first among equals and to govern by power of his own character. Often this headman is chosen because of his ability in magic. He is aided by a shaman, or religious leader, whose office may also be hereditary.

The most important governing unit among the Lao Theung is the extended family, with the eldest man as head. The Lao Theung society is patriarchal. Family goods pass from father to son, and men are active in government. Men decide how to divide the farm land and when to abandon a farm site.

The Lao Theung practice slash and burn agriculture, seeking land in the tropical forests, slashing trees and undergrowth and burning them to clear farm land. The land is turned into rice paddies and plots for growing maize, legumes, and vegetables. The land is prepared for planting with the aid of water buffalo, animals that are cherished among the dwellers of the mountain slopes. Lao Theung families also raise chickens, pigs, and cattle.

Lao Thueng people are animists, venerating a wide range of spirits and ancestors. To appease these spirits and enlist their aid in curing illness or growing crops, sacrifices are made to the appropriate spirits. Often these sacrifices include the destruction of the most prized of Lao Theung possessions, the water buffalo.

Unless flooding or other natural disasters occur, Lao Thueng agriculture produces an excess of rice. This rice is used to barter with other Lao and the Chinese for consumer goods such as cloth and for medicines.

Lao Soung. One of the tribal groups included among the Lao Soung, the mountain-top Tai, is the Hmong. While representative of the lifestyles of the Lao Soung, the Hmong isolated themselves from the others by forming, under the United States Central Intelligence Agency, a secret army that worked for many years with the Americans in their war against Communist forces in Laos. Hmong lives have been dominated by persecution as a result (see HMONG).

Stringing their wood and bamboo homes, thatched with leaves, along nearly inaccessible mountain ridges, the Lao Soung also practice slash-and-burn agriculture. In this mountain area the rice crops are augmented by planting and harvesting opium poppys. Opium can be grown in seasons other than the rice season and is traded in the towns below for such needed items as salt, iron, and textiles. Small, sturdy horses help in the farming and in transporting goods over the rugged mountain trails.

The village is a collection of related families; families are the most important social unit among the Lao Soung. A village headman is selected because of his personal leadership attributes but is usually the oldest male family member. He serves under a clan chief whose position is hereditary.

Although Buddhism and Christianity have come to the mountain peaks, many animistic beliefs are still held there. Divination and ancestor worship are parts of the village religious practices. Even so, each village has a Buddhist center, along with other places designated for veneration of ancestors.

In the tradition of the mountain people, the Lao Soung have little to do with the national government—even opposing it through an organization called Chao Fa (God's disciples).

Lao Loum. The Lao who inhabit the Mekong River valley and the adjacent mountains are, for the most part, Buddhists. As with other Lao they are village dwellers. (The capital, Vientiane—now Viangchan—has a population of just over 200,000 and is Laos' largest city. The other famous city, Luang Prabang—now Louangphrabang—has fewer than 50,000 residents.) These people, too, are rice cultivators, using irrigation to flood rice paddies that are cultivated with plows driven by water buffalo and oxen. The language of this group is the national language, Lao (Laotian).

The lowland Tai also live in villages (*muongs*) of related families. Each village is ruled by a local headman or prince called *chao muong*. Under his leadership, except in times of disaster, life for Lao men is tranquil. Men construct the irrigation systems, then plant the rice. About 100 days later, the rice is harvested, leaving the rest of the man's time for leisure. Women grow vegetables, weave cloth, make clothing, cook, and tend the children. As soon as they are able, the children tend the livestock.

Each village of wooden houses on raised pilings contains a Buddhist *Wat* (pagoda), and Buddhist *bouns* (festivals) are frequent. Buddhist monks tend the pagoda and assist in the festivals, in return for which they are cared for through alms from the community.

The Tai people who live in the mountains bordering the Mekong Valley are divided into three groups according to the color of the traditional dress of the women: red (Tai Deng), white (Tai Khao), and black (Tai Dam). The Tai Dam are noted for their ability to breed and raise small, sturdy horses.

Common elements among the Lao. Lao are rice farmers. Under the French some became teachers, police, army officers, and government workers, but most of these positions fell to the Chinese in Laos. The French, then the Americans, and finally the Communist government have sought to develop a manufacturing base in Laos. The manufacture of such items as cigarettes, soft drinks, beer, soap, detergents, plastics, and light furniture has arisen mostly in Vientiane. However, probably fewer than 15,000 Lao are employed in industry. A few workers serve in the developing mining and forestry industries.

Almost all Lao are village dwellers, living in houses made of wood and bamboo and raised on pilings above flood danger at ground level. Most are peasant farmers. In earlier times, an aristocracy grew up around the royal family based at Luang Prabang. This aristocracy grew mostly from family ties with the royalty. However, fewer than 200 families claim this aristocratic heritage.

Lao women, although they have only recently gained the right to vote, are treated with near-equality to men. This is particularly evident in the new industry of the country, where women work alongside men at the same rate of pay.

Lao are mostly Buddhists although there are a few Christians and animists. However, most of those who hold to animism or claim Christianity incorporate these beliefs into some form of Theravada Buddhism. So almost every village in Laos has, as a focal point, a Buddhist Wat. Thousands of monks tend these Wats. At one time, many young men often attained an education by becoming monks for a few years.

Under the new government, education is free wherever it is available. Not all remote villages have schools, but the government has placed an elementary school in most of them. There are more than 7,000 village schools. School is not mandatory; still, two-thirds of the people of school age attend. School begins at age six and continues for five years. Secondary school begins at eleven and continues for six years.

Most Lao are conversant in the Lao language, which is used in the schools. For many years, Laotian literature was tied to that of Thailand. Still, a dozen newspapers serve the country and nearly ninety percent of the people are able to read them. There are four book publishing companies creating books in Lao—all of them located in Vientiane.

Lao celebrate three national holidays. April 13–15 is the Lao New Year, May 1 is labor day, as it is in other Communist countries, and December 2 is national day. Other holidays are celebrated locally and are mostly centered on Buddhist events.

For More Information

Khan, Azizur Rahman, and Eddy Lee. *Employment and Development in Laos: Some Problems and Policies*. Bangkok: ILO, 1980.

Stuart-Fox, Martin. *Laos: Politics, Economics, and Society*. Boulder: Lynne Rinner Publishers, 1986.

Zasloff, Joseph J. and Leonard Unger, editors. *Laos: Beyond the Revolution*. London: Macmillan, 1991.

MAINLAND CHINESE

(mane′ land chi neez′)

People of the People's Republic of China, the most populous country in the world.

Population: 1,000,000,000 (1991 estimate).
Location: People's Republic of China.
Languages: Mandarin Chinese; other Chinese dialects.

Geographical Setting

China, the world's third-largest country in area after Russia and Canada, is the most populous. About one in every five of the world's people is Chinese. With just slightly more area than the United States, China holds over four times as many people. The Han Chinese, comprising ninety-three percent of China's population, have historically been centered in the east in the great plain around the Yellow River (Huang He). This cradle of Chinese civilization–a broad swathe of land extending south from Beijing–was isolated by huge deserts to the north and by the harsh Tibetan Plateau to the west. The Chinese were not a seafaring people, so the Yellow Sea to the east also acted as a barrier. Today, the Chinese heartland includes this northern plain–still the nation's best agricultural land–plus South China, which the Han had settled by about A.D. 800. The south stretches east from Vietnam and includes the major ports of Canton, Macau, and Hong Kong–though the last two have been administered by European powers. The South's closeness to the busy trade routes of the South China Sea have made its people more outward-looking than the isolated northern Chinese; in fact, nearly all of China's emigrants have been from the southern provinces.

The Han heartland comprises the part of China east of a line drawn from Beijing south to the Gulf of Tonkin, next to Vietnam.

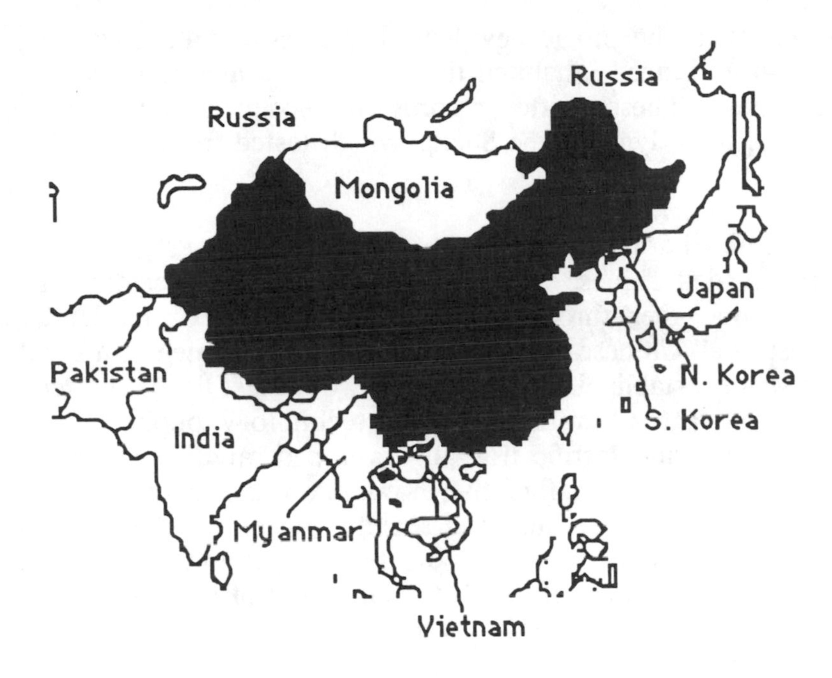

West of this line live most of China's so-called "national minorities"–Mongols, Tibetans, Turks, and other non-Chinese peoples, who together make up seven percent of the population. The eastern half of the country–the Han part–includes vast and inhospitable deserts, huge sunken basins (including the Tarim Basin, the world's largest), and high rolling grasslands and plateaus. Much of these areas are sparsely inhabited.

China's climate is as complex and varied as its terrain. Monsoon winds dominate patterns of rainfall, with cold, continental winds sweeping south in the winter, and hot, humid ones blowing in from the southern seas in the summer. Rainfall is highest in the south, becoming less reliable as one goes farther north. Temperatures vary seasonally, with cold winters in the north.

Historical Background

Long timeline. China boasts the world's oldest continuous civilization, which means that today's Chinese can look back over 4,000 years of unbroken cultural traditions. In earliest times, the legendary Xia Dynasty is believed to have held sway from about 2100 to 1600

B.C. Recent archaeological evidence indicates that a bronze-using urban culture indeed inhabited the sites which later records say were Xia centers. These written records—in recognizable Chinese—date from the next dynasty, the Shang, which lasted from about 1600 to 1027 B.C.

The hundred schools of thought. The Zhou Dynasty (1027 to 221 B.C.) extended Chinese culture from the immediate area of the Huang He (Yellow River) throughout the plains of North China. Under this longest of all Chinese dynasties, civil and governmental institutions took shape, establishing patterns that would last to the modern age. Commerce, agricultural and military technology, public works such as irrigation, and fortification all developed rapidly in this time of advancement. Most influential, however, was the growth of ideas about man's role in nature and society. So many different philosophies emerged that the middle of the Zhou period is referred to as the "hundred schools of thought." The ideas of Lao Zi (Lao Tse, c. 580 B.C.) and Kong Zi (551–479 B.C.), called Confucius in the West, had the greatest impact. Lao Zi is credited with developing Taoism, which urges men to find harmony with nature's way, or *tao*. Confucius, by contrast, laid out guidelines for social interaction and good government. These complementary systems—one for private life, one for public—shaped Chinese thought for thousands of years.

Rise of central authority. During these early dynasties, or governmental regimes, power ebbed and flowed among a number of small "warring states" (as the last period of the Zhou Dynasty is called). By the end of the Zhou period, a concept of Chinese identity had evolved, in which China (*Zhong-guo* or the "Middle Kingdom") lay at the center of the world, superior in culture to the uncivilized peoples around it. In the following centuries, this idea—combined with Confucian traditions of government—gave rise to a series of dynasties in which China was united in a single empire. The most important of the early imperial dynasties were the Han (206 B.C. to A.D. 220) and the Tang (A.D. 618 to 907).

Han Dynasty. Under the Han Dynasty, Confucian ideals were used to create a powerful civil service based on competitive examinations. China expanded her power westward, defeating the "barbarian" tribes on her northern and western borders and making them tributaries (paying subjects) of the Han government. Trade was established as far west as the Roman Empire, to which the "silk route" carried valuable Chinese silk across Asia and the Middle East. Technological advances, such as the invention of paper, also occurred in this age of development. Eventually, in a pattern to be repeated, the Han Dynasty became rigid and corrupt, finally collapsing in A.D. 220.

Disunity and Tang recovery. China again fell into disunity, and for nearly 400 years individual warlords—local rulers backed by their own armies—feuded among themselves. Technological advances continued, however, most notably in the invention of porcelain. Buddhism, introduced from India during the Han Dynasty, gained in popularity in the 400s and 500s, accompanied by the spread of Chinese culture to non-Chinese peoples in the north and south. Eventually the Tang Dynasty asserted central control, ushering in another period of cultural growth and territorial expansion. Art and literature flourished, with literature becoming available to wide audiences through the invention of block printing about 50 B.C. A Tang ruler also perfected the Confucian-based civil service system developed earlier during the Han period. Finally, Buddhism became thoroughly integrated into Chinese traditional culture. Tang power had declined by the mid-700s, however, weakened by northern invasions, economic trouble, and popular unrest, and the dynasty was overthrown in 907.

Mongol rule. After another short period of civil strife, the Song Dynasty (960–1279) reunified much of Chinese territory. Economic revitalization marked the Song period, as growing trade created a new class of wealthy merchants to share power with the scholarly civil servants. By the mid-1200s, the vast Mongol armies of Genghis Khan had conquered an area from North China to the Black Sea, twice invading Western Europe. In 1279, the last weakened remnants of the Southern Song Dynasty collapsed, inaugurating almost 100 years of Mongol rule in China (1279–1368). During this rule, Han Chinese were excluded from power. Culturally, however, the period was one of great fertility, as influences came to China through the vast Mongol network. Western musical instruments, for example, first reached China during the Mongol period, as did the Venetian traveler Marco Polo; at the same time, Chinese porcelain, playing cards, and printing slowly made their way west.

Ming Dynasty. Chinese rebels overthrew a decayed Mongol regime in 1368, establishing the Ming Dynasty, which lasted until 1644. In the early, dynamic years of Ming rule, Chinese armies reconquered territory as far west as Vietnam, and huge naval fleets explored and collected tribute throughout Southeast Asia, sailing as far as India and East Africa. By 1433, however, the last fleet had returned, and for unknown reasons, the Ming rulers fell back into the old inward-looking attitude of a China holding itself aloof from the surrounding, inferior world.

The West and the Manchus. Ming vitality began ebbing just as Europe entered its most energetic era, the age of exploration and colonization. The Portuguese arrived in the 1500s, followed by the Spanish, Dutch, and British. The insular northern government limited trade to a few ports—most important, the southern port of Guangzhou (Canton). The Ming Dynasty fell in 1644, weakened by internal unrest, and Beijing was taken by the Manchus, a non-Chinese people from the north. The Manchus absorbed Chinese culture, however, and adopted the same Confucian civil service and isolationist posture as the Mings. Resistance to the Manchus was strong, especially in South China, where Ming naval commanders fought from their base on the island of Taiwan. In order to consolidate its rule, the Manchu Qing Dynasty laid waste to the South China coast, where wealthy Chinese merchants had their headquarters. By eradicating Chinese merchants, many of whom fled abroad, and discouraging other Chinese from trade, the Manchus opened the way for European economic dominance.

Opium Wars and the Taiping Rebellion. By the 1800s, China had become subject to great pressures, both external and internal. Britain, by this time the main Western power, had come to rely on the sale of opium in China to balance its trade for tea and silk. The Qing government attempted to curtail trade in the drug, which resulted in Britain and then other European powers orchestrating a series of invasions into Chinese territory. These four "Opium Wars" (1839–1860) each ended in humiliating defeat for the Chinese; the Qing government was forced to sign treaties giving the Europeans territorial and economic concessions. Unprecedented floods, famines, and droughts added to China's problems, and popular dissatisfaction with Manchu rule took root, particularly in South China. The Taiping Rebellion, the largest mass-uprising in modern Chinese history, originated in the south and combined anti-Manchu feeling with religious ideals. Only with Western help was the Qing government able to suppress the revolt—leaving the government further under the power of the West.

Revolution. Further rebellions, rising anti-Western feeling, military defeat by Japan in 1895, and failed reform within the Qing administration had paralyzed China by the early 1900s. In 1911, Western-educated Sun Yat-sen, born in the southern city of Canton, led a revolution that toppled the last Qing emperor. Sun Yat-sen was unable to consolidate his rule immediately; Qing weakness had allowed the rise of powerful regional warlords who were able to triumph over Sun's military forces. Help came from the Soviet Union, which also aided the small Chinese Communist Party, allied to Sun's Guomindang (Nationalist Party). On Sun's death in 1925, leadership of the Guomindang passed to Chiang Kai-shek. By this time, the Communist movement within the Guomindang was growing, but Chiang was able to suppress it enough to claim control of all China by 1927.

Invasion and civil war. In the early 1930s war broke out between the Guomindang and resurgent Communist forces, led by Mao Tse-tung, in the early 1930s. At the same time, Japan invaded Manchuria (in the far north) and began pushing farther south, reaching Beijing in 1937. Until the defeat of Japan in 1945, at the end of World War II, the Guomindang and the Communists fought against both each other and the Japanese occupiers. Famine and violence brought severe hardship to the people, especially the peasants, who were already used to trying times. More and more of the people came to support the Communists, who appeared to speak for the peasants. With the departure of the Japanese, the Communists gradually began to win out, finally forcing the Guomindang to retreat to the island of Taiwan in 1949. Since then the Mainland Chinese have been under Communist control, while the Guomindang has maintained a rival government on Taiwan.

People's Republic of China. Victory brought great enthusiasm to the early years of the People's Republic. Facing huge challenges, the Communist government was aided by wide popular support. Industrial recovery, land redistribution, and military success against the United States in Korea all brought high morale to the Chinese. The failure in 1959 of the next step, an economic program called "the Great Leap Forward," took the edge off these early victories. Mao Tse-tung took responsibility for the failure, and by the mid-1960s "moderates" such as Deng Xiaoping had come to power. The moderates wished to liberalize the economy by allowing private ownership of land and permitting limited free markets.

Cultural Revolution. Mao Tse-tung, thinking that China was straying from the Communist path, loosed a reaction to the moderates that became known as the Cultural Revolution. From 1966–70, the Cultural Revolution raged throughout China, as all public expression—from politics to art and religion—was forced to toe the Communist Party line. Those suspected of "bourgeois obstructionism" (Communist jargon for supporting capitalist ideas) were sent to camps in the countryside to labor with peasants and to be "re-educated" in "Mao Tse-tung Thought." The "Red Guards"—young people's groups of mysterious origins—soon took over the Cultural Revolution, denouncing teachers, professors, Communist Party officials, and other authority figures, as well as writers, artists, and intellectuals. By 1967, the Red Guards had to be suppressed by Mao himself, as they turned their violence and suspicion against each other. In 1970, firmly in control once again, Mao ended the upheaval.

Propaganda, Chinese style. *Courtesy of David Tuch.*

Reform and Tiananmen Square. By 1973, the moderates—led by Premier Zhou Enlai and by Deng Xiaoping, brought back to power after falling out of favor—had staged somewhat of a comeback. For the next few years, until Zhou's and Mao's deaths in 1976, the moderate and hard-line factions struggled for dominance. With Mao's death, the hard-liners lost decisively. Within a month, four hard-line leaders—the "Gang of Four," including Mao's influential widow—had been arrested, and the moderates were once again in power.

In the 1980s and early 1990s, China again underwent a cycle of liberal reform and authoritarian backlash. By the mid-1980s, much of China had been transformed by experiments in free enterprise and by new openness to Western ideas, fashions, and investment. Political reform failed to keep pace with economic and social change, however, and demonstrations in favor of greater democracy occurred with some regularity. In the spring of 1989, these demonstrations spread nationwide, culminating in huge student protests in Beijing's Tiananmen Square. After several months, during which thousands of students occupied the square, the government finally acted to suppress the students and their supporters in the general population. On June 4, 1989, tanks and soldiers attacked the square, scattering the protesters and killing an unknown number, probably at least 300. Since then, in an atmosphere of renewed authoritarianism, many leaders of the democracy movement have been tried and executed or imprisoned.

Culture Today

Aging leadership. As the remaining leaders (like Deng Xiaoping) who fought alongside Mao reach the age of 90, China faces the problem of who will succeed them. During the 1980s, China seemed to lead the way among reformers in the Communist world. Then came the rising protests and the deeply traumatic events of June 1989. After the crackdown, China's government seemed as rigid as ever, while the rest of the Communist world seethed with rapid, revolutionary change. Tourism and foreign investment, having advanced rapidly in the 1980s, dropped sharply after the Tiananmen Square event and have not yet really begun to recover. The brief taste of freedom, followed by harsh repression, has made many—especially the young and the educated—cynical and disillusioned towards the government. The Chinese leaders are faced with the need to establish their legitimacy among people who have seen old-style Communism discredited—not only at home, but around the world.

Communism and tradition. Mao Tse-tung's vision of Communism fits in with some important aspects of traditional Chinese culture and rejects others. Chinese traditions tend to put common interests—for example, the good of the family or of society as a whole—over individual ones. Thus traditional values stress the individual's obligations and duties to society, rather than his or her rights within it. This strand in Chinese culture agrees with Communist ideas, which emphasize the good of the many over that of the few.

Of the traditional values that Communism has rejected, most important is probably the ancient Confucian model of social relations. The Confucian tradition stressed the obedience and respect owed by one member of society to another: for example, by subject to ruler, by son to father, or by wife to husband. This hierarchical system became closely identified with the imperial government, bound up as it was in the emperor's civil service. In traditional society, Confucian scholar/civil servants had the most prestige, followed by farmers, then by artisans, merchants, and soldiers. By contrast, Mao attempted to "level" society, to create a classless "people's dictatorship," in which one owed obedience only to the state—which represented "the people."

Urban-rural divide. Such a leveling has proved an elusive goal, however. Even before the reforms of the last decade, for example, significant differences existed between city and country life. Wages, living standards, and education are all far better for city-dwellers, while huge areas of rural China remain backward and isolated. Furthermore, since the late 1950s, it has been illegal to move to the cities from the countryside without state permission, and one's position as rural resident is inherited legally. Mobility is thus very difficult, creating what amount to permanent classes of country- and city-folk. (On the other hand, mostly because smaller towns have grown, the percentage of the population classified as urban rose from twenty percent in 1982 to over forty percent in 1992.) Economic opportunities offered by the reforms have further widened the gap between city and country. Free enterprise on any significant scale is largely urban, and is strongest in the traditionally commercial southern cities.

Food. Chinese cuisine is one of the world's most varied and sophisticated. In broad terms, the greatest division in food (as in culture)

A Chinese peasant man in a typical wide straw hat.
Courtesy of David Tuch.

is between the north, centered around Beijing, and the south, centered around Canton. The northern staple grain has been wheat, eaten in bread, noodles, dumplings (*mantou* or *baozi*), and meat- or vegetable-filled pockets of dough (*jiaozi*). The northern climate restricts the variety of vegetables available; northern cooking has thus been relatively plain, making up for the lack by using lots of garlic, onions, and chilies in preparation. As in the south, favorite meats are pork and chicken. The most famous northern dish, Peking Duck, is one of many comparatively sophisticated dishes invented in the emperor's kitchens (Peking is the old English version of Beijing).

Rice, the staple grain of the south, accompanies most of the complex and varied southern dishes. Of the many southern regional cuisines, most famous are Cantonese and Szechwan. Because of the high proportion of emigrants from Canton, Westerners think of this as "Chinese food." The dishes balance sweet and sour flavors and crunchy and smooth textures, using few spices and short cooking time to bring out natural flavors. Seafood is used more than in the north. Exotic specialties abound, such as shark's fin soup and "1,000-year eggs"—which are soaked in horse's urine. The spicier Szechwan cooking, which has recently also become widely popular in the West, evolved in the isolated and landlocked southern interior province of Szechwan. Across China, tea is the favorite drink. The growth and fermentation of tea leaves is an ancient art, and many varieties are believed to be beneficial to health.

Clothing and shelter. In past times, China was known for its exquisite textiles, especially silk, first cultivated by the imperial court. The Communist era has been dominated by the "Mao jacket" (as it is known in the West), a drab gray or blue cotton jacket, buttoned to the neck, worn with pants and a cap of the same simple cloth. Since the outward-looking 1980s, however, Western fashions have become popular, and more brightly colored clothes are now worn by many of the people. T-shirts and jeans have become the uniform of the young, and the most stylish T-shirts bear slogans printed in English (though they may be made in China).

Rural houses are mostly simple structures of stone or wood, built in a variety of regional styles. Perhaps the most distinctive traditional houses are the huge, round stone structures built by the Hakka, a northern people who migrated south to escape persecution. The persecution persisted, and to protect themselves, the Hakka communities banded together, all living in what amounted to a large stone fort or castle. Urban housing throughout China is in high demand, and the government provides subsidies and controls allotment. Wealthy families as a rule live in conditions similar to the less well-off, so that neighborhoods in Chinese cities seem more financially equal than in the West.

Family life. Family remains the center of Chinese society, although the state has taken over some traditional family roles. Great differences divide urban from rural family structure. Rural peasants have relied on large families to share work and increase household income. Sons are preferred to daughters, who cannot work in the fields and will eventually join their husbands' families. Until 1982, under the

Chinese schoolchildren illustrate the trend toward Western clothing.
Courtesy of David Tuch.

collective farming system, each family's income was based on how many workers it could supply to the collective group or work unit. "Decollectivization," begun in the 1980s, allowed greater family freedom in such matters as crop choice, with the result that smaller families are now able to raise more profitable crops. With only about ten percent of its land suitable for farming, China faces severe problems in feeding its people; smaller families thus reduce population pressure, and have been encouraged by the government. Legal incentives are offered to one-child families. With greater freedom to sell what they produce for their own profit, farmers have begun to seek educational advantages for their children.

Economic reform has changed life less for urban families (as opposed to individuals), for whom the work unit offers housing, care in old age, and other benefits that the family provides in the country. Families are smaller, playing less of a role also in matters such as marriage. In general, city life revolves more around friends from work or elsewhere than the still-conservative country life, where family members heavily influence one's choice of friends and spouse.

Carpet weaving is a major industry in some parts of China. *Courtesy of David Tuch.*

Women have taken an increasingly active role in society since the advent of Communism. Where before they were restricted by the Confucian idea that they should be subservient to men, modern Chinese women have generally achieved equality both at home and in the workplace, where they occupy positions of authority alongside the men.

Religion. While Communist China is officially atheist, traditional religion remains an important aspect of Chinese society. In stark contrast to Western religions, Chinese religion tends to be inclusive, combining various aspects of different faiths in a lively and colorful mix. The three dominant strands, melded together over the centuries, are Confucianism, Taoism, and Buddhism. Confucianism, originally more of a philosophy than a religion, acquired religious aspects over time. While no longer connected to the state, Confucian ideas of social order continue to shape Chinese society. Confucius himself came to be regarded as a god after his death. Taoism, also dating from the

Silk is an important product of China. This is a rack in a silk factory. *Courtesy of David Tuch.*

500s B.C., still incorporates its original ideas of harmony with nature, but eventually came to include a number of mystical beliefs such as faith healing, fortune telling, and magic. There is also a wide variety of Taoist gods and goddesses. Buddhism, originally from India, holds as its central belief the idea that all life involves suffering, which is linked to one's desires, so that one must eliminate all desire in order to achieve spiritual peace (called *nirvana*). Many different versions of Buddhism are practiced, often varying by region.

Chinese temples—large, colorful structures—can be dedicated to all three religions, featuring ornate statues of different deities. In daily life, religion most often concerns praying for luck or success, appeasing the spirits of dead ancestors, or attempting to tell the future. *Fengshui* is the ancient technique of arranging one's physical environment in order to achieve such goals. The placement of a doorway, for example, or an ancestor's grave, is believed to have an important influence on the family fortunes.

Holidays. The adoption of Communism added a holiday to the Chinese year. May 1, Labor Day, is now celebrated with parades and political shows as it is in other Communist countries. However, the Chinese still celebrate the coming of the new year with fireworks and parades as in the past. This holiday falls on the first three days of the first moon of the Chinese lunar calendar. The moon is also the subject of a fall celebration that occurs in September. In addition Mainland Chinese celebrate Women's Day in March, Army Day in August, and National Days on October 1 and 2.

Language. Chinese does not use an alphabet, relying instead on characters—originally pictorial representations of ideas—in writing. Thus, identical characters may be pronounced differently. This system has the advantage that speakers of the many dialects, often mutually incomprehensible, may communicate with each other by writing if not by speech. The official dialect is that of Beijing, often referred to as Mandarin, and spoken by about seventy percent of the population. Chinese grammar is simple, relying on word order rather than changes in the forms of the words. Spoken Chinese is tonal, which means that similar words may mean different things depending on the tone—rising, falling, falling/rising or high—that one uses. Although around 50,000 characters exist, only about 5,000 are used commonly.

Literature and the arts. China's literary tradition, stretching back almost 4,000 years, is the world's longest and one of its greatest. Among the oldest classics are the ancient works of Confucianism and Taoism, as well as a collection of popular songs collected and recorded by Confucius himself. The Tang Dynasty (618–907) marks the beginning of the golden age of Chinese poetry; works of prose fiction date from the Ming Dynasty (1368–1644). One of the best known is the *Jinpingmei* ("The Plum Blossom in a Golden Vase"), which gives a lively and realistic account of social conditions in the 1500s. Formerly regarded with some scorn by high-minded scholars, prose came into its own in the 1900s, as China went through the upheaval of revolution and civil war. Recently, a number of women writers have emerged, the best known in the West being Zhang Jie. Her novel *Heavy Wings* examines corruption and disorder during the Cultural Revolution. Like many Chinese writers, she has walked a tightrope between government control and artistic expression, often angering authorities. Censorship, relaxed during the 1980s, has again become a common part of writers' lives.

Since ancient times, painting and calligraphy (the art of beautiful writing) have been among the most revered of Chinese arts. Unlike in the West, where tradition is punctuated by revolutions in artistic technique, Chinese artists have carried on unbroken styles which changed only minimally over the centuries. In both calligraphy and painting, ink, brushes and paper are exquisitely refined, and used with religious concentration. The artist's spiritual state is regarded as vitally important to successful execution of the extremely sophisticated works in such materials as jade, ivory, metals, porcelain and silk. Queen of the performing arts is Chinese opera, which dates from the 200s B.C., and has evolved into regional variations, each offering colorful and dramatic beauties to the music lover. Opera is particularly popular among older people.

For More Information

Fairbank, John King. *The Great Chinese Revolution, 1800-1985*. New York: Harper & Row, 1986.

Morgenstern, Manfred, ed. *Insight Guides: China*. Singapore: APA Publications, 1990.

Schell, Orville. *Discos and Democracy: China in the Throes of Reform*. New York: Pantheon Books, 1988.

Worden, Robert L. *China: A Country Study*. Washington, DC: Department of the Army, 1988.

MALAYS

(may' lays)

People of the southern region of the Malay Peninsula and the islands of Singapore and western Borneo.

Population: 16,000,000 (1990 estimate).
Location: Malaysia, Indonesia, Thailand, Singapore.
Language: Malay, an Austronesian language.

Geographical Setting

From the southern extreme of Thailand, the Malay Peninsula ends in a bulging tip 350-miles long—the peninsular portion of the Federation of Malaysia. At the end of this tip is the state of Singapore, and 500–700 miles east is the island of Borneo. Malay people migrated to this area from mainland Asia. Malaysia, Singapore, and a western portion of Borneo—Sarawak—form the home of the Malays. From this area, Malays settled in the Pacific Islands, reaching as far as the Philippines. Over the centuries, some of these people have been absorbed into the cultures surrounding them. However, there remains a large group of Malays, mainly in Malaysia, who speak a Malay language, live according to Malay family customs, and follow a Malay form of Islam. This group of Malays in Malaysia is discussed here.

This is a tropical land; temperatures vary little during the year and remain warm. Rain falls most days of the year, usually in the late afternoon or evening. From June to November the rains are intensified by monsoon winds. It is a region of tropical jungles, rubber plantations, and pineapple farms.

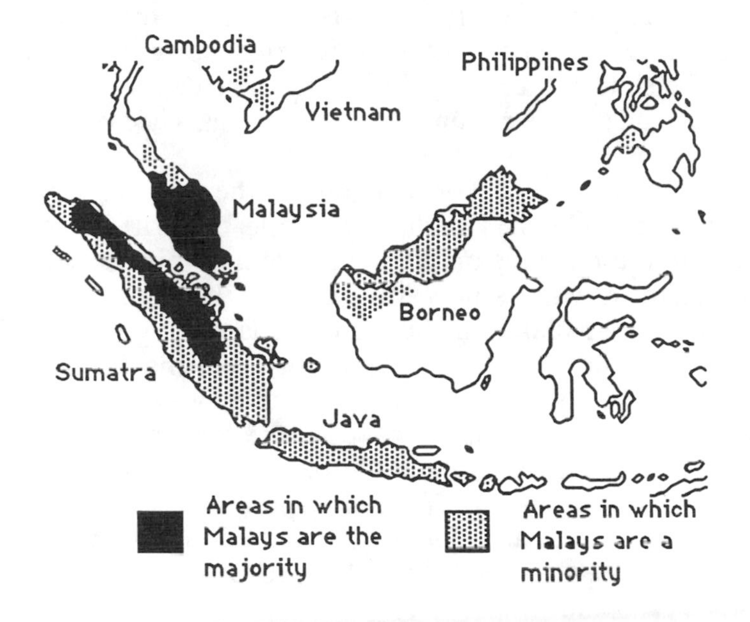

Historical Background

Sri Vijaya. While the Malay people today claim to have come to the Malay peninsula from the island of Sumatra, ancestors of the Malays probably migrated south to the peninsula before 2000 B.C. The early people settled throughout the peninsula and neighboring islands.

That they came from Sumatra is suggested by the discovery that an early Malayan empire was based at Palembang, which lies in the south of that island. This empire thrived on piracy and on tariffs exacted from traders traveling to and from China and India. Eventually, this first empire, Sri Vijaya, controlled the island of Sumatra and much of the peninsula across the Malacca Strait. For more than 400 years, Malays ruled the ocean trade routes until the empire fell to a new force in the region, ruled from Java in the eleventh century.

Empire at Malacca. About A.D. 1400, a disfavored ruler from Singapore fled north about 100 miles and established a second kingdom at Malacca. This port became a great trade center and was a focus of immigration from India and China. The migrants from India brought Hinduism, which left traces on the Malay society; but they also brought Islam and, aided by Arab missionaries, carried this religion throughout the many tribal units of Malays that had grown over the centuries. Malacca grew to its greatest power about the beginning of the sixteenth century, just as the Portuguese were taking an interest in trade in the region. In 1511, Portugal claimed Malacca.

European influences. The Portuguese held the area for 130 years, then were driven out by the Dutch. Meanwhile, the British had begun to take an interest in the region. By the 1700s, a number of sultanates had taken form in what is now Malaysia. In the northwest corner bordering today's Thailand, the Sultan of Kedah ruled over a section of the mainland and an island, Penang. In 1786, the British leased this island from the sultan. Later, this same sultan was to grant Britain rights to land on the mainland. In 1819, the British administrator there, Thomas Raffles, was granted the right to establish a colony on another island, Singapore. By 1824, Singapore had been sold to the British East India Company. The Dutch had established themselves at Malacca and in 1825 ceded this colony to Britain.

British expansion. In 1874, the British increased their hold on the region at the request of two small states seeking British protection from their neighbors. Two sultanates arranged similar protection agreements before 1889. In 1895 these four sultanates united to form the Federated Malay States with a British governor. By 1914, five other regions had been given to the British. The Europeans had established rubber plantations and industries in Malaysia along with tin-mining. Under the British, these industries thrived, and Malaysia became more prosperous—but at some expense to the Malay people. Needing workers for their plantation systems and mines, the British brought indentured workers in large numbers from India and encouraged Chinese workers to immigrate to Malaysia.

Independence. World War II saw the region occupied by the Japanese. At the end of the war, Britain returned and formed its protectorates and territories into the Malayan Union. In 1948, this union became part of the Federation of Malaya as a step toward independence. Communist forces, which had helped to overthrow colonialism, immediately began campaigning in the country and continued to press their demands for the next ten years. However, independence was agreed upon in 1957 and, in 1962, a new state of Malaysia had

The rulers of the nine original Malay states still dominate Malaysia.

formed, including the old Federation as Western Malaysia and Sarawak and Sabah on Borneo as Eastern Malaysia. The result is that Malays have a wide variety of experiences over an expanse broken by 500 miles of sea and segments of Indonesia. One example of the cultural variations that have developed from these experiences is the matrilineal structure of some Malay groups in the Indonesian state of Sumatra. Among the Indonesians and on the Malaysian island states of Sarawak and Sabah, Malays are often in the minority. They are a strong majority, although representing mostly the poorest class, in the northern states of the Malay peninsula. In Malaysia, the government aims to place nearly one-third of the country's economy under Malay control. In Malaysia, Malay strength in government has been assured as the new structures grew out of old structures.

Government, new from old. Malays played a dominant role in the new nation of Malaysia. Formed of thirteen states (of which eleven have separate governing units), nine former sultanates, and the two original British settlements at Penang and Malacca, the new government grew out of the old. Nine hereditary rulers—the sultans of the states of Johore, Kedah, Kelantan, Pahang, Selangor, and Trengganu together with hereditary leaders of Negri Sembilan and the Raja of Perlis—form a council that elects a king to serve for five years. The old British settlements of Malacca and Penang along with Eastern Malaysia's Sarawak and Sabah, in which Malays are minorities, do not have a voice in this election. Thus, Malays are assured of a strong and usually dominant voice in the government of Malaysia. The king (who must be Malay) and council appoint members to a senate, while a house of representatives is elected by popular vote. The king also appoints a prime minister to guide the daily activities of government. In recent years, government has been uneasy. While the same prime minister has guided government since 1976, he has been frequently at odds with various members of the cabinet. Various states (the old sultanates continue to be ruled by their hereditary rulers) have protested what they see as unequal treatment by the central government.

Culture Today

Religion. A binding force among almost all Malays and a force that separates them from the large Chinese minority in the country of Malaysia is religion. Malays are Muslims of the Sunni sect. But, unlike their Javanese neighbors, the Malays have incorporated some of their older religious beliefs into Islam, while still adhering to Muslim principles. Animistic ideas of local spirits and demons are widespread, as are Hindu-Buddhist symbols, particularly for rituals of marriage and healing.

Often a religious ceremony begins and ends with Islamic rituals while its content is based on Hindu or Buddhist ideas. Malays have no difficulty in merging earlier religious ideas with Islam, claiming that successful actions of spirits (magic) or other beings depend on their acceptance by the one supreme god, Allah. Malays regularly make pilgrimages to Mecca, observe the fasting month of Ramadan, pray five times daily while prostrating themselves facing Mecca, and celebrate Islamic holy days and religious feasts.

So important is this religion to the Malays that some residents of Malaysia have gained recognition as Malays simply by becoming Muslims. To be converted to Islam is sometimes said to take on Malay ethnicity (*masok melayu*). No person is properly considered Malay if that person adheres to a religion other than Islam.

There have been many attempts through the years to reform the Malay Muslim faith. One of the strongest ones was *dakwah*, a missionary movement begun in the 1970s to convince Malays that their older traditions and some Western innovations are not in keeping with Islam. Other groups work to maintain Malay customs within the Islamic faith. Still others are concerned with integrating Islam with ideas of industrialization.

Family life. Except that the family order among some Malay groups depends largely on descent from the mother's hereditary line, Islam has dominated Malay family life. Marriages between Muslims and non-Muslims is discouraged. Since the organization of the government in 1957, the ease with which Muslim men secured divorce has been restricted by government regulations and the divorce rate has decreased. At the same time, the Islamic custom of taboo against marriage within a clan has been relaxed so that now marriage is discouraged only among first cousins.

In the Muslim tradition men play dominant roles in public affairs, while Malay women have more power within the home. They manage the household budgets and attend to the children. These children are the focus of the Malay family. Married couples who are childless frequently adopt children to complete the Malay family. Malay children attend school. They are expected to grow, mature, and, above all, to marry.

The reliance on a strong family is seen in Malay proverbs:

> Water hacked is not severed. (A family is not severed by a quarrel.)
> If a tree has roots many and firm, there is no need to fear the tempest.
> (Winstedt 1957, p. 27)

Village life. Malays are the small-scale agriculturalists of Malaysia. When the Europeans began to plant rubber trees on large plantations and to mine the rich tin and aluminum ores of Malaysia, they imported Chinese and India Tamil workers. These workers, especially the Chinese, increased and became the business people and tradesmen in many of the large towns and cities. About forty percent of the Malaysian population is Chinese and most of these live in the towns. (When the federation was first formed, Singapore was part of it, but that colony was encouraged to withdraw, largely because its great Chinese population would have given the Chinese dominance over the Malays in the federation.)

There are only eleven cities of population greater than 100,000 in Malaysia, accounting for about eighteen percent of the population. Most of the Malay people live in small villages—clusters of homes built of bamboo and other wood and with thatched roofs. Often the homes are elevated on pilings to avoid the wet ground. Much of the Malay peninsula, particularly in the south, is swampland.

Villages are most often clusters of related families who share work and problems, sometimes working together on a plantation of which the village forms a part. The village of one's birth is important, as is the village in which one is married. Young villagers who leave the village for work in the factories of towns and cities return frequently for celebrations and contribute to the financial welfare of the village whenever possible.

The majority of Malays form the poorer class in Malaysia. More than sixty percent of them live below the income level that has been defined as the margin of poverty by the Malaysian government. Nearly eighty percent of the Malays live in the small villages and work as rice farmers. Rice growers do not yet produce enough food for the growing population, but new strains of rice grown in the north of the country provide crops every four months, nearly doubling the productivity of the fields. In addition, the Malaysian government has promoted expansion of the amount of land used for food growing.

Men and women work together in the rice fields. Men plant the rice in nurseries and plan and tend the irrigation systems. Women transplant the rice seedlings in the fields and help with the harvest. Rice is the most important agricultural produce, even though many villages are associated with rubber plantations. Rubber is a cash crop and is subject to great changes in value as the world market changes. In the south, pineapples are an important cash crop and some Malays work in the processing plants around Malacca to prepare pineapples for market.

Since the 1970s, particularly, Malays have joined other people on Malaysia in a move to the larger towns and cities. While the Malays who now live in the city make up less than twenty percent of the total Malay population, the number of city and town dwellers has grown by more than 100 percent in the last twenty years. About one-fifth of the Malay workers have found jobs in small industries in towns and cities. They process foods, assemble electronic equipment, and prepare raw rubber or make rubber products for market.

Cities and towns. Malay society has been described as based on three ideas: *gotong royang*, help among neighbors; *ummak*, shared Muslim faith and responsibilities; and *malu*, self-respect. Self-respect grows from accepting the responsibilities of community and religion. As Malays move to the cities and towns to take positions in industry, business, and government, they are separated from their original communities and merged with people of other religious backgrounds. Family structures are greatly pressed as younger family members move away from the community. Family units tend toward nuclear rather than extended units. These trends are evident in Malay townspeople. Even so, Malays for the most part cling to the ideas that their group is identifiable through adherence to Malay customs and to gotong royang, ummak, and malu.

Education. The national government and regional ones support schools in Malaysia. Most Malay villages have two village centers, an elementary school, and a mosque. Education takes place in both centers. Government-aided schools provide free education from the ages of six to nineteen. In the elementary schools, students learn in the official language of the country, Bahasa Malaysia. English is sometimes taught as a second language. Children attend the village primary school from age six to twelve. Some then continue to a secondary school until they are seventeen. At that age, students may qualify to study two more years to qualify for the university, or they may elect to study two years in a trade or vocational school. Seventy-eight percent of all young people of these ages are in school. The government interest in education has reduced adult illiteracy among the Malays from nearly one-third of the people in the 1960s to less than one-fifth of the people (13.5 percent of men, 29.6 percent of women) in the 1990s.

Social structure. Even though the customs of the Malays make it unacceptable to display wealth, Malays are divided into classes according to landholdings and secure incomes. As people leave the small family farms, wealthier Malay farmers have increased their acreage. Some have come to control the once-British rubber plantations. Plantation owners are at the top of the economic system—the wealthiest of the Malays. Below them in the economic class system are teachers and small business people, and below them, former government workers (soldiers and police officers on pensions). Religious figures, Muslim teachers, and mosque officials, once prestigious figures in the society, have fallen in the economic scale toward near poverty. The language and courtesies of the Malays, both formal and informal, reinforce the various social stratifications based on wealth, relationships, and age. So strict are the social customs of politeness and harmony that the Malays have invented *mengamok* ("running wild") as moments when letting off steam is acceptable.

Clothing. Dressing comfortably for work in the warm and humid weather, the Malays once wore a single piece of clothing, a sarong. This was wrapped around the waist and was the sole garment of the men. Women wore a light blouse atop the sarong. As Malays found work on the plantations, and some moved to the larger towns, the men have abandoned this costume except during periods of relaxation. Work clothes are Western in style, although men often wear trousers or shorts that are loose-fitting and of light material. The man's dress is topped by a fez or a turban. The Malay women still wear the sarong and blouse as their most common dress, choosing under Islamic custom to cover their arms and legs and sometimes covering their heads with scarfs or shawls.

Holidays. Traditional costumes can be seen throughout the Malay villages during periods of celebration. The Malay celebrations reflect the varied ethnic makeup of their country. Chinese New Year on the first two days of the first moon of the lunar calendar is celebrated with parades, music, and dancing. Muslim religious holidays are universally celebrated with appropriate feasts and worship: Hari Raya Puasa (the end of Ramadan), Hari Raya Haji (the Feast of the Sacrifice), and the birthday of Muhammad. In addition, the birthday of His Majesty Yang di Pertuan Agong ("The Supreme Head of Malaysia") is currently celebrated in June.

Arts. The wide range of languages to which Malays have been introduced and in which their literature has been written is illustrated by the newspaper publications in Malaysia. Five daily newspapers publish in English, six in Chinese, five in Malay, two in Punjabi, and two in Tamil in Western Malaysia. There are publications in Malay, Chinese, and English in Eastern Malaysia.

Music and dance are popular among the villagers. Dramatic actions suggesting past histories of violence and sword play characterize the dancing, which is accompanied by drums and pipes made of bamboo. One popular dance re-enacts the deeds of ancient warriors. Men dress in traditional sarong and shirt, add a sash and a turban, and dance with swords and shields in this dance, Ota-Ota.

For More Information

Bunge, Frederica M., editor. *Malaysia: A Country Study.* Washington, DC: American University, 1985.

Jones, Gavin W. "Malay Marriage and Divorce in Peninsular Malaysia: Three Decades of Change," *Population and Development Review,* 7, No. 2, June 1981, pp. 255–78.

Snodgrass, Donald R. *Inequality and Economic Development in Malaysia.* Kuala Lumpur: Oxford University Press, 1980.

Winstedt, Sir Richard. *Malay Proverbs.* London: John Murray, 1957.

MAORI

(mau′ ree)

Pre-European Polynesian inhabitants of New Zealand; the largest ethnic minority in the area today.

Population: 326,325 (1991 census).
Location: New Zealand.
Languages: Maori; English.

Geographical Setting

Composed primarily of two islands, New Zealand became home to the Eastern Polynesian people known as the Maori a thousand years before Europeans sighted the area. Over thirty major Maori tribes occupied separate territories, mainly in the north half of North Island.

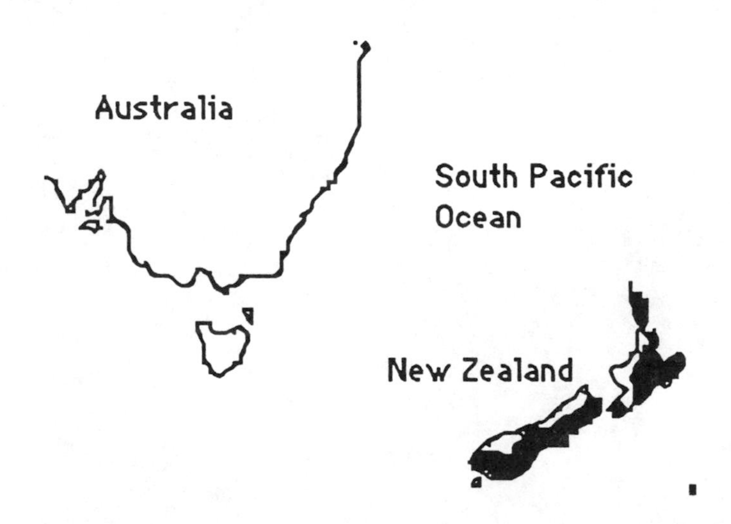

Roughly ten percent now occupy South Island, ninety percent, North Island. Seven of every ten Maori live in the north half of North Island. Once a rural group, in the 1950s the Maori migrated almost en masse to cities, favoring Auckland in particular.

New Zealand's climate ranges from subtropical in the north to very cold in the south. Average temperatures vary from 55 to 48 degrees Fahrenheit. Southwest to northeast, a mountain chain stretches across most of the terrain. The land is subject to both earthquakes and volcanoes. Resources include fish from rivers, lakes, and the surrounding ocean. Until 300 to 500 years ago, another rich resource—the flightless, ostrichlike moa (some stood twelve-feet high)—provided food. From the flax plant came material for clothing; greenstone was shaped into jewelry or weaponry.

Historical Background

Origin. The Maori have their own mythic explanation for the creation of both themselves as a people and New Zealand. First there was only cosmic night. Then came Earth Mother (Papa) and Sky Father (Rangi), who produced male offspring. These male gods tired of the lightless space and rebelled; Tane, god of creation, pushed his parents apart. A child of Tane, Tiki, became the first man, the Maori Adam. He was followed by demigods, including Maui, a mischiefmaker who fished up New Zealand's North Island from the ocean floor. Legend has it that he smuggled himself aboard his brothers' fishing canoe. Much to their chagrin, Maui caught a huge fish. His brothers hacked it to pieces. In anger, the earth made the sun rise and harden the fish's flesh. Its surface grew rough and mountainous due to the brothers' mutilation. This, says the myth, explains the origin and terrain of the North Island, the fish of Maui.

Oral tradition of the Maori further recounts their coming to North Island from Hawaiki, a homeland in Eastern Polynesia. Great stock is put in a major migration made in canoes, the final wave of eight canoes arriving about 1350. Today's Maori trace their ancestry to these eight canoes. However, scholars debate the accuracy of the tale. Some regard it as a historical account of voyages between the tropical Pacific and New Zealand. Others regard it as an account of internal voyages from one part of New Zealand to another. In fact, archaeolgists suggest, the first settlers of New Zealand set out in search of fresh land from Eastern Polynesia, probably from the Cook Islands, sometime between A.D. 600 and 1100. Polynesian and Maori physical traits probably stem from these Cook Island migrants, who trace their own origins to earlier migrants who moved to Polynesia 2,000 years ago.

Classic culture. It is thought that others lived in New Zealand before the Maori, surviving mainly by fishing and hunting moa (large flightless birds). Slowly the Maori absorbed this population and over the next four centuries developed a classic culture. Beginning with a few Eastern Polynesian customs and some imported plants (yams, taro, kumara), the people adapted to their new environment.

A tribal social organization evolved, which traced its origin to the ancestor-founder, one of the migrants who had sailed over in a canoe. Tribes were loose associations of from one to ten thousand members. It was the smaller subtribe, or *hapu*, that operated as the effective everyday unit of society. Hapu members cooperated closely for daily survival, living together on a certain stretch of tribal land, constructing canoes or meeting houses together. A hapu assigned fishing stands and farming plots within its area to its various families.

Most basic in Maori society was the *whanau,* or extended family—a head man, his wife or wives, unmarried children, married sons and their families, and slaves. While separate sleeping spaces were assigned to the small, nuclear families, they were regarded only as subsets of the whanau.

Elderly people such as these widow elders are highly respected in Maori society. *Courtesy of Wayne Mitchell.*

Communities ranged in size from a few to several hundred households. In each community were five types of buildings: *whare mehana*, or sleeping houses; communal cook houses; storehouses; shelters for wood; and in the nineteenth century a community meeting house. Most of the year the Maori lived in unprotected communities, but when threatened by conflicts (over fishing rights, marriages, and the like), the people retreated into fortified strongholds. Called *pa*, these strongholds were surrounded by walls and ditches, much like World War I trenches; if possible the pas were strategically located, on, for example, an inaccessible hill.

Each major settlement had a *marae*, an open space for gathering—in later years the site of the community meeting house. Two of the most prevalent forms of art in Maori society—carving and speechmaking—were exhibited on the marae. Carvings of ancestors adorned meeting houses; speechmaking was common at *hui*s, or gatherings for peaceful purposes. A Maori legend, *Ponga and Puhihuia*, illustrates the pivotal power of speech and reasoning in Maori society. Puhihuia, a beauty of wide renown falls in love with Ponga, a lad of lesser rank, and elopes to his hapu. Enraged, her people discuss war to avenge the theft of the beauty; Puhihuia's clever words to her mother convince them to act otherwise:

> I am now of marriageable age. Am I wrong in following the example of Kauataata [a sacred ancestress] . . . She selected Tiki [the first man] as her husband, and you are descended from her. If I am wrong, your ancestress was wrong . . . The wrong did not originate with me. It is from you and before you. You saw the one you liked and nothing would stop you. You opened the way and I have followed in your footsteps, so blame yourselves, not me.
>
> (Fletcher 1908, pp. 41–42)

In descending order, society moved from chiefs (*rangatira*) to commoners (*tuta*) to slaves (*taurekareka*). There were finer rankings too. In the legend above, both Puhihuia and Ponga came from chiefly families but the maiden belonged to a more sacred line of ancestors than the lad. Members of chiefly families generally entered into marriages arranged by their elders. Commoners exercised more choice. Lowest in society were the slaves, as a group sometimes kindly treated but hard-worked. Their lives were on occasion sacrificed to gods, Maori masters eating the human flesh.

Values. Central to Maori values were the concepts of *mana*, *tapu*, and *utu*. *Mana* is an individual's spiritual power. According to Maori belief, people inherit an initial store of mana and can increase or

Ornate wood sculptures mark this Maori building.
Courtesy of Wayne Mitchell.

decrease it by their actions. It may also be drained away by improper contacts. Existing to protect a person's mana were rules known collectively as *tapu*, meaning "under religious restriction." (The English word *taboo* stems from *tapu*.) Male aristocrats, for example, were restricted from touching the calabash when they drank; slaves held it for them. Opposite of tapu was *noa*, meaning "ordinariness" or freedom from restriction. Whether positive (gifts or compliments) or negative (bodily harm or insults), deeds in Maori society had to be reciprocated. *Utu* means "compensation," a basic Maori value. Status in Maori society was measured by how much was given away and by how generously the gift was reciprocated. Like gifts, crimes were also subject to the principle of utu, or compensation, and this was often exacted in a *muru*, or raid, the offended party plundering the criminal's area as repayment for a misdeed. Warfare was seen as a means of exacting compensation by shedding blood. The standard Maori attack was to raid rapidly, then withdraw. Some of the victims became slaves; the rest were murdered and eaten, for protein and to complete the revenge by reducing the offenders to food.

Maori-European relations—an overview. The Dutch navigator Abel Tasman gave New Zealand its name (calling it "Nieuw Zeeland") in 1642. He had little contact with the Maori, but three later expeditions (1769, 1773, 1774) drew New Zealand into the larger world. Led by Captain James Cook, these later expeditions brought a host of beneficial new "goods" into the Maori world, including cloth, iron tools, pigs, and potatoes. However, they also introduced guns and diseases.

For nearly a century after European contact, Maori society continued to dominate the area. The *Pakehas*, or Europeans, had to adjust to its sway. Slowly they began to affect Maori ways. The tides turned in distinct periods:

1. Maori independence prevails—1769–1863.
2. The tide of independence turns—1863–1869.
3. Pakeha society becomes dominant—1869–1970s.
4. Maori strive for bicultural society-1970s–present.

Whalers and missionaries. First whalers, then missionaries, introduced Pakeha ways into Maori culture. Sealers and deep sea whalers arrived in New Zealand in the 1790s, setting up camps in South Island, killing off most of the whale herds. Most of the whalers departed within thirty years, although commercial whaling continued. During their stay, the whalers greatly affected Maori culture through trade. They introduced pigs and cattle to the Maori, and whaleship captains became a major source of guns. The captains would hire Maori men to cut whale blubber and the like, but their crews regarded the Maori as inferior and mistreated them at times. Applying the principle of utu, described above, the Maori would react vengefully, sometimes killing crew members. Of course, there was peaceful contact too. Some of the whalers joined the tribal societies, taking Maori wives and even adopting Maori dress.

In 1814 Reverend Samuel Marsden founded a mission in New Zealand. Both islands had been seething with intertribal warfare, the guns (and diseases) brought over by the Pakeha exacting a heavy toll.

The missionaries served as peacemakers, providing welcome relief. First the chiefs, then the people accepted Christianity. The missionaries convinced them to also adopt European clothing, a change of questionable worth. Wearing European dress around 1840, a group of Maori looked to one outsider like beggars in rags. At the behest of the missionaries the people abandoned other long-standing customs: polygamy, slavery, and cannibalism.

The 1830s saw the European population jump from 150 to over 2,000. Captain William Hobson arrived during this time. Drawing up the Treaty of Waitangi, he had Maori chiefs sign away control of the islands to Britain in exchange for British protection and citizenship. Fifty chiefs signed the treaty on February 6, 1840; 500 more added their signatures later, but other chiefs refused to sign and protested:

> We, we only are the chiefs, the rulers. We will not be ruled over. What! thou a foreigner up and I down. Thou high and I . . . low! No, no, never, never.
>
> I will not agree to the mana [spiritual power] of a strange people being placed over this land. Though every chief in the island consents to it, yet I will not.
>
> (Kawharu 1989, pp. 263, 268)

Nevertheless, Britain recognized the treaty as valid. There was misunderstanding about how much power the chiefs were signing away, due partially to different versions of the treaty in the Maori and English languages. In English, for example, the treaty said the chiefs forfeited to the Queen *sovereignty* over New Zealand's affairs. In the Maori translation, the people ceded *governorship*. Disputes would follow about exact meanings. Meanwhile, the Queen guaranteed possession of their lands to the Maori, reserving for the Crown the right of pre-emption—the first option to buy Maori lands that were for sale.

Land wars. There followed twenty years (1840–1860) of incorporation of Pakeha goods and customs into Maori society. At the same time, conflict brewed. In 1844, one chief, Hone Heke, cut down a flagstaff, a symbol of British sovereignty. About 1,000 warriors supported him in a revolt that took a year to quell. This outbreak foreshadowed future strife. It is important to understand that the Maori did not operate as one unit but as a collection of separate tribes whose lands were threatened. Pakehas kept coming. Already they had occupied nearly the whole South Island and much of the North Island; by 1858, they outnumbered the Maori. In self-defense, some tribes decided to elect a Maori king and form a central government. Not all tribes joined the King Movement, but it endured, acquiring a monarch (its first being Te Wherowhero), a flag, a code of laws, a police force, and a territory (called the King Country).

Meanwhile, skirmishes between the Maori and Pakeha escalated into land wars from 1860 to 1870. They were fought by groups of Maori here and there, never on a national scale and not over an unbroken period. Furthermore, the wars did not cleanly pit one people against the other; some of the Maori fought for the British government. Using guerrilla tactics, the hostile tribes won victories but in the end were defeated by superior British fire power. Their fighting, though, had impressed the enemy.

Most memorable among wartime engagements is the 1864 Battle of Orakau, fought by 200 warriors and 100 women and children. Without a water supply or escape route, the choice of battle site was uncharacteristically unsound for the Maori. Yet the rebels resisted five assaults in three days before the situation inside the pa, or military stronghold, became hopeless. Still, they refused to surrender, instead choosing to break forward through the British line, their women and children in the center and best warriors up front:

> We rushed that line. They shot us and stabbed us with bayonets. We strove to break that line. As we reached it a soldier tried to bayonet me. I parried the point and shot that soldier . . . a man from the rear line stepped forward into the vacant space. I shot that man with my second barrel and darted through the line.
>
> (Belich 1986, p. 172)

Estimates placed British dead and wounded at sixty-nine, Maori at eighty.

Most notable among the rebel soldiers were Titokowaru and Te Kooti. In his exploits, Titokowaru employed a modern type of pa, which consisted of only earthworks below ground. He used this modern pa to wage a kind of trench warfare that proved extremely effective against enemy fire. The Maori rebels retreated from one pa to another until the late 1860s. Fighting longer than all the rest was the rebel Te Kooti. Te Kooti first supported the government, but one day was wrongfully arrested, then deported to Chatham Islands. Escaping from prison, he returned to wage the wars' most effective guerrilla campaign against the government. British forces, including Maori soldiers, doggedly pursued Te Kooti for three years, but the wily rebel eluded them. He became a master of the sudden raid, splitting his force into small parties for a flash attack. Over time, despite Te Kooti's deft warfare, the persistance of pro-British forces took its toll. His army grew ever weaker until 1872, when, undefeated but with only six remaining followers, Te Kooti finally retreated into King Country, an area closed to Pakehas.

The government ultimately confiscated 1,400,000 acres of Maori land to pay for the fighting during the Land Wars.

Integration. The next century saw the blending of the Maori into Pakeha society. Most of the land that had been left to the Maori was ultimately transferred to Pakeha hands. According to the Crown, all property belonged to the Maori and could not be taken without their consent or payment to them. So the Europeans set up a court to acquire Maori land. Formed in 1867, the Native Land Court transferred land owned collectively by an entire hapu to individual members of that hapu, who then could sell their parcels to outsiders. Some unsavory outsiders promptly advanced credit to Maori, who then had to sell their land in order to pay off their debts. By 1960 only four million acres remained in Maori hands.

There were efforts in politics and education to merge the Maori into larger society. In 1867 a southern, a northern, an eastern, and a western voting district were formed to elect four Maori members to the House of Representatives. That same year Native Schools opened in Maori settlements. The schools insisted on Maori students speaking English only, neglecting Maori language and history. Thus, the military power of the Pakehas was succeeded by cultural power. Their society became dominant, the population of Maori tribes dwindling until some predicted they would ultimately disappear. However, from the beginning of the twentieth century, the population began to recover.

By 1890, even the hostile Maori had emerged from the King Country to join larger society, taking paid, unskilled jobs, building roads, shearing sheep, and the like. In the interest of Maori rights, the people set up their own parliament, the Kotahitanga, in 1892. Dealing with the national government, it met for eleven years before being replaced by local councils. Some individual Maori gained stature in the national government, too; for example, Sir James Carroll (1853–1926) becoming New Zealand's acting Prime Minister.

Despite all this activity, the Maori remained segregated from the Pakehas in the first half of the twentieth century. In fact, the different tribes remained isolated even from one another, especially the commoners in Maori society, who were not allowed to attend intertribal celebrations.

Bicultural society. World Wars I and II brought far-reaching changes. In the First World War, the Pioneer Battalion of Maori fought with such bravery at Gallipoli and in France that it became difficult for Pakehas back home to exclude the Maori from full participation in national life. Still, legislation forbade the Maori from buying alcohol, for instance, or receiving government financial aid for housing. Then came World War II. Over 17,000 enlisted in the Maori Battalion, which fought valiantly in North Africa and Italy (a Maori, Moananui-a-Kiwa Ngarimu, won the Victoria Cross). Back home, 11,500 more Maori filled vacancies in factories and others formed a supporting Maori War Effort Organization. Tribalism was still a factor, resulting in disputes over leadership within the Maori Battalion itself, for example. Overall, though, these wartime organizations moved members beyond their tribal roots; they had begun to function as a single people.

The 1950s saw mass movement of the Maori to the cities, where they faced discrimination in employment, hotels, and the like because they were Maori, not because they belonged to a certain tribe. Treated as one people, they reacted in kind, not losing their tribal identities but placing them within the larger context of a Maori people. It was not until the 1970s, however, that many Maori viewed themselves as one distinct people. The early 1970s saw radical protest in relation to the Treaty of Waitangi and Maori land rights. In 1975 the Waitangi Tribunal was established as a vehicle through which Maori could air grievances about land. The Tribunal agreed to hear claims from Maori citizens who considered themselves prejudiced by any legislation or policy that was out of keeping with the Treaty of Waitangi. That same year, in the interest of not losing any more land to Pakeha owners, a woman named Whina Cooper led a land march from the far north to the seat of Parliament in Wellington. In keeping with Maori tradition, Whina addressed the marchers each morning, continually reminding them of the tapu (sacred) nature of their task; they should refrain from violence even if provoked by hostile bystanders. In the end 30,000 activists joined the Land Rights Movement, aiming to save the last three million acres of Maori territory. Without it, they feared, Maori culture would disappear. In 1977 the activists occupied, later winning back, disputed territory that had been earmarked for housing (Bastion Point). Such activism reflects a new approach by the Maori. They are reclaiming their place in New Zealand society.

Culture Today

Politics. Today's Maori comprise about ten percent of New Zealand's population. They continue to hold four Maori seats in Parliament, representing an eastern, southern, western, and northern Maori electorate in the country. Passed in 1974, an Electoral Amendment Act gives the people the right to choose if they will vote on the Maori or the general electoral ballot. About 400,000 claimed to be Maori. There are Maori activists who see participation in the general election as vital; also, considering the four seats in Parliament a token gesture, they advocate additional seats for Maori legislators.

Within the culture, politics once rested in *rangatiras* (chiefs) of a tribe's hapus, or subsections. They wielded power in daily affairs, though there was an overall tribal chief (called the *ariki*). Currently, most tribes have not one chief but a few elderly spokesmen for the tribe. The King Movement has endured, but its activity is now largely limited to regular gatherings and a coronation celebration.

Locally the Maori are organized into 400 government councils. The councils issue liquor permits and the like, communicating with Parliament through a national New Zealand Maori Council. At the grass roots level, the people have organized groups (for example, Nga Tamatoa in 1970) to combat racial discrimination in New Zealand. The minimum of racial strife here as compared to other societies is often lauded. Yet there has been enough inequality to stimulate such groups, despite the existence of a government Ministry of Maori Development to attend to the people's needs.

Economics. In the time of Classic Maori Culture, the Maori labored in teams. Men applied their digging sticks, chanting as they turned the earth, moving as if they were one person to the beat of ancient rhythms. The people seemed to work together whenever possible, even at tasks that could be performed alone. Besides planters, there were *tohunga*s, or specialists in different trades: the *tohunga whakairo* (carvers), the *tohunga whaihanga* (master builders), the *tohunga ahurewa* (priests). The period of assimilation in the late 1800s took the people into farming, forestry, and seasonal jobs such as road construction. With the move to the cities after World War II came entrance into a host of occupations, from engineering to medicine. Those who became self-employed tended to concentrate in the clothing industry.

The Maori still carry on their Polynesian tradition as boat men.
Courtesy of Wayne Mitchell.

Jobs on Maori land now provide employment for a minority of the Maori population. There are family farms and land corporations. Such a land corporation might, for example, divide 100,000 acres into separate sheep and cattle stations, which are controlled by an overall management committee.

In general, participation in the national work force has been lower for Maori citizens than for others in New Zealand society. In 1986, the Maori unemployment rate reached 14.9 percent, in contrast to the non-Maori rate of 5.8 percent.

Food, clothing, and shelter. Like other New Zealanders, the majority of Maori live mainly in single-story homes of wood, brick, or concrete. Traditional ideas of family often continue, despite the move from a rural to an urban setting. An individual, the Maori believe, is part of a family group, whose life outlasts that of any particular member. In keeping with this belief, and in contrast to the Pakehas' focus on immediate family, the Maori identify with anyone of their "bones," or any relative of a common ancestor. *Family*, in Maori society, normally means "large family"—thirty to fifty family members who are the descendants of a common ancestor plus their spouses and children. While Pakehas emphasize independence of the small family; the Maori stress continuity and interdependence among related small families. Today small Maori families occupy houses of their own, but nearly one-third of these households are shared with related kinfolk.

The closeness of the large family is evident in labels. Elders call their nieces' and nephews' children *grandson* and *granddaughter*, for example, as well as children of their own children. Such loose definitions enable Maori children to move freely between households, enjoying eating and sleeping privileges. Disrupting this custom to some degree, the mass movement to the city has resulted in members of the larger families not always living close by. So the Maori have adjusted to this changed condition by forming "kin clusters," looser groups of relatives who may not descend from the same ancestor.

Coastal and forest tribes first met their dietary needs by fishing, fowling, rat trapping, crop raising (yams, taro), and gathering (berries, shellfish). The Maori ate two meals a day, cooking in a pit (*hangi*) and eating their fare from small green flax baskets. European whalers introduced whale meat into the diet for a time. Also introduced were potatoes, which, along with other imports (see NEW ZEALANDERS), remain dietary staples.

At the height of Maori society, high fashion was the domain of the chiefly men, not the women. Flax, swamp grass, and the like served as material for belts, kilts, leggings, capes, and cloaks. Highly esteemed was the full-length dogskin cloak, its bottom and sides rimmed with a *taaniko* border (triangle, zigzag, diamond motifs). Among the accessories were white feathers in the ear, greenstone neck tikis, and for the men, facial and body tattoos. Women had tattoos etched into their chins.

Unique to the Maori was the art of carving a man's entire face. An artist would study the facial lines of the man to decide which ones needed accentuating. As he lay on the floor, his head on the artist's knees, the design was traced onto the face, then chiseled into the lines.

Tattooing was ultimately abandoned by the Maori, but certain garments have remained in use. A performance costume that gained favor with twentieth-century women was a kilt (worn over a European-style underskirt), taaniko bodice, tiki around the neck, taaniko-pattern headband, and shark earrings. Men favored a feather headband, taaniko bandolier (soldier's belt across the chest), and kilt worn over shorts. Today, the Maori normally wear European clothing, but they continue to lay an old-style cloak over a coffin after someone dies, in tribute to the full costume of earlier times. Traditional designs such as the taaniko pattern have found their way into present-day clothing.

Arts. Carving and oral arts (speeches, stories, proverbs, songs) have been dominant in the society. Maori carving features the tiki, more exactly the tiki-mania—an image with a birdlike head on a humanlike body that has arms and legs. While people may be able to identify the spirit or ancestor that a tiki is intended to represent, little is actually understood about the meaning of symbols used in the carvings.

On a larger scale, carving continues today in the building of *marae*s, or meeting houses. Figures of ancestors are carved in panels of the meeting houses—one-story rectangular structures with a deep-gabled porch. Regarded as places where spirits dwell to protect the living, the houses are not only named after an ancestor but also thought to represent his or her body. The front window is his eye, a visitor steps through the door into his chest, and the central rafter is his backbone. In today's cities there has been vigorous building of urban maraes. These urban maraes have helped inspire a larger than tribal identity among the people.

Traditionally the owners of a marae are entitled to special rights, most important being the right to speak there in public as host. The highly valued art of speechmaking has featured orators whose

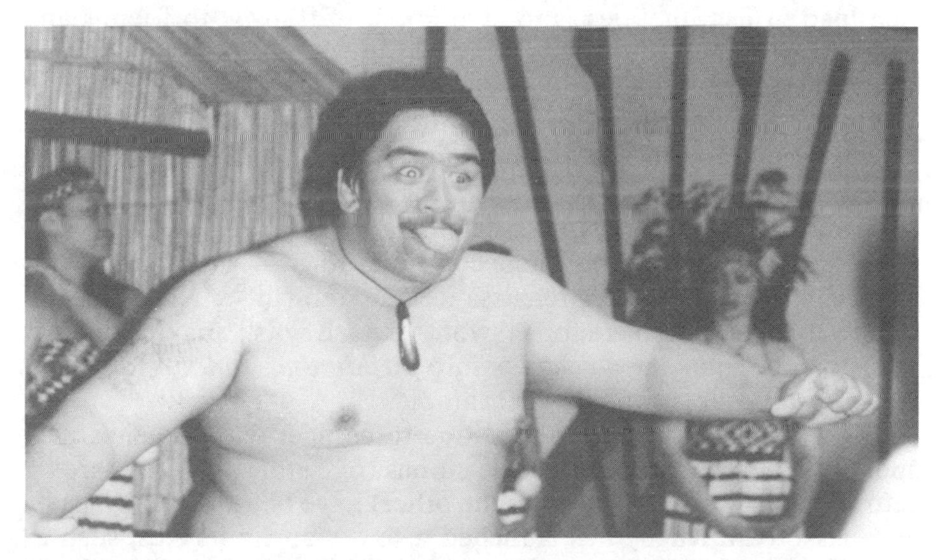

A Maori dancer sticks out his tongue as a symbol of defiance and independence. *Courtesy of Rebecca and Richard Harms.*

speeches are dramatic performances. They stride back and forth and utter words rhythmically, adding dramatic gestures from time to time, perhaps stamping their feet in the ten or fifteen minutes during which they speak.

Maori literature ranges from myths to poems about relations with the Pakehas. It was not until the 1970s that a written literature sprang into being. Renown among authors is Witi Ihimaera, who also edited an anthology of Maori writing. In it, the poem "Go Home, Maori" features a school child who is taunted by Pakehas:

how dare people here
become so incensed
about conditions
in countries
other than the lucky one
when the lucky one
does this
to its own?

(Ihimaera 1982, p. 289)

Values today. Without money at first, the people regarded gift giving as a highly valued activity. It was tied in to the idea of reciprocity, doing unto others as they have done to you, whether good or bad. Today this value remains alive, the obligation being to reciprocate good gifts. If someone, for example, wins at the races or hauls in a rich load of fish, the idea is to give much of it away to friends and relatives who will return the favor in times of need. From the high value placed on such generosity comes a tendency among the Maori to spend rather than save cash earnings.

Also valued is the Maori language. Though the people now speak mainly English, many of them are bilingual. At least seven variations of the Maori language exist, associated with different regions of the country. The language as a whole continues to grow, and is a positive sign of a general "Maori renaissance" or rebirth in New Zealand society today. Maori has adopted words from English, making distinct adjustments, changing *policeman* into *pirihimana*, *window* into *wini*, and *blanket* into *paraikete*, for example.

New values have been added due to contact with Pakehas. Old sports like kite flying and knuckle stones (five stones rapidly thrown into the air and caught one after the other) have been joined by rugby and basketball. Rugby has launched a few Maori atheletes, such as Tom Ellison and Bill Nepia, into national if not international fame. More subtly, rugby has encouraged harmony among the Pakehas and

Maori as well as Maoriness—the sense of belonging by the various tribes to one larger group. Urban life has also seen the growth of *komiti*, or associations among Maori—for example, a Maori Women's Welfare League.

Religion. Religion remains a priority. In the Classical period it was based on belief in eight major gods and a supreme god. During the mid to late nineteenth century, prophets (said to receive direct revelations) were the spiritual leaders. Today over one-fourth of the population belongs to the Anglican Church. Others belong to the Mormon Church or a native religious movement, notably Ringatu or Ratana. Revered as a saint, the rebel Te Kooti (see Historical Background) founded the Ringatu movement. The Ratana movement, begun by Tahupotiki Wiremu Ratana, set aside tribal allegiances to unite the Maori as one faithful remnant. Its leader broke sacred rules (of tapu) to demonstrate that the time was ripe for change in the organization of Maori society.

Education. Maori have experienced difficulty with Pakeha-style schooling. New Zealand's educational establishment is a Pakeha invention, based on Pakeha values. Maori culture originally trained its children by apprenticing them to *tohunga*s, specialists in different fields. A select few entered the *whare wananga*, a school of learning run by the priests, which taught children to value cooperation above competition and physical and social skills above intellectual achievements. With this heritage the Maori entered Pakeha schools, which placed a premium on individuality, competition, and the intellect. The clash has resulted in Maori students progressing more slowly than their Pakeha counterparts, and in a lower proportion receiving advanced degrees. Only recently have schools begun to teach the Maori language and aspects of the cultural history. Progress and subjects in formal schooling for Maori youth remain widespread concerns.

Holidays. Although New Zealand experiences less intercultural hatred than other Asian and Pacific Island societies, in recent years the Maori have influenced one of the nation's major holiday celebrations. Waitangi Day commemorates the Maori-Pakeha treaty. Protesting against the hypocrisy of "celebrating" so controversial a treaty, the Maori have over the years convinced the government to tone down the holiday into one of commemoration rather than celebration. Their protest is evidence that the Maori are now striving vigorously for a bicultural nation. The aim is to retain their identity, perhaps separately, but more likely in a way that ensures their economic growth and their equality in a partnership that could be an exciting bicultural model.

For More Information

Belich, James. *The New Zealand Wars and the Victorian Interpretation of Racial Conflict*. Auckland: Auckland University Press, 1986.

Ihimaera, Witi and Long, D. S., eds. *Into the World of Light: An Anthology of Maori Writing*. Auckland, New Zealand: Heinemann, 1982.

Kawhara, I. H., ed. *Waitangi: Maori and Pakeha Perspectives of the Treaty of Waitangi*. Auckland: Oxford University Press, 1989.

Orbell, Margaret. *The Natural World of the Maori*. Dobbs Ferry: Sheridan House, 1985.

MENANGKABAU

(min ang′ ka bau)

One of the peoples of Sumatra and Malaysia;
sometimes spelled *Minangkabau.*

Population: 6,000,000 (1990 estimate).
Location: Sumatra, Malaya.
Language: Javanese.

Geographical Setting

Sumatra, the fifth-largest island in the world, lies divided by the equator south of the Malay peninsula. More than 1,000-miles long and about 260-miles wide, this island includes flat plains on the eastern side and a range of mountains, the Barisan Mountains, on the

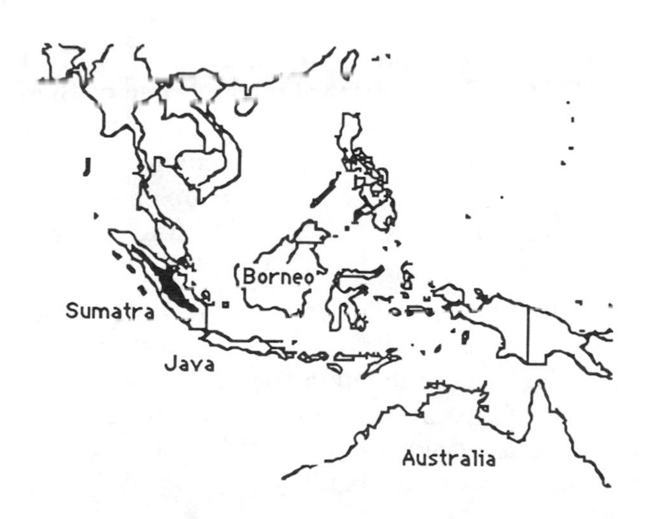

west side stretching the entire length of Sumatra. Midway on the coast below this mountain range is the city of Padang, believed to be the center of the early Hindu kingdom that ruled most of the island. A Malay people, the Menangkabau live in the central mountains above Padang.

Historical Background

The Menangkabau are a Malayan people who once founded a separate kingdom in the highlands of central Sumatra and who still live in that area, although members of the group have spread throughout the Malay peninsula. At one time they were the center of a Hindu-Malayan empire that controlled the plateau region.

Emerging power. The Menangkabau first emerged as a politically powerful people in Indonesia before the fourteenth century, at a time when the Hindu empire Srivijaya controlled large portions of Sumatra and Malaya. The royal family that established itself in Sumatra during this period were Menangkabau. Among their accomplishments was the development of trade with outside peoples in the sixteenth and seventeenth centuries. Contact with outsiders brought conversion to the Islamic religion in the seventeenth century. In the eighteenth century, the Menangkabau extended their influence by conquering the area of Johore on the Malay peninsula.

They remained in control until Sumatra was taken over by the Dutch in the nineteenth century. By that time, the Menangkabau had spread through Sumatra and Java while keeping their base near Padang. North of Padang, another group, the Asahan, had settled and established a more strict Islamic tradition. Some of these, the Padri, or fervent Muslims who had made the mandated trip to Mecca, attempted to impose their beliefs on the Menangkabau, in direct contrast to the matriarchal pattern of this people. Thus, the Menangkabau came to look on the Dutch as protectors of their lifestyles.

Civil war. Taking advantage of this inner conflict, the Padri War (1803–1837) between the new Islamic religious leaders and the traditional rulers, the Dutch entered the war in support of the traditional rulers, subsequently assuming control of the area. They reorganized government, established schools, created towns, and introduced modern business and industry into an agricultural society.

Independence from Dutch. A movement for independence from the Dutch developed in Sumatra in the early twentieth century and gained popular support when the Japanese occupied the country during World War II. The Menangkabau played an active role in the Indonesian revolution against the Dutch, which began in the 1930s but climaxed after liberation from the Japanese forces from 1945 to 1949. A Javanese/Balinese leader, Sukarno, led this revolution aided strongly by two Menangkabau political leaders, Mohammad Hatta and Sutan Sjahrir. On December 27, 1949, Indonesia became independent, the Dutch withdrew, and the Menangkabau began playing a prominent role among the political leaders of the new democratic republic. However, they soon found themselves at odds with the Javanese largely because of the style of politics in the two groups. Menangkabau built political parties based on respect for all members and wide dispersal of information. Javanese politics was based on the older structures of a political elite and peasants. Nevertheless, since he represented the largest group, Sukarno soon gained complete control, disbanded the legislature that had been defined by a constitution, and began to rule as a dictator. In recent years, the differences have led to some agitation for separate governments, agitation that has been stimulated by the unequal production of goods in Java and Sumatra. Sumatra has become the supplier of necessary goods to an ever-growing Java population.

Culture Today

Women. According to legend, the people of Sumatra owned a starving female calf that defeated a champion bull from Java. *Minang* means "winning" and *kebau* names the animal that was defeated. The people were named Menangkabau in celebration of this victory. The old story illustrates the importance of women in Menangkabau society. Although men represent the Menangkabau in government and business, women dominate other aspects of the people's life. Women own all the property of the Menangkabau family. The community house is the property of a headwoman, her sisters, their daughters and their children. Husbands have no homes of their own but live in the homes of their mothers and are only visitors in the homes of their wives.

Homes. The community house is a large, ornate, rectangular structure raised high above the ground. A saddle-shaped roof covers the house, and most of the inside space is devoted to a main room. Adjoining it are small living compartments for different wives, daughters, and their children. The Muslim religion allows the family to include four wives. In Menangkabau society, men are visitors in the homes of their wives, living near their mother's community house, helping with the farm chores of the mother, but mostly free to engage in politics (in which a man represents his mother's clan) and business. A man also serves as chief of his mother's clan under her direction.

Government. Men have always been the main participants in the government of the people. The Menangkabau divide themselves into clans made up of related families from neighboring community houses. A male member of each house represents the family in a council that makes decisions for the clan. Representatives of several clans then participate in the largest council of traditional government, the *negari.* On the national level, men from Menangkabau communities participate in Indonesia's House of Representatives (Dewan Perwakilan Rakyat) and the People's Consultative Assembly (Majelis Permusyawaratan Rakayat) when the constitution is in force.

Religion. The Menangkabau have practiced Islam since the seventeenth century but continue to include previous Malayan religious practices. They have resisted Islamic tenets that would weigh against their matriarchal structure. In addition, professional magicians conduct ceremonies to produce rain, inspire love, or thwart enemies. Mediums provide ancient cures for illness and practice soul-catching. Thread is fastened around the wrists of women during childbirth to prevent their soul from escaping during delivery.

Economy. The traditional economy of the people was agricultural and it continues to provide more than half of the livelihood. Women own the fields and perform most of the labor, growing rice, maize, peanuts, fruits, vegetables, and tapioca for their families. Rubber, clove, and coffee are grown as cash crops. Sowing and planting is done by the women, but men return home from their *rantau* (temporary places to which they migrate) to assist with the harvesting.

Food. The farming provides grains, fruits, and vegetables for everyday foods. Buffalo are kept for their milk, which is eaten as a thin yogurt, and fish are a regular food in the diet. Both men and women buy and sell farm products, household goods, and cloth at weekly markets.

City life. In Malaya, Menangkabau men are becoming important in commercial agricultural production and as wage laborers in businesses. In cities they work as factory managers, restaurant owners, hotel clerks or owners, and teachers, for example. The villages are largely empty of men during a large part of the agricultural season. Modern business has provided the men with new avenues for success and is changing the balance of importance between male and female in Menangkabau society.

For More Information

Kahn, Joel S. *Minangkabau Social Formations: Indonesian Peasants and the World Economy.* London: Cambridge University Press, 1980.

Lewis, Reba. *Indonesia: Troubled Paradise.* New York: David McKay Company, 1960.

Thomas, Lynn L. and Franz von Brenda, editors. *Change and Continuity in Minangkabau.* Columbus: Ohio University Press, 1985.

MONGOLS

(maun′ gols)

The various peoples of Mongolia and northern China.

Population: 3,000,000 (1990 estimate).
Location: Mongolian People's Republic, China.
Language: Many dialects of Mongol.

Geographical Setting

Sweeping across southern Russia and present-day Mongolia is a vast grassland, or steppe. Across this region, nomadic herders and hunters once roamed freely. Here the winters are harsh, but the other seasons produce abundant grasses on which great numbers of cattle, goats, sheep, camels, and horses can graze. In Mongolia, this steppe is broken by a mountain range, the Khangai, then drops to a plateau three- to four-thousand-feet high. The plateau gives way in the southeast to the Gobi Desert, which extends into China. The entire area is a dry land, averaging from ten to fifteen inches of rain annually, except in the Gobi Desert, where less than five inches is normal annual rainfall.

Mongolia is the present home of the largest population of Mongols, who once ruled much of the land from Hungary through China. However, many Mongols live in the Inner Mongolia area of the People's Republic of China.

Historical Background

Origin myth. According to Mongolian legend, a wolf and doe mated to produce the first Mongols. After twelve generations, a Mongolian woman, Alan Gooa, had three sons who were fathered by a beam of

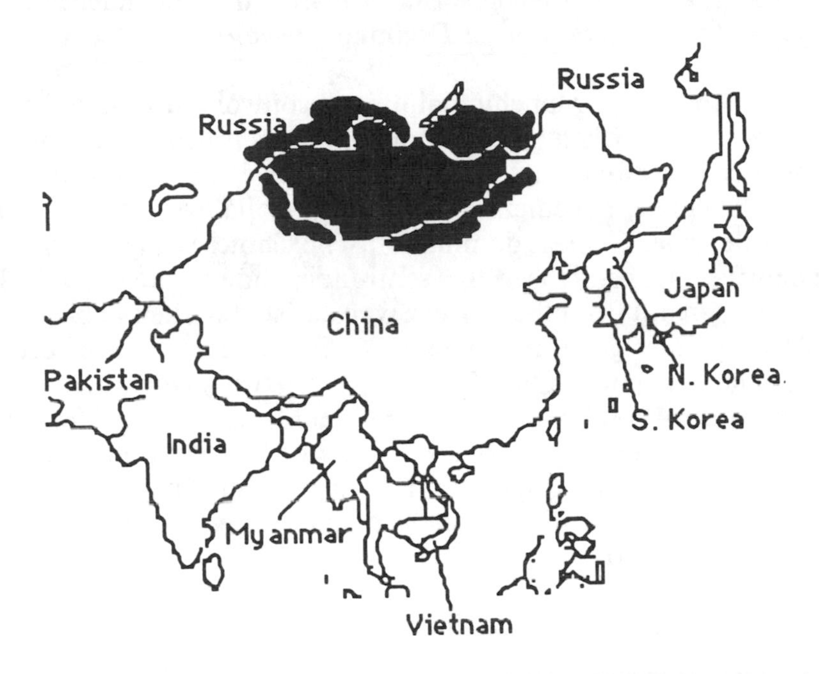

light. The youngest son began a line of descendants that, after nine generations, produced Genghis Khan.

Early history. Historical records show that the first Mongol empire began in 1206 when the chieftan Temujin changed his name to Genghis and was elected khan, or prince, of the people. Genghis was the first to unite groups of Mongol and Turkic peoples into a warrior force. Superior military strategy and tactics brought success in one assault after another until the Mongols controlled much of Asia. Northern China was conquered in 1215, a portion of Turkistan was overrun around 1220, and southern Russia was seized in 1223. War in China brought death to Genghis Khan in 1227.

Division. The empire was divided among sons in succeeding generations so that khans ruled over increasingly smaller portions of territory. Genghis's grandson Kublai Khan united northern and southern China under one Mongol kingdom for the first time in the 1260s, and his empire lasted until 1368. Then various Mongol princes fought amongst themselves until the last emperor, Ligdan Khan, died in 1636. The Manchu invaded and conquered Mongol territory in the early 1600s, and the Mongols formally lost their independence to the Manchu at the Convention of Dolonnor in 1691.

Independence. The Manchu maintained control until the successful rebellion of 1911, when leading Mongol nobles proclaimed Mongolia an independent monarchy. War with China in 1915 was inconclusive but resulted in an agreement to reduce Mongolia from independence to self-rule under Chinese domination. The Chinese general Xu Shuzeng deprived Mongolians of this semi-independent rule in 1920. The people sought aid from the Soviets, who assisted in the establishment of a Communist government in 1921 and a secret police force in 1922. Another portion of the original territory remained under Chinese control and became known as Nei Mongol (Inner Mongolia). A portion became the People's Republic of Mongolia in 1924, and the country adopted a constitution modeled after that of the Soviets. Later, during World War II, some of the Mongolian territory was absorbed by the Soviet Union.

Dictatorship. In 1936, Mongolia fell under the dictatorship of Marshal Choybalsan, who controlled the people using methods as severe as those of Joseph Stalin in Russia. A long series of political purges and an anti-religious campaign resulted. The old guard of Mongolian revolutionaries and intellectuals was largely liquidated on false charges of treason. About 130,000 Mongols were sent to forced labor camps or resettled in Siberia and Central Asia. Many fled to China. The existence of Mongolian culture was routinely denied. No Mongol literature was permitted in the schools, and churches were destroyed. Choybalsan died in 1952 and Mongol literature was permitted again in 1956, but the Communist policy prevented displays of national loyalty. The 1962 celebration of the eight-hundredth birthday of Genghis Khan was cancelled because it might encourage feelings of nationalism at the expense of loyalty to Communism.

Recent development. The five-year plan (1981–1985) set specific targets for industry as well as housing and agriculture. The people of Mongolia do not operate any major industry, but there is limited output of coal, cement, bricks, knitwear, footwear, meat, and other consumer goods. The seventh five-year plan (1986–1990) confirmed an economic union with the now disintegrated Soviet Union under which Mongolia would receive aid in developing much needed power plants. In 1990 a government infused with representation from new factions in Mongolia recognized the weakness of collectivization of agriculture as it had been practiced in that country for more than forty years and opened all livestock holdings to private ownership.

Culture Today

Appearance. Mongols tend to have stocky builds. Their skin varies from yellow to dark brown, they have short heads covered with dark hair, and the cheekbones on their round faces are high. While the angles of their eyes and nose create the impression of flatness, the tilted axis of their black or brown eyes gives the impression of a slant. Their stature is short, averaging five-and-one-half feet.

Cities, villages, and nomads. Traditionally the Mongols have been nomadic herdsmen. Organized under Ghengis Khan into a military order based on tens, hundreds, and thousands, the Mongols of the 1200s and 1300s lived in circular tents—yurts—which they sometimes mounted on wagons for permanency and easy transportation. Before that time, the Mongol people probably supported themselves by herding cattle, sheep, goats, and some camels, and by hunting. Today close to forty-five percent of the people live in towns and twenty-two percent of the population has settled into permanent communities in the rural areas. The remainder lead the traditional nomadic lifestyle, mostly raising sheep, goats, cattle, and horses. Flocks of camel, oxen, and yak are less commonly found among the Mongol herds.

Family life. In the 1300s and 1400s, at the peak of their world importance, the house-unit was a single family, with a father who was a serf to an under-chief and served mostly as a warrior, a wife whose duties were endless, and their children. Men made the carts and wagons and built the frames of the houses. They also made bits and saddles for the horses and their own weapons of war. The training and care of the horses were men's responsibilities, including the milking of the mares, and beating the milk in leather bags to separate the kurd from that part used to make *kumiss* (fermented mare's milk). When the family moved to better pastureland or to a battle site, women drove the carts and dismantled and set up the tents. They also milked the cows, made butter, tanned the hides, sewed clothing, made the felt for clothing and tents, cooked, and cared for the children. The family conserved their limited water supply by not laundering their clothes or washing out food containers.

Some of these tasks and the division of labor still exists among the nomadic Mongols. However, more than half of the people of Mongolia in the 1990s live in cities and towns where food can be bought in the marketplace, and where men work for wages in a growing number of industries, such as clothing manufacturing and brick and concrete making. Their age-old dependence on animals continues. The making of woolen cloth, clothing, and carpets are major occupations.

Cooperatives. Under the Great Khans from Genghis to Kublai, Mongol families were required, under penalty of death, to adhere to a strict set of behaviors. Their cooperative action was to fight under a mandate said to have come from the supreme God to subjugate all other people. But while fighting or at peace they were to honor all religions, protect the innocent, respect learned and wise men everywhere, love one another, share provisions, not steal, not commit adultery, not bear false witness, not betray anyone, and spare the aged and poor. While each family was expected to serve the Khan in his battles to extend Mongol territory, each was expected to find its own food and water supplies.

Today, Mongol herders and agricultural workers are in the process of reversing Communist collectivization in Mongolia and are now breaking up cooperatives and state farms. There were 200 herding cooperatives and 60 state farms. The government owned and controlled the farms. Workbooks were issued and kept by farmers who were paid according to the amount of labor performed. Mainly the farmers raised cereals, potatoes, and vegetables. The herding cooperatives were organized into a number of brigades, each with its assigned territory and tasks. A brigade was further subdivided into bases; a base might have included two households looking after a set number of livestock. Decollectivization began in 1990 and will require some years to fully disband this highly organized structure.

Food, clothing, and shelter. Today, as in the past, the livestock of nomadic Mongol households provide material for clothing as well as food products. In the past meals were chiefly meat—mutton and wild game, occasionally supplemented by beef. From the herds came milk that was made into cheese and cheese-curd. Some grain and rice were added to the diet as they were imported from conquered countries. Milk was a popular drink, as was *kumiss*, a slightly alcoholic beverage made from mare's milk. Today meat, milk, cheese, and butter form the main foods in the traditional diet. The amount of meat is limited. Tea is popular, and fermented mare's milk is also a common Mongol beverage.

As in earlier days, the livestock of nomadic Mongol households provide material for clothing as well as food products. The followers of Genghis Khan and his successors, of both sexes, wore trousers covered by long woolen robes, fastened over the chest. Boots of leather or felt, felt caps, and sometimes woolen overcoats completed the dress. For the summer months, the woolen garments were replaced with cotton or silk obtained from China by those who could afford to do so. Since war was the occupation of all able-bodied men, weapons were a constant and integral part of the male dress. Each man wore a sword and a light sabre along with a bow or two and separate quivers for light and heavy arrows. In battle the warrior wore a steel cap with a leather neckpiece and a short jacket (jerkin) of lacquered leather. He might also carry a metal or leather shield.

The yurt has remained the home of some of today's nomadic Mongols. As in the days of the Great Khans, parents and children live in this traditional Mongol dwelling. The yurt is a circular tent with an expandable frame that measures twenty to thirty feet in diameter. More ornate today, the yurts began as simple circular felt tents most often divided into two parts by curtains that separated the husband's room from that of the wife and children. Some of the yurts in the days of the Khans were too large for easy assembly and disassembly and were mounted permanently on large wagons.

The long-lasting advantage of the yurt was and is that it can be assembled by two people within one-half hour. First, a collapsible wood floor is laid. The floor is usually thickly carpeted, providing a cushion for the traditional bed, which is a sleeping pad. Then, four-foot-high lattice walls are placed around the floor and a red door installed. Finally, the frame is covered with layers of heavy felt made from yak or sheep's wool and held in place by ropes. A lighter material, canvas, might be used as a covering in the summer. However, many nomads today have substituted a low spreading tent, a *maikhan,* for the yurt. The maikhan requires less wood, a material not readily available on the western steppe.

Increasingly, today's Mongols are becoming settled and new customs are finding their way into the household. In Mongolia in the 1990s, 225,000 households have radios and about 125,000 have television sets. Television broadcasting has been expanded so that fifty percent of the people of Mongolia have access to this medium.

Government. In the days of the Great Khans, land was owned by the Khan and managed by nobles who were in charge of the tens, hundreds, and thousands of warriors. There was little dependence on agriculture, and the horses and other animals were allowed to roam over large areas of grasslands to graze. The grazing lands were shared by all the warriors.

Land and natural resources, along with industry, are basically still owned by the government in Mongolia. Cooperative ownership is mainly related to livestock; there is a limited degree of private ownership of sheep, goats, cattle, and horses. Political power rests in the People's Great Hural (Assembly) whose members are elected every four years by the people. Political divisions include eighteen *aymags*, or provinces, which are further subdivided into *hoshuns*, and then *sumuns*. Among the nomads, there is the unit known as the *bag*, which includes ten to fifteen households that may travel over a strictly regulated distance.

Social structure. All the Mongols ruled by the khans were divided into family units. The men of these units were organized under a lesser chief by tens, and these by tens, and tens again, to make an important fighting unit. But after the decline of the great Mongol empires in the 1500s and 1600s, social status was associated with livestock owned and with hereditary rank. At the lowest level were the masses of free nomads, or *arat*. Above them were the nobles, or *taiji*. The *khans,* or princes, occupied the highest level and, for a time, power and social status passed from princes to religious leaders of the Mongols. This structure has tended to break down under government pressure for Communism.

Religion. The oldest religion of the Mongols is animism. The followers believed in spirits of the mountains, forests, rocks, winds and other natural forces. The ancestors of today's Mongols during the period of the Great Khans were also shamanists who believed in spiritual leaders that used magic to influence natural forces for good or evil. However, the Mongols then believed in a supreme God of Heaven, Tengri, and in a Goddess of Earth, Nachigai. Prayers and offerings were made to these gods, whom the Mongols believed had decreed that they should be warriors and determined their successes or failures in battle. Some houses also had idols made of felt to protect the man and his wife, called the master's brother and the mistress's brother. These thirteenth-century people believed in an afterlife; it is reported that some chiefs were buried sitting on their horses and with other horses, along with food were buried alongside.

As these fighters came into contact with Chinese and other Asians, some of them became followers of Lamaism, a compromise religion that was a combination of the original animist practices and Buddhist beliefs. A number of Mongols in the former Soviet Union adopted Christianity and now belong to the Russian Orthodox Church.

Before the Communist takeover of Mongolia, the Mongols there, as well as the Mongols of Inner Mongolia, were Mahayana Buddhists, led by priests, or lamas. In the 1930s, religions were discouraged. Images of Buddha were replaced by pictures of Karl Marx and the Islamic mosques of the Kazakh neighbors of the Mongols were destroyed. Although later revisions of the Mongolia constitution separated church and state and permitted religious activities, only part of the Mongols now profess Buddhism. There is one chief monastery (Gandantegchinien) in the country, at Ulan Bator, and it houses about 100 lamas.

Recreation. Popular recreation includes archery, wrestling, horse racing and chess. Epic literature has been written on the athletic ability of Mongol heroes of the past. It cannot be universally enjoyed, however, because schooling among the nomads has been limited.

Education. Under the rule of the Great Khans, there were no schools, although the Mongols widely respected the educated people among those they conquered.

Even today, the nomadic life does not encourage all children to attend school, even though schools have been built by the government in the cities, and boarding schools have been built for nomadic families with the goal of raising the proportion of children enrolled. In the 1990s 45.6 percent of the Mongols in Mongolia attended school. Special secondary schools and technical schools train both nomadic and settled students for agricultural, service, and industrial jobs. Consequently the future lifestyle of the nomads may differ from that of their parents.

For More Information

Phillips, E. D. *The Mongols.* New York: Frederick A. Praeger, 1969.

The Europa Yearbook, 1991. Europa Publications Limited, 1991.

The Far East and Australia, 1992. Europa Publications Limited, 1992.

NEPALESE

(neh′ pah leez)

Native inhabitants of the Kingdom of Nepal.

Population: 20,000,000 (1991 estimate).
Location: Nepal, in south-central Asia.
Languages: Nepali and various Hindi and Tibeto-Burman dialects.

Geographical Setting

Landlocked, oblong-shaped Nepal lies between northeastern India and Tibet. About the size of Florida, Nepal can be geographically divided into four vertical regions. A strip of fertile plain called the Tarai, about five-to-twenty miles wide and 500-miles long, runs along the Indian border. The Tarai is home to about one-third of Nepalese, but produces two-thirds of the nation's agricultural output. Rising abruptly from the Tarai run two close-set, jumbled mountain ranges, the Siwalik Hills and the Mahabharat Lekh. These ranges, sparsely populated because of their poor soil, reach heights of 2,000 to 5,000 feet. North of them, around the central Katmandu Valley, spread low-lying hills and valleys that are home to over half of Nepalese. Katmandu, the capital, has a population of 400,000.

Looming high over the hills to the north, pushed skyward by India's ancient collision with the Asian continent, rise the mountains for which Nepal is famous—the Himalayas. This massive range has its heart in Nepal, though it extends farther eastward and westward. Among its jagged peaks are nine of the ten highest in the world, eight of which lie in Nepal or on its borders. They include Mount Everest, at 29,028 feet the world's highest point. Called Sagarmatha (Brow of the Ocean) by the Nepalese, it straddles the border with Tibet.

Nepal's climate varies with its terrain. In the Tarai, part of India's Ganges Plain, summer temperatures often exceed 100 degrees Fahr-

enheit. Climate in the Katmandu Valley is more moderate—although it lies over 4,000 feet above sea level, its latitude is about that of Florida. While winters have some frost and snow, the people can usually bring in three harvests each year. In the Himalayas, by contrast, short cool summers limit farming. Hardy potatoes and barley provide staples in the sparsely populated Himalaya valleys. Winters are severe—windy and cold, with heavy snowfall.

Historical Background

Kirati civilization. Few records of the Nepalese's origins survive, save in the myths and legends of the ancient past. The area is mentioned in such ancient Hindu epics as the *Mahabharata* and the *Ramayana*, showing cultural connections with northern India from about 800 B.C. A people called the Kiratis are said to have invaded from the east at about that time, establishing a kingdom in the central Katmandu Valley. The Mahabharata recounts how their first king, Yalambar, died in the epic's great battle. For perhaps 1,000 years, Kirati culture, rich in export crafts and architecture, held sway in the central valley.

Siddhartha Gautama. During this time, in the 500s B.C., Nepal became the birthplace of one of the world's great religions, Buddhism. In about 550, a Hindu prince named Siddhartha Gautama was born near Lumbini, in the western Tarai. As a young man, Gautama decided to devote his life to searching for spiritual wisdom and enlightenment. Eventually, he became the Buddha, or Enlightened One. He spent the rest of his long life preaching his enlightenment, which is called Buddhism. This reflective, non-violent religion, stressing compassion and self-restraint, ultimately spread throughout Asia (see ASIAN RELIGIONS).

Licchavi rulers and Tibet. Around the A.D. 300s, a northern Indian people called the Licchavis invaded and overthrew the last Kirati rulers. By the 500s, the Licchavis had established a powerful state in the central valley, in which a Hindu aristocracy ruled over a largely Buddhist population. At the same time, a strong kingdom centered in Tibet emerged north of the Himalayas. For the first time, extensive trade arose through the Himalaya passes, and Nepal became a meeting ground of Asian and Indian cultures. These connections helped spread Buddhism north of the Himalayas, and as far east as Japan and Korea. Tibet became firmly Buddhist, while Nepal—the land of Buddha's birth—over the centuries became more and more Hindu. Still, a Buddhist undercurrent remained, fed by Tibetan and other Asian immigrants in remote areas of the north and east.

Malla Dynasties. From the 1000s to the 1700s, Nepal fell under a new group of Hindu rulers, who collectively came to be known as the Mallas. Eventually, three Malla kingdoms shared the Katmandu Valley with the rest of what is now Nepal, ruled by dozens of smaller independent Hindu kingdoms. Malla origins are unclear, but it seems likely that the new rulers came to escape Muslim invaders in north India. During the long Malla period, the basic pattern of Indian aristocracy and Asian subjects became more firmly established. Links between the ruling classes of the various kingdoms were common, with intermarriage occurring frequently between powerful families.

Shah kings and modern Nepal. One of these kingdoms, Gorkha, in western Nepal, benefited from both a strategic location and a line of politically astute rulers, the Shahs. In 1768, King Prithvi Narayan Shah of Gorkha invaded and conquered the Katmandu Valley, a small part of which was called Nepal. King Prithvi Shah used the central valley as a power base, creating the first unified Nepalese state. After consolidating rule in Nepal, the Shah rulers began a campaign of expansion. An invasion of Tibet ended in defeat by Chinese troops. In the south, Shah ambitions were frustrated by defeat at the hands of the British, India's colonial rulers. After a two-year war, the Shah king signed a "Treaty of Friendship" in 1816, giving up much of Nepal's conquered land and establishing borders similar to those today. (The Nepali soldiers, many from the Gorkha region, had impressed the British, who drafted a number of them into the British army. These are the famous Gurkhas, who still serve in the British and Indian armies today [see GURKHAS].) After these defeats at foreign hands, the Shah kings closed Nepalese borders to all foreigners. With few exceptions, the borders remained closed until 1951.

Rana ascendance. In 1846, an army general named Jung Bahadur Rana took over the Nepali government, assassinating his opponents in what came to be known as the Kot (Courtyard) Massacre. Rana named himself prime minister and made the position hereditary. The Shah kings, stripped of power, remained as figureheads. In the 104 years in which they held power, the Ranas made some attempts to modernize Nepali society. They abolished forced labor and built schools and colleges, including a college for women. However, the lot of the common farmer remained a poor one, while Rana friends and relatives received the best land and other advantages. By the mid-1900s, the Ranas themselves had become numerous and divided. As dramatic regional developments followed World War II, political events caught up with the Ranas in 1951.

Shah return. In the late 1940s, Nepal's two giant neighbors underwent violent upheavals. To the southwest, India freed herself of British rule and underwent a brief but bloody civil war. India's new government opposed the Ranas, threatening to take over Nepal. To the northeast, Chinese Communists, after a long civil war, finally ousted the Nationalist Party of Chiang Kai-shek. The new Communist government, reviving China's ancient claims on Tibet, annexed that country in 1950. Thousands of Tibetan refugees fled to Nepal. In this turbulent atmosphere, a Nepali movement arose to restore the king, Tribhuvan Shah, viewing him as a supporter of democracy. King Tribhuvan, with Indian support, took over peacefully in 1951.

Panchayat democracy. Over the following decades, Tribhuvan and his successors experimented with different forms of government. In

1962, Tribhuvan's son King Mahendra established a system of local and national congresses called *panchayats*, elected without political parties and limited by the king's power. In a national referendum held in 1980 under Mahendra's son King Birendra, Nepalese voted to continue this unique system of government.

Culture Today

Harmony in diversity. While the general cultural divide in Nepali society is between Hindu- and Tibetan-based blocs, each bloc itself comprises a complex mosaic of ethnic groups. Furthermore, in many if not most of these groups, Hindu and Tibetan strands have become interwoven. Thus, an Indian Hindu from the Tarai will more than likely share some beliefs with the most remote Buddhist villager. This fusion, cemented by political unity under Shah kings, gives Nepalese their own distinctive character. It has also given rise to tolerance and cooperation, preventing the ethnic strife that plagues other culturally diverse lands. Although their resources are scarce and poverty is widespread, Nepalese seem always happy to get along with each other.

The Tarai. In the Tarai, populated by Hindus and separated from the rest of Nepal by the Siwalik and Mahabharat mountain ranges, Nepal turns its face toward India. Here Nepalese tend to be conservative, retaining the rigid caste system that divides Indian society. They move freely over the border with India, a border which is frequently spanned by marriage or business connections. Most live in small farming villages. Of the caste groups, the largest are the Brahmans and Chetris, formerly the priestly and warrior classes of ancient times. Smaller groups include the Tharu, descendants of the Tarai's earliest inhabitants, and the Danuwar, Majhi, and Darai.

Katmandu and the middle hills. Brahmans and Chetris also live in the hill districts west of Katmandu Valley. With them, and dispersed north and east of Katmandu, live the numerous groups sometimes referred to collectively as Gurkhas. These tough, resilient hill peoples—Gurung, Magar, Rai, Limbu, Yakha and Sunuwar—have traditionally supplied the famous soldiers of the same name. (No single ethnic group goes by the name Gurkha.) Dominating Nepal's heartland, the Katmandu Valley, are the Newars, who mix Tibetan and Indian heritages. Newari cultural traditions provide the core of Nepal's artistic inheritance (see below). In Katmandu itself can be seen

Nepal's ethnic diversity in a nutshell. Newari merchants and artisans, Magar sheep farmers offering animals for sale, weavers, or farmers from various hill villages, uniformed schoolchildren, Western tourists, and Himalayan villagers—all mix together on the city's colorful, dusty streets.

Peoples of the high mountains. In the sparse, poor villages of the Himalayan valleys live Tibetan-speaking, Buddhist peoples. These farmers of small plots and yak-herders eke out a high-altitude existence. The yak, a long-haired Asian ox, provides milk as a staple food, while its hides and wool are used in clothing and shelter. The Tamang people are farmers and artisans, often specializing in wicker-work or basketry. The Thakalis, Nepal's most successful entrepreneurs, traditionally dominated the ancient salt trade between Tibet and India. Today they have transferred their enterprising energy to business fields such as construction, as well as areas such as politics, the arts, and the academic world.

"Tigers of the Snow." Most famous of all Himalayan peoples, however, are the Sherpas. From their villages in the high mountains of north-central and eastern Nepal, they have acquired a worldwide reputation for strength and endurance. Since the early 1900s, Sherpas have served as porters and guides on Himalayan mountain-climbing expeditions. Bred to the demands of high-altitude exertion, Sherpa men and women for decades have cheerfully carried loads of up to 120 pounds in conditions that would leave the average Westerner gasping after a few steps. It was a Sherpa, the now-legendary Tenzing Norgay, who shared the first ascent of Everest in 1953 with Sir Edmund Hillary of New Zealand. Since then, Sherpas have become world-class mountaineers in their own right, though many still make a good living as guides or porters for the thousands of climbers and hikers who visit Nepal each year.

Food, clothing, and shelter. Owing to regional diversity, Nepal has never developed a distinctive style of cooking. The most flavorful dishes, borrowed from Indian cuisine, are found among Tarai peoples and the Newari. They include spicy curries of lamb or chicken with vegetables, served with rice, the staple of the fertile plains. Rice is also commonly eaten with *dahl*, a thick lentil soup. Barley, potatoes, and dairy products are staples of the high altitudes. Barley is ground raw and mixed with milk or water to make *tsampa*, which is used instead of rice. Potatoes, introduced in the 1700s, have done much to improve the diet of the high villages. They are eaten boiled, baked, or made into pancakes called *gurr*. Cheese, yogurt, and clarified butter called *ghee* are eaten alone or mixed with other foods. Tea is the national drink, brewed with milk and sugar or, in the mountains, mixed with yak-butter, Tibetan-style. Mountain people also enjoy *chang*, a strong beer brewed from fermented barley.

In the Tarai and elsewhere, Brahmans and Chetris dress in the Indian way. Women wear cotton or silk *saris* (wraparound skirts) and tunics with loose pants. The men frequently wear Western-style shirts and pants, especially in cities and larger towns. All Nepalese women favor jewelry, the most common being bead necklaces, ear-

A Nepalese pagoda. *Courtesy of Shiva Rea Bailey.*

rings, and nose rings. In the temperate middle hills, the men dress in loincloths, perhaps with a simple wool shirt or sweater. Thick wool and felt outergarments are necessary in the mountains (especially in winter) and are often colorfully embroidered. The more affluent guides—mostly Sherpas—have begun wearing Western gear, and down parkas have made their way to the most remote villages.

Homes also vary by region, and are generally simple and functional. Nepalese rely entirely on local materials. In the lowlands, bamboo frames thatched with reeds are common, though more prosperous villages have modest wooden homes. In Katmandu, most buildings are of red brick with tile roofs, lending a distinctive look to the city. The red brick is also standard in the lower-lying hills and plains of the central valley. Mountain peoples build sturdy homes of stone cemented with dried mud and roofed with thatch. In eastern Nepal, some hill peoples weave slender branches together to form outer walls, supporting the structure on stilts or stone columns.

Family life. The Nepalese are generally a warm and cheerful people, and families tend to be fun-loving and closely knit. One of the main problems the people face, however, is educating their children. Poverty and a high birthrate make schools scarce and the children's labor very helpful to the family. Both the government and private organizations (such as Sir Edmund Hillary's Himalaya Trust) have made much progress, building hundreds of village schools in the past twenty years. Hunger, poor housing, and inadequate medical care take an especially high toll on children's health. About twenty-five percent of Nepalese children do not reach the age of four.

In the face of such hardship, the family provides a stronger source of emotional and material support than in most Western societies. This support also means that the individual has strong duties and obligations. In the Newari family structure, for example, the pattern of daily life is determined by a series of rituals and tasks on behalf of the family. Often these duties are religious. Particular gods or goddesses, which the family has traditionally prayed to, need to be calmed. Family shrines need maintenance, the elderly need caring for, and various chores and favors are waiting to be done. The Newari extended family may consist of thirty or more members. Many duties are divided among larger units, the *guthi*, which include both more distant relatives as well as family friends. The guthi provide services and support on a community-wide basis.

Religion. Though ninety percent of Nepalese are officially Hindu, most combine their Hinduism with elements of Buddhism. Many rural peoples also incorporate elements of animism and shamanism, some of which can be traced to origins in Mongolia and Siberia. Nepali religious life is thus a lively and easygoing mix that reflects the culture as a whole. Religion pervades daily life, with hundreds of small rituals performed as a matter of routine. For example, men, women, and children may start the day by carrying offerings called *puja* to Hindu or Buddhist temples. The puja are small metal bowls filled with rice, red powder, and flower petals. After praying, they mix the puja with clay, dabbing a small amount on the center of their foreheads. Called *tika*, the marks symbolize the presence of the divine.

Hinduism and Buddhism find common ground in Tantrism, which combines Hindu gods with the Buddhist idea that all things are interconnected. Tantrism, once popular in India but now surviving mainly in Nepal, influences virtually all aspects of Nepalese religious beliefs. Nepalese Buddhists readily worship the Hindu trinity of Brahma, Shiva, and Vishnu as representing earlier manifestations of Buddha. Nepalese Hindus, for their part, see the Buddha as a divine incarnation of Vishnu.

Not surprisingly, this temple in Katmandu is known as the monkey temple. *Courtesy of Dr. W. Paul Fischer.*

Festivals and holidays. Aside from personal rituals of daily life, Nepal's many festivals provide opportunities for fun and noisy collective worship. Indeed, to some visitors, Nepal seems to be celebrating a single ongoing festival. The occasions average about one a week, with some overlapping into the next. In all, about a third of the year is set aside for the celebrations, with the greatest concentration coming from August to October. Festivals are often held at a single site, on which crowds of singing, dancing, colorfully garbed Nepalese converge. Most are attended by both Hindus and Buddhists, such as the *Indrajatra*, a spectacular eight-day celebration held in the Katmandu Valley in September. The Indrajatra features everything from military parades to kite competitions to animal sacrifices. (Such sacrifices, held on the final day, are the central element of most festivals.) Other festivals, such as *Dasain*—also held in September, and celebrating fertility—take place throughout the land.

Language. Nepali, the official language, is related to Hindi. The language of the Brahmans and Chetris, it is spoken by only perhaps sixty percent of Nepalese, however. Most ethnic groups speak their own languages, with individuals fluent in Nepalese as well. There are as many as thirty-six distinct languages, and numerous dialects. With tourism thriving since the 1980s, many Nepalese speak some English, especially in Katmandu and Pokhara.

Literature and the arts. The earliest-known Nepalese writings are stone inscriptions in Sanskrit (the ancient Hindu language) from the Licchavi and Malla periods. Nearly as old, manuscripts of Hindu religious texts such as the *Mahabharata* and the *Ramayana* also survive. Newari and Sanskrit were used for religious works and family chronicles from about 1300 to 1700. After the mid-1700s, Nepali emerged as the language of secular (non-religious) poetry, in the hands of pioneers such as Bhanubhakta Acharya (late 1700s). Poetry has since been extremely popular among educated Nepalese, many of whom write verse for recreation. Among modern writers, the popular political leader B. P. Koirala has written novels and short stories dealing with modern themes such as sexuality.

The rich artistic heritage of the Nepalese dates from the 200s B.C., when the Buddhist Indian Emperor Ashoka is said to have erected four *stupas*, or monuments, which still stand at the religious center of Patan, south of Katmandu. Several classical ages of religious art and architecture followed. From the A.D. 300s to 800s, Licchavi artists produced elegant stone statues and inscriptions still admired throughout the Katmandu Valley. During the Malla period, Newari genius, spurred by influences from India, Tibet and China, created elaborate statues and temples decorated with stone and metal statuary. Later Newari artists continued the tradition, expanding it into painting and wood carving. Painting remains a vital art form, both in the traditional *thangka* religious scrolls and in modern adaptations. Sherpa paintings, for example, show Himalayan landscapes in a distinctive and colorful style similar to the thangkas.

Nepal and the outside world. Shortly after Nepal's long isolation ended in 1951, the 1953 ascent of Everest catapulted the land and its people into world attention. The attraction of climbers to the world's most formidable mountains in the 1950s and 1960s exposed the Nepalese to the ways of Westerners for the first time. During this period, Katmandu, with its tolerant, exotic, and spiritual atmosphere, became a focal point for hippies and others seeking escape from the West. More recently, "trekking in Nepal" has become a popular vacation for energetic and adventurous tourists. They have brought income to the Nepalese, but many have been careless of Nepalese ways and culture. Environmental degradation has affected the busy trails and camping areas of the middle hills. Yet the Nepalese, by nature tolerant and easygoing, have so far managed to weather the assault of modern goods, movies, televisions, and soft-drink cans without excessive disruption of their own culture. Their resilience puts them in a more favorable position than most other developing peoples.

For More Information

Hillary, Louise, *High Time.* London: Hoddard and Stoughton, 1973.

Hoefer, Hans J. ed. *Insight Guides: Nepal.* Singapore: APA Productions, 1985.

Rose, Leo E. and Scholz, John T. *Nepal: Profile of a Himalayan Kingdom.* Boulder: Westview Press, 1980.

Van Beek, Steve. *Our World in Color: Nepal.* Hong Kong: The Guidebook Company, Ltd., 1990.

NEW ZEALANDERS

(new zea′ land ers)

People, mostly of British ancestry, living in New Zealand.

Population: 3,434,950 (1991 census).
Location: Two islands southwest of Australia.
Language: English.

Geographical Setting

Home, to New Zealanders, is an archipelago of two large islands and a number of lesser ones. Together these islands form a land area slightly larger than the British Islands, from which most of New Zealand's original settlers came. Most New Zealanders live on the North Island, which is less mountainous than the South Island. Peaks

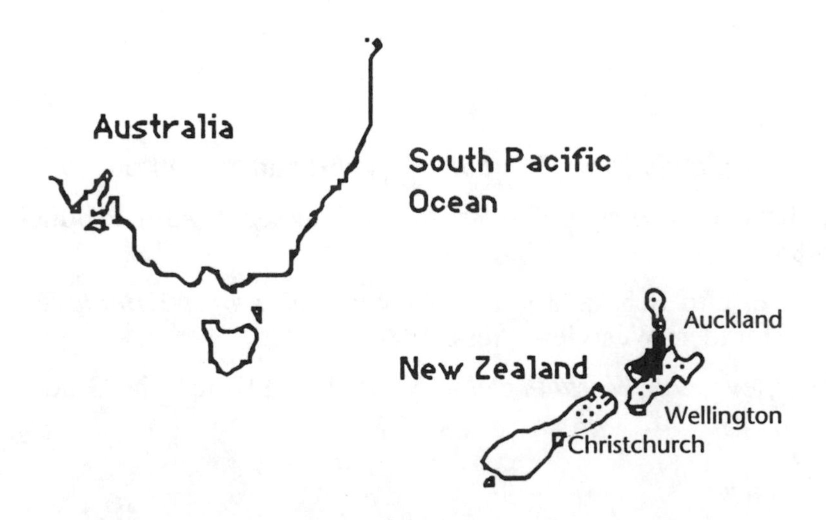

in the South Island range from altitudes of 5,000 to over 12,000 feet. On the North Island the three highest peaks are volcanic and not quite as tall. Overall, the islands are forty-nine percent mountains, twenty-five percent steep hills, fifteen percent rolling hills (lowlands), and only eight percent plains. Once well-forested, it is terrain best suited for grazing livestock.

New Zealand lies almost as far south of the equator as the British Isles are north of it. However, New Zealand has a greater range of climate. The weather is changeable, often windy with short calm or tempestuous periods. Floods, dry spells, snow, earthquakes and volcanic eruptions occur quite regularly in some areas. Colder-than-usual summers in 1991 and 1992 were blamed on the Mount Pinatubo eruption. New Zealand's North Island has a more temperate climate than the South Island.

Historical Background

Origin. Archaeological evidence suggests that sometime around 1000 A.D. Polynesian navigators found their way to the islands that they called Aotearoa and settled mostly on the North Island. Estimates place about 250,000 settlers on the islands when the first Europeans found their way there. In 1642, the Dutch sailor, Abel Tasman circled the islands and gave them their name, but did not make landfall. Then in 1769, Captain James Cook landed on the islands and claimed them for Great Britain. His claim was quickly refuted by the British parliament.

The Maori (the Polynesian inhabitants—see MAORI) were a collection of tribes. Quick to avenge any offense, these tribes were experienced in war. They sometimes traded peacefully with the European visitors and at other times fought the Europeans. Two months after Cook's visit, the French sailor De Surville arrived and so mistreated the Maori that the memory lingered and demanded revenge. Three years later when another French ship arrived, the Maori massacred its leader. In 1809 one Maori man signed on as a sailor on the *Boyd* in order to return to New Zealand. Offended by his treatment aboard, he later convinced his tribe of this mistreatment, causing the entire crew to be killed.

It was not until British missionaries had moved to New Zealand (1814) and a French party was being organized to settle there (1840) that the British government reluctantly commanded a Captain Hobson to establish a colony on the islands. Captain Hobson landed near a Maori settlement on the north end of the North Island, Waitangi, and claimed the islands for Great Britain. Later that year some colonists settled on the southern tip of the North Island and founded Wellington. A number of other British settlements would be established on both the North and South islands. Captain Hobson met with some Maori chiefs and in the Treaty of Waitangi reached an agreement. It would enable his agents to purchase land for British settlements while guaranteeing the Maori rights to their lands and assuring these people that the British government would work to preserve Maori culture. It has been argued that for many years the Waitangi Treaty was not well upheld, but it has begun to be recognized as the founding document of modern New Zealand and commands popular respect and attention today. The treaty is included here not as written originally in English, but as translated from the Maori language.

Early settlers. At first, while the European settlers were a minority, they abided by the terms of the Waitangi Treaty. But within twenty years there were so many British immigrants carving more and more grassland from the bush in which the Maori lived that a series of wars broke out in several parts of the country between Maori tribes and British settlers. In part these wars were the result of British hunger for land and the zeal to stamp British sovereignty over the Maori.

The Points of Agreement in the Treaty of Waitangi

1. The chiefs of the Confederation and all the chiefs who have not joined the Confederation give absolutely to the Queen of England forever the complete government of their land.
2. The Queen of England agrees to protect the chiefs, the sub-tribes and all the people of New Zealand in the unqualified exercise of their chieftainship over their lands, villages, and all their treasures. But on the other hand, the chiefs of the Confederation and all the Chiefs will sell land to the Queen at a price agreed to by the person owning it and by the person buying it (the latter being appointed by the Queen as her purchase agent).
3. For this agreed arrangement therefore, concerning the Government of the Queen, the Queen of England will protect all the ordinary people of New Zealand and will give them the same rights and duties of citizenship as the people of England.

(from New Zealand's *National Report to the United Nations Conference on Environment and Development,* December 1991)

Another likely cause was British misunderstanding of the Maori tribal structure, which resulted in purchase of land from some Maori chiefs that, under the Maori structure, were the holdings of other chiefs. As a result of the Maori (Land) Wars, some tribes retreated from the lowlands and plains into the interior bush and mountains. The situation was aggravated by more British settlers after gold was discovered in the mountains of South Island in 1861, although this was not an area heavily populated by the Maori, and at Westland on the east side of the island. British settlers had already established Christchurch on the eastern plain of South Island in the 1850s and founded other settlements on this island. By 1900, there were about equal numbers of British settlers on each of the islands.

Independence. As the gold fever waned, the larger expanses of lowland and flatland on North Island became more attractive for British sheep herders and dairymen. As time passed, sheep rose in number and the dairy industry grew. The colony quietly prospered, largely by supplying meat to the British Islands.

New Zealand received little attention from Western countries in the early twentieth century, yet it did begin to assume an independent role in international affairs. New Zealand soldiers joined those of Australia in the famous World War I battle at Gallipoli and fought gallantly there and throughout the war. After the war, New Zealanders claimed their right to participate in the war's-end Treaty of Versailles. In 1931 New Zealanders were granted full independence within the British Commonwealth through the Statute of Westminister, a statute they accepted only in 1947 after World War II. Thereafter New Zealand began a process in which the government would play a dominant role in guaranteeing a comfortable life for all its citizens.

Industrialization. Agriculture remained the dominant economic factor and led to industries for processing foods, beverages, and tobacco. Sheep herding gave rise to industries for processing wool and creating fabrics. New Zealand's abundant forest resources were channeled into manufacturing wood products and into pulp and paper industries. Fishing developed with the introduction of tuna freezing and processing plants, and a number of small factories were established to produce plastic and woodcraft articles. From New Zealand's abundant resources came material for metal products and chemical manufacturing. In sum, a highly diversified economic base developed in the islands as a result of independent and government support. Some of New Zealand's industry was nationalized—for example, automobile fuels.

Recession. In recent years, New Zealand's declining economy and increasing immigration has caused considerable turmoil. There have been other periods of turmoil in New Zealand's history. In the 1930s government passed wide-ranging social reforms that introduced a modern welfare state, which was in keeping with an already adopted pattern of government involvement in private life. Almost from the start European New Zealanders had turned to the central government to solve their problems, in insurance, transportation, business, education, and the like. This approach held until the 1980s, a decade of upheaval in which government relinquished much of its role in private life.

Two major political bodies, the National Party and the Labour Party, have dominated New Zealand politics. Long governed by a Labour Party oriented toward a welfare state, New Zealanders began in the middle of the 1980s to make radical changes in their government in response to a downturn in the economy. They attempted to eliminate some regulation of industry and to change some government-owned enterprises to private ownership. Compulsory membership in trade unions was abandoned. In a series of changes of leadership, the National Party took control of government, wresting it from the Labour Party in 1990. The new government continued to be pressed to live up to the agreements of the Waitangi Treaty, under which ownership of a number of properties, rivers, and forests in the country was contested by Maori groups.

Culture Today

The tensions in New Zealand have reflected a struggle in the culture itself to create an independent identity. First there was the question of whether to consider itself a colony or a nation, then whether to identify more closely with Europe or neighbors in Asia. In general New Zealanders have been slow to create a separate culture, following the lead of Britain and America into the 1970s. They have since acted to crystallize a separate identity. It is characterized by vigorous arts and craft, some literature of international interest, and a growing infusion of Maori and, more recently, Polynesian culture into the mainstream.

A changing farm economy. The source of much of New Zealanders' incomes continues to be dairy farms and sheep ranches. There were once more than 62,000 farms of about 6,000 acres each in the country. However, as in other growing economies, New Zealanders are moving to the major cities. Industrial growth and continued immigration has resulted in most of the society becoming urbanites. Three-quarters of the New Zealanders live in cities, of which Auckland, with a population of more than one million, has become the largest, followed by New Zealand's capital, Wellington (300,000), and South Island's Christchurch (280,000).

In the 1990s the number of sheep has decreased from the 80 million of the 1980s to 60 million today, while the cultivation of fruits, vegetables, and plants has increased. The raising of kiwi fruit, apples, flowers, and berries for export is a growing part of the economy. Also raised is livestock other than sheep, which was first imported from outside countries: pigs, cattle, and horses.

Seven percent of the New Zealand income is derived from its forests, and fishing remains a large part of New Zealand's export (recent legislation has granted a large part of this resource to the Maori). While coastal cities in particular have seen the growth of industry (freezing plants, dairy processing factories, and lumber shipping facilities), the smaller towns are dotted with hundreds of small businesses, often attached to a living quarter.

Regulation. New Zealanders once led a highly regulated life. Until the last decade, for example, all businesses closed on Saturdays and Sundays and were open on weekdays from 9:00 A.M. to 5:30 P.M. (except for Fridays and sometimes Thursdays when the stores were open until 9:00 P.M.). Gasoline, until recently, could be purchased at the same price everywhere in New Zealand—a price controlled by the government.

There is a flat fee prescribed by the government for medical care and unemployment benefits, and a progressive income tax that, until 1991, paid each family three dollars weekly for each child under sixteen and provided for a family allowance after fourteen years of marriage. In 1991 child benefits were eliminated from the welfare system, and benefits for unemployed and single parents were reduced.

Family, food, and shelter. The allowances for children reflected the New Zealander's belief in the traditional family structure of husband, wife, and children. Only since the 1960s has it undergone significant change. Pressure from women's groups resulted in gains in the 1980s of social legislation for maternity leave and equal pay. Also ten women were voted into parliament in the 1984 election. New Zealand women today often work outside the home to help support the family, some in the thousands of small businesses. But a primary obligation is still care of the family.

Meat, milk, eggs, fruits, and vegetables, particularly potatoes, have been the mainstays of a rich New Zealand diet, which averages 3,000 grams (about six pounds) of food daily. The trend since the 1960s has been toward increased variety in the diet.

Most houses in New Zealand are simple frame homes—the average about 1,200 square feet, in which dwells a family of between three and four people. Seventy percent of these homes are powered completely by electricity. To make their homes unique, families often paint them with gay colors and add their own decorations. The government builds many of the living quarters and finances others, after a twenty percent down payment. A State Advances Corporation until recently built homes for rental and sales, and still lends money for home purchases. Although New Zealanders can choose to finance and build their own homes independently, many have lived in government-built houses. The state corporation continues to support housing for the very poor.

Although the government has been encouraging New Zealanders to live in closer proximity to their neighbors, the tradition has been for homes to be built with much space around them. As a result, New Zealand towns and cities tend to sprawl over large land areas. In the 1980s and 1990s, this tendency began to erode, especially in such large metropolitan areas as Auckland. Nearly one-fifth of all New Zealanders now live in the Auckland area.

Majority-minority relations. The similarities among homes suggest the egalitarian attitude of a society that has moved toward accepting most everyone as equal and toward including the large Maori minority into the mainstream. Less sizeable minorities include Pacific Island Polynesians (Samoans, Tongans, Cook Islanders, Niveans), Chinese, and Indians.

New Zealand is often praised for its interracial harmony in comparison to other societies. Yet the atmosphere has not been entirely conflict-free. Friction has erupted among minority groups as well as between the Maori and whites. Still, New Zealanders in general have been drifting away from ties with the British Isles and gravitating to ties with their Southern Pacific and Asian neighbors.

Religion. Beginning in 1814, British missionaries attempted to convert the Maoris to Christianity. At first unsuccessful, by 1840 the missionary workers had begun to bring many Maori into Protestantism. A large portion of the general population today claims affiliation with Protestantism. New Zealanders enjoy freedom of worship, and nearly one-third of the non-Maori have clung to their British tradition by participating in the Anglican Communion. One-eighth are Catholic, and a small number attend other Christian churches. Still, religion is not a strong influence among New Zealanders, as indicated by the fewer than fifty percent who profess membership in any organized religion.

Government. New Zealand, like England, has no written constitution. Instead, bodies of law and policy govern the actions of all the people. Under these laws, New Zealanders of voting age are required to register to vote. The people emphasized their separateness from other parts of the British Commonwealth in 1974 by changing the title of the queen. From that year, the Queen of the British Commonwealth was known in the islands as the Queen of New Zealand. Still, the executive power in New Zealand lies with Queen Elizabeth II, whose will is executed by New Zealand's Governor General and Commander-in-Chief. Since 1990, that post has been held by a woman, Dame Catherine Tizard. Dame Tizard is obligated by New Zealand law to defer to the majority of an Executive Council, the head of this council being the Prime Minister. Thus, despite rule by the queen, actual direction of government rested with an elected New Zealander and a single-body legislature of eighty-seven elected members—of which four must be chosen from the Maoris. In 1992, however, New Zealanders voted to elect a legislature of mixed membership more closely tied to the proportions of each cultural group in the population.

Recreation. "Down under, they're mad over their rugby, racing, and beer" (Johnston 1976, p. 134). The deep interest of New Zealanders in a wide variety of sports is internationally known. Peter Snell was a world champion distance runner of the 1960s. Other examples of distinguished New Zealand athletes include Dennis Hume in motor racing, and Bob Charles, a highly successful professional golfer. New

Zealanders enjoy watching and participating in these sports, but the favorite pastime in the country is rugby, seconded by cricket. There is a national rugby team, the All Blacks, and a national cricket team. Moreover, nonprofessional New Zealanders are participants in these and other sports, perhaps more than any other people. Water sports as well as land ones occupy much of the people's time. Surfing carnivals are events of mass participation, competitions, and play. Many New Zealanders swim and there are small pools open to the public even in some elementary schools. Others are active in team sports. For many, fitness is a goal, and the outdoors is the place to exercise for fitness. Jogging, mountain climbing, and just walking are popular sports. This type of activity has given New Zealanders at least one claim to international fame. Sir Edmund Hillary was the first person to climb the world's highest mountain, Everest.

Most families with individual homes in New Zealand have gardens and care of these gardens occupies many homeowners. Like sports, gardening points to the New Zealander's fondness for outdoor activities. Many of them extend this interest to explorations of the dense bush that covers the hills and mountains not cleared for agriculture. Horse breeding (for horse racing) is another traditionally popular outdoor activity.

Arts and literature. As in other aspects of culture, the development of distinctive arts and literature has been slow in New Zealand. In the 1970s artists finally came into their own on a worldwide scale, beginning with pottery makers such as Beverly Luxton and Richard Parker. At the same time literature was coming to maturity.

Few New Zealanders have gained international popularity as authors. John A. Lee wrote of politics during the worldwide depression of the 1930s; Janet Frame and Dan Davin wrote stories whose characters were drawn from New Zealand's small towns; and Katherine Mansfield won international acclaim for her writing. Among authors who have recorded New Zealand history are W. H. Oliver in *The Story of New Zealand*, Keith Sinclair in *A History of New Zealand*, and Michael King in *Maori*. In the 1970s authors finally attracted attention for literature that raised universal questions in New Zealand settings. Greg McGee's play *Foreskin's Lament* is one example; it concerns a young rugby player's struggle to try moving in new directions in a confining society.

The year 1992 saw the fourth International Festival of Arts at Wellington. It featured more than 500 shows, involving than 100 performers and spread through 42 buildings. New Zealand has seven continuing theatrical groups that performed at this festival along with the highly acclaimed New Zealand Symphony Orchestra. Playwrights John Broughton and the late Robert Lord each brought out a new work (*Marae* and *Joyful and Triumphant*). Several authors introduced new books at the festival as part of "Readers' and Writers' Week"—John Cranna and Barbara Anderson among them. To encourage the arts, the government had by this time created a new national post, Minister of Cultural Affairs. This minister oversees the nation's heavy commitment to the arts through such organizations as the New Zealand Symphony Orchestra, New Zealand Film Archive, New Zealand Film Commission, and the Queen Elizabeth II Arts Council of New Zealand.

Education. As with most aspects of their lives, the education of New Zealanders has been highly regulated by the government. There is a national curriculum, which is required by both public and private schools. Elementary education is required for all young people from ages five to fifteen. Students enter secondary school at age twelve and soon begin to vary their courses of study according to whether they will continue with technical or university education. Separation along these tracks is done each year of secondary school. By age seventeen students are prepared to take examinations for higher education. According to interests and success on these exams, a student may be admitted to university education, to study in a teacher's college, or to advanced technical training.

Holidays. Saturdays and Sundays have, for the past eighty years, been universal days off for New Zealanders. Also, there are many memorable days in their history and religious background. Christian holidays are generally celebrated as in other Christian-dominated nations. A New Zealand national holiday, Waitangi Day, commemorates the signing of the Waitangi Treaty with the Maori tribal chiefs on February 6. Another national holiday commemorates New Zealand's most glorious day in international battle, the landing of troops at Gallipoli in World War I. ANZAC Day is April 25. June 3 is recognized as Queen's Day (the Queen of New Zealand's birthday), and December 26 is Boxing Day, which began in England as a day of gift giving to servants and service providers.

For More Information

Binney, Judith, Judith Bassett, and Erik Olsen. *The People and the Land: An Illustrated History of New Zealand*, 1820–1920. Wellington, New Zealand: Allen and Unwin, 1990.

Department of Statistics. *New Zealand Official 1992 Year Book.* Wellington: Department of Statistics, 1992.

Johnston, R. J. *The New Zealanders: How They Live and Work.* New York: Praeger Publishers, 1976.

New Zealand's National Report to the United Nations Conference on Environment and Development. Wellington: Ministry of External Relations and Trade, 1991.

Sinclair, Keith. *A Destiny Apart: New Zealand's Search for National Identity,* Wellington, New Zealand: Allen and Unwin, 1986.

OVERSEAS CHINESE

(oh′ ver seez chi neez′)

People of Chinese ancestry living in Asian countries other than China, mainly in Southeast Asia.

Population: 25,000,000–35,000,000 (1991 estimate).
Location: Southeast Asia.
Language: Chinese and the languages of adopted countries.

Geographical Setting

Nearly all the Chinese who have left China have come from a relatively small area along the South China coast. Starting in the west, this coastal strip includes parts of the provinces of Guangxi, Guangdong (Canton), and Fukien. Isolated from China's imperial and cul-

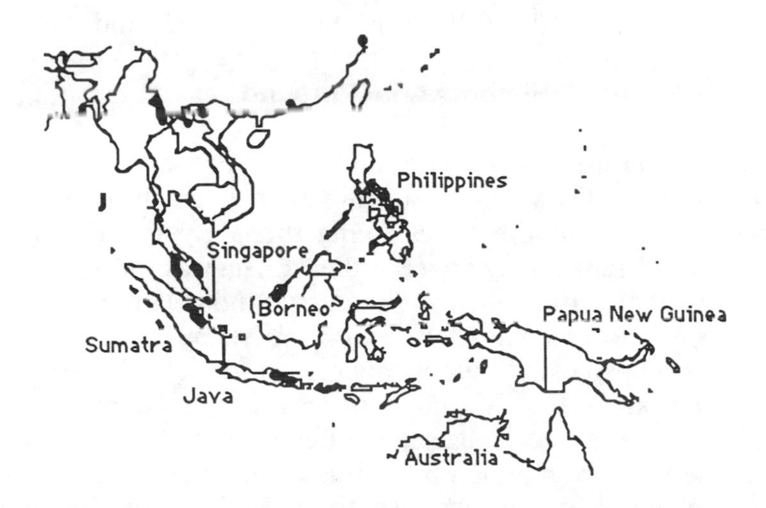

tural capital, Beijing, in the north, living close by the waters of Southeast Asia, the southern Chinese have had both social and geographical reasons to emigrate. They have been more open to foreign influences—first from Southeast Asia, later from the explorers and merchants of Western Europe—than their inward-looking northern cousins. The poor soil of South China often brought crop shortages of famine, making even harsh labor overseas attractive. The four main South Chinese peoples who have dominated emigration are the Cantonese (from Guangdong), the Hakka (dispersed along the coast), the Teochiu (from the Guangdong-Fukien border area) and the Hokkien (from Fukien).

While the term "Overseas Chinese" is used to include Chinese who settled as far away as Europe and the Americas, this entry will focus on those who came to Southeast Asia. Most countries in the region have significant Chinese populations. Thailand, Malaysia, and Indonesia have the largest, with up to 6,000,000 each. Firm numbers are difficult to affirm, not least because generations of intermarriage and assimilation have blurred "Chineseness." On the other hand, persecution or simply a desire to blend in have often led the Chinese to keep a low profile when it comes to matters such as declaring their ethnicity.

The tiny island city-state of Singapore, at the southern tip of the Malay Peninsula, is dominated by its Chinese (over 2,000,000), who make up about eighty percent of the Singapore population. Cambodia, Vietnam, and the Philippines each have up to 1,500,000 citizens of Chinese descent. Smaller numbers live in Myanmar and Laos, or are scattered throughout the Pacific Islands and Australia.

Historical Background

Early explorers and traders. The Chinese did not settle South China until about the 600s, when Han Chinese moving from the north absorbed the non-Chinese tribes living there. By the 1200s, trade between South China and nearby Southeast Asia was well established. Fleets of wooden ships, called junks, carried porcelain, jewelry, and fine textiles to ports such as Malacca, on the Malay coast. Returning, they would bring spices, drugs, or raw metals to the Chinese imperial court. In the late 1200s, Marco Polo traveled as far as India and Persia in one of the trading fleets. Though sponsored by the government, the fleets were manned by South Chinese because the northerners looked down on commercial activity. In the early 1400s, during the first forty years of the Ming Dynasty, the Chinese government undertook an impressive but one-time-only burst of naval activity. Massive fleets of up to sixty ships and 27,000 men sailed in seven separate expeditions. Commanded by the superb navigator Cheng Ho, the fleets sailed as far as East Africa and established contact with about forty states. They enrolled many Southeast Asian states as tributaries (taxed subjects) of the imperial government.

Rise of private trade. Official interest in such seafaring expeditions flagged after Cheng Ho's time, however. The Ming rulers reverted to the old northern-based, landlocked mentality, and China never again became a sea power. Instead, imperial trade dropped off in favor of increasingly adventurous private merchants. Although such private trade was officially banned until 1567, the 1400s and 1500s saw greater and greater Chinese commercial expansion in the southern seas. Piracy and smuggling expanded as well, and the line between pirates, smugglers, and traders was often blurred.

Settlers, refugees. The first Chinese to settle abroad were merchants and ships' crews. They stayed in foreign ports to establish outposts that took advantage of local trade conditions. After 1644, when the Ming Dynasty fell to invading Manchus, their numbers were added to by refugee Ming loyalists fleeing Manchu rule. In Taiwan, the Ming commander Koxinga established a base that drew on wealthy Ming loyalists who had fled to the Philippines and Vietnam. Koxinga resisted the Manchus for nearly twenty years (see TAIWANESE). Fighting in the south continued through the mid-1600s, and refugees left in a steady stream. In 1661, the Manchus ordered the evacuation of coastal areas, burning boats and entire villages. They succeeded in breaking the sea-based Ming resistance, but also broke China's private merchants, many of whom fled after losing their homes and possessions. Manchu policy thus helped open China to enterprising European traders who had been on the scene since the 1500s.

Western power. By the time of the Ming collapse, Chinese merchants in the Philippines and on the Malay Peninsula had done business with Portuguese and Spanish traders for nearly 150 years. Chinese junks brought silks, gunpowder and other goods to the Spanish-founded port of Manila in the Philippines, for example. From there, Spanish galleons transported the goods across the Pacific to Mexico. The Spanish paid with Mexican silver, which the Chinese then brought back to China. During the 1600s, Dutch ships gradually muscled in on trade with China and Asia, at the expense of the Spanish and Portuguese.

Over the next 200 years, European state-backed trading corporations (such as the Dutch East India Company) became immensely powerful. Spain, Holland, and, later, France and Britain supported the merchants, colonizing most of Southeast Asia and parts of China. The Chinese government, by contrast, had no interest in colonization or commerce. Without the backing of an energetic, Western-style state, Chinese merchants could not operate on the scale of their European counterparts. They continued to thrive, but as middlemen or service-providers. As the Europeans developed commercial interests in areas such as Indonesia and Malaysia, they created a huge market for unskilled labor—a market that came to be filled largely by Chinese immigrants.

Coolie trade. The unskilled Chinese laborers were known as coolies, and were shipped in large numbers not only to the tin mines of Malaya or the sugar and rubber plantations of Indonesia, but as far as Hawaii, South Africa, Peru, and California. Sometimes the laborers were kidnapped or lured into service by misleading promises. They were transported under the harshest conditions, and the work was often backbreaking. Many thousands died on the ships or in the fields and mines they worked. Yet famine and unrest in South China encouraged many to try their luck overseas. Emigration grew steadily through the 1700s and mushroomed in the late 1800s, with over 2,000,000 leaving China between 1848 and 1888.

Pull of China. While the northern-based imperial government looked down on the emigrants, effectively washing its hands of them, in the south emigration became an integral part of village life. A young man was often expected to seek his fortune abroad, but was equally expected to return home once he had done so—"returning in silk robes," as a saying went. Once he had established himself, younger male relatives would follow. Men from the same village or region would emigrate to the same place, so that Chinese communities abroad were almost always formed by migrants with regional affiliations. Even when the goal of returning faded—as it often did—with time and age, wealthier emigrants sent their sons to be educated in China.

The constant interchange of people opened South China to new ideas. In 1911, it was Western-educated Sun Yat-sen, a Cantonese, who led the rebellion that finally toppled the Manchus. Sun's older brother had emigrated to Hawaii, where Sun joined him and went to school, later returning to the British colony of Hong Kong. Sun's movement owed much of its success to his support among Overseas Chinese.

World War II and Communist China. During World War II, after Allied forces had been driven from the Pacific, it was often the Chinese immigrants who offered the strongest resistance to the Japanese occupiers. In Malaya, for example, the fiercest resistance was put up by Chinese Communist guerrillas. Communism was introduced to the Malay Chinese by radicals of Sun Yat-sen's Nationalist Party (Kuomintang). It eventually became a power in its own right among the Chinese at home and abroad (though it never enjoyed the widespread support the overseas Chinese lent to Sun Yat-sen). The Malayan Communists, almost all Chinese, resisted not only the Japanese but also the British after the war. After 1949, when Communists under Mao Tse-tung won power in China, such movements caused great suspicion towards the Chinese in Southeast Asia. From the 1950s to the present, native populations in Southeast Asian countries have at times viewed Chinese residents with hostility, as representing the interests of Communist China. Their hostility has been increased by economic dependency on the Chinese, who usually represent a minority of the population but often control the economy.

Culture Today

Assimilation. The Chinese populations have been assimilated to widely different degrees in different countries. The greatest assimilation has occurred in Thailand, where most Chinese have adopted Thai ways. Thai Chinese have intermarried with Thais for generations and have often adopted Thai names. Chinese husbands, thought to be good providers, have been popular among Thai women; the daughters of such unions were in turn thought desirable by Thai men. Thailand was less influenced by European powers than colonial Malaysia or Indonesia, where the Europeans encouraged the Chinese to remain apart by ranking them above the local people. Hostility toward the Chinese became bound up in emerging nationalism in these post-colonial countries, where in the 1950s and 1960s, thousands were killed in anti-Chinese riots. While in Thailand, Chinese men who married Thai women assimilated to Thai culture, the

Chinese immigrants (most of whom were men) who married Indonesians or Malaysians gave rise to new cultures that mixed Chinese with native ways. This mix is called Baba in Malaysia and Peranakan in Indonesia. The Babas and Peranakans have married mostly among themselves, and have traditions going back 400 years.

Work ethic. The mark of the *Hua ch'iao*, as the Overseas Chinese are called in Cantonese, has remained their drive to succeed in business. In the past, this goal ideally included a glorious return to one's home village with wealth that would improve the family lot. This incentive gradually changed, as the immigrants put down roots, to improving the lot of oneself and one's new family in the adopted land. The dream of a fortune stiffened the backs of Chinese laborers, whose endurance amazed Europeans and Americans. The laborers went into business for themselves at the earliest opportunity. One day's laborer might be selling goods from a cart the next week, setting up a shop the next month, and distributing imported goods to several of his own shops by year's end. The Chinese business is traditionally distinguished by low-profits, high-turnover, family participation, and the willing extension of credit to customers.

Commercial empires. Today's Hua ch'iao form a low-profile network of business and financial interests, often allied by marriage or friendships between powerful families, that cuts across international boundaries. With an estimated combined wealth of nearly $200 billion, the Overseas Chinese dominate Southeast Asia's industry, trade, finance, and real estate. The greatest fortunes began in commodities trading, when Chinese stepped into the vacuum left by departed Europeans and defeated Japanese after World War II.

Indonesia's Liem Sioe Liong (Sudono Salim in Indonesian), exemplifies the Hua ch'iao success story. Born in Fukien, China, in 1916, Liem came to Indonesia in the 1930s, joining his older brother, who had come twelve years earlier to help their uncle run a small business trading peanut oil. The village they settled in was also the center of the *kretek* (clove cigarette) industry. Japan took over commodities trading on occupying Indonesia in 1942, and Japan's defeat in 1945 thus left many markets up for grabs. Liem made his early fortune smuggling cloves to supply the kretek makers, as well as sugar, medical supplies, and arms. He supplied the arms to Indonesia's independence movement, which was fighting to keep the Dutch from reestablishing their pre-war control of Indonesia. One of the independence leaders he got to know was Suharto, Indonesia's president since 1965. With such political contacts, he won contracts to export rubber and coffee. Today, Liem has interests in manufacturing, finance, construction, and real estate, and his companies account for almost five percent of Indonesia's gross domestic product.

Connections. Liem's story also reveals the complex networking that supersedes national boundaries, binding the Hua ch'iao of different countries together. He has major partners in Hong Kong, Singapore, and Malaysia, one of whom is Malaysian billionaire Robert Kuok, also Chinese. Kuok in turn controls an empire spanning the Philippines, Singapore, Hong Kong, Thailand, and China. Kuok's Thai connection is the Sophonpanich dynasty, founded by Chin Sophonpanich, born Chen Pi-ch'en to Chinese parents in Thailand in 1917. The Sophonpanich fortune is founded on ownership of the powerful Bangkok Bank, with branches throughout Southeast Asia, and which is known for having lent start-up money to countless Overseas Chinese businessmen who could not find loans elsewhere. Chin's parents were Teochiu, and regional loyalty still figures in the bank's affairs. For example, the Hong Kong branch of the family bank, headed by Chin's oldest son, Rabin, specializes in financing Teochiu clients.

Singapore. Founded in 1819 by British empire-builder Stamford Raffles and long a British colony, Singapore is unique among Southeast Asian nations in having a Chinese majority. Under the leadership of former Prime Minister Lee Kuan Yew since its independence in the mid-1960s, Singapore has become one of the region's major financial centers, a tiny city-state whose economy equals those of many European countries. Lee's Hakka great-grandfather arrived in Singapore shortly after its foundation, and his mother was the daughter of a wealthy Baba family in Malaya. Educated in England, the flamboyant and controversial leader has shaped Singapore's character, embodying at once a colonial past, a foundation of Chinese culture, and the immigrant drive to get ahead.

Food, clothing, and shelter. The Hua ch'iao's daily lives reflect varying mixtures of Chinese and local influences. Chinese food, popular worldwide, has influenced cuisine throughout Southeast Asia. Food is one of the strongest markers of Chinese culture, and many Hua ch'iao fortunes have been made supplying it to eager immigrant customers. One exception is Malaysia, where Baba families tend to favor the spicy, oily Malay food rather than Chinese. Southeast Asia has long supplied exotic delicacies to China. Most famous are the nests used in bird's nest soup, which are taken from caves in Indonesia, Burma, and Thailand. Constructed of leaves, hair, and feathers stuck together with saliva, the nests are believed to have mysterious health giving properties. The trade remains immensely profitable, but its most famous practitioner was the Hokkien immigrant Wu Jang, who arrived in Thailand in 1750. Allying himself with the Thai king, Wu won the right to export the nests and founded a great dynasty of bird's nest sellers.

Most Hua ch'iao men, like other businesspeople in Asia, wear Western-style clothing on both formal and informal occasions. Women may still wear the traditional *cheongsam*, a tight silk tunic, as well as Chinese jewelry.

In Malaysia, Baba homes combine Chinese and Malay furniture and decoration. If possible, the houses are built Chinese-style, with a central hall for burning incense in honor of the family's illustrious ancestors, and separate rooms for each son and his wife.

Family life. In general, Hua ch'iao families tend to be more conservative than those of Mainland China, where Communism brought changes such as women's rights. Among immigrant families in North Borneo, for example, women with feet bound in traditional fashion could be found into the 1970s. Families are tightly knit, and children are expected to be dutiful and obedient. Couples are chaperoned before marriage in Singapore, and marriages are frequently arranged.

Religion. Most Hua ch'iao are Buddhist, and their religion has played a major role in influencing assimilation. It made Chinese more acceptable in Buddhist Thailand, for example, while preserving segregation in Muslim Indonesia and Malaysia. In particular, a resurgence of Islamic values in Malaysia in the 1980s has led to friction between Chinese and Malays.

Language. Baba families have spoken a mixture of Chinese and Malay unique to themselves, although Malay has become more common in recent years. While native languages are generally spoken, Hua ch'iao families often encourage the study of Chinese, either Mandarin (spoken in the north) or the family dialect of the south (Fukien or Teochiu, for example). English has become the language commonly used in business transactions, especially international ones.

For More Information

Heidhues, Mary F. S. *Southeast Asia's Chinese Minorities.* Hawthorne, Australia: Longman Australia, 1974.

Gosling, L. A. Peter, et al. *The Chinese in Southeast Asia.* Singapore: Maruzen Asia, 1983.

Mitchison, Lois. *The Overseas Chinese.* London: The Bodley Head, 1961.

Pan, Lynn. *Sons of the Yellow Emperor: A History of the Chinese Diaspora.* Boston: Little, Brown & Co., 1990.

Sender, Henny. "Inside the Overseas Chinese Network," *Institutional Investor*, September 1991: pp. 37–41.

PAPUA NEW GUINEANS

(pap′ yoo uh new gin′ ee uns)

The native inhabitants of Papua and New Guinea.

Population: 3,700,000 (1990 estimate).
Location: The eastern portion of an island complex north of Australia in the Pacific Ocean and bordering on the equator.
Languages: English and 700 Papuan languages.

Geographical Setting

Papua New Guinea is composed of the eastern half of the island of New Guinea and a number of lesser islands located in the southern hemisphere of the Pacific Ocean north of Australia. The western border of Papua New Guinea is the province of Indonesia called Irian Jaya. To the north of the mainland, the mountainous islands of Manus, New Ireland, and New Britain are all provinces of Papua New Guinea. The eastern provinces include the islands of Milne Bay and North Solomons. The total national area of all of the islands is 178,700 square miles.

The main island consists mostly of mountainous highlands with deep ravines, torrent rivers, and rain forests. The central spine of Papua New Guinea is a high range of mountains, with peaks over 12,000-feet high, that runs east to west across the island. From the mountains many rivers flow down to the sea, the two largest being the Sepik River in the north and the Fly River in the south. Most of Papua New Guinea is covered in a dense blanket of rain forest with a wide variety of birds, reptiles, snakes, and tree kangaroos. So dense is this forest and so rugged the mountains, that travel through the main island is largely by footpath or by air. The central Highland valleys are some of the most fertile and populated—containing almost

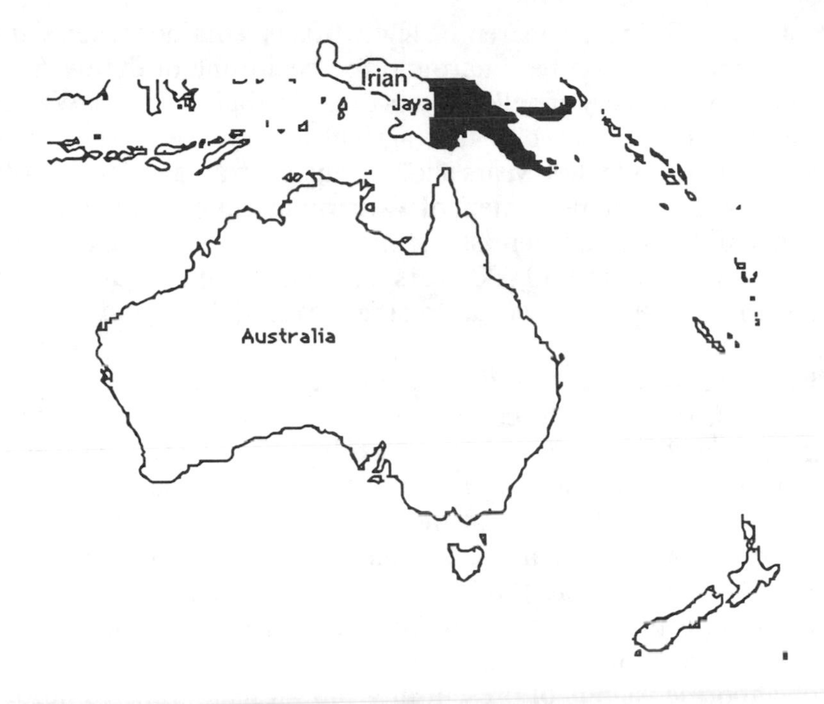

40 percent of the population. Until the 1930s the tribal populations of this area were unknown to outsiders.

The climate of Papua New Guinea is tropical, although there is some variance between the lowland and highland temperatures. In the lowlands the mean high temperature ranges between 86 and 90 degrees Fahrenheit with a low between 73 and 75 degrees. The highlands are cooler; night frosts are common above 6,500 feet. The seasons in Papua New Guinea are based upon the rainfall patterns with wet and dry seasons occurring at different times according to the proximity of the region to the mountains or the coast. The capital of New Guinea, Port Moresby, is one of the driest areas of the island, receiving an average of forty inches of rain a year. In the highlands, average annual rainfall ranges from eighty to 180 inches, while the western coast averages more than 240 inches a year.

Historical Background

Early origins. Most of the early history of the Papuan New Guineans is based upon historical speculation and the oral history of the people themselves. Relatively little archaeological work has been carried out in Papua New Guinea. Apparently, few artifacts remained when significant European contact began around the beginning of the twentieth century. The discovery of pollen layers in the Wahgi swamp in Western Highlands Province suggests that agriculture was practiced on the main island around 9,000 years ago. Extensive drainage canals at the site also suggest the development of water management by the early inhabitants of the island. Scientists estimate that the first people arrived in New Guinea around 50,000 years ago, when the island may have been nearly connected as two landmasses covered the region.

First European contact. A Portuguese explorer, Jorge de Meneses, was the first European to contact New Guinea, in 1512. He called the land Ilhas dos Papuas or "Island of the Fuzzy-Hairs," borrowing from the Malay word *papuwah*. While the first European attempt at colonization was in 1793 by Lieutenant John Hayes, a British naval officer, few outsiders actually settled on the island until the nineteenth century. The Dutch were the first to assert authority primarily over the western portion of the island. One of their purposes was to keep other European powers from interfering with their dominion over the neighboring islands of present-day Indonesia. A limited amount of trade in items such as exotic feathers was then occurring among the coastal peoples of New Guinea and Malay and Indonesian traders. However, due to the lack of valuable trading resources, European traders focused their efforts elsewhere.

Claims for New Guinea. In 1824, the British and Dutch agreed that the Dutch claim would include only the western portion of the island, known today as Irian Jaya, and a Dutch token settlement was established on the coastline at Vogelkop. A whole series of British claims in the east followed. Whenever a British ship sailed by, a British flag would fly in order to claim the island as part of the territory of Queen Victoria. At the same time, the Germans began to trade in northeast New Guinea and the newly independent government of nearby Australia began to oppose the presence of European powers. In 1884, the southeastern quadrant of New Guinea was annexed by Great Britain and in the same year the German New Guinea Company quickly raised the German flag over the north coast of the island.

Australian administration. In 1906, the control of British New Guinea was handed over to Australia, which renamed the area Papua. In 1914, during World War I, the Australians attacked Blanche Bay in the northeast of the island and gained control of German New Guinea. In 1921, the Australians officially took over the German part of the island as a mandated territory of the League of Nations, calling this section New Guinea. Sir John Hubert Murray was governor of the Territory of Papua and New Guinea from 1908 to 1940 and created many programs in village development throughout the island. Murray established a system of village councils and constables to work in cooperation with the colonial government. Schools, hospitals, and aid-posts where also built to aid the native populations. Village plantations of coconuts, coffee, cocoa, and rice were also begun, but without much success in attracting the colonial investments that were desired. The discovery of gold at Wau and Bulolo in the north in the 1920s and 1930s created more investment and also a greater difference in wealth between the peoples of the north and south.

Discovery of the Highland Peoples. In the 1930s, about 1,000,000 native people previously unknown to the outside world were discovered living in the central highlands of New Guinea. These highlanders were viewed as a boon to the plantation owners, who used them as mass labor in coastal plantations. Cash crops such as coffee and cocoa had been introduced to the region to small landholders and plantations and required a great deal of manual labor. By the end of World War II, cocoa and coffee had swiftly spread across the highlands increasing the economic prosperity of the region.

World War II. At the beginning of World War II, the Japanese invaded Papua New Guinea and quickly occupied most of the north coast by 1941. As the Japanese moved south, the Australians were able to maintain their control of Port Moresby and little more until the Japanese began to withdraw their troops slowly in 1942. It was not until 1945 that Australia, with help from the United States, ousted the Japanese and restored its administration of Papua and New Guinea. After the war, Australia combined its administration of Papua and the mandate to govern New Guinea into a single government of the Territory of Papua and New Guinea with a common capital at Port Moresby. Despite the lack of economic development in Papua, Port Moresby grew rapidly and drew large numbers of migrant workers from the poorer areas of the island. Under a system of indentured servants, workers were contracted to work for a number of years in exchange for room and board and a small salary to be paid at the end of their term. This system generally strained the family life in the villages with the strong men leaving the family unit for work outside. In 1950, the system of indentured servants was abolished and replaced by a system of private contract.

Independence. In 1962, Dutch New Guinea passed into Indonesian control and in 1969, the western half of the island became Irian Jaya, a province of Indonesia. Although guerrilla factions within Irian Jaya have protested for independence from Indonesia, Irian Jaya remains a province of Indonesia. Anti-colonial protests against Australia's rule of Papua and New Guinea rapidly escalated in the 1960s. In 1964, a House of Assembly was formed with sixty-four members, which included forty-four openly elected members. The first genuine elections for the House of Parliament were held in 1968 and 1972. Self-government was attained on December 1, 1973, and in 1975, Papua New Guinea became fully independent from Australia. The first prime minister of Papua New Guinea was Michael Somare, a popular native-born politician who built the foundations for Papua New Guinea's political future.

Papua New Guinea today. Since the 1960s, Papua New Guinea has survived many challenges presented to this new democracy. In spite of linguistic diversity, tribal antagonisms, and a low rate of literacy, Papua New Guinea has managed to sustain a degree of solidarity amongst its people. In 1980, Somare's government fell to Sir Julius Chan from the island of New Ireland. Once deputy prime minister to Somare, he and his People's Progress Party tempered the strained relations with neighboring Indonesia and controlled violence that had begun to erupt in the towns and the highlands over the high unemployment, population pressures, and alcoholism. Today, the prime minister of Papua New Guinea, Right Honorable Paias Wingti, is facing the challenge of moving his country into the world economy of the twenty-first century.

However, the Papua New Guineans have increased their population at a rate that has exceeded the national income. About one-third of the country's income comes as grants from Australia, and Papua New Guinea is currently courting stronger support from Japan. The base for international trade remains agriculture, despite the mining of some gold and copper, principally on the outlying island of Bougainville. From the beginning of independence, this small island has threatened to secede from the nation and has been the site of violence. As a result, copper production from the Bougainville mine in recent years has temporarily ceased.

Culture Today

Heritage. The Papuan New Guineans are a mixture of heritages, cultural backgrounds, and traits—the result of a history of isolation in the mountains and intermarriage with other peoples along the coast. Although Irian Jaya, the western Indonesian province of the island, shares the basic history, geography, and cultural similarities with its eastern neighbors in Papua New Guinea, less is known about the people of central Irian Jaya; this entire entry focuses on the peoples of Papua New Guinea. Anthropologists divide the genetic background of the people into two groups: "Papuans," the original inhabitants of the island, who most likely came to the island when it was more accessible to Asia; and Austronesians, who are more closely related to the peoples of Polynesia. The Papuans are darker in skin color and live primarily in the highland areas. The Austronesians are inhabitants of the coastal areas. They are believed to have arrived in New Guinea later than the Papuans.

Languages. The rugged geography of New Guinea has kept many groups in isolation. One result is a remarkable diversity of languages, with over 700 mutually indistinguishable languages spoken in Papua New Guinea. Although Papuan New Guineans comprise only one-tenth of one percent of the world's population, they speak over fifteen percent of the world's languages. Many of these languages are spoken by fewer than 1,000 people and some are spoken by fewer than twenty. The diversity of languages has resulted in the Papuan government's designation of English as the official language. However, *Tok Pisin* (Melanesian Pidgin) is now the most widely used language of communication between people of differing groups.

Religion. The earlier religions of the Papuan New Guineans have been called animistic—the belief that all objects in the natural world are imbued with spirits. Thus there are spirits of rocks, trees, and animals, along with the ancestral spirits of people. Within a tribal group, a man or woman who is spiritually gifted may become a shaman or priest who interacts with the ancestors in the spirit world to receive information from them and attempt to remedy illness and conflicts and to prophesy. Shamans can practice both a beneficial "white magic" or an adversely affecting "black magic" on the recipient.

The arrival of Europeans brought Christianity. The new religion was introduced by missionaries and blended with animism. Since the arrival of missionaries in the mid-1800s, Catholic, Anglican, Lutheran, Methodist, and Seventh Day Adventist churches have been established in order to spread Christianity to the towns, villages, and remote areas and to operate development projects in education, health care, social services, and industry. One result was the development of cults known as "cargo cults."

Cargo cults. Cargo cults are a phenomenon unique to Papuan New Guineans but similar cults are found throughout the Pacific Islands. The Papua New Guinea cargo cults arose as a way of responding to the impact of Westerners and explaining the origins of their technology, wealth, and power. Many anthropologists (e.g., Lawrence, Worster, and F. E. Williams) have studied the cults and trace their origins to a village, Vailala in Papua, where there was an earlier example of a cult. In 1919, a cult developed there known as "Vailala Madness." The villagers were told by a shaman that ancestral spirits would return bringing the material wealth of the white man, called "cargo." Stories were passed that a cargo abundant with goods and foods would be coming for the locals not the Europeans. The villagers abandoned their gardens, killed their pigs, and prepared for a great festival. They waited in vain for the prophesied cargo. Eventually the first believers abandoned hope and returned to their gardens. Reappearance of the "cargo cults" was noticed after the end of World War II, when the United States and Australian armies left behind supplies and machinery. In the 1960s, the cargo cults began to appear on the island of New Ireland, where inhabitants decided not to pay their taxes and instead to put the money into a fund to "buy" American president Lyndon Johnson, who was believed to be the source of Americans' wealth. Because of their blend of Christian and native beliefs and practices and their goals of dramatic social change, the cargo cults are one of the most studied social and religious movements and continue to occur in segments of the population.

Food, clothing, and shelter. In the villages of the eastern highlands, circular huts are the most common form of shelter. These huts are built on the ground (without stilts). The roofs are dome-shaped and made of grass with high peaks rising from the centers. In the urban areas, modern Western architecture is used for buildings and homes.

Gardening is the most important subsistence activity for most rural Papuan New Guineans. Yams, taro (a type of tuber), sago (a starch), and bananas form the staple of the lowland populations. In the highlands, sweet potato is the primary food. Growing cash crops such as cocoa and coffee is common for landholders and on plantations in the highlands. Tuna and prawn (shrimplike crustaceans) are food products from the coastal areas. Copra, palm oil, and timber are the main exports from the coastal areas.

Papuan dress adornment is colorful and creative, drawing from natural materials, paints, found objects, bird and animal feathers, and skins to make headdresses and ornaments. In the Mount Hagen area, the inhabitants wear aprons made of string created by twisting and plaiting blades of grass. When the weather becomes cold in the evenings, rugs are worn like cloaks to keep warm.

***Sing-Sings* and pig feasts.** The *sing-sing* is a traditional gathering of song, dance, feasts, and ceremony among the Pacific Islanders. Before the arrival of Europeans, these sing-sings were an important part of the economic, ritual, and political life of the Papua New Guineans. When the missionaries came to Papua New Guinea, they considered sing-sings to be pagan and un-Christian. Many were stopped. At present, some sing-sings continue but are primarily held for tourist functions, large exhibitions, festivals, or celebrations such as marriages and funerals.

In addition to sing-sings in the highlands, pig feasts are large ceremonial events which bring people together for celebrations focused around the distribution of pigs and other goods. Among high land tribes, leaders, called *big men*, are recognized for their wealth, power, and generosity. A big man may decide to sponsor a pig feast in order to gain status within his tribe. Younger members of the community are solicited to build a long, rectangular dance house, in addition to smaller houses that will serve as dormitories for guests from distant villages. Three months or longer is needed to prepare for the elaborate feasts, during which time the big man and his kin collect the necessary food and pigs for giving away at the pig feast. The actual pig feast may last for days, bringing a few hundred or several thousand people. Pigs are both slaughtered by the sponsoring group for distribution to guests and given as gifts. The feasts serve as important social, economic, and political gatherings.

Education. Formal schools were first set up among the Papuan New Guineans by Christian missionaries who came to the area under the colonial administrations. English is now the primary medium of instruction in the school system, which is operated by the government. The educational system is based upon the Australian system of education. Technical colleges, a National Arts School, and the University of Papua New Guinea are available for those desiring higher education. Although these opportunities for education exist, many of the village populations are so isolated geographically and by language that they do not have access to educational facilities. In addition, there is growing distrust of the pressure of Western educational systems as there are not enough jobs for educated Papua New Guineans.

The arts. Most Papua New Guinea are historically centered around functional and ceremonial artifacts. These have created great interest around the world for their vibrant, bold, and diverse styles. Villages only a few miles apart have their own unique specialty and style for artifacts such as masks, statues, bark cloth, baskets, ornaments, and pottery. Today these articles are collected worldwide and have therefore produced a demand for their continued manufacture. The Sepik region is the traditional artistic center famous for its decorative canoes, wood carvings, clay models, drums, and flutes. The best-known pottery is from the village of Aibom near the Chambri Lakes. There the delicate pots are noted for their white, red, and black painted relief faces. Spears, bows and arrows, and shields are decorated items which are used for hunting and for the spiritual protection of the warriors in highlands. In the Gulf Province, wooden boards are used to carve reliefs of village ancestors, which serve as the guardians of the village. The boards also serve to illustrate important events in the life of the villages. Large and dramatic masks that are found throughout Papua New Guinea are primarily ceremonial pieces to be worn in rituals or to adorn sacred places. In the Sepik region the masks are carved with bold patterns and often decorated with shells, teeth, hair, and rattan.

Traditional forms of money. In the highlands of Papua New Guinea, items such as shells and animals are often used in exchange for needed goods. Kina shells are among the most valuable and prestigious forms of traditional money. The kina are large crescent-shaped shells derived from the gold-lipped pearl shell. They are worn as personal ornaments during ceremonial occasions. Kina can be traded as bride wealth and for pigs or other ceremonial objects. Another traditional display of wealth in the highlands is the *aumak*, a pendant of tiny bamboo rods worn around a man's neck. Each rod indicates that the wearer distributed ten or so kina shells. Thus, a long row of the small bamboo rods is an indication of great wealth. Cowry shells were also once a traditional form of money but are now primarily used as decoration. Pigs are the most important form of payment in trade, gift giving, and compensation for any wrongdoing.

Family life. Family life in the rural areas, where most of the population lives, is strong and centered around the extended family. Family celebrations such as marriage are large events in which a bride wealth in the form of cowry or kina shells, pigs, or money is offered to the family of the bride by the groom and his relatives. The presentation of the bride wealth may involve dramatic dancing by the groom's family in order to increase the donations given by the family.

Wife, husband, and children work together within their clan (an extended kinship group) to increase the group's status and fortune. Children are able to care for themselves from an early age and help with gardening, hunting, household chores, and community functions. Today, children have the opportunity to go to school to receive a formal education in addition to learning the skills from their parents.

Government. Although the Papuan New Guineans who live mostly in the highlands of the country are citizens of the country of Papua New Guinea, the difficulty of transportation throughout the country has made for little relationship of the inland villagers with the central government in Port Moresby. As a result, this government has found it necessary to decentralize, placing much responsibility for government in provincial institutions. One result has been frequent rebellions of the provinces. One example is the copper strike and its aftermath in the province of Bougainville. Even some provincial governments have difficulty communicating with all the Papuan New Guineans in their area. The effective government of the Papuan New Guineans, therefore, lies in about 160 local governmental councils and elected village councillors who tie the local government to the government of one of the nineteen provinces, who in turn interact with the national parliament and prime minister. Thus, the government of Papua New Guinea is a democracy.

For More Information

Lawrence, Peter. *Road Belong Cargo: A Study of the Cargo Movement in the Southern Madong District, New Guinea.* New York: Waveland Press, 1989.

Strathern, Andrew. *Rope of Moka.* London: Cambridge University Press, 1975.

The Far East and Australasia 1992. 23rd edition. London: Europa Publications, 1992.

Williams, F. E. *Vailala Madness.* Honolulu: University of Hawaii, 1977.

Worsley, Peter. *The Trumpet Shall Sound.* New York, Schocken; 1987.

PUNJABIS

(poon jahb′ eez)

Hindu, Muslim, and Sikh inhabitants of the Punjab.

Population: 68,700,000 (1991 estimate).
Location: Northern India and Pakistan, including the disputed region of Jammu and Kashmir.
Languages: Punjabi; Hindi; Urdu; English.

Geographical Setting

The Punjab is a landlocked area in the northwestern Indian subcontinent; the name refers originally to the region, rather than to the people who occupy it. The term "Punjab" comes from the Persian *panch ab*, or "five waters": the Jhelum, Chenab, Ravi, Beas, and Sutlej rivers, whose waters laid down the fertile Punjab plain. In southern Punjab, the five rivers join to form the Indus, which flows to the Arabian Sea. The Punjab's borders have shifted in the past, though in modern times its shape has been roughly that of a butterfly. Today, the Punjab is divided between Pakistan, which has the western, larger wing of the butterfly, and India, which has the eastern, smaller wing. The Indian part is further divided into the states of Punjab, Himachal Pradesh, and Haryana (see below). Traditional boundaries have been the Himalayan foothills in the north, the Rajputana Desert in the south, the valley of the upper Ganges River in the east, and the Indus in the west. Major cities in Indian Punjab are Chandigarh and Amritsar, and in Pakistani Punjab, Lahore and Peshawar. To the south lies the capital of India, New Delhi, and the large metropolis of Delhi.

The hills of the northern Punjab are cool in the summer and cold and snowy in the winter. Temperatures in the plains, mild during

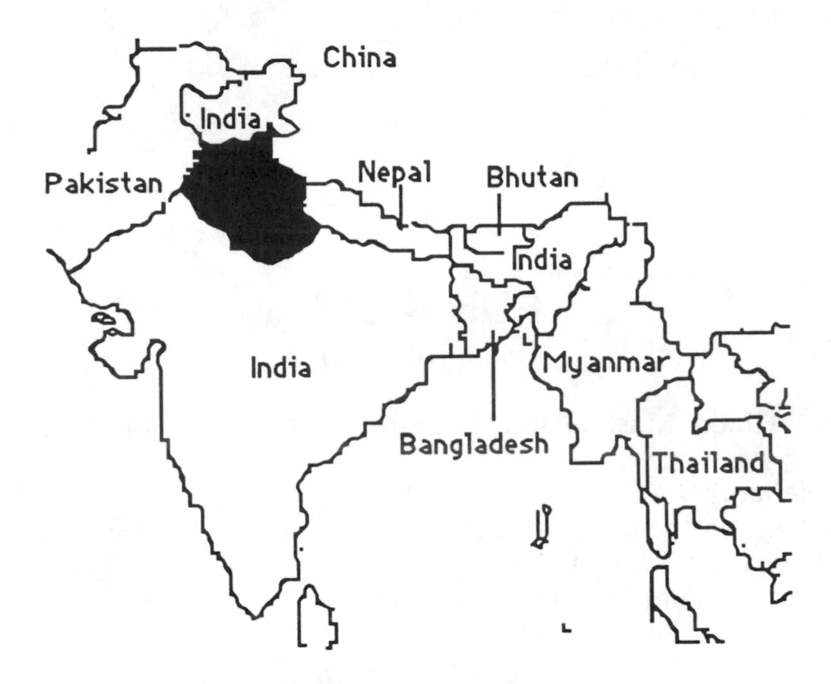

the short winter, can reach 120 degrees Fahrenheit before the monsoons (heavy seasonal rains) begin in June. The rains are heaviest in the northern plains and hills; the central and southern plains receive less dependable rainfall. In the distant past, settlements in the central and southern plains were largely restricted to the riversides, where the availability of water permitted farming. More recently, however, agriculture in these areas has been assisted by an extensive irrigation system, most of which was built during British rule in the late 1800s.

Historical Background

Invaders through the mountains. The Punjab was part of one of the major cultures of the ancient world, the Harrapan civilization of the Indus Valley. This agricultural society flourished for over 1,000 years, beginning about 2700 B.C. By about 1500 B.C., Aryan peoples, migrating through the Hindu Kush mountains of eastern Afghanistan, had conquered the Harrapans. The Aryans eventually extended their control throughout India, dominating and mingling with the Dravidian peoples who had lived there before. Punjabi culture, like that of India as a whole, derives from mixed Aryan and Dravidian elements. The mixture gave rise to the Hindu religion, which spread southward throughout India (see ASIAN RELIGIONS). However, the Aryans were only the first of a long line of invaders who would use the strategic mountain passes of Afghanistan to conquer the Punjab—and sometimes much of India—from the northwest. Darius, the mighty Persian emperor, brought the Punjab under Persian control in the 500s B.C.; in the late 300s B.C., Alexander the Great destroyed the Persian empire, bringing his Greek armies as far east as the Punjab. There he defeated a local ruler before being turned back by his homesick and uncooperative troops.

Battleground of empires. Over the coming centuries, empires arose both to the east, in India, and to the west, beyond the mountain passes. At one time or another, they invaded Punjabi territory, each leaving its mark on the ethnically and racially mixed Punjabis. The Mauryan empire was the first to unite India's various kingdoms. Its founder, Chandragupta Maurya, defeated Alexander's successors about 300 B.C.; under the Mauryas, Buddhism spread across India. The Mauryas ruled the Punjab until their empire broke up (c. 150 B.C.). After that, another wave of western invaders began: the reappearance of Alexander's Greek successors, not allied with Bactria, an ancient desert country of southeast Asia (c. 170–75 B.C.); the Sakas, Parthians and Kushanas (c. 75 B.C. to A.D. 150); the re-emergent Persian empire (A.D. 200s); and the White Huns (A.D. 400s–500s).

Coming of Islam. Although Arabs entered Baluchistan and Sind (to the south of Punjab) in A.D. 711, it was not until about 1000 that Islam took root in the Punjab. Islam was brought to the Punjabis by yet another conqueror from the northwest, the Muslim Turks. The new religions displaced Buddhism and, to some extent, Hinduism. The Turkish-Afghan leader Mahmoud of Ghazhni (979-1030) conducted raids into the Rajput kingdoms south of the Punjab, eventually establishing a base in the Punjab itself. By the early 1200s, his Turkish successors had created a new sultanate (kingdom) centered on Delhi, a major city on the eastern edge of Punjabi territory. The Sultanate of Delhi controlled most of India by the early 1300s; and within 200 years, Turkish-dominated Islamic rule covered the entire subcontinent.

Hindus, Muslims, and Sikhs under the Mughals. In 1526, another Muslim ruler from Afghanistan, Babur, invaded India, defeating the

Sultan of Delhi. Descended from the Mongol conqueror Genghis Khan, Babur founded the Mughal (Mongol) empire, which would rule much of India for over 200 years. During the Mughal period, although Hinduism remained widespread and Islam grew in popularity in the Punjab, an important new religion appeared. This new faith originated within the Punjab itself. Its founder, Nanak Dev (1469–1539), combined elements from both Hinduism and Islam in a strict code of personal morality. Nanak took the title of *guru* (teacher); his followers were called *sikhs* (disciples). Nine gurus succeeded Guru Nanak, each adding new elements to the Sikh code. Often, the Mughal government persecuted the Sikhs, and two gurus were executed in the 1600s. The last guru, Gobind Singh (1675–1708), initiated the most drastic changes, transforming the Sikhs into what amounted to a military brotherhood. During the 1700s, the Sikhs struggled against a weakening Mughal grip on power. In 1799, under the leadership of a warrior and statesman named Ranjit Singh, the Sikhs established a state that included the Punjab and surrounding areas.

British conquest. One of the main causes of the Mughal empire's disintegration was the growing power of the British in India. Using Bengal, in the far northeast of the subcontinent, as their headquarters, the British gradually extended their influence during the 1700s (see BENGALIS). By the 1830s, the Punjab, now the heart of the Sikh state, was the only significant region of the subcontinent not controlled by Britain. Ranjit died in 1839, leaving an unstable Sikh government; ten years later, after defeating the Sikhs in two bloody wars, the British had conquered and annexed the entire Punjab.

Punjabis and the British *Raj*. British rule brought profound and lasting changes to Punjabi society. The British built new roads and railways, increased agricultural production through an extensive system of canal irrigation, imposed English laws, changed the system of land ownership, and built schools that taught both English and native languages. The pressures of colonial occupation also deeply transformed the way Punjabis viewed themselves and their culture. Two main trends emerged. First, divisions between the main Punjabi religious groups—the Muslims, Hindus, and Sikhs—became more sharply defined than they had been in the past (see below). The second development was that Punjabis—particularly Sikhs and Muslims—rapidly came to dominate the British Indian Army. After Bengali

Muslims, formerly the army's backbone, led a year-long rebellion within the army in 1857, the British turned increasingly to Punjabis for military manpower (see BENGALIS). By World War I (1914–17), Punjabis, though less than ten percent of India's population, made up about sixty percent of the army. Over 750,000 Punjabi soldiers fought for the British "Raj" (empire) in the trenches of Europe, the sands of Arabia, and the bush of East Africa.

Rural protest. During the early 1900s, even as they served the British with great distinction, Punjabis, and Sikhs in particular, carried on sustained protests against colonial rule. In 1919, 379 Sikh protesters were killed and over 1,200 wounded when British soldiers opened fire on them in the Sikh holy city of Amritsar. From 1920–1925, Sikhs undertook the Akali movement, in which rural Sikh farmers used both violent and nonviolent means to oppose the British. These protests occurred in an atmosphere of growing violence throughout India, as Hindu and Muslim leaders campaigned for Indian independence.

Partition. Independence came in 1947, and British India was divided into a Hindu state (India) and a Muslim one (Pakistan). Although most of British India had been Hindu, two areas had had Muslim majorities: the Punjab and Bengal. Pakistan included parts of these two areas, which were separated by over 1,000 miles of Indian territory, thus forming a single state in two distant halves. In the western half, the new boundary ran right through the Punjab, between the cities of Lahore and Amritsar.

Partition came at a high cost: hundreds of thousands died in riots pitting Hindu and Sikh against Muslim Punjabis, and twelve to fifteen million were forced to leave their homes. Over five million Sikhs and Hindus fled eastward, from Pakistan to India, and about seven million Muslims fled India for Pakistan. In 1965, war erupted between India and Pakistan over the disputed territory of Jammu and Kashmir (north of the Punjab). Violence flared again in 1971, when East Pakistan (Bengal) declared independence and became Bangladesh. Punjabi Muslims, who dominated the West-Pakistani military, were responsible for the massacre of many thousands of Bengalis in the bloody civil war that followed. The war ended when India came to the Bengalis' aid, defeating the West-Pakistani forces.

Culture Today

Old and new patterns. Today, Punjabis are more rigidly divided by religion than ever. Pakistani Punjab is virtually 100 percent Muslim. About 63,000,000 Punjabis live there; at over sixty percent of Pakistan's population, they form the country's dominant ethnic group. Indian Punjab was split in 1966, with the Hindi-speaking southern plains (including Delhi) comprising the new state of Haryana, and the northern Himalayan foothills becoming Himachal Pradesh. The leftover land remained the state of Punjab, which is now much smaller than the old region of the same name. Of an estimated 12,000,000 Sikhs, perhaps eighty percent live in Punjab, where they make up about fifty-five percent of the state's population. Most of the rest live in Haryana, which is dominated by Hindus. As in the days of the Raj, Sikhs continue to serve in high proportions in the Indian military. Whether Hindu, Muslim, or Sikh, Punjabis share common characteristics inherited from their turbulent history. They have a reputation for being good fighters, and are thought of as adaptable and adventurous. Since partition, many Punjabis have emigrated, mostly to Britain, African states such as Kenya, or America, where they are quick to take up the ways of their new homes.

Old Delhi, one of India's large cities, lies on the border of Punjab. *Courtesy of Dr. W. Paul Fischer.*

India's Punjab crisis. In the past, relations between Sikhs and Hindus were close and friendly. During the centuries of Mughal rule, Sikh warriors often protected Hindus from Muslim raids. Sikhism was viewed as a special branch of Hinduism, and members of the two faiths intermarried freely. A Hindu family in the Punjab might raise its oldest son as a Sikh, and families sometimes switched between Sikhism and Hinduism from one generation to the next. Despite occasional conflicts, Sikhs and Hindus essentially lived as a single community.

In the 1980s, however, this once peaceful situation exploded into violence. In 1984, Sikh extremists occupied the Golden Temple at Amritsar, the most holy Sikh shrine. Defying the Indian government, they demanded respect for their religion similar to that given to all other religions. Barring that freedom of religion, the Sikhs would accept the creation of an independent Sikh state, "Khalistan," in what is now the state of Punjab. (This desire, shared to some extent by many Sikhs, originated in the days of partition, and was in fact partly responsible for the division of the Punjab in 1966.) The Sikhs, who kept weapons on their persons and in their temple as required by their religion, were led by Sant Jarnail Singh Bhindranwale, who had conducted a campaign of assassination and violence against the apparent Hindu movements to destroy all Sikhs in the Punjab.

Eventually Prime Minister Indira Gandhi ordered the Indian Army to attack the Temple, and over 1,200 Sikhs were killed, including Bhindranwale. In retaliation, Gandhi was assassinated by her own Sikh bodyguard, who she had refused to dismiss after the trouble began. (The Sikh guard had, while on leave from his duties, learned that his entire family had been killed by the Hindu forces.) After the assassination, enraged Hindus rioted against Sikhs, killing perhaps 3,000. Most were killed in Delhi; rioting was also severe in other areas of Haryana and Punjab. However, there was and continues to be a great deal of violence in Amristar, a city built by the Sikhs to be the capital of Punjab.

The result of this tragic chain of events has been to make extremists out of those who were once moderate. Formerly moderate Sikhs, appalled at the violation of a sacred temple and at the riots, now openly support the militants. Many Hindus who might once have sympathized with Sikh aims now cannot forgive the assassination of Gandhi. Violence has continued: in 1988, for example, over 1,500 Sikhs were killed in terrorist incidents in the state of Punjab.

Religion. In the Punjab as in the rest of the subcontinent, the religions that have created such tensions—Islam, Hinduism, and Sikhism—have been shaped by one another and by the cultures they have in common. When Punjabis converted to Islam, often they did so because a family or tribal leader had decided to take the new faith. Consequently, folk religion—such as belief in the evil eye, in astrology, or in magic amulets or potions—and Hindu elements found their way into Punjabi Muslim belief. Sufism, the mystical tradition found throughout the Muslim world, also has had a pervasive effect on Punjabi Muslims. Sufism's emphasis on personal morality and on the individual's direct interaction with the divine undoubtedly influenced Guru Nanak, Sikhism's founder.

Sikhism also grew out of a reaction to ideas found in Hinduism, in particular the perceived injustice of the caste system, which Sikhs reject. The separation of Hindu society into castes has less force in the Punjab than elsewhere in India, perhaps partly as a result of Sikh influences. There is a Sikh religious mandate to bear arms in defense of the weak and poor. Hindus perceive this as a threat and differ on other issues as important as the difference in belief in castes. Sikhs see themselves as completely divorced from Hinduism, while Hindus treat the Sikhs as a rebel sect of Hinduism.

Years of Muslim rule meant that local Brahmans—the priestly Hindu caste—were never allowed to achieve the power and respect in Punjabi society that they enjoyed elsewhere. Similarly, the repeated destruction of Hindu temples by Muslim raiders lessened the role that temples played in Punjabi society. (Temples generally have high social as well as religious importance in Indian societies [see TAMILS].) In all three faiths, a wide range of competing activist groups further fragments the already complex situation.

Language. The Punjabis' linguistic scene is as complex as their religious one: they have a saying that language changes every fifteen miles. Punjabi, which exists in many dialects, is the most widespread spoken language in both Pakistani and Indian Punjab. In the past, educated Punjabis spoke Punjabi and wrote Persian. Later, Urdu replaced Persian as the written language. Urdu, closely related to India's most important language, Hindi (spoken in Haryana), gradually absorbed elements of Persian and is written in an Arabic-based Persian script. Urdu became identified with Punjabi Muslims and is Pakistan's official language—though only about ten percent of Pakistanis speak it as a first language. Always socially prestigious, now it is favored by young Pakistani urbanites. Muslims abandoned Punjabi as an official language partly because Sikhs adopted it, developing an alphabet for it and making it their scriptural language. During the Raj, English vied with Urdu as the language of prestige and is still spoken widely.

Literature and the arts. Because Punjabi was in the past unwritten, little literature exists outside of Sikh religious texts. Indeed, Punjabis pride themselves on their reputation as a practical, rough-and-ready people, a tradition not in keeping with a strong literary past. Instead, they have a rich heritage of legends, songs, and oral poems. These stories are recounted to children, and feature ill-fated lovers, magical characters, and great kings and warriors. Punjabi arts are similarly geared toward the practical: woven cloths, jewelry, embroidery, and metalwork, for example.

Food, clothing, and shelter. Punjabi foods feature the hot, spicy dishes found elsewhere on the subcontinent. The main difference between Hindu or Sikh dishes and Muslim ones is that Muslims eat beef, which Hindus do not. (Hindus regard the cow as sacred.) Most meals include a spicy curry made of meat, fish, or vegetables, served with a round, flatbread called *chappatis* or with rice. Tea is the most popular drink; Muslims and most Sikhs drink no alcohol.

There is also little difference in clothing between Muslims and Hindus. Muslim women may wear the *burqa*, a special gown that covers them from head to foot. Traditional women's dress is the Punjabi *salwar kameez*, which consists of a long dress worn with baggy trousers. Women may also wear the *chownk*, a cup-shaped ornamental cap. Men generally wear loose-fitting trousers with light cotton shirts. Business suits are common for men in the cities. Among Sikh men, clothing includes the "five K's," which are outward signs of their devotion: *kesh*, or uncut hair and beard; *kangha*, the comb they carry; *kara*, a steel bangle they must wear; *kach*, their knee-length shorts; and *kirpan*, the dagger they must wear. Men who observe the five K's are *Khalsa*, or pure. Male members of the Khalsa take the middle or last name Singh (lion); women admitted to the Khalsa take the name Kaur (princess). (Sikh women enjoy greater independence than their Muslim or Hindu sisters, often taking part in public life.)

Punjabi villages, traditionally agricultural, in the past were built around the *mohalla*, a block of houses surrounding a central courtyard, and acting as the neighborhood unit. The mohalla was made of dried-mud bricks; rooms were spacious and furnished sparsely. Today, many villages now consist of separate cottages or houses. City dwellers live mostly in modern apartment blocks.

Family life. Family descent plays a central role in Punjabi society, determining not only a member's religion but also his or her social standing. The basic unit is the household or *ghar*, which is organized within a village by *biraderi*. The biraderi is a tightly knit kinship group of households whose members are descended from a single ancestor. Muslim Punjabis traditionally marry within the biraderi, while Hindus marry outside of it. In both cases, marriages are still arranged, although bride and groom tend to have more say about the match than in the past. Also, it is rare now for boys and girls to marry before the late teens (for girls) or early 20s (for boys). Among both Hindus and Muslims, traditional society is organized in social ranks, associated with hereditary professions. For the Hindus, the system is formalized as a series of *varnas*, or castes; the Muslims adopted a similar system, though it was never given religious sanction.

For More Information

Fox, Richard G. *Lions of the Punjab*. Berkeley and Los Angeles: University of California Press, 1985.

Nyrop, Richard F., ed. *India: A Country Study*. Washington, DC: Department of the Army, 1985.

Nyrop, Richard F., ed. *Pakistan: A Country Study*. Washington, DC: Department of the Army, 1984.

Talbot, Ian. *Punjab and the Raj, 1849–1947*. New Delhi, India: Manohar Publications, 1988.

SAMOANS

(suh moh' ans)

Polynesians of the cluster of islands that make up American Samoa and Western Samoa.

Population: 210,000 (1990 estimate), including 40,000 American Samoans and 170,000 Western Samoans.
Location: Three major islands—Savai'i, Upolu, Tutuila—and many lesser islands in the Pacific Ocean 2,300 miles southwest of Hawaii and 1,500 miles north of New Zealand.
Languages: Samoan; English.

Geographical Setting

The native Samoans are Polynesians, a term that refers to a group of islands lying in a triangular area over the east-central Pacific Ocean. Each side of the triangle is approximately 4,500 miles in length with the apex located at the Hawaiian Islands and the base of the triangle forming at New Zealand in the west and Easter Island in the east. The basis of the grouping is cultural rather than geographical for the islands are physically diverse from each other. The native peoples of these islands share a common cultural, linguistic, and genetic heritage which has become known today as Polynesian. There are two main cultural areas of Polynesia—western Polynesia and eastern Polynesia. Western Polynesia comprises Tonga, Samoa, and adjacent groups; eastern Polynesia includes the Hawaiian, Society, Southern Cook, Austral and Tuamotu islands and the Marquesas, Easter Island, and New Zealand.

While sharing many cultural traits, these regions have also undergone separate development and have their own unique history, customs, and style of arts. The Samoans since the nineteenth century

have been divided among various Western nations (1899–1919, Germany; 1919–1960, New Zealand). Until the 1960s, Savai'i, Upolu, and their neighboring small islands were governed by New Zealand. Since the early 1900s, Tutuila and six nearby islands have been governed by the United States. Western Samoa is now an independent nation. Most Samoans live on the islands of Western Samoa, which has a total of 1,090 square miles of land as compared to American Samoa's 76 square miles.

Like the Hawaiian Islands, the Samoan Islands are volcanic, with rugged terrain formed from the volcanic activity which created the islands and continues to add to their shapes. These islands have heavy precipitation (nearly 200 inches a year) and lush vegetation resulting from the rich soil. The islands are surrounded by barrier reefs that make a more calm waterway 200 yards to two to three miles wide, providing a natural transportation route. The centers of these islands are volcanic peaks that slope down to more gentle hills and then to coastal plains that vary in width.

Trade is restricted because of the rugged coastline in which there are few safe harbors. In Western Samoa, these harbors face north and are subject to cyclonic winds from December through March. The rains fill streams that cut down the sides of the mountains swiftly, forming deep and steep channels. This cutting adds to the ruggedness of the islands, a ruggedness that is disguised by the abundant vegetation that covers the rocky mountain slopes and hills. The roughness of the land is illustrated by the largest island, Savai'i, which has an area of 700 square miles (roughly an area 70 miles by 100 miles), but which has an interior so rough and with such dense vegetation that it has yet to be fully explored.

The climate of Samoa is tropical and the islands are covered with tropical forests with their heavy underbrush. Before the arrival of Polynesians to the island, they were without much that is needed today for human habitation. Most of the useful plants and all of the domestic animals that are utilized by Polynesians today were brought to the islands by the Polynesians themselves.

Historical Background

The native Samoans are Polynesians who originated from the Malay Peninsula of Southeast Asia and migrated throughout the islands of the South Pacific over a period of 2,000 years. The long period of migration and the wide ocean expanses separating the many island groups gave the people of each island cluster a separate identity. So, while Samoans, Hawaiians, Maori, and others probably migrated from Malaysia, over the course of time the Samoans developed their own unique social structure, language, and culture.

Origins. The only clues to the early history of the Samoans is the archeological record. Clues include skeletal and cultural artifacts, such as pieces of pottery, that help to reconstruct the unwritten history. A subject of great debate, how or when present-day Samoans migrated to the area, has yet to be determined. According to one of the most accepted archeological theories, the Polynesian migrants could be the descendants of Mongoloids from the East Asian mainland heritage who may have expanded into Southeast Asia from Asia. From the Malay Peninsula they traveled by outrigger canoe across the Pacific Ocean to the various islands during the Paleolithic or Old Stone Age. Intermarriage with the people of Australoid background who also inhabited parts of Southeast Asia has lead to the unique physical features of the Polynesian peoples.

***Lapita* culture.** The earliest Polynesian artifacts include a distinctive style of ceramics that is identified as belonging to the Lapita Culture. Finding and dating the Lapita Culture pottery provides a record of the rapid movement of the Polynesians, eastward from New Guinea to as far as Samoa, between 1500 and 1000 B.C. The pottery itself is highly distinctive and can be distinguished from all other Melanesian ceramics by the types of designs and figures that decorate the pots. By 1300 B.C., the Lapita-style pottery had spread from early Philippine and New Guinea sites to Tonga and Samoa.

Western Polynesia: 1500 B.C. to A.D. 1. Archeologists are fairly certain that the Lapita people were the first to penetrate into western Polynesia (or any part of the Polynesian triangle). The Samoan Islands were among the first islands to be inhabited. Dating from around 1000 B.C., pottery, pendants, chisels and fishhooks have been found in Western Samoa. Gradually, these seafaring explorers created settlements along the coast and spread into the valleys of the islands. The early Polynesians in Samoa were farmers and lived in scattered homesteads. They developed villages and chieftancy in later years.

The tropical chiefdoms: A.D. 1200–1800. Eventually, powerful chiefdoms did develop and the Samoans became characterized by frequent warfare, outstanding religious architecture and monuments, highly developed navigational and fishing skills, and powerful classes of chiefs and priests. Over the centuries, the more powerful chiefs consolidated some of the people. In the Western Samoan islands the central government came to include a king who ruled from the small island, Manono, between the larger islands Savai'i and Upolu. Two royal families, Malietoa and Tupea, ruled the two large western islands and the smaller ones surrounding them through a council of chiefs. Large stone mounds such as the Pulemelei on Savai'i, the largest prehistoric monument in Polynesia, are remnants of the great chieftancies of Samoa. In contrast to the Western islands, the easternmost ones continued to be ruled as independent small chieftancies.

European contact. The Samoan Islands were first sighted by a Dutch seaman, Jacob Roggeveen, in 1722. But since he failed to discover valued minerals or spices there, little attention was paid to them. They were not visited again until 1768 by Louis de Bougainville, and received little attention from the West except for runaway sailors until John Williams of the London Missionary Society settled there in 1830. Williams found a land that had just passed through a series of violent wars that established one dominant chief. By mid-century, British, German, and American seamen had established trade bases in the islands and had begun to take an interest in Samoan politics. As these three nations sided with various groups of chiefs, they added firepower to the already brutal tribal warfare. Attempting to bring order to the warring chiefdoms in 1889, British, American, and German forces agreed on a neutral government set up under King Malietoa Laupepea. Soon the British withdrew, granting their rights to Germany. Western Samoa then became a protectorate of Germany, while the far southeastern island remained under United States control. In 1904, the chiefs of Tutuila ceded their rights to the American government. Conditions changed once more at the onset of World War I. In 1914 New Zealand troops captured Western Samoa and began a rule that was planned from the beginning to grant independence to Western Samoa. This independence did not come soon, and in 1927 some of the Samoan residents, both Samoans and Europeans, formed a group called the Mau to force government action through civil disobedience. For nearly ten years, the Mau and the New Zealand-guided government were at odds. Ten years later, in 1946, Western Samoa fell under United Nations rule, but New Zealand remained as administrator. After a cabinet had been formed and a constitution approved, Western Samoa became independent in 1962. At that time, a decision was made to ignore the constitutional call for elections of a prime minister every four years, and to retain their leader for a lifetime. Slowly, Western Samoans began to reject the old idea of rule by a council of chiefs and move toward universal suffrage, but this was not accomplished until 1990. Women were soon allowed to vote for legislators to serve in the body still called a Fono as in the days of the council of chiefs. By 1990, Western Samoa had appointed its first female cabinet member, Fiame Naomi, as Minister of Education and Labor.

While under United States Navy supervision before 1961, Samoa's one reliable harbor, Pago Pago, was enlarged and an international airport constructed nearby. The 40,000 Samoans on Tutuila began to become Westernized. Many small plantations arose to grow coconuts and other products for export, and two canning factories were built to prepare tuna for shipment to other countries. This region, too, underwent a series of changes in governmental forms and constitutions. The most recent constitutional proposal still calls for vote by the chiefs of the various small groups of Samoans, not for universal vote.

Isolated by the lack of a good harbor and service by airlines, Western Samoa has continued the patterns of small farms and plantations with much slower economic changes.

Culture Today

Samoa today is a mixture of settlers who are considered to be of Polynesian heritage and new inhabitants from Europe, Asia, and the Americas, which has created a multicultural society in this island region. Despite the pressure for change from the newer immigrants, the traditional Samoan culture continues to influence religion, the arts, family and social structure, and political relationships.

Religion. Most Samoans profess to be Christians, and, in fact, the most impressive buildings on the islands are the Christian churches. However, their form of Christianity incorporates many traditions of an older religion. The central characteristic of the Samoan religion is a belief in *mana*, a sacred supernatural power that pervades all things, animate and inanimate. The power of mana in people, buildings, stones, tools, canoes, and foods was preserved through an elaborate system of rules and collective ritual called *tapu*. Tapu (from which Europeans and Americans derived the word "taboo") provided order and harmony to the Samoan universe and still guides Samoan decisions. Groves, trees, temples, and parts of the islands could not be entered by ordinary people (they were "tapu" to them) because they were pervaded by the mana of a high-status person or god. If an ordinary person stepped over a chief's tool left on the ground, he or she would nullify the mana of the tool, rendering it powerless. Women were not allowed to enter canoes because it was believed that they would defile the canoe. In many societies, the men had to follow certain tapus regarding their food and the company of women to preserve the power of their mana. The punishment for violating major tapu or prohibitions was a swift execution. Other lesser tapu violations would bring illnesses or bad luck on the wrong doer. The great gods and goddesses of the Samoan pantheon were worshipped by local priests and chiefs with rites which often involved human and animal sacrifice, chants and recitations, feasting and fasting, music and dance. The belief in mana extended religion into all aspects of Samoan life.

Christianity has been eroding the ancient beliefs since the 1880s. The completeness of Samoan adoption of this religion can be seen throughout the islands. Large church buildings of cement, stone, and wood are uniquely designed and decorated, with spires and domes rising far above the neighboring homes.

The arts. Samoan art draws on materials locally available; artistic works include bark cloth making and design, basketry weaving, and featherwork. Found throughout the islands, crafts organizations were a means for organizing and training specialists in canoe construction, wood carving, and tattooing. Today, cultural centers, schools, and universities as well as traditional apprenticeships form the basis for artisan training.

Tattooing is highly prized among Samoans and a large number of Samoans are skilled at this art. However, as with most other crafts, only those few with extraordinary talents are recognized with special rankings. In Samoa, artisans who exhibit the small differences that make for superior craftsmanship, such as the ability to make tattoos that are more detailed than average, are recognized with titles and with leadership in their crafts.

Music. Dance and song are important art forms throughout Polynesia and are performed for festivals, ceremonies, and social gatherings. The dance and song was often originally part of the religious expression of the people done in praise of the gods and goddesses of the indigenous religion and the natural world. Major events in Samoa are celebrated by donning the earlier native costumes, preparing large feasts, and spending long hours or even days in song and dance. This recognition of a special event with song and music is known as a *sing sing*. The sing sing celebrating the tenth anniversary of Samoan independence was an islands-wide festival that lasted for three days.

Shelter. Samoans live in small villages on the more level coastal plains of each island. A typical village is a neatly arranged row of Samoan homes situated along a dirt or sandy road. Each family home is an open building erected on a foundation of rock. Poles in the center support the homes, which are often built on elevated rectangular platforms, with the height and size dependent on the status of the owner. As with houses in other Polynesian islands, Samoan homes were mostly made of wooden framework and thatched roofs. The houses were typically open all the way across the front, creating a veranda where most of the household activities took place. Inside, the houses were covered with woven mats. Polished coconut logs served as seats or pillows for sleeping at night. Among the cluster of houses, a ceremonial plaza, or *tohua*, would serve as the focal point of the community.

Samoan villagers gather for a village photograph. *Courtesy of Wayne Mitchell.*

In recent years, Samoans have tended to adopt styles of Europeans, Americans, or Asians, particularly in home furnishings as well as in clothing for the people in the larger towns.

Language. Polynesian people speak about thirty closely related languages that form one branch of a widespread family known as Austronesian, which includes the languages of Micronesia, Indonesia, the Philippines, Madagascar, and parts of mainland Southeast Asia. Although Samoans have developed their own language over the years, their common base with other Polynesian languages is seen in the many similar terms for the same items. Samoan words for the plants, animals, and terms that describe the way of life of the early Polynesians have their bases in more ancient languages, some appearing to have been derived from the ancient language of India, Sanskrit.

Family life and social structure. Family life in Samoa is based upon a closely knit extended family and a well-defined line of kinship that links people with their ancestral heritage. The typical family unit consists of two to three generations living together within the household of the senior male. The lineage of a family can often be traced back to the original migration of the family to Samoa. These kinship ties form the identity of a family group and define how it interconnects with the whole community. A group of related families comes together under a chief chosen by his people from men, or less frequently women, who earn lesser titles because of their personality, speaking ability, and strength. Today, as in the past, there are two types of lesser chiefs: *ali'i* (titular chiefs over small groups of people) and *lonfale* (chiefs by virtue of their speaking abilities). All chiefs in Samoa are referred to as *matai*. Within a large extended family called an *aiga*, matai ruled small segments and came together in a *fono* (a council of chiefs) to choose their leader. Samoan chiefs still wield great influence—more in American Samoa, where they control voting rights, and less in Western Samoa, where their New Zealand overlords led them more rapidly toward voting rights for all adults.

Food. Traditionally the sea provided much protein for the Samoans. Gardens supplied fruits and vegetables. Fish, mollusks, and crustaceans are important food sources, as are the major native Samoan crops—taro, breadfruit, bananas, sugar cane, and coconuts. Breadfruit is not picked until it is overripe and then it is beaten into a pulp and stored to turn into a fermented breadfruit paste. The coconut is important as a food source and also as a source of leaves, which are used to make baskets, ropes and thatch. The trunk of the coconut palm was once hollowed out to make canoes. In recent years, as the islands' population has grown, Samoans have traded copra and other abundant products for imported food to supplement the food grown at home.

Clothing. While most Samoan people today wear Western-style dress due to European influence, traditional Samoan clothing is worn on special occasions and for cultural festivities. Vegetable material was a source of clothing. Cloth was made of beaten bark known as *tapa* derived from mulberry or banyan trees. Bark cloth is still made in the islands but now is produced for sale to tourists. The material is beaten into small sheets and then assembled to produce loincloths, capes, skirts, and headdresses—and, today, sportshirts and other goods for the tourist market. Tapa cloth is decorated by painting and water markings. Jewelry made from shells, tropical flowers, such as hibiscus and frangipane, and leaves are traditional adornment.

The village and larger society. Samoan society has a highly stratified, but equally highly fluid, structure. That is, Samoan leaders are chosen on the basis of ability, and the rank and authority of the Samoan varies with the task. A village chief, for example, would be

A Samoan fisherman. *Courtesy of Wayne Mitchell.*

chosen from family leaders on the basis of his ability to make judgments and to lead. The best fisherman is another high-ranking leader. When the village chief fishes in the fleet of the best fisherman, he must take the rank of a typical fisherman and oarsman even though he has made the decision about when to set sail. The village chief who fishes is assessed his share of the catch for a village feast just as the other fishermen. As families grew and divided, more people came to have the title of chief, matai, and this proliferation of leadership titles has created difficulty in forming a European-style democracy. Many matai aspire to the fono, the national legislature, and their aspirations have become the basis on which the various political parties have arisen.

Each village has a chief and also a princess. The princess has privileges and rights of her own and leads the young women of the village. But here is another example of the fluidity of Samoan society. Should a group of young ladies be engaged in some activity in the absence of the village princess, another young woman is quickly acknowledged to be the acting princess. Through this female structure, women have definite tasks and their own spheres of influence. In the 1990s, some women have risen through the societal hierarchy to become high-ranking officials in the national government.

The oral literary tradition. The oral tradition of Samoans, a tradition shared by many Polynesian peoples, is rich in mythology, legends, and facts about Samoan history and their worldview. Studying the oral tradition, along with searching for artifacts, is one of the primary ways in which the past of all Polynesian peoples is reconstructed. For instance, the legend of Maui, a prominent god among many Polynesian peoples, tells the story of how the Polynesian archipelago was created and provides insight into the life of the early migrations of the Polynesian explorers. The legend tells of a voyage Maui made with his twin brother eastward into the Pacific Ocean. After traveling for many days and nights by canoe without sight of land, they finally found an island in the horizon—the home of the god Tonga. Maui and his brother were given fishhooks by Tonga in order to help them find their own land far from his own. The next morning they sailed away until they were far from Tonga's home to fish. As they fished, they began to pull islands up from the water. Continuing their journey throughout the Pacific Ocean, they pulled up many more islands.

When they finally returned home, they found that their own home had become overpopulated and threatened by enemies from the north. Maui told the other Polynesians to build canoes and sail eastward to the islands he and his brother had fished from the sea. He told the people how to use the stars and sun for navigation and what they would need for their voyage. He also promised that he would call to the people through the coconut trees, through the wind across the waves and valleys and through the rain until all of the islands were inhabited. Maui's call has not been heard for over a thousand years.

For More Information

Bellwood, Peter. *The Polynesians: Prehistory of an Island People.* London: Thames and Hudson, 1978.

Buehler, Alfred. *The Art of the South Sea Islands.* New York: Greenstone Press, 1964.

Fox, James W. and Kenneth B. Cumberland. *Western Samoa.* Christchurch, New Zealand: Whitcombe and Tombs, 1962.

Siers, James. *Samoa in Colour.* Rutland: Charles E. Tuttle Company, 1970.

SHAN

(shahn)

People of eastern Myanmar and northern Laos who speak a northern Tai dialect.

Population: 3,100,000 (1990 estimate).
Location: The mountain and hill valleys of eastern Myanmar, Laos, and southern China.
Languages: Shan, a Tai language; Burmese.

Geographical Setting

The Shan are mountain people. In Myanmar, where there is a large Shan population, they live on the Shan Plateau of the east central part of the country. This plateau consists of rolling hills, cut steeply by the waters that flow into the Salween River. The Salween originates in China and drains into the Gulf of Martaban just east of the Bay of Bengal. Throughout Myanmar (formerly Burma), the climate is tropical, warm and damp. The constant 80-degree temperature of most of the country is tempered by the altitude in Shan territory, where temperatures are 10 to 15 degrees cooler. Rainfall there is about 70 inches yearly, but varies with the location. The soil in this region is not as arable as along the Irrawaddy River in central Myanmar. Much of the land has been damaged by leeching.

The Shan are rice farmers who prefer to live and work in the many valleys among the mountains and steep hills. In these valleys, they are scattered so that the population density is much less than along the Irrawaddy River. Making up one-sixth of the population of Myanmar and spilling over into Laos, the Shan are spread over nearly half the land.

Historical Background

Origin myth. According to Shan legend, two figures, Khun Lun and Khun Lai, descended from heaven to found a kingdom of the Shan (who call themselves Tai) in upper Burma and southern China. These two were tricked by one of their servants, Pang-Ku, who became king of Muang Kae. Regardless of the questionable truth of this tradition, by A.D. 568 Tai people had founded a kingdom in upper Burma with its capital at Muang Maorong (near present-day Tagaung).

Early history. With other Tai people, the Shan migrated south from China after the migration of the Khmer and Mons of Thailand and Cambodia. It is believed that the people of Burma left southern China to escape the bloody struggles between the Chinese and Tibetans. Shan, Miao, Lao, and other peoples, all who call themselves Tai, settled in the northeast and central Burma locations before A.D. 1000. By 1200, there had been established a kingdom in southern Myanmar with its capital at Prome. This kingdom expanded and eventually moved its capital to Ava, farther up the Irrawaddy River, which had become the capital of the Shan people as they migrated south. All the while, the Shan people in their mountain strongholds were ruled by local chiefs. In the early 1500s Shan soldiers under the sawbwa (prince) of Mohnyin established themselves on the Irrawaddy and reached the Burman capital city of Ava. The Sawbwa captured that city and turned it into a Shan city. In a reign of terror against the Burman, he burned their libraries and ordered Burman monks to come to his palace, where he burned them alive. Once established, the Shan kings of Ava initiated a golden age for Burman literature—preferring that language to the earlier Pali. Shortly, however, the various Shan groups around Ava began to quarrel among themselves.

Meanwhile, a great Burman king, Tabinshwehti, had set out to conquer the Mon people of the south of present-day Myanmar. Having accomplished that, Tabinshwehti moved north up the Irrawaddy River to capture first Prome and then the army of the Shan moving down from Ava. The defeat of the Shan and their inclusion into a Mon-Burman kingdom occurred in 1541.

British rule. Under the British who claimed Burma as part of India in the 1700s, the Shan were used to counter threats to British rule by the Burman and Khmer. Several Shan states were recognized in the plateau area to which the Shan of the Irrawaddy Valley had withdrawn. In 1937, to strengthen their support of the British, the Shan states formed the nucleus of a separate British colony of Burma.

Independence. Always pressing for independence, the many peoples of Burma banded together. In 1947 the Shan agreed to join with the Burman and others, and in 1948 the Union of Burma was formed. Under the agreement of union, Kachin and Shan areas were organized into states with considerable autonomy. The constitution of the new government provided for a trial period of ten years during which the Shan would be free to withdraw from the Union. That permission to secede was soon revoked, however, and an unstable Union held together. Its government provided for a Chamber of Nationalities made up of twenty-five local princes. Eleven years later, the sawbwas of the Shan drew together in rebellion to form the Shan State Independent Army, even though local rulers among the Shan gave up their independent rule in 1960. That rebellion spread throughout the various peoples of Burma and finally (1962) resulted in a military takeover of the government. The government of Burma responded with force and diplomacy, finally securing enough tranquility that it could offer amnesty to all the rebels who would cease their insurgency.

(Actually this came about by a Burman offer to allow freedom of trade to any dissenters who would join the Union.) In 1974, a new constitution was approved by the voters of Burma. This constitution did not mention the previous autonomous states. Since that time, the Shan as part of renamed Myanmar have struggled with the economic problems of that country.

Military government. Resistance by Kachin, Shan, and other minority groups to a united Myanmar continues today. The constitution of 1974 provided for a government by a Peoples' Assembly and for various local and regional assemblies. However, the military government suspended the Assembly from 1988 to 1990 and in 1992 had not yet recognized the authority of the Peoples Assembly except to construct a new constitution.

Chinese communism. Supported by the Chinese, people of the north, Kachin, established a White Flag party that has worked to develop communism within all of Myanmar and has disrupted the national government's efforts to enforce boundary restrictions between the Shan state and China. This group has been joined by Mon people to the south of the Shan in rebellion. Burman and Shan have dealt harshly with these rebels, resulting in the flight of more than 50,000 Karen, Mon, and others to Thailand.

The country of Myanmar continues to be centered in the heavily populated central and southern Irrawaddy River valley, which is predominantly Burman. Surrounding this basin in a horseshoe shape are the mountain and hill regions inhabited by minority groups—Arakan, Chin, Kachin, Shan, Karinni, and Karen—all seeking insurance of their own ethnic integrity and continuing to fight for it with the dominant Burmans.

Culture Today

Villagers. Two-thirds of the Shan are rice cultivators living and farming the valleys and leaving the mountaintops and high hilltops to other people. In the valleys of eastern Myanmar and Laos, they prefer to live in villages and travel to their farm plots from there each day.

A typical Shan village is an irregularly spaced cluster of houses on either side of a road or a stream. Under their own rule, the Shan villages united with nearby villages in a political unity called a *khaing* under a local leader, a *myothugy*. However, the British focused on each village as the governmental unit and recognized a village headman as the local leader.

Larger villages may include small businesses and schools and many contain Buddhist pagodas.

Family life. Shan villages are clusters of related families who clear the valley areas, plant, and irrigate rice crops. An important second crop for many is opium—because it can be grown in the off-season for rice and because it brings a small income to the farmer. This income is, however, quite small as the opium is sold to regional merchants, frequently Chinese, then transported to Thailand to be refined into heroin. Families are male-dominated, although Shan women enjoy considerable status and have, as recently as the 1960s and 1970s, been strong leaders of the Shan (leaders of the rebellion and unifiers of the several Shan fighting factions).

Children are important to the Shan family, both as a source of workers for the fields and as the hope of the future. This is to be seen in their view on education. Education is provided wherever possible by the national government, for six years beginning at age five. This education and the subsequent six-year secondary schooling is not compulsory. Still about two-thirds of the Shan of school age attend school, and illiteracy among Shan adults amounts to less than one in five.

Houses. Shan houses are not unlike other Myanmar houses. They are constructed of bamboo or wood frames supporting a thatched roof. Walls are of woven bamboo strung between the upright frames. Windows and doors may be covered with plaited bamboo curtains.

Inside, the home has several sleeping rooms separated from a special cooking area, again by bamboo screens. There is either an outhouse or no disposal facilities in many of the homes. Furnishings are equally sparse, consisting of grass mats for sitting and sleeping, a low table or two, a wood box for storing clothing, and necessary tools for cooking. These may include forks and spoons, although most often eating is done using fingers as tools for the food.

Food. Boiled rice or a rice with a mild curry sauce is the staple food of the Shan. Two meals a day, one in late morning and one in early evening, consist of the same menu. A typical meal includes the rice, a clear soup, and salad or vegetable. Ngapi, a paste made from salted fish or shrimp, is a popular addition. Between the two main meals,

Shan snack frequently on sweets and fruits. Tea is the most popular beverage at these snacks, although it is not often taken with the meals.

Clothing. The centuries-old, traditional dress is still most popular among the Shan. Men wear a jacket over loose-fitting trousers and complete this dress with a turban. Tattoos are very popular among the male Shan as among other peoples of Myanmar. A boy in this country is often tattooed from knee to thigh. Women wear tight-fitting, long-sleeved jackets and colorful silk skirts. Women, too, wear turbans. Necklaces are popular items of jewelry as are earrings. For a long period in their history the Shan were admiring adversaries of the Burman and adopted some of their ways. Shan girls, as do many others in Myanmar, almost universally have their ears pierced for large earrings about the age of eleven.

Language and literature. In language, too, the Shan have borrowed from their Burman neighbors and conquerors. The language of the Shan is a Tai dialect related to the languages of Laos and Thailand. However, the written script employs the Burman symbols to represent Shan sounds. Under British rule, some of the local languages of present-day Myanmar were destroyed (e.g., Mon) and others were ignored. Shan was ignored as English and Burman became the languages of the British colony. Not until the 1950s, when a Shan prince and president of the Union, Chao Shwe Thaike, was instrumental in translating Buddhist texts from the ancient Pali (then thoroughly Burmanized) into Shan was a new age of Shan literature initiated. Still, this literature is hidden by the Burman government's closing of most of the Shan state to foreign visits, and by the continuing anti-nationalism and consequent military unrest in the area.

Religion. The Shan, along with the Burman, follow Therevada Buddhism, although this religion accommodates some Hindu influences and retains older beliefs in good and evil spirits.

For More Information

Anderson, John W. et al. *Area Handbook for Burma.* Washington, DC: American University, 1971.

Htin Aung, Maung. *A History of Burma.* New York: Columbia University Press, 1967.

Thaike, Eugene (Chao Tzang Yawnghwe). *The Shan of Burma: Memoirs of a Shan Exile.* Singapore: Institute of Southeast Asian Studies, 1987.

SINHALESE

(sin ha leez′)

The largest group of people living in Sri Lanka.

Population: 7,000,000 (1990 estimate).
Location: Sri Lanka (Ceylon).
Language: Sinhala, an Indio-Iranian language related to the ancient Sanskrit.

Geographical Setting

Sri Lanka, formerly Ceylon, is a large island south of the tip of India. Extending from near India like a giant teardrop, the country is 270-miles long (north to south), and at its widest point, 140-miles east to west. Mostly, the island is a lowland with elevations below 1,000 feet except for mountains in the south-central region. The whole island lies just north of the equator and is therefore warm, humid, and covered with lush growth, including palm trees and hardwoods. Monsoon rains sweep over the island, giving the highlands more than 200 inches of rain each year. In lower lands, rainfall is a more moderate forty inches annually.

The independent country is made more accessible to mainland India by several smaller islands that form a bridge to the tip of the continent.

Historical Background

Origin. According to Sinhalese legend, many years ago the daughter of a king in India was carried away by a man whose totem was the lion. The princess and the man fell in love. Their marriage produced a son and daughter and, later, a grandson, Vijaya, who was exiled

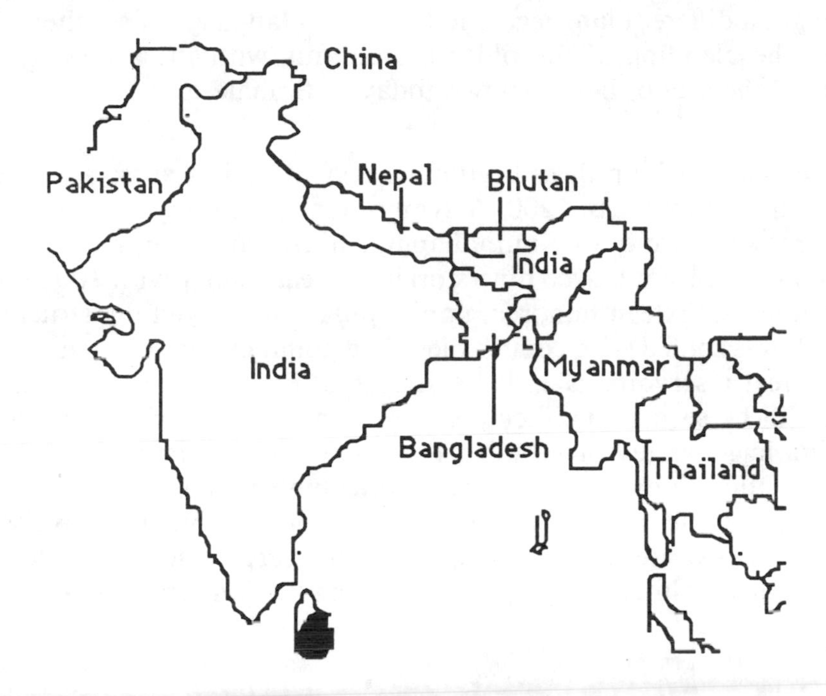

for suspected evil-doing and moved to a nearby island to establish his own kingdom. The island, formerly known as Ceylon, is now Sri Lanka.

In the epic Hindu story *Ramayana,* the settling of Ceylon is attributed to one man, Rana, who crossed the series of sandbars from the mainland to the island known now as Adam's Ladder to recover his wife, who had been stolen by a king of the first inhabitants of the island. (Whatever the pattern of migration, Sinhalese settlers on the island found earlier residents there who earned their livelihood possibly by hunting, an occupation suggested by the name given them—Vedda [in Hindi, "hunt"].)

Sinhalese written history tells of the first Sinhalese king, Vijaya, who sailed from the Bay of Bengal in 483 B.C. with several hundred followers, married a local princess on the island, and became King of Ceylon. These early inhabitants were probably worshippers of Hindu deities but soon were converted to Buddhism, a religion which was brought to the island in the third century B.C.

These first settlers in Vedda country were joined through the centuries by other migrants from the continent. The later settlers brought new art and culture to the land, and eventually some of them brought a different language, the Dravidian language of southern India. The blending of the older immigrants with these newcomers formed the group that is known today as Sinhalese.

Early history. From these beginnings a great society arose and flourished until about A.D. 1200. A symbol for this society was the magnificent capital city of Anuradhapura, filled with beautiful temples and a magnificent palace nine-stories tall, each story with 100 lavish apartments. Sixteen hundred granite pillars supported the structure, which was roofed with copper tiles. The grand city had paved streets and great reservoirs as early as 1000 B.C. Evidence of its greatness can still be seen in architecture and paintings. Elsewhere, a palace with a huge white dome built 244 years before Christ still stands at Tissa. Other domed masonry structures built with six different variations of dome shapes are used to house Buddhist relics of days past. These *dagaba* are lavishly sculptured structures made of brick and plastered in white. The largest dagaba have diameters approaching

A Hindu wedding party of earlier years illustrates the traditional clothing of the Sinhalese. *Courtesy of the Smithsonian Institution.*

300 feet. In other places artificial hills made of masonry and rising several hundred feet form supports for shrines. The monument, built by King Parakrama (A.D. 1156–1186), contains two outstanding examples of rock sculpture: a statue of Parakrama and images of Buddha. Metal castings can be dated to the period between the fifth and twelfth centuries A.D. Another great city, Pretnapura, became famous as "the city of gems," for its mines that produced a wide range of precious stones.

Union and division. The attractive society was subjected to frequent invasions from India. One such visit, chronicled in the *Mahavamsa,* brought a sacred Buddha Tooth to Sri Lanka in the third century.

In 760, the great city of Anuradhapura fell to the Cholas, invaders from what is now the Madras State of India, and the Sinhalese moved their capital to a new city, Polonaruwa. Beginning in 944, Tamil people began to move across the narrow strip of water. By the eleventh century, Tamil people had conquered the island. They were to hold it for fifty years until a new Sinhalese king, Vijcyabahu V, regained the throne. This king ruled for forty years before the country again fell into many separate parts. The nation remained fragmented until it was reunited in 1153 by Parakambaku. However, the death of this ruler brought a new decline in the land. Fifteen kings attempted to control the kingdom in the next quarter century, until the land of the Sinhalese was subjected to a Hindu ruler from Southern India.

Dutch. When Portuguese sailors accidentally stumbled onto the land in 1505, they found the island divided into three kingdoms—a northern Tamil stronghold, mountain Sinhalese in the area of Kandy, and lowland Buddhists in the south. In the 1600s, Dutch invaders seized control of the government of the Sinhalese after a twenty-year dispute with the Portuguese, and in 1796, British interests took control of the coastal areas. In 1802, the Peace of Amiens formalized the British claim to the coast. Meanwhile, in the mountain areas, the King of Kandy held a kingdom and treated his subjects with such great atrocities that some of them pleaded with the British to intervene. This accomplished in 1815, the British held control of the island from then until its independence in 1948. The British outlawed the rigid caste systems that had been the standards for Sinhalese populations both in the lowlands and in the mountains and initiated changes in land use. European traders began to influence Sinhalese culture. The tradition of rice farming by small groups or families gave way to a system of large plantations, where the Sinhalese began raising tea, coconut, and spices for trade.

British Commonwealth. In 1948, Ceylon became an independent member of the British Commonwealth and the name of the country was changed to Sri Lanka. With this have come many economic and social changes in the Sinhalese system. A decade of tension began in 1956 between the Sinhalese majority and the Tamils, who formed the largest minority. A major issue was the official language of Ceylon, which at first was declared by the government to be Sinhalese only, but later came to include Tamil as well. In order to control the large Tamil minority, the Sinhalese government first attempted to move the Tamils from their northern stronghold by banning fishing in northeastern waters, then by inviting India to send troops to keep peace. The tension between the two groups led to states of emergency in Ceylon in 1977 and 1983 and to continued unrest through 1991.

Sinhalese control. The Sinhalese dominate politics in the Democratic Socialist Republic of Ceylon. The president is directly elected by the people and the Sinhalese comprise seventy-four percent of the population. Their dominance has been responsible for much violent conflict, which the current government has attempted to resolve by conferences with the Tamil people. In 1989, the Sinhalese rulers again attempted peace with the Tamil minority, this time by requesting immediate withdrawal of the Indian military. This withdrawal was made conditional upon the relinquishing of weapons by the Tamils and establishment of nearly autonomous territorial governments in Sri Lanka. Tamils have, throughout, sought a voice in the government through the Tamil United Liberation Front, a political party opposed by the Sinhalese Sri Lanka Freedom Party. Outside of government, a major force for Tamil independence was the Liberating Tigers of Tamil Eelam. In 1990 the Sri Lankan Sinhalese-dominated government declared its intent by passing a law eliminating separation of the country as a solution to the unrest.

Culture Today

Economy. Agriculture has always been the base for Sinhalese life. The Sinhalese place those people who engage in agricultural pursuits in a higher caste. The tiller of the soil has traditionally been the most noble of occupations. This attitude has persisted to the degree that

Women work in the fields picking tea in Sri Lanka. *Courtesy of the Smithsonian Institution.*

present-day urban professional families and civil servants still own their own farmlands. The major crop grown for food is rice. Fruit and vegetables are grown as well.

The British formed a plantation system for the growth of cash crops, which upset the Sinhalese village economy at first. Tea soon accounted for half of all Sinhalese income, with rubber and coconuts also grown as cash crops. Most of the tea, rubber, and coconut plantations of the country are now owned by the Sinhalese, but their development has seriously affected the lives of the Sinhalese. The growth of cash crops was accompanied by a decline in production of rice and fish—the Sri Lanka food crops. In the 1990s, food production must be enhanced by imports, a situation that drains the nation's economy.

Today, much of the old Sinhalese way of life has vanished. Social and political tastes have been shaped by associations with Western countries, particularly among the Sinhalese who live in the low country. Twenty-five percent of these people now live in the cities. The capital city, Colombo, and its suburbs now house nearly two million people, while on the Pacific coast, Jaffna has a population of 120,000. About one-sixth of the people now find work in light manufacturing.

Villages. Each of these hill communities might contain as many as 1,000 people, whose homes are clustered together below a rain-fed reservoir for water. There is cooperation among the people of a village because of their mutual dependence on water. The villagers, who are usually closely related, share the water, which is carefully allotted to each plot of land.

Social structure. In spite of the British ban on the traditional castes of Sinhalese society in the 1800s, remnants of this system still pervade the society. Throughout the land among all the peoples of Sri Lanka, people who own agricultural land are among the highest rank, whether or not their agricultural efforts produce great incomes. Below these *Goyigama,* there are subcastes of holders of royal appointments, popular leaders, cowherds to the king, royal clerks, temple servants, wood choppers, some domestic servants, fishermen, cinnamon peelers, soldiers, and toddy tappers. Lower castes include craftsmen, tailors, lime burners, laundrymen, sugar confection makers, potters, barbers, grass cutters, tom-tom beaters, dancers, mat weavers, funeral drummers, and beggars. As the Sinhalese have moved to the larger cities and towns, these castes, which are hereditary and somewhat inflexible in the villages, become more flexible and more related to wealth. In a city of two million, for example, some claim to be Goyigama by heredity or success (and are separately identified from the country folk by the name Colombo Goyigama). These castes are closed networks of families based on occupations and on an element Sinhalese hold to be "ritual purity."

The social structure is further complicated by religion. The Buddhist temple priests control more than 100,000 acres of agricultural land, which is farmed by tenants or share croppers. In addition, the Buddhist faith disdains commercial activity as demeaning. The buying, manufacturing, and selling of goods is therefore left to Hindu Tamils and Christians. Buddhists prefer to work in government service.

Family life. The rigid social structure determines the members of a family. Mores related to the traditional social positions are so fixed that formal marriages are rarely necessary. Parents arrange for the marriages of their children and often provide a dowry for the marriage of a daughter. The male-domination in the family begins before marriage. A man can refuse to accept a marriage arranged by his parents, but a woman lacks this power of veto. Nevertheless, the various castes prescribe who shall marry, so that a formal marriage is rarely necessary. A woman who cooks for a man is considered to be his wife. There are widespread economic differences between groups of Sinhalese, however, and marriages are usually arranged by parents in the interest of protecting their holdings. Tradition prescribes that sons inherit land from their father in equal degrees. And the same arrangement stands for the property, if any, of the wife. Husband and wife, in the more traditional highland families, do not share property. In the lowland cities, this practice has changed by Dutch law to one of communal property between husband and wife

Sinhalese families are male-dominated. This is seen in marriage arrangements which sometimes contract for the woman not to work outside the house. In many Sinhalese homes, the husband has his own room; wife and children share another. It is also seen in the eating habits of the family. Men are served first and eat separately. Women and children eat together later. That the role of women is changing can be seen from their participation in sports.

Food, clothing, and shelter. The basic food of all the Sinhalese is rice. This is eaten at all the most important meals, even though it must now be imported in great quantities to meet the country's needs. Those who can afford to do so eat several times daily. A typical breakfast may consist of *sambal*, a hot dish of chilies, onions, fish, and coconut. Another breakfast is prepared from boiled yam. And, of course, rice is available for breakfast. A mid-morning break allows time for tea or coconut milk. Sinhalese eat their heaviest meal at noon. Rice with vegetables or fish forms the main dish and is often supplemented with a coconut soup, *pol-hodi*. Fruits are also included in the noon meal. A mid-afternoon tea is the time for a bun or sweet pastry. Then in the evening, Sinhalese eat a lighter meal of rice and curry.

These meals are taken in a single-family home, which, in the country, is a two- to four-room building surrounded by and separated from other houses by a garden. In the growing cities and large towns, houses are packed close together and gardens are relegated to the back of the house. Mud and plaster walls are topped with roofs made of tile or palm fronds. The average village house is lighted by an oil lamp, and food is prepared in a fireplace using tools made from such materials as coconut shells. There is little furniture. Overcrowding in the cities has resulted in government construction of flats or apartment buildings along with some individual family homes. These homes are made by building wooden frames for the walls and filling them with mud, which is then compacted. These homes most often include electricity and running water. Another solution to urban crowding is to offer, at government expense, to move people to rural areas and then employ them for a time building their own water and sanitation systems. Between 1965 and 1970 some 400,000 people were relocated under this program. This included many of the nearly 40,000 people who had begun to crowd the ancient city of Anuradhapura, which was considered to be a sacred site by the Sinhalese. In the late 1960s and early 1970s, a new town was built next to the old one in order to preserve the sacred sites.

In the cities, businesspeople and workers dress in Western-style clothing during the workday, then return home to change to the time-honored common dress of the Sinhalese. For men, this includes a sarong, a wraparound skirt that is ankle length and is worn with or without a colorful shirt. For women, daily dress is the sari, a long piece of cloth wrapped to form a skirt and draped over the shoulder. A blouse completes the woman's dress. In contrast to the men, women wear the traditional dress outside the home, then some change to a Western-style robe to do housework.

Education. Schools are organized on a British pattern and even religion has been affected by Western influence. Officially, education in Sri Lanka is compulsory between the ages of five and fifteen, and education is free from kindergarten through the university. Three types of schools have proven successful among the Sinhalese: state schools, Perivenas (Buddhist schools), and Christian church schools. By 1990, the rate of illiteracy in Sri Lanka had been reduced to below twelve percent.

Religion. There have been developments of Roman Catholic and Protestant groups among the people, and there are some followers of

Islam on the island. Buddhism continues to be, however, the dominant religion, and its influence is particularly strong in the hill communities, where the more traditional Sinhalese live.

The chief of the local temple, the *Bhikku,* and the local doctor specializing in herbal medicine, the *ayervida* are the most important people in a Sinhalese village.

Recreation. Many holidays and festival days are associated with religion in Sri Lanka. The Sinhalese, mostly Buddhists, celebrate Wesak, the festival of the birth, enlightenment, and death of Buddha, with home decorations and lights on public buildings. This celebration is held in May. In the fall, the Tamil neighbors in the cities, most of them Hindu, celebrate Deepvali, a festival of lights to honor the return of the Hindu god Rama from Sri Lanka to India. Each year, the highland city of Kandy presents Perahera, a pageant in which a casket containing relics of the Buddha are paraded through the streets on the back of the largest available elephant.

Young people enjoy the sports brought to them in colonial days. Cricket and soccer teams are organized everywhere and are major items in the news. Boys learn to play soccer in school.

Girls have much less leisure time than boys. Beginning at an early age, they are expected to complete their school work and then return home to help with the household chores. Still some girls participate in track and field contests and there is an All-Sri-Lanka Women's Hockey Team.

Arts and literature. Early Sinhalese art and writing was inspired by religion. Adopting much from India, early Sinhalese built magnificent temples that included areas for sacred rites, a bathing tank, a sacred tree, and a *stupa.* The stupa was a bubble-shaped dome built over the bones of an ancestral hero. Over the years, the typical stupa was enhanced with a wooden or stone railing, and later a brick cube around the dome. From this, a stone pillar arose adorned by one or more umbrellas.

The temples were decorated with figures of deities, and with paintings of tongues of fire and of various animals symbolizing such events as birth and death. Paintings, bas-relief, and giant stone figures depicted the Buddha. Paintings in the temples and on cave walls featured figures of maidens. Later art focused on the Buddha's spiritual struggle, with tongues of flame, whirlwinds, and demons standing in sharp contrast to the tranquil Buddha figures.

Modern artists represent the traditional themes and have extended these ideas to include Western-style expressions. A group known as the '43 Group successfully introduced a Picasso style to Sri Lankan painting. Other artists, such as Pushpananda Weerasinghe, have recently experimented with abstract sculpture.

Early literature, too, was of religious import. The *Mahavamsa* is the earliest-known religious history, and includes instructions about the building of a stupa. This work was written by a Buddhist monk, Thera Mahanama, in an older Pali language Other early literature includes translations of religious works from earlier Sanskrit or Pali and poetic works. Popular among these were message poem-prayers to a god asking for favors—called *sandesa.*

Modern literature included, until 1940, works in both Sinhala and English. The first Sinhalese novel appeared in 1905, but the first modern works also emphasized religious themes. Two authors are credited with developing the novel in Sinhala, Simon de Silva and Piyadasa Sirisena. Both chose as themes the decay of traditional Sinhalese life under British urbanization. Simon de Silva's best novel was *Our Religion*; Piyadasa Sirisena's, *Happy Marriage,* a story of two lovers who could not marry until the man, a Christian, renounced his religion in favor of Buddhism.

Still on the theme of Sinhalese tradition, Martin Wikramasinghe more recently wrote *Ape Gama* (Our Village) and *Gam Peraliya* (Changing Village).

Music and dance were inhibited in the revival of Sinhalese arts by the disdain of Buddhist monks, who were not allowed to encourage these art modes. Still, males dance dramatic roles and rhythmic dances in the highlands of Kandy dressed in an ornate costume that includes thirty-two or sixty-four different ornaments. In the 1940s, women began to dance in the hill country, and their dancing has been accepted under government sponsorship. Formerly, women dancers were considered to be of very low caste.

By the 1970s, traditional dances had been reinterpreted in successful ballets under the direction of Chitra Sena.

For More Information

Nyrop, Richard F. and others. *Sri Lanka, A Country Study*. Washington, DC: American University, 1982.

Wriggins, W. Howard. *Ceylon: Dilemmas of a New Nation*. Princeton: Princeton University Press, 1960.

TAIWANESE

(tie′ wahn eez′)

Descendants of Chinese settlers and immigrants on the island of Taiwan.

Population: 21,000,000 (1991 estimate).
Location: Western Pacific Ocean.
Languages: Taiwanese Chinese; Mandarin Chinese.

Geographical Setting

The island of Taiwan lies approximately 120 miles off the south-central Chinese coast. Its shape is usually compared to that of a tobacco leaf. About one-and-one-half times the size of Vermont, the island is roughly 250-miles long and eighty-miles wide in the middle.

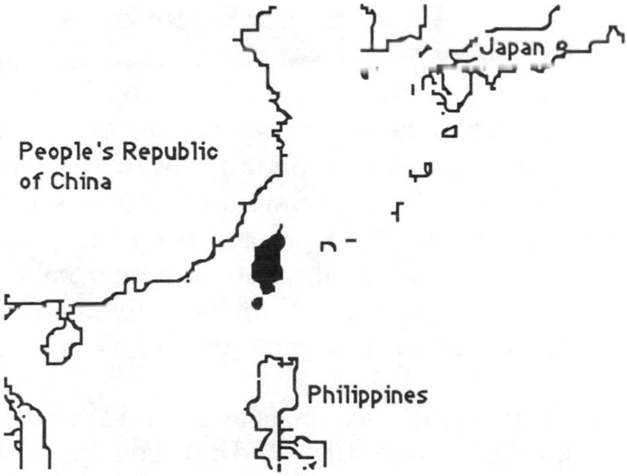

To the west, across the Taiwan Strait, lies mainland China; to the south, about 200 miles over the Bashi Channel, begin the Philippines; eighty miles to the east and northeast lie the Ryuku Islands, Japan's southernmost extension; northward stretches the South China Sea and the central Chinese coast. Taiwan controls a number of smaller islands, notably the Pescadores (Peng-hu), close to the west coast, and two island groups (Quemoy and Matsu) close to mainland China. Rugged mountains, with fifty peaks near or over 10,000 feet, run down the eastern two-thirds of the island, right to the coast. The western one-third, with fertile plains and tidal flats, holds most of the population and all of the major cities. The capital is Taipei, near the northern tip.

Known officially as the Republic of China, Taiwan is also called Nationalist China. Since its defeat on the mainland and withdrawal to Taiwan in 1949, the "Nationalist" government has remained hostile to its rival, the Communist regime of mainland China.

Taiwan's latitude is roughly equal to that of south Florida, and its climate is subtropical, though snow and frost occur in higher mountains in winter. The abundant rainfall comes in two monsoon seasons. During the northern monsoon (October to March) temperatures can plunge suddenly in areas such as Taipei, as cold winds sweep in from north China. The southern monsoon (April to September) brings south Taiwan most of its rain, as well as ocean-bred typhoons. These violent tropical storms, the Pacific's equivalent of hurricanes, cause frequent damage to property and crops throughout the island.

Historical Background

Early peoples. Little is known about Taiwan's early history, though archeological evidence indicates that people lived there as early as 8000 B.C. Taiwan's earliest inhabitants were not Chinese, but are thought to have come from Malaysia or Indonesia. Some scholars believe that non-Chinese Miao people from south China also settled Taiwan and mixed with the Malaysians. These tribal peoples evolved into two distinct groups: farmers who occupied the western plains and less sedentary hunters and warriors who lived in the mountains.

Hakka settlers. For centuries, the island had little or no contact with the mainland, and Chinese rulers did not consider it part of China. The earliest Chinese reference calls the island the Land of Yangchow;

later, during the Han Dynasty (206 B.C. to A.D. 222), it was known as Yinchow. In A.D. 239, a government expedition of 10,000 men is said to have explored Taiwan, but did not claim or colonize it. Not until the Tang Dynasty (618 to 907) did the first Chinese come to live there. The Hakka, originally from northern China, had fled southward to escape harsh persecution by their neighbors. Settling coastal areas across from the island, they became fishers and traders, thus learning of Taiwan and its surrounding islands. Eventually, pressured by continuing persecution, they migrated first to the Peng-hu Islands and then to Taiwan itself. They settled the southern plains, forcing the aboriginal occupants into the mountains.

Fukien immigrants. During the Ming Dynasty (1368 to 1644), growing numbers of Chinese from Fukien province, just over the Taiwan Strait, also began to occupy the island. They took over the southern and western plains, pushing some of the Hakkas farther inland. During the 1400s and 1500s, Taiwan also became a refuge for pirates, who preyed on ships and on coastal areas of the mainland. The fall of the Ming Dynasty to the Manchus brought a large wave of Fukien refugees, so that about 100,000 Chinese altogether lived on Taiwan by 1650. Eventually, the Fukien Taiwanese would call themselves *ben-di-ren* ("this-place-person" or native), and Taiwanese Chinese would evolve out of the Fukien dialect.

Koxinga and the Dutch. In 1517, Portuguese sailors, spotting Taiwan on their way to Japan, had cried out "ilha formosa" ("beautiful island"), giving the island the name by which Europeans would know it, Formosa. But it was the bitter rivals of the Portuguese, the Dutch, who became the main European presence on Taiwan. In the 1620s much of Taiwan came under the Dutch East India Company, for which Taiwanese peasants grew sugar cane and other cash crops.

As the Ming Dynasty came under increasing threat from the Manchus, the last Ming emperor appointed a Taiwan-based pirate, Cheng Chi-lung, as commander of the Ming navy. Despite winning several battles, Cheng could not prevent the defeat of the Ming forces on the mainland in 1644. Cheng's son, Cheng Cheng-kung (known in the west as Koxinga), carried on the struggle against the Manchus. Like his father, he scored some successes but was unable ultimately to defeat the Manchus, who would rule the mainland until 1911 (see MAINLAND CHINESE). In the early 1660s, Koxinga turned his attention to the Dutch, who up until then had not considered him a threat. He besieged the sparsely manned Dutch forts, which held out for nearly two years before surrendering. Koxinga died soon after expelling the Dutch, in the midst of plans to drive the Spanish from the Philippines. Today, the Taiwanese revere him as a national hero.

Manchu period. Koxinga's successors, weakened by internal feuding, were unable to maintain Taiwan's independence, and in 1683 they surrendered after Manchu troops landed on the island. Manchu rule lasted for 200 years, but the unruly island was often governed more in name than in fact. Trade flourished, despite the lack of a strong central government. Chinese immigration from Fukien, stepped up under Koxinga, continued to grow, so that the Chinese-descended population was about 2,500,000 by 1890. During this period and increasing in the late 1800s, Western powers contributed to the island's prosperity, as Taiwanese ports took advantage of booming trade.

Imperial Japan. Responding to Taiwan's riches and to the weakness of Manchu control, Japan mounted a brief military invasion of the island in 1874. Full-scale war broke out between China and Japan in 1895, after Japan's invasion of China's ally, Korea. The Japanese victory resulted in the cession of Taiwan to Japan, and the island became Japan's first imperial possession. Brutally crushing a brief Taiwanese rebellion, the Japanese imposed an often harsh law and order on the formerly turbulent island. The fifty years of Japanese rule brought material benefits: the Japanese built a network of roads and railroads, as well as schools, hospitals, and industrial facilities. Yet the Taiwanese chafed under Tokyo's oppressive rule, which ended with Japan's defeat in World War II (1945).

Taiwan and the Guomindang. From the Manchu collapse in 1911 to the defeat of Japan (which had invaded China in the 1930s), mainland China endured long years of widespread death and destruction. Along with the brutality of the Japanese invasion, conflict persisted between the Nationalist government (Guomindang) and the Communist rebels. In 1949, Communist forces defeated the Guomindang, thereby gaining control of the mainland. Chiang Kai-shek, the Guomindang leader, withdrew with his forces to Taiwan. With him came 1,500,000 mainland Chinese, including about 600,000 soldiers, bringing Taiwan's Chinese-descended population to 7,500,000 in 1950.

Chaing Kai Shek, an earlier leader of the Taiwan Chinese, is honored with this memorial in Taipai.
Courtesy of Dr. W. Paul Fischer.

At first, Chiang Kai-Shek hoped to reconquer the mainland. As this hope faded, the mainlanders' children and grandchildren came to consider themselves more and more Taiwanese. Taiwan's strongest ally has been the United States. All the same, in 1971 Taiwan was expelled from the United Nations and replaced by the mainland People's Republic of China, which the United States recognized in 1979 as the legitimate Chinese government. Yet despite diplomatic isolation, the Taiwanese have prospered in the world of international trade; since the mid-1960s the island has regained the boom town flavor of its pre-Japanese past.

Culture Today

Growing unity. Today, distinctions between Taiwanese ethnic groups have become less divisive than in the past, as economic prosperity and the passage of time have acted to break down barriers. At about 1.5 percent of the population, the aborigines have become largely assimilated. They speak Taiwanese and have adopted Chinese ways, though most still live in less-populated mountain areas. Like other native peoples, they have been treated harshly in the past and sometimes still are, even as their artistic and other cultural traditions have acquired a certain trendiness. The isolation of these native peoples continues as intermarriage is less between them and the Chinese immigrants than among the Chinese groups themselves.

The various Chinese groups also maintain some elements of their self-identity. The Hakkas (about five percent of the population) still pride themselves on being the earliest Chinese immigrants, and maintain their own dialect as well as speaking Taiwanese. They traditionally favor railroad and police jobs. At seventy-five to eighty percent of the population, the Fukien Chinese comprise an easy majority, dominating many aspects of business, agriculture and local politics. Mainlanders (about fourteen percent) continue to dominate education and national government, tending to live in cities such as Taipei. Still, such differences mean less and less, especially among the young, who tend to view themselves simply as Taiwanese.

Classical Chinese culture. In contrast to the Communist regime of mainland China, the Guomindang government has consciously preserved and emphasized the glories of China's ancient culture. From acupuncture to Zen Buddhism, from the martial arts to the ancient art of calligraphy, Taiwan has become a bastion of traditional ways that have often disappeared or fallen into neglect on the mainland. In this respect, as in Taiwan's role as political haven from mainland enemies, the Guomindang era closely parallels that of Koxinga. The seventeenth-century hero, with whom Chiang Kai-shek is often compared, kept Ming culture and government alive in Taiwan, opposing Manchu rule on the mainland. Similarly, Chiang's personal leadership encouraged artists and other cultural figures to ally themselves with the Guomindang. The mainlanders who arrived in 1949 represented every aspect of Chinese culture—repeating the pattern of those who found refuge under Koxinga in the 1600s.

Frontier tradition of free enterprise. In addition, Taiwan today cherishes an older and more robust island tradition, born of earlier days as a prosperous, unsettled and lawless frontier. The Taiwanese "economic miracle" has brought the people Asia's highest standard of living after Japan. Rags-to-riches stories are common, and many is the self-made millionaire who began his career in a lowly position. Government regulation has traditionally amounted to little—leading some from other countries to say that the Taiwanese idea of free enterprise is a little too free. Taiwanese companies have made copies of brand-name products—"Rolex" watches, "Gucci" shoes, "Cartier" lighters, for example—to be sold cheaply without regard for copyright or patent infringement. After years of complaints, however, the Taiwanese government has recently taken some measures to restrain such freewheeling practices.

Government. Officially, Taiwan's Guomindang government has insisted on retaining the name Republic of China, maintaining also that Taiwan is a part of China and refusing to recognize the mainland Communist government. This position has been the major stumbling block to diplomatic recognition by other countries, as well as to participation in international sporting events such as the Olympics. Under Chiang Kai-shek, the Guomindang kept a tight grip on power. Chiang died in 1975, and was eventually succeeded as president by his popular oldest son, Chiang Ching-kuo. The younger Chiang initiated some democratic reforms, such as legalizing opposing political parties. In 1987, he abolished martial law, in force for nearly forty years. Upon Chiang Ching-kuo's death in 1988, the Taiwanese-born Lee Teng-hui succeeded him, symbolizing greater participation by Taiwanese in the national government. All over Taiwan, statues honor Chiang Kai-shek and his predecessor, Dr. Sun Yat-sen, who founded the Guomindang and the Republic of China in the early 1900s. Even today, the Guomindang governs by Dr. Sun's Three Principles: Nationalism, Livelihood, and Civil Rights.

Food, clothing, and shelter. Food occupies a primary place in Chinese social life, and Chinese cuisine is famous all over the world for its complexity and variety. Taipei is a major center for Chinese cooking. Everywhere in the bustling city one sees evidence of food being transported, prepared, or enjoyed. Chinese cuisine has many regional variations, and all may be found in Taipei. Because most of the mainlanders and most of the Taiwanese themselves come from the southeastern province of Fukien, that region's dishes are most widespread in Taiwan. Seafood and rich, tangy sauces are often featured.

The Taiwanese have taken to Western clothing, and in daily life most Taiwanese wear clothing similar to that found on the streets of America or Europe. Older men especially often wear hats fashioned from straw in Western styles or in the shallow, conical style traditionally worn to keep the sun off. Sandals and shorts are also popular.

Most Taiwanese live in modest but comfortable houses or apartments. Virtually all homes have electricity—and own at least one television set, as well as other electronic conveniences. Taiwanese like the noise and activity of city life, finding the constant uproar comforting rather than disturbing. Many families who work in the country commute from the city, where they prefer to raise their children.

Family life. The preference for city life comes from the deep importance that Chinese attach to human interaction, a desire for constant companionship rather than solitude. Accordingly, the family holds pride as the most important social unit. Chinese children are loved and indulged, remaining dependent on their parents long after Western children go out on their own. Indeed, the idea of children going "out on their own" is foreign to the Chinese family.

Throughout life, family connections remain paramount in all aspects of Taiwanese activity, from the job one gets to exchanges of favors in minor daily matters. As they grow older, the children look after their parents, and failure to take care of older relatives is considered a serious moral failing. Families are patriarchal, and a woman who marries is considered to have joined her husband's family. Friendships—slowly made but lifelong—serve to augment family connections in business and daily life. Each Taiwanese can count on a network of family and friends for support in times of trouble.

Literature and the arts. Because literature was discouraged under Japanese occupation, most Taiwanese writers are young. Western trends in literature and art are popular. Taiwan boasts Asia's most vibrant film industry and is the home of the "kung fu" movie, which draws on Chinese martial arts to please young audiences in both East and West. In general, though, Western culture tends to find favor among the young, while traditional Chinese art forms appeal to older and more conservative Taiwanese. In dance, music, and theater, a number of artists and companies creatively blend both Western and Eastern influences. The Cloud Gate Dance Ensemble is perhaps the most acclaimed of these groups, winning worldwide recognition in its European tour in 1981. Older people enjoy Chinese opera, calligraphy (the art of beautiful writing, a favorite of Chiang Kai-shek), painting, and traditional music and dance (see MAINLAND CHINESE). Of these arts, perhaps calligraphy is the most tradition-bound. Profound importance is attached to the materials (brushes, inks, and paper, which the Chinese invented in the 100s) and to the artist's own spiritual approach to the art.

Religion. The artist's technique should flow from the inner harmony that the Chinese admire in all respects of life, and which is reflected also in Chinese religion. Unlike Western religions, Chinese religions are not separate or mutually exclusive, tending instead to merge with each other and often to take on aspects of philosophy. Thus, most Taiwanese would think of themselves as practicing both Buddhism and Taoism, with a strong overlay of Confucianism. Each of these religions has many temples throughout the island, some temples are devoted to two of them or even to all three. About 2 to 5 percent of Taiwanese are Christian, though the Christians tend to be highly visible and often occupy powerful positions in society. Chiang Kai-

A Confucian temple in Taipei, Taiwan. *Courtesy of Dr. W. Paul Fischer.*

shek, for example, was Christian, having converted after marriage to a devout Christian woman.

Holidays. Taiwanese holidays fall into two categories, determined either by the lunar (Chinese) calendar, or by the solar (Western) one. The lunar holidays can fall on different days by Western reckoning and represent traditional folk or religious celebrations. They are the most colorful and chaotic, often involving crowded, festive, and noisy street celebrations. The chief lunar holiday is the Chinese New Year, lasting three days; others include Lantern Day (also involving crowded festivities and lots of fireworks), Dragon Boat Festival (with colorful, televised boat races), and the birthdays of Taoist deities such as Kuanyin, goddess of mercy, and Matsu, goddess of the sea. Solar holidays celebrate occasions associated with the state: Founding Day, on January 1, celebrates the founding of the Republic of China; Restoration Day, on October 25, celebrates Taiwan's return to Chinese rule after the Japanese occupation; Sun Yat-sen's and Chiang Kai-shek's birthdays are also observed, on November 12 and October 31, respectively.

Language. Mandarin Chinese, Taiwan's official language, is taught in schools and used by the media. Most Taiwanese, however, speak Taiwanese Chinese in their daily life. Descended from the Fukien dialect, Taiwanese is a spoken language only. While the two languages are similar, they are not mutually intelligible. Young people, having grown up after the mainlanders' arrival, all speak Mandarin; many older Taiwanese can still speak Japanese, but have no Mandarin. While older children study English in school, few speak it well, though most can read and write simple English.

For More Information

Copper, John F. *Taiwan: Nation-State or Province?* Boulder: Westview Press, 1990.

Knapp, Ronald G. *China's Island Frontier.* Honolulu: University Press of Hawaii, 1980.

Reid, Daniel P. *Insight Guides: Taiwan.* Singapore: APA Publications, 1989.

TAMILS

(tah′ milz)

A mostly Hindu, Dravidian people of South India.

Population: 5,100,000 (1991 estimate).
Location: Tamil Nadu (India) and Sri Lanka.
Language: Tamil.

Geographical Setting

The vast majority of Tamils live in the Indian state of Tamil Nadu, an area about the size of Kansas on the far southeastern tip of the Indian subcontinent. Tamil Nadu ("Land of the Tamils") is bounded to the north by the state of Andhra Pradesh, to the northwest by the state of Karnataka, and to the east by the state of Kerala. Eastward lies the Bay of Bengal, which meets the Indian Ocean and the Gulf of Arabia at Cape Comorin, India's and Tamil Nadu's southernmost point. From the coast, a broad plain rises gradually to meet the southern extension of the Eastern Ghats, a chain of hills running down India's eastern coast. West of the hills, the land continues to rise westward in a plateau, until it meets the Western Ghats. Extensions of these hills separate Tamil Nadu from Kerala. Several rivers run west through the plateau and hills to the Bay of Bengal, largest of which is the Cauvery. The largest city is Madras, India's fourth most populous, on Tamil Nadu's northern tip.

About three million Tamils live on the independent island nation of Sri Lanka, off Tamil Nadu's southeastern coast, where they make up about twenty percent of the population. They live mostly in the island's north and east.

Climate in Tamil Nadu is tropical, rising to 110 degrees Fahrenheit in the summer and rarely falling below 65 degrees Fahrenheit

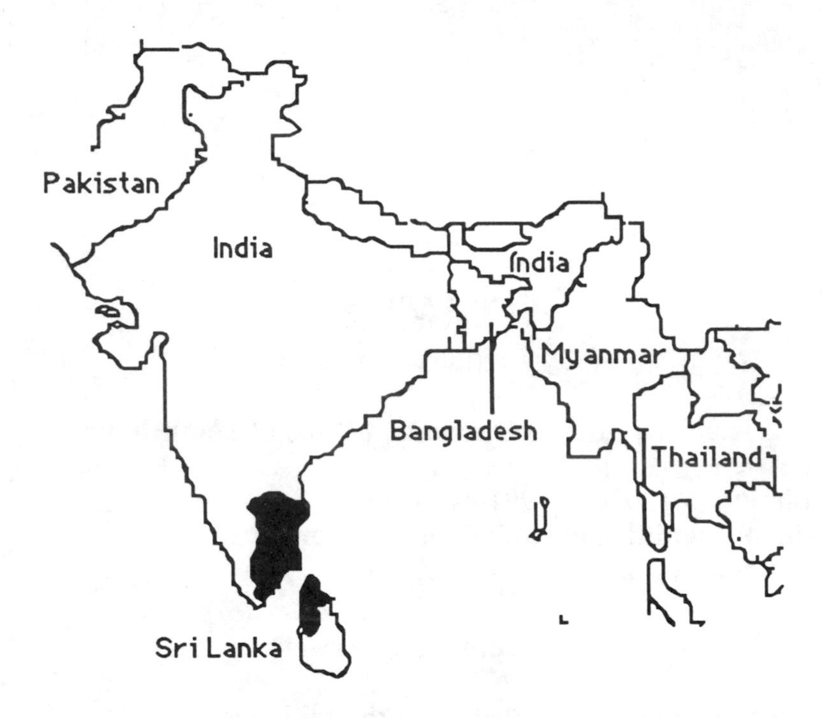

in the winter. Rainfall comes mostly during two monsoon seasons. The southwest monsoon lasts from June to September and can bring an average of two inches a day in some places. The northeast monsoon, from October to December, can be even heavier, and often causes flooding in coastal areas. The northeast monsoon is accompanied by storms and cyclones.

Historical Background

Dravidians and Aryans. The Tamils represent the most culturally distinct remnant of the Dravidian group of peoples, who are thought to have occupied India before the arrival of the Aryans around 1500 B.C. The mixture of Dravidian and Aryan cultures produced elements (such as the Hindu religion) that eventually pervaded the entire subcontinent, giving rise to a common cultural backdrop to the Indian patchwork. Because the Sanskrit-speaking Aryans arrived from the north, however, it was in North India that their influence was strongest. In South India, particularly in Tamil Nadu at the southern tip, the people kept Dravidian ways alive. Especially in their language and the ancient literary works associated with it, the Tamils, of all

Indian peoples, show the smallest Aryan influences (see DRAVIDIANS and INDO-ARYANS).

Early kingdoms. Beginning around 500 B.C., several different Tamil kingdoms arose. Under these dynasties—the Cholas, Cheras and Pandyas—northern influences were brought to the south mostly by the Jain and Buddhist religions. The Tamil kingdoms competed with each other, and the exploits of their heroes are celebrated in a body of poetry called the *Sangam*. Until the A.D. 500s, Tamil bards (performing poets), called *panar,* added to the *Sangam*, establishing the classical foundation of Tamil literature.

Pallava Dynasty. By the 500s, the growing kingdom of the Pallavas, centered near Madras, had gained control of Tamil Nadu and surrounding areas. Believed to be descended from Sanskrit-speakers of North India, the Pallavas promoted Hinduism, suppressing Buddhist and Jain institutions. Yet Tamil language and culture adapted to this change, as a new order of poets working in Tamil emerged. Called *Nayanars*, they were part of a distinctively Tamil religious movement devoted to the Hindu god Shiva (*bhakti*). Under Pallava rule, art and architecture also flourished, and cultural as well as commercial exchanges occurred between South India and Southeast Asia.

Imperial Cholas. The early Chola kingdom, one of those described in the *Sangam*, was based in the valley and delta of the Cauvery river. In the 800s, after centuries of Pallava rule, a new Chola kingdom emerged and overthrew the Pallavas. Like the old Cholas, the new ones based their culture in the rich Cauvery River Valley. There they built ornate and elaborate temples, still visited today, which formed the nucleus of their social and economic lives. Chola rulers controlled much of South India by the 900s; later kings such as Rajaraja (ruled 985–1014) and Rajendra (ruled 1012–44) conquered parts of Sri Lanka and the Maldive Islands. Their powerful navy controlled the Bay of Bengal, and contacts with Southeast Asia and even China were strengthened. Tamil culture, expressed in literature and temple art, flowered during Chola rule, particularly in the 1100s.

Vijayanagara. The Cholas were defeated in the late 1200s by the resurgent Pandyas; by the 1400s most of South India had fallen under a new empire, that of Vijayanagara. This new power arose north of Tamil Nadu, in present Karnataka. In the 1500s, at the peak of Vijayanagara glory, the Tamils were ruled by Telugus, a non-Tamil Dravidian-speaking people of Karnataka and Andhra Pradesh. During this time, substantial numbers of Telugus settled in less populated areas of Tamil Nadu, where they still constitute a sizable minority. Temple building, using huge slabs of native granite, continued to flourish in Tamil Nadu under Pandya and Vijayanagara rule. Vijayanagara power declined in the 1600s, as Muslims expanded into South India (see BENGALIS and PUNJABIS). By the 1700s, the Tamils had come under Muslim states established in Karnataka, although Muslim control of the far south existed more in name than in fact.

European presence. In the late 1700s, however, Muslim rule in Karnataka was swept aside by a new conqueror, the British. European contacts with South India had begun in the late 1400s, with Portuguese landings on the western coast. In the 1500s and 1600s the Dutch and French also established profitable trading settlements. The major Portuguese settlement was at Goa, on the west coast; the major French one was Pondicherry, in Tamil Nadu. The earliest British outpost, and long the most important, was in Madras, also in Tamil Nadu (1639). The earliest British territorial acquisition came in the northeast, however, in Bengal, which by the mid-1700s became the center of the growing British influence. By the early 1800s, the British controlled all of South India as well, having defeated both the French and the Muslim rulers of Karnataka.

British rule. Until 1857, the Tamils were included in the Madras Presidency, the vast southern administrative unit of the English East India Company. Control passed to the British Crown in 1857. Under the British, many Tamils emigrated to work as day-laborers. Over 500,000 went to Sri Lanka between 1896 and 1928, and over 300,000 to other parts of the British Empire, such as South Africa, where their descendants still live. The British brought many material improvements to India: roads, railways, universities (including one in Madras), postal service, and telegraph service. Yet Indians were generally excluded from positions of power or social prestige. Nationalist movements, aimed at self-rule for India, gained support in the late 1800s and early 1900s. For the Tamils, these impulses often expressed themselves in a renewed interest in the ancient Tamil literary and cultural heritage. Independence came in 1947.

Tamils in Sri Lanka. Comprising about twenty percent of the Sri Lankan population, Tamils in Sri Lanka are descended from two different groups. So-called Sri Lankan Tamils (about 2,000,000) are those whose ancestors settled on the island during past periods of imperial expansion, such as that of the Cholas. The Indian Tamils (about 1,000,000) are the descendants of the laborers imported by colonial owners of tea plantations in the late 1800s and early 1900s. Neither group has assimilated to the majority Sinhalese population, descended from Sanskrit-speakers from the north. Instead, they have kept their Tamil culture, though they do not mingle between each other either. Since the 1950s, tension between the Tamil and Sinhalese communities has erupted repeatedly. It has resulted in Sinhalese riots against the Tamils, and in Tamil separatism, which finds its most extreme expression in the terrorist group, the Tamil Tigers. The violence has spread at times to Tamil Nadu, and the Tigers are suspected in the bombing assassination of Indian prime minister Rajiv Gandhi in May 1991.

Culture Today

Culture in South India. The Dravidian south, of which Tamil Nadu may be considered the heartland, is marked by several strong cultural differences from North India. As discussed above, Aryan influences are stronger in the north. Just as that difference stemmed from geographical causes, so did the relative peace in which southern culture

Highly decorated temples dot the region of the Tamils in India.
Courtesy of Shiva Rea Bailey.

evolved. In the north, passes through the high mountains between India and Central Asia allowed successive waves of conquerors to disrupt society (though they also stimulated cultural change). The Aryans were the first such wave; others included Persians, Greeks, and Muslim Turks. The most extreme effects of these incursions may be seen by comparing two cultures of the far north and south. In the Punjab, whose fertile plains bore the brunt of the invasions, the constant warfare created a culture shaped by upheaval (see PUNJABIS). Where the Punjabis for centuries had their Hindu temples ransacked by raiding Muslims, the Tamils' temples stood for centuries, evolving even as they provided a material link with the past. Where the Punjabis never developed an alphabet, much less a body of literature, Tamil language and literature are among the world's richest and most ancient.

Art and architecture. Temple art and architecture represent the core of the Tamil cultural heritage. In addition to their function as religious centers, the temples served as schools, hospitals, courts, banks, grain stores, markets, and theaters. Thus, while northern temples tend to be smaller and more self-contained, Tamil temple complexes often comprise the heart of a town, with walled enclosures that include areas for various civil functions. Tamil temples are distinguished by the *gopuram* (gateway), over which is constructed a concentric ring of rectangular bands, one on top of the other, giving a pyramidal shape to the resulting tower. Each level is decorated with intricate stone sculptures honoring the god to whom the temple is dedicated. Larger complexes have several such gateway towers, which act as landmarks for the pilgrims (journeying worshippers) who come to pray at the temple.

Aside from the many stone sculptures, images of gods and the animals associated with them are also cast in bronze. Weavers create the silk and other cloths in which the figures are draped. Classical dance, involving years of training, is another important art form; dances such as the Bharata Natyam, the Tamils' classical style, are taught, performed, and enjoyed in Madras as nowhere else in India. Dancers and musicians perform at the temples, and epic poems are also read; often, the sculptures illustrate scenes from these ancient works, allowing the audience to follow along.

As elsewhere in India, movies are highly popular, and Tamil filmmakers turn out many thrillers and romances.

Languages and literature. Tamil is older than any contemporary European language and is the oldest Dravidian language (others include Malayalam, Telugu, and Kannada). It is actually two languages, one colloquial, or spoken, and the other formal and literary. Today, Tamil writers use both: colloquial language for dialogue, and literary, "classical" language for narrative passages.

The many Tamil works from the Sangam period (c. 300 B.C.–A.D. 500) fall into two classes: *akam* ("interior") poems, which consider aspects of love; and *puram* ("exterior") poems, which deal with kings, warriors and social behavior. Epics composed after the Sangam period include the *Silappadhikaram*, which tells the story of a passionate woman who avenges the death of her unfaithful husband. In the 1100s, the greatest Tamil poet, Kampan, adapted to Tamil the Sanskrit epic *Ramayana*, a narration of the life of the god Rama. In modern times, as Tamil writers were exposed to Western literary forms, many authors have specialized in the short story or the novel. Some have retold old tales and myths; others have written stories based on patriotic or historical themes.

Religion. Over ninety percent of Tamils are Hindus; about eight percent are Muslims or Christians. Smaller numbers of Jains and Buddhists also survive from early times. The Jains especially have contributed to Tamil culture, both in literature and in the many Jain temples still active. Hindus have a range of gods to worship; among Tamils, as among other Indians, the most popular are Vishnu and Shiva. In particular, Tamils have participated in the movement called *bhakti*, or the devotional worship of Shiva, which has spread throughout India. Most Tamil temples are devoted to one or the other of these two gods. Pious Tamils bathe in a river, the sea, or a temple tank before praying. Different gods require different rituals. For example, devotees of Ganesh, the elephant-headed son of Shiva, break a specific number of coconuts before the shrine.

In South India the caste system, by which Hindus are divided into hereditary social ranks, tends to be more strictly observed than in the north.

Food, clothing, and shelter. Vegetarian dishes are more popular in the south than in the north, though prepared with the often hot spices used throughout India. Many such spices are combined to make curry, the English version of the Tamil word *kari*, which merely means sauce. Different combinations of spices such as cumin, ginger,

Buddha takes many forms in the temples and shrines of India. *Courtesy of Shiva Rea Bailey.*

tamarind and cardamon are mixed; the hotter ones include various chilis. The vegetables—eggplant or potatoes, for example—may be cooked in a stew with the spices, then served with rice, lentils, and yogurt. When meat is eaten, it is most often mutton or chicken, and always as spicy as the vegetables. Tamils also favor seafood, such as fish or shrimp with ginger. Coffee is widely drunk in the south, whereas tea is more popular in the north.

Tamil women's clothing features colors and contrasts brighter and more extreme than in most other regions of India. Their *saris* (lengths of cloth draped over one shoulder and wrapped around the body) feature combinations such as orange with purple, or bright green with pink. Such colors are worn especially during the many public festivals

South of Madras, India, a worship site has been carved from a single massive rock overlooking the Bay of Bengal.
Courtesy of Dr. W. Paul Fischer.

and holidays. Men generally wear *lungis* or *dhotis*, a length of cloth wrapped around the waist and hanging to the knees or ankles, most often with a Western-style shirt.

With about thirty percent living in towns or cities, Tamils are more urban than most other Indian peoples (the average society is about eighteen percent urban). Middle-class city-dwellers live in modest houses or apartments. Though poverty is less apparent in cities such as Madras than in other large Indian cities, the poorest occupy slums of shanties or other makeshift shelters.

Family life. Religion and tradition continue to shape family life for most Tamils. The most important unit is the nuclear family, within which duties and rights are clearly delineated by sex. The men's job is to protect and support the family; men thus dominate public life. Women are expected to care for the houschold and children and, in agricultural families, are in charge of weeding and assisting the men at harvest time. These roles are less fixed among the upper and middle classes, where women are more and more gaining access to education and careers, both formerly reserved for men. The caste system, while now illegal as a basis for discrimination, still influences popular attitudes. Among Tamils in Sri Lanka, for example, it explains why

This Tamil family group is preparing rice for a meal. *Courtesy of Shiva Rea Bailey.*

Sri Lankan Tamils and Indian Tamils–who together comprise the Tamil minority on Sri Lanka–do not mix with each other, though both have preserved their Tamil identity (see above). The Sri Lankan Tamils, who emigrated centuries ago, are of a higher caste than the Indian Tamils, who came as laborers under the British. Caste is hereditary and places the family and thus the individual in a fixed social position.

For More Information

Adler, Jack. *Hippocrene Companion Guide to Southern India.* New York: Hippocrene Books, 1992.

Embree, Ainslie T., ed. *Encyclopedia of Asian History.* New York: Charles Scribner's Sons, 1988.

Kalidos, R. *History and Culture of the Tamils.* Dindigul, India: Vijay Publications, 1976.

Nyrop, Richard F. *India: A Country Study.* Washington, DC: Department of the Army, 1985.

Ross, Russell, ed. *Sri Lanka: A Country Study.* Washington, DC: Dept. of the Army, US Government, 1990.

THAI

(tie)

People of Thailand who are related to the southern Chinese.

Population: 51,000,000 (1991 estimate).
Location: Thailand.
Language: Thai, one of a family of Asian languages that includes Lao and Shan.

Geographical Setting

The country of Thailand lies south of China and is bordered by Malaysia, Myanmar, Laos, and Cambodia. It is a region distinguished by great rivers and mountain ranges. Thailand is separated from Laos by the Mekong River, which flows through Cambodia to the South China Sea. On the west, the Bilauktaung Mountains mark the boundary with Myanmar. These mountains drop to the east to a fertile river basin. The northern Wang, Ping, and Nam rivers converge at the city of Nakhon Sawan, then the single river divides again to form the Chao Phraya and the Nakhon Chai, which empty into the Gulf of Thailand. The central section of this river system is the heart of the Thai rice-growing region and of Thai population.

Northeastern Thailand is a high plateau, the Khorat, that rises in the north to the mountains of northern Myanmar and Laos. These mountains separate Thailand and China, with which Thailand has no boundary, even though the Thai people are believed to have originated in China and are regarded by the Chinese as relatives.

The rice-growing areas of the western rivers and the Mekong are tropical monsoon regions in which heavy and sometimes disastrous rains fall in the months of May, June, and July.

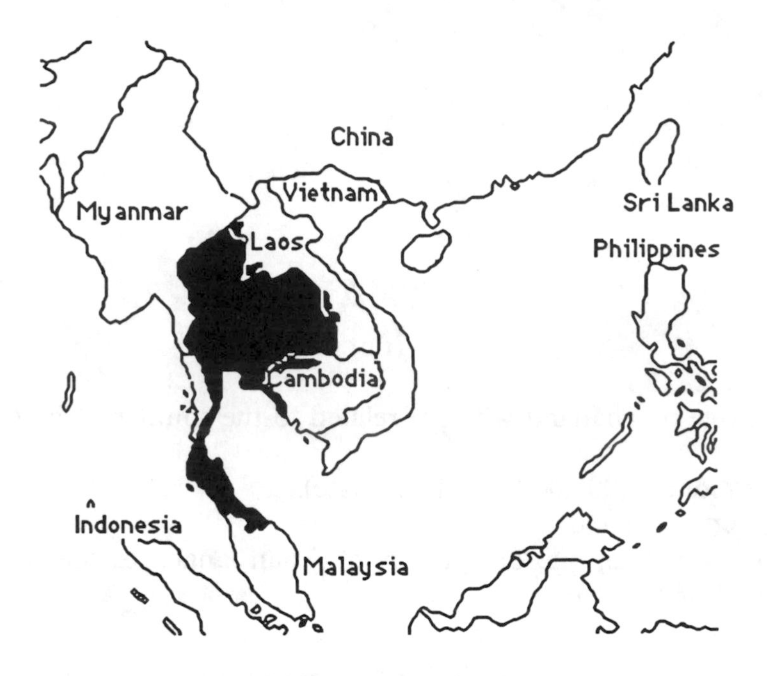

Historical Background

Origin. The first mention of people who spoke the Tai (called Thai in Thailand) language is recorded in Chinese documents about the area in the south of China known as Yunnan in the sixth century B.C. By the first century A.D. the Tai-speaking people had formed an independent kingdom in the south of China and had established themselves as rice growers and skilled workers in bronze casting. These people grew apart from their earlier association with the Chinese except that there were some common elements in the languages and customs. Over the years, the Tai people formed separate political units in what is today Thailand, Laos, and Vietnam. Those who established kingdoms in what is now Thailand separated themselves from the Tai in other regions, eventually changing their name to Thai. Later they became known as Siamese.

Sukhothai. The Thai built a thriving economy in the Chao Phraya valley of western present-day Thailand, where the people became known as rice growers, wood cutters, and elephant trainers. This kingdom replaced a former Khmer (see KHMER) kingdom with its capital at Sukhothai, 200 miles north of the present city of Bangkok on the Mae Nom Yom. The first great Tai kingdom began here under Phra Kuang, said to be the first ruler of all the Thais. By 1350, the kingdom was well established under a king who claimed ownership of both land and people by divine right.

Kublai Khan. In 1253, the Mongol ruler, Kublai Khan, moved southward from China into Myanmar, Laos, and Thailand, temporarily interrupting the Thai kingdom. Reunited again by the most famous of the Thai rulers, Ramthamhaeng (Rama the Great, 1277–1317), the Thai kingdom expanded to include parts of Myanmar and Laos and to reach farther south on the peninsula.

Buddhism. By 1350 the kingdom had come under the rule of Rama Thibodi, who moved the capital southward and built a great city near the mouth of the Chao Phraya, Ayutthaya (Ayuthia). This ruler accepted Buddhism as his religion and imported monks from the north to instill Buddhist beliefs among the people. He also developed a legal code, the Dharmashastra, which guides the Thai people even today. Rama Thibodi continued to expand the Thai realm, capturing the Khmer capital of Ankor and attempting, but failing, to move down the Muslim-dominated Malay peninsula. Following his rule, the Thai kingdom disintegrated into a number of smaller feudal states. But by 1378 the kingdom was reunited, with its capital at Ayutthaya, bound by a king who had become a symbol of religious purity. By now, association with the Khmer people had introduced Hinduism to the Thai, a religion that merged easily with their own Buddhism. The king became *dwaraja*, a divine ruler who was thought to be the earthly incarnation of the Hindu supreme god, Shiva.

The country retained its feudal system. The king ruled over local lords (*nai*) who supervised servant land tenants (*phrai*), and had his own servants who were also protectors of the throne, the *luang phrai*.

Castes. King Trailok, who ruled from 1448 to 1488, was to expand this simple organization of nai, phrai, and luang phrai into a system of castes based on land distribution. This was the beginning of a caste system based on wealth that endured in Thailand until recent years.

Foreign interaction. Shortly after King Trailok's reign, in 1511, the Thai kingdom was first visited by Europeans. Beginning a long tradition of accommodation, the Thais in that year established a trade pact with the Portuguese visitors. Eighty years later, the Dutch were to gain a similar trade pact (1592). This was to be followed by pacts with the French, British, and Japanese.

Meanwhile, in 1569 Burmese forces overran the Thai kingdom, which was betrayed by one of its rebel citizens, Dhammaraji, who had set himself up as a king. His son, Naresuan, embarrassed by his father's treasonable act, reestablished the Thai government and, in order to prevent a repetition of the treachery, changed the status of all phrai to luang phrai—therefore claiming all Thais and their lands to be owned by the king. Siam became a wealthy feudal state governed by a king who was an absolute authority in all matters, including Buddhist religious issues.

For all this early history, there was almost constant war with Cambodians and continuous claiming of Cambodian land by the king of Siam. The capital city of Ayutthaya grew to rival any of the European cities of the time. Then, in 1664, the Dutch attempted to use force to expand their trade agreement. The Thais at first turned to the French, who were in neighboring Cambodia, for help. But the final result was that all foreigners were requested to leave Siam in 1568, and there began 150 years during which no foreigners were allowed in the country.

Burmese control. In 1767, Burmese troops again entered the country and destroyed the capital city of Ayutthaya, But the kingdom was soon reestablished under Phraya Takin. By 1782, Chakkai, a Thai general, had taken over the government as Rama I, King Yat Fa. He moved the capital from Ayutthaya farther south down the river to Bangkok.

British influence. In 1855 the Siamese ruler formed an agreement with Britain that gave the British control over ninety percent of Siamese trade. British advisers became part of the Siamese court and were a great influence on the people of Siam. The relationship between Siam and Great Britain under King Mongkhut was glamorized in the motion picture *The King and I*, an adaptation of a Broadway play based on Margaret Landon's novel *Anna and the King of Siam.* Although this movie was a fictionalized story of two real people, King Mongkhut actually was well acquainted with British customs.

Britain and France. In the late 1800s Britain and France met to define their claims and roles in Indochina. The agreement between them assured Siamese independence. The country flourished under this assurance and the British trade agreement. The tradition of accommodation (bending like a bamboo in the wind) gradually resulted in a changing culture. Siam was influenced toward Western-style life and government. By the early 1900s slavery had been abolished, a university had been established, railroads were under construction, and a system of free education had started for young people from seven to fourteen. But the Westernization of Siam brought unrest.

A constitution. In 1932, the Westernized upper class of Siam revolted and forced the king to establish a constitutional monarchy that included others in the government of the country. Siam was independent under this constitutional government until 1942, when the country sided with anti-Japanese forces in World War II, was defeated, and then ruled by the Japanese until 1945. The old government was destroyed in this period, so that when Siam, now called Thailand, was freed from Japanese control, it fell under military rule. Since then, the nation of the Thai has experienced a series of military coups and has been under continuous military government. Since 1932, the constitution under which Thailand is governed has been rewritten twelve times. Also, during this period, the Thai population increased so that Thailand, which was one of the least densely populated countries just after World War II, with only 22,000,000 people, has more than doubled this population today.

The year 1957 was a turning point in Thai history. While the Thai people had venerated their king and had been loosely united under a constitutional monarchy and under a military dictatorship since World War II, in that year the government fell to Field Marshall Sarit Thanarat. With aid from the United States, Marshall Sarit built roads, upgraded education, and promised more democracy to the Thai people. His rule succeeded in turning Thailand toward a world economy. Even though his death in 1963 revealed a mire of misappropriated funds, Thais mourned the Marshall who had attempted to bring them into the future.

In fact, this seemingly benevolent dictator may have made life more difficult for future military dictatorships. Improved education brought restlessness for more voice in their own government among the Thai people. In 1973, the military rule of generals Thanom and Praphat collapsed, leaving the country without effective leadership. A caretaker government proved distant from the Thai people's desires for more liberalism. The unrest resulted in a new military dictatorship in 1976. The establishment of this government began with a bloody attack on university students. A disappointing military rule then lasted until 1988. Although a general led the country from 1988 to 1991, the country experimented with parliamentary rule. But in 1991, military rule resumed under a "peace-keeping" council headed by General Sunthorn Kongsompong. This government has met with strong opposition, particularly among the students of Thailand.

Today, Thai veneration of its king continues while the Thai people experiment with democratic ideas, struggle with military rule, and rebel in favor of non-military government—all the while maintaining their belief in the leadership of the king.

Culture Today

Industry. In spite of the large and long-established city of Ayutthaya and its replacement, Bangkok, eighty-three percent of the Thai people are still employed in agriculture and live in smaller villages. Rice, maize, rubber, and hardwoods such as teak are grown in an industry that has increasingly centralized landownership at the expense of the small farmer. The Thai peasant today is often landless, working as an employee for large landowners or as an urban factory employee. Much of the industry centers around the hardwood harvests and mining and exporting of the rich tin, tungsten, and lead resources.

The Thai spirit of cooperation is reflected in the efforts of all the villagers to maintain the village temple, which is seen as community property. Thai villagers cooperate in working on systems of dams, canals, paths, and bridges, with each villager contributing a share of the work.

Religion. Buddhism became the state religion of the Thai kingdom in the thirteenth century and has guided Thai thought and action since before that time. In the sixth century B.C., Siddhartha Gautama, who became the Buddha, began to exhort the people of Asia to follow a Noble Eightfold Path that would lead to eternal peace. His teachings were written in the Pali language in the first century A.D. and in the Thai language by the sixth century. The main body of the teachings of Buddha are contained in three "baskets," or sections of the document. The first section contains instructions to the *sangha*, the monastic order charged with preserving the faith. This section also contains information about *karma*, the all-pervading spirit of life and reincarnation, a concept important to Buddhist belief. The second "basket" is the *dharma*, or doctrine of Buddhism, and the third contains commentaries designed to help with understanding of the dharma. The second basket describes the Four Noble Truths: suffering exists, suffering is caused by cravings for worldly pleasures, suffering can be made to cease by ceasing these cravings, and suffering can be made to end by following the Noble Eightfold Path. This Path involves right view (understanding the Four Truths), right thought (without cravings), right speech, right action (for example, no killing), right livelihood (work not harmful to living things), right effort, right mindfulness (a condition similar to the Christian notion of development of mind, body, and spirit), and right concentration (which can be achieved through meditation).

Even the smallest villages have Buddhist temples with carved and colored gables. The Thai peasant may spend as much as one-fourth of his or her total income on this temple and the support of the monks who maintain it. The Buddhist monks are historically so important to the Thai that nearly every family includes a sum for maintenance of the monks in the family budget. The *sangha* (order of monks) was for a long time the only source of education for the Thais and continued to serve as teachers even after education became na-

Wat Phra Keo is the home of the Emerald Buddha that was moved by the Thai from Burma (Myanmar) to Thailand. *Courtesy of Dr. W. Paul Fischer.*

tionalized and universal. The village temple is the site of lavish ceremonies for novice monks who are conducted into the order through a symbolic death and passage into a new life. Thai youth can be initiated into the Buddhist religious order at age twelve. Many candidates enter the order to study then withdraw and return to village life and to their families.

The goal of the laity is to refrain from taking life, stealing, lying, unchastity, and drinking. To watch over this process of purification, the Thai religion includes *phi*, spirits who are permanent parts of everything on earth. There are also *chao*, guardian spirits. Supplication to and celebration of these spirits and the gods (which often include Hindu gods) is done at individual home shrines or at a community spirit house.

Several rites are related to the religion and to growing up. These include the rites of shaving the hair and knotting it at the top and of entering the priesthood.

Family life. The family home in the village is a wooden structure made of bamboo or teak depending on the wealth of the family. There, mother and father share equally in the decision-making, and younger members are subordinate to any elders who live there. The home may shelter several sub-families. Married couples often spend years in the wife's family home to help with the work.

Strict social customs guide Thai behavior. For example, the father of the family must sleep in the northeast corner of the house. When sitting, men sit cross-legged, women sit sideways. Members of the family may not sit in positions that would place them higher than their guests. Even deaths in the family are controlled by custom. One door of the house is designated for passage of the dead, who may not be removed through any other passage.

Women play a strong role in Thai society. Inheritance is matrilineal. That is, mother and father share the house and land jointly but the youngest daughter has traditionally inherited the family home.

Groups of related families often cluster together in a village neighborhood. The families band together to provide financial aid for the monks, to help in house raising, build irrigation systems, and other jointly beneficial projects.

Village life. A typical Thai village is a cluster of bamboo or wooden homes built around a *Wat*. The Wat is a large structure that serves many purposes for the villagers. It is a place of worship, the center

Thai peasants of the Kaw tribe on their way to work in the fields. *Courtesy of the Smithsonian Institution.*

of a system of charity, monks' quarters, the local center of Buddhism, astrology, and magic, and a community meeting house. The spirit of accommodation that pervades Thailand has, however, brought Western ideas to even the small villages. Now most towns have a business area and are developing a more prosperous elite class.

Many of the actions of the villagers are guided by religion. The Buddhist's goal is to become an *arhat* (saint), ready to achieve an even higher goal of emptiness from cravings, a state called *nirvana*. In daily life, this involves gaining of merits. Caring for monks, giving to charities, helping neighbors, etc., provide *bun* (merits), while misdeeds to others or to animals gain *bap* (demerits).

Society's divisions. Thai social rankings have long been based on landholdings, with the owners of the largest tracts of land holding the highest rank in the society. Since he is the religious as well as the governmental head of the state, the king of Thailand holds much land. He and his hereditary nobility hold the highest rank, followed by lesser government bureaucrats and some military officers. Since Buddhists disdain business dealings, much of the trade was left to Chinese immigrants, who became prosperous and, therefore, hold the next highest rank. They are followed by the highest salaried workers, and then the peasantry.

Clothing. Today the traditional Thai dress of a jacket and pantaloons and long flowing skirts is perpetuated in the colorful Thai dance and theater. But the Thai people are restless, anxious to have more voice in government; to express their independence and modern thinking, they are becoming more Westernized in dress.

Literature. The classic literature of the Thais has been poetry. Often the subject of this poetry was secondary. Thais placed great value in the rhythm and blend of sounds; the beauty of the language was more important than the content. Still-popular historic literature in this style include Khun Phan's *Romance of Khun Chang*; *Ramakian*, the Thai version of the Indian Ramayana; *Adventures of a Javanese Prince*, by Inao; *Sam Kho*, a Chinese romance spanning three kingdoms; and *Phra Abhirnani*, a romantic verse. The *Ramakian* details long-held Thai social values: gratitude, integrity, fidelity, and belief in the law of karma.

In the 1980s and 1990s a new wave of authors brought "boldness" to Thai writing. These writers began to use the language to explore contemporary Thai issues—crime, the ecology, university life and activity, government corruption, waste, and other current issues. Titles such as *The Chao Phraya River Is on the Verge of Dying*, *Telephone Conversation*, *The Night the Dog Howled*, and *What Kind of Boat?* began to reveal concerns of the people of Thailand.

Change has not been so rapid in other arts. Thai painting has traditionally been, and remains, dedicated largely to temple murals. Painted without shadows or real perspective, these temple paintings include ancient stories such as the temptation and defeat of Mara, Buddha in many poses, scenes of the Intaka story (an ancient poem written in the Pali language), and still lifes. A few artists, such as

Angkara Kalyaenaphong, have combined writing and art to express concerns of today.

Thai drama is unique. The major form, *lakhon*, is ornately costumed and designed and features graceful and slow-moving actions.

Holidays. Representative of Thai concern for self-government—even though it seems to be confused by a preference for military power—is a single national holiday. This holiday, December 10, commemorates the day in 1932 of the acceptance of the first Thai constitution—even though that constitution has been frequently violated or set aside, and has undergone twelve revisions.

Economy in the 1990s. Borrowing heavily from world resources, Thailand has begun to change from a subsistence rice-growing economy to a diversified one in which cash agricultural crops such as sugar cane have increased and the Thai forests carefully exploited to build a lumber industry. A series of five-year plans has moved Thai economy rapidly into the world market. Mining, fishing, cotton-growing, and some development of petroleum resources have led to this economic growth. One result, as elsewhere in the industrialized world, has been an increase in the population of Thai cities. Most of the economic development has aided the region around Bangkok and that city has grown to nearly 6,000,000 people. As a result, the benefits of economic growth have been concentrated there and little felt in other regions of Thailand and among Thailand's minorities.

For More Information

Cultural Survival Report 22. South East Asian Tribal Groups and Ethnic Minorities. Cambridge: Cultural Survival, 1987.

Mulden, Niels. *Everyday Life in Thailand.* Bangkok: Drang Kamol, 1979.

Phillips, Herbert. *Modern Thai Literature.* Honolulu: University of Hawaii Press, 1987.

Poolthupya, Srisurang. *Thai Customs and Social Values in the Ramakian.* Bangkok: Thammasat University, 1981.

TIBETANS

(tih bet′ uns)

The inhabitants of the Tibetan Autonomous Region of China.

Population: 1,300,000 (1971 estimate).
Location: Autonomous region of China, bordering Nepal, India, Bhutan, and China.
Language: Tibetan, a Tibeto-Burman language.

Geographical Setting

Tibet has been called "the rooftop of the world" as it occupies about 471,700 square miles of plateaus and mountains of Central Asia including the highest mountain in the world, Mount Everest. The country is surrounded by mountains ranges—the Himalayas to the south and west, the Kunlun Mountains to the north, and the Khams to the east.

The Tibetan country is rich in natural resources. While traditional beliefs about disturbing the land prevented the mining of its mineral resources, the Chinese government has begun to exploit the gold, iron, and coal deposits and other mineral resources. The greatest woodlands exist in the Khams district, with virgin forests covering some 17,300 square feet. Tibet is also valued as a primary source of water for Central Asia. The Indus River, known in Tibet as Seng-ge Khabab—"out of the lion's mouth"—flows from the melted waters near Mount Kailas, a mountain sacred to both Hindus and Buddhists. Of the country's many lakes, Lake Manasaroswar is the largest and most sacred.

Although Tibetans refer to their homeland as Kha-ba-can (Land of Snows), Tibet is relatively dry—the country receives an average of eighteen inches of snow a year. The perpetual snow line begins at

16,000 feet in the Himalayas, which act as a barrier to the monsoon precipitation from the south. While the temperature at the higher elevations are cold, the lower valleys and plateaus are mild, with the greatest variations in temperature occurring during a twenty-four-hour period. Temperatures reach a low of 18 degrees Fahrenheit at night and high of 45 degrees during the day. Because of the cool climate, food items such as grains, meats, and butter can be stored for long periods of time without spoilage.

Historical Background

In its difficult-to-reach mountain retreat, Tibet long maintained a policy of isolation with the outside world, although cultural and economic exchange took place between the bordering countries of China to the east and north, and India, Nepal, Sikkim, Bhutan, and Burma to the south. During the 1950s Tibet was invaded and then annexed by the Chinese government, causing Tibet's religious and political leader, the fourteenth Dalai Lama, his government, and thousands of refugees to flee from Tibet and to live in exile throughout the world.

Early Origins. Based upon physiology, historians have speculated as to the origins of the earliest Tibetans. The Chinese T'ang annals (tenth century) retrace Tibetan origins to the Ch'iang tribes, recorded about 200 B.C. as inhabiting the mountainous northwest region of China. Physical anthropologists generally refer to types of Tibetan people according to their physiological characteristics. Round-headed people are related to the early Chinese and Burmese people of the Yellow River Valley in China. Long-headed people found amongst the nomads of the north and the nobility of Lhasa are more closely related to the Turkic peoples of the west. A chronicler of the ninth century traces the lineage of Tibet's rulers through thirty-six generations to a semi-divine king, Nyag-khri btsan-po.

Tibetan Kingdom. Written records of Tibet's history begin in the late sixth century, when the Tibetan kingdom was formed under the Spu-rgyal btsan-po, who passed on the title of *btsan-po* or "mighty" to the kings that would follow. The next ruler, Gnam-ri slon-btsan (A.D. 570–619), imposed his reign over the Ch'iang tribes on the Chinese border. His grandson Slon-brtsan-sgam-po is remembered as the first *chos-rgyal* (religious king) of Tibetan culture and for extending the Tibetan kingdom into Nepal, western Tibet, and parts of China's border land. To strengthen political alliances, he took as wives a Chinese, Tibetan, and Nepalese bride; the last is credited with introducing Buddhism to Tibet.

After the death of Slon-brtsan-sgam-po and until the reign of Khri-slon-ide-brtsan (755–797), Tibet's rulers were in constant competition with each other and in defense of the frontiers with the dynasties of China. Khri-slon-ide-brtsan was able to recapture Tibet's eastern borders and extend his rule into northern India. Khri-slon-ide-brtsan was known as a great champion of Buddhism, who invited Buddhist teachers from India and China to spread the religion, which had been confined mostly to the royal households. In 710 he founded the temple Bsam-yas, where Tibetans were trained as monks. As Buddhism became more involved with the management of the kingdom, with monks being appointed to government posts, the religion became the focal point of noble rivalries. After the death of Khri-slon-ide-brtsan in 815, the Tibetan kingdom began to disintegrate when his successor Ral-pan-can was assassinated and a relative, Glang-dar-ma, enthroned, only to be killed by a monk seeking revenge. Members of the old royal family migrated to western Tibet, and, by 889, Tibet was once again separated into lordships.

Ninth to fourteenth century disunity. With the disintegration of the kingdom, Tibetan generals and chieftains established separate territories, for which they chose their people's religious affiliation. For a time, Buddhism faded until it was brought back to life in central Tibet by the Indian missionary Atisa and thereafter Buddhism spread into every aspect of Tibetan life. Tibetan religious men began to gather into communities and expand upon different aspects of the doctrine. Atisa's own teaching became the basis for the strict practices of the Bka'gdams-pa sect. Soon other sects were formed. The Tibetan scholar Dkon-mchog-rgyal-po established the monastery of Sa-skya (1073) and other lamas (religious leaders) founded several monasteries of the Bka-brgyud-pa sect. These sects eventually became stable as prosperous noble families began to patronize them. In all of the sects except the Bka'gdams-pa succession was by reincarnation, rather than by lineage.

Mongol intervention. With timely submission, Tibet was able to avoid invasion by the world-conquering Mongolian Emperor Genghis Khan in 1207. However, failure to pay tribute to the Mongols after his death led to many damaging raids on Tibet. In 1247, the Sa-skya lama was summoned to Mongolia and appointed viceroy of Tibet. Throughout the Yuan dynasty founded by Kublai Khan, the Sa-skya lamas would rule Tibet on behalf of the Mongols. The Mongols reorganized Tibet into thirteen smaller districts to have tighter control of government. However, monasteries of the Bka-brgyud-pa sect contested the Sa-skya authority, and domestic dissension brewed under the distant leadership. The collapse of the Yuan dynasty in 1368 led to the eviction of the Mongols by the Ming dynasty and the end of the Sa-skya control of power. Tibet regained its independence and a flowering of Tibetan culture followed.

Rise of the Gelug-pa sect. In the fifteenth century, as various Buddhist and Bon sects continued to wrestle for internal governmental power, another sect, the Gelug-pa, or Yellow Hat order, began to emerge. Founded by the saintly scholar, Tsong-kha-pa, the sect was built upon the teachings of Atisa and was a reformist movement against the political and economic fetters that affected the monastic lives of the various sects. Soon the Gelug-pa sect was drawn into the political arena as well. Although they won influence and acceptance by mediating between the more powerful sects, the Gelug-pa met conflict with the ruling Karma-pa sect and the allies of the Rin-spungs princes in power. In 1578, the Gelug-pa were invited to visit the ruling Mongol leader Altan Khan. The Altan Khan is responsible for bestowing the title "Dalai," or "oceanwide," Lama, which was to be applied to every succeeding lama up to the current fourteenth Dalai Lama, Tenzin Gyatso, who currently governs the Tibetan government from exile. With the patronage of the Mongols, the Gelug-pa sect was protected by armed bands of Mongols against the rivalry of the Red Hats or Karma-pa sect. In 1640, Gushi Khan championed the rise of the Gelug-pa sect and enthroned the Dalai Lama as the ruler of Tibet, while keeping the title of king and military protector for himself. Lhasa became the spiritual as well as political capital of the country while Gushi's troops enforced the rule of the Gelug-pa over the other sects. The grandeur and prestige of the government was enhanced by reviving the religious ceremonies of previous kings and building the great Potala palace as a symbol of the unified government of Tibet's past history.

Manchu Supremacy. The installation of the fifth Dalai Lama at Lhasa in 1642 coincided with the rise of the Manchu Dynasty in China. Until the nineteenth century, the Manchu Dynasty would serve as overlords to the Tibetan country with relative peace between the countries. In 1792, a Manchu edict excluded all foreigners from Tibet, ending Christian missionary and British diplomatic relations. However, as the Manchu dynasty declined, Tibet gradually increased its independence. When Tibet refused to cooperate with British diplomats seeking greater trade routes to China, armed forces were sent into Tibet, causing the Dalai Lama to flee to China. Eventually a treaty was signed between Britain and Tibet without Chinese adherence. In 1906, the Chinese skillfully turned the tables on Tibet by achieving a treaty with Britain without Tibetan participation that recognized the Chinese suzerainty over Tibet. Then in 1910, China used direct force against Tibet for the first time in ten centuries and the Dalai Lama was again forced to flee, this time to India.

Tibetan Independence. After the Chinese Revolution in 1911, Tibet expelled all Chinese from Tibet and declared independence for their new republic, seeking Britain's support. The British government conducted a three-way conference between Tibet and China and prepared a treaty which would ultimately grant Tibet its autonomy. However, China withdrew and Britain and Tibet were left to sign the treaty on their own. Although the Chinese never recognized the treaty as valid,

Tibet sustained its independence until 1951. During this time, the fourteenth and present-day Dalai Lama, Tenzin Gyatso, was discovered. In 1939 at the age of four, he was recognized as the reincarnation of the Dalai Lama. This established him as the political and religious head of Tibet.

Chinese conquest. Throughout Tibetan independence, China still persisted in its interest in Tibet. In 1949, with the rise of the Communist Party in China, the Tibetan government once again took up the fight for Tibet's "liberation," and in 1950 the Chinese government launched an invasion of eastern Tibet. Although the Dalai Lama appealed for support from the United Nations, India, and Britain, assistance was denied. In a 1951 delegation to China, the Tibetan government signed a treaty designed by China that would grant Tibet religious freedom and autonomy but would make provisions for a Chinese civil and military establishment in Tibet. While the Chinese government built roads, schools, and hospitals within Tibet, tensions began to escalate amid the oppressive indirect rule of the Chinese. In March of 1959, the Chinese military surrounded the Potala Palace in Lhasa, but thousands of Tibetan people put themselves between the arsenal and the palace to protect the Dalai Lama. The Dalai Lama, his ministers, and many followers narrowly escaped across the Himalayas to take refuge in India. In Tibet, a military dictatorship was established and the religious and social fabric of Tibetan life began to disintegrate. In Dharamsala, India, the fourteenth Dalai Lama set up a government-in-exile.

Tibet today: Struggle for self-autonomy. The Chinese legacy to Tibet has primarily been destructive. Since 1949, more than 1.2 million Tibetans have been killed, about one sixth of the population. More than 6,250 monasteries have been destroyed, along with over sixty percent of Tibet's philosophical, historical, and biographical literature. Today, one out of every ten Tibetans is imprisoned, while the rest of the population has undergone intensive reeducation meetings held by the Chinese Communist government. Tibetans live under restricted movement, limited health and education services, and cultural repression. Deforestation is another serious problem as entire mountainsides have been cleared for China's use.

This destruction has not gone unnoticed. The Tibetan government-in-exile in Dharamsala, headed by the Dalai Lama, spearheads a worldwide effort to regain Tibetan autonomy through negotiation

When the Chinese army took control of Tibet, many Tibetans fled to northern India. This is a Tibetan refugee center in the Punjab region. *Courtesy of Shiva Rea Bailey.*

and protest. In 1990, the Dalai Lama was awarded the Nobel Peace Prize for his nonviolent approach to the Tibetan struggle for independence. Since 1954, many refugee centers have been established in India and Nepal, where Tibetan culture continues to survive through the monasteries, the arts and crafts, and Tibetan family life.

Culture Today

Religion. Buddhism came to Tibet in the eleventh century from Nepal, India, and China. It developed into the unique form of Buddhism that is practiced by Tibetans today, having replaced the former religion, called Bon, which had been incorporated over the years into the ritual life of the lay (nonmonastic) people of Tibet. The Tibetan religion, often called Lamaism, is a unique form of Mahayana Buddhism. Religion pervades Tibetan life and forms the basis for the government, literature, arts and crafts, and daily life of the people. In many aspects of Tibetan life, it is difficult to separate the religious and the secular. The head of the Tibetan government is by tradition the supreme religious leader, the Dalai Lama. According to Tibetan beliefs in reincarnation, the Dalai Lama is believed to be reborn and a search party for the next Dalai Lama is conducted by the state until a child with the right characteristics is found. The present Dalai Lama is the head of the state and also of one of four sects of Tibetan Buddhism, the Geluk-pa Sect. The other sects, the Sa-gya, the Nying-ma, and Ga-gyu, have their own monasteries and authority.

Family Life. The practice of Tibetan Buddhism is an important part of the social and cultural fabric of Tibetan family life. Before the Chinese occupation, every Tibetan household would contribute one boy or girl to become a lama (monk) or nun in one of the many monasteries situated around the country. Today, this practice continues only within the refugee communities where thriving monasteries have been established.

The conical hat is a style worn by elders in Tibet. *Courtesy of Shiva Rea Bailey.*

Religious festivals involve home preparation of special foods and butter sculptures which are placed upon the family altar. Prayer flags enscribed with thousands of repetitions of the Tibetan spiritual phrase, or mantra, "Om Mani Padme Om" are hung outside the family dwellings. Tibetan marriages are predominantly monogamous, although the custom of polygamy (marriage to multiple wives) and polyandry (marriage to multiple husbands) is practiced on a limited scale.

Dress. The clothing of Tibetans is determined by tradition and by social class. Nomads usually wear thick clothes made of sheepskin

Prayer wheels are common sights in Tibet. *Courtesy of Shiva Rea Bailey.*

or yak hair. Farmers, tradesmen, and monks wear woven cloth out of the wool of sheep. Women today commonly wear a colorful apron wrapped over long dresses made of wool or silk. Women's traditional headdresses are another sign of dignity and status. Strands of turquoise and coral, the preferred stones of Tibetans, can be woven into the hair. The jackets of the men characteristically have exaggerated sleeves which hang over the hands. The monks uniformly wear long, dark purple or maroon robes draped like togas across the upper body. During festivals the monks and particularly the lamas wear elaborate ceremonial headdresses. Before the Chinese purge, nobility of Tibet wore clothes made of fine Indian and Chinese silks brought over the Himalayas by caravan traders.

Food. Tibetan foods are derived from the available resources of this mountainous region. Due to the cold climate, grains, dried meats and cheeses, and butter keep without spoilage for long durations. One of the mainstays of the Tibetan diet is *Tsampa,* a roasted barley rolled into balls and eaten with fingers. Tsampa is served with meat and vegetable soups and stews as a hearty meal in the cold climate. Another staple is a Tibetan dumpling called *Momo,* stuffed with meat, bacon, lamb, and vegetables. Tibetan buttered tea made from yak milk is a daily beverage in the homes and monasteries. Fermented beer known as *chang* is a drink of social and celebrative occasions.

Language. The Tibetan language is related to the Burmese languages in its origins, although today a speaker of one language cannot understand ideas spoken in the other language. The Tibetan language is comprised of many regional dialects although the Lhasa dialect of Tibet's capital is the national language. The spoken language is divided into two levels of speech: the honorific or *zhe-sa* and the ordinary or *phal-skad,* depending on one's social status. Since the Chinese occupation of Tibet in the 1950s, the Chinese language has been imposed upon the Tibetans. The written language of Tibet utilizes a script derived from that of the Indian Gupta in 600 A.D. The script itself has four subdivisions depending on its use, *dbu-can* (Buddhist textbooks), *Khyg-yig* and *phal-skad* (general use), and *bru-tsha* (decorative writing).

Literature and the arts. Tibetan literature and art is largely a religious expression of Tibetan Buddhist ideals and philosophy. The written literature of the Tibetans is primarily comprised of religious texts that have been developed over the centuries since the founding of Tibetan Buddhism. Texts on logic, cosmology, philosophy, ethics, and history are labored over by Tibetan monks preparing for their degrees while lamas are the key figures in writing new treatises. Folklore and mythology are part of a rich oral tradition shared within the family life.

The monasteries of Tibet were once great training centers for the art that decorated temples and homes. Gilded bronze sculpture and paintings called *Tankas* are some of the most treasured expressions of Tibetan art and are exhibited in museums around the world. The Buddha, revered lamas and sages, and deities are portrayed in the paintings and sculptures. Tanka is the Tibetan word for banner and refers to the mounting of the paintings onto silk material that hangs from poles in temples.

A unique form of Tibetan sculptures is made of yak butter and takes several months to create for ceremonial occasions such as the Tibetan New Year, *Losar*. As a symbol of the mortality of all things, the sculptures are destroyed the day after the ceremony. Tibetan rugs are also world-renowned for their superb hand-weaving and are a primary source of income for some Tibetan refugees living outside of Tibet. Religious dances or *cham* are performed by the monks on

Many places of worship, such as this one, have been closed since the coming of the Chinese to Tibet.
Courtesy of Shiva Rea Bailey.

Tibetans continue their weaving work even as refugees in a camp in India. *Courtesy of Shiva Rea Bailey.*

religious holidays. The dances, involving masks and music, enact the myths of the Tibetan deities. Performed in the open courtyard of the monasteries, these spectacular events bring Tibetan locals together in celebration of their faith and culture. Folk songs, dances, and drama are also an important part of the fabric of the village life of the various regions.

Shelter. There are several types of dwellings among the Tibetan people, which vary according to social status and function: the monasteries for the monks and nuns, the houses of the nobility, the houses of the peasants, and the dwellings of the nomadic populations. The Tibetan nobility live in multilevel stone houses with a courtyard and chapel as part of the quarters. The majority of Tibetan peasants live in single- or two-story buildings made of clay with an earthen floor and flat roofs. Nomadic pastoralists live in tents of yak hair about twelve-to-fifty feet long. The monasteries are the most unique expression of Tibetan architecture and are a result of the financial support of the surrounding community.

Tibetan monasteries. Tibetan monasteries are cultural learning centers for the preservation and continuation of Tibetan culture. Built into the stark hills and mountains of the Tibetan plateau, these majestic monasteries of rectangular shape rise out of mountains and can be identified by their hundreds of small windows. Before 1950, Drepung, Ganden and Sera, three of the largest monasteries in the world, were in the surroundings of the Tibetan capital, Lhasa. These great monasteries were bases for Tibetan religious culture. Drepung Monastery, with some 10,000 monks, was the largest Buddhist monastery in the world. Today, under the Chinese government, only a dozen of the approximately 6,000 monasteries are still standing. The others have been destroyed and evacuated. Since the Chinese occupation, Tibetan monasteries in Nepal and India have been founded by the Tibetan refugee population.

For More Information

Gyatso, Tenzin H. H. *Freedom in Exile: The Autobiography of the Dalai Lama.* New York: HarperCollins, 1990.

Rowell, Galen. *My Tibet.* Berkeley: University of California Press, 1990.

Snellgrove, David. *A Cultural History of Tibet.* Boulder: Prajna Press, 1980.

VIETNAMESE

(vee et′ nah meez′)

The majority of the people of Vietnam.

Population: 64,500,000 (1990 estimate).
Location: Vietnam, Cambodia.
Language: Vietnamese, an Austro-Asiatic language related to Chinese.

Geographical Setting

The land of the Vietnamese is a long thin strip along the Pacific Ocean coast, separated from the rest of a peninsula northeast of the Malay Peninsula by mountain ranges and hill country. Some of the mountains extend south to form a spine along the edge of the peninsula known as Indo-China into Malaysia.

Climate and geography are the forces that dominate the Vietnamese way of life. The region is tropical and subject to heavy rains in summer, sometimes with heavy winds. The wind-driven rains are called monsoons. In spite of the large cities and the rich mineral resources in the mountain areas, nearly two-thirds of the people are farmers and fishermen. These people live in lowlands, where they have access to water for raising their principal crop, rice, but risk destruction by the rivers that frequently flood the region. The Red River, for example, has been known to increase its normal flow by forty times in the wet season. In addition, the arca has been struck by violent cyclones and earthquakes. In 1897, buildings throughout the region were destroyed by one of the world's most violent earthquakes, which was followed in the same year by a cyclone that claimed many lives. The instability of the land and sea has influenced much of Vietnamese life, creating periods of famine among the people, and

contributing to a population that is less concentrated than that of its larger neighbors, India and China.

Farming the floodlands demanded that the people construct drainage ditches and flood-control systems. Maintaining these systems bonded the people into village, regional, and state units. At one time, the land of the Vietnamese was divided into three sections, with Chinese residents of Annam holding their own empire in the north.

Historical Background

Origin. Before 1000 B.C. people who were closely akin to the Southern Chinese had settled along the Red River near the border separating present-day Vietnam and The People's Republic of China. This area, on the Tonkin Bay, is known today as Tonkin. Gradually, the settlers extended their region to far beyond the center of present-day Vietnam to Cochin-China, a southern region inhabited by settlers from India. In the north, a country called Au-Lac was established before 214 B.C. In that year, Au-Lac was overrun by the Chinese emperor but continued to be more influenced by another kingdom in the area, Yunnan, until the present northern and central Vietnam was included in the Chinese empire of the Han in 112 B.C.

Dinh Dynasty. Renamed Annam, this area of present-day Vietnam became a province of the Chinese empire for the next 1,000 years. The people of Annam adopted the teachings of the Chinese religious leader, Confucius, as well as Taoism and Mahayana Buddhism. However, control of Annam by the Chinese was loosely held and, with the fall of the Chinese Tang dynasty and assimilation of northern Vietnam into a new Chinese rule, the Vietnamese rebelled. In A.D. 938 a Vietnamese chief, Dick-Bo-Lank, succeeded in breaking from the Chinese and establishing an independent Vietnamese reign known as Dai Viet. Under the line of rulers of this dynasty, the Vietnamese gradually increased their territory along the course of the Indo-Chinese Peninsula. The Vietnamese grew strong enough to resist further Chinese intrusions from the Song (1075–1077) and Mongols (1282–1288) and to seize land from a Hindu group in south Vietnam who lived along the coast and had a long-standing kingdom there called Champa. Champa finally was included entirely in Dai Viet in 1685. The two groups, one of the Chinese tradition (Vietnamese) and one influenced by the Hindus of India (Cham), make up most of the population of the present-day Vietnam coast.

Nyugen rule. The rule of the Vietnamese flourished until 1407 when the land was again claimed for a few years by China. It was regained by the Vietnamese under the leadership of Le-Loi, who incorporated more of the land by defeating the Cham people in 1470. However, by the seventeenth century, the Vietnamese government was split between two clans, the Trinh in the north and the Nguyen in central Vietnam. The stronger Nyugen clan eventually prevailed and began an expansion that was to bring both Champa (southern immigrants from India) and some Khmer (Cambodian) peoples under Nyugen control. However, as the Vietnamese rulers expanded their territory into Cambodia, they came face-to-face with European colonization.

Colonization. European influences in the area had begun with Dutch and English trade visits to Hanoi in the 1600s. In the 1700s the Nguyen rulers were overthrown and then regained control with the aid of the French. The Nyugen leader of the south, Nyugen Ahn, took the capital of Hanoi and, under the name of Gia-Long, became emperor over all of Vietnam in 1802. Gia-Long proclaimed himself

Emperor at Hué. His successor, Minh-Mang (1820–1841), began an expansion into Cambodia, where he met French resistance. Seeking to expand their trade influence, the French attacked various areas of the country throughout the next 100 years, beginning with joint French-Spanish naval attacks on Da Nang and Saigon. Having lost their claims in India to Great Britain, the French sought easy routes to the great markets of China. At first they thought this easy route would be along the Mekong River in the south of the Indo-Chinese Peninsula and, in 1854, captured the southern city of Saigon. But the Mekong River proved unpredictable and unnavigable, so from their base in the Saigon area (Cochin-China), the French expanded all the way to the Chinese border and in 1874 signed a Franco-Vietnamese treaty agreement that recognized French rights to, at first, three Vietnam provinces and, later, the entire territory.

By 1887, the French had gained control of the areas now known as Cambodia (Kampuchea), Vietnam, and Laos, and established the federation of French Indo-China. The French established businesses such as rubber plantations, raised the taxes of the peasants and provided an education system that disrupted traditional values. However, Vietnamese opposition to French control grew during the late 1800s, led by such Vietnamese heroes as Truong Cong Dinh, Phan Dinh Phung, and Hoang hoa Tham.

Although the French established a trade base in Vietnam, built several new cities to develop coal mining potentials, and cultivated crops such as rubber, most of the Vietnamese saw little change in their lives other than increased taxes. Eventually, the Vietnamese and Cham became more openly opposed to French government and skirmishes broke out, most of them in the south. During the early 1900s two strong leaders appeared, Phan Chau Trinh (who spent time in prison after 1908 and then lived in exile in France until 1926) and Phan Boi Chau (who wrote revolutionary material from China, was arrested in Shanghai, and confined to Hué). The revolutionary spirit grew into a peasant movement supported by the Communist Party of Indo-China in the 1930s.

Struggle for independence. During World War II the Japanese succeeded in forcing the Vichy French government to allow them military bases in Vietnam, and just before the end of the war, Japan took full control of the area. The end of the war saw a split in Vietnam as China was given the responsibility of accepting peace terms from Japan for the north of the country and from Britain for the south.

Following World War II, a new anti-colonial movement resulted in the formation of a northern resistance group, the Viet Minh, under the leadership of Ho Chi Minh. This group became increasingly anti-French and anti-Japanese (the Japanese having become a new force seeking a stronghold in Indo-China during World War II). The Viet Minh resisted Japanese intruders who had entered the country with the approval of the wartime French government in 1940.

In 1945 the Japanese yielded control of Vietnam to a national political party and this party declared independence from France. In that same year, Chinese troops entered north Vietnam with the co-operation of the Viet Minh for the stated purpose of helping rid the country of the Japanese, but withdrew after an agreement was reached with the French. After the Chinese withdrew in 1946, the French returned to Vietnam under a seemingly agreed-to condition in which the Republic of Vietnam would be a free state within a French Indo-Chinese Federation that included Cambodia and Laos. However, the Viet Minh, the old group still headed by Ho Chi Minh, with help from the United States, resisted French intervention, winning a decisive victory at Dien Ben Phu in 1954. After this defeat, the French agreed to withdraw from north Vietnam. An agreement to divide the country was arranged at Geneva. Later in that same year, the French withdrew from southern Vietnam as well.

For twenty years following the Geneva agreement, southern Vietnam was an independent state, supported by the United States. But French interests in other parts of Indo-China precluded absolute abandonment of Vietnam. A long guerrilla war began in which the French and later the United States led the south in battles against a successor of the Viet Minh headed by Ho Chi Minh in the North. Looking for support in his efforts to unite Vietnam, Ho Chi Minh espoused Communism and was aided by China and the Soviet Union. Vietnamese opposed to Communism fought on the side of the French and were supported by troops from the United States beginning in 1961. The United States reportedly became involved because of its fear that actions in Korea and Vietnam indicated a Communist threat to take over Asia. Committed to stopping this threat, President John F. Kennedy had placed 8,000 United States soldiers in south Vietnam by 1962. The ruler of South Vietnam, Ngo Dinh Diem, a Catholic, was assassinated in 1963, after having aroused the distrust of Buddhist monks. The remaining government was hampered by corruption from within and threatened by movements of the Viet Minh from the north.

In the same twenty years, north Vietnam had developed a government under Communist leadership and had set about eliminating the power of large landowners to control the lives of villagers by redistributing the land. Supported by the Soviet Union and China, the Communist leaders continued to press for a united and Communistic Vietnam.

In 1973 the United States withdrew from the turmoil. In an atmosphere of governmental indecision and dissension at home, its armed forces in Vietnam had swelled to more than 500,000 soldiers and still lacked home support sufficient to dislodge the Communist forces. The forces of Ho Chi Minh were victorious, and in 1976 the land of the Vietnamese and Cham was unified into the present country known as the Socialist Republic of Vietnam. Shortly after its establishment, Vietnam began incursions into the land of its neighbor, Cambodia, eventually taking some control of a country that had been renamed Kampuchea by the revolutionary Khmer Rouge. Much of what has happened in Vietnam since that time is obscured by government restrictions of press and foreign interaction with Western countries. However, the Vietnamese began a program of nationalization of agriculture and development of industry. The country contained rich mineral resources and found ready markets for its coal in the Soviet Union and China. In the 1980s relationships with both these trading partners began to fade, and in 1987 the government of Vietnam began to try to attract other international markets. At the same time, the Vietnamese began to withdraw from Kampuchea and that country again assumed the name Cambodia. This effort was seriously hampered by the United States' refusal to establish amicable relations with Vietnam until complete withdrawal from Cambodia was accomplished and all missing American soldiers in the Vietnamese conflict were accounted for. In the 1990s both Vietnam and the United States appear to be moving toward resolution of the problems separating them.

Culture Today

Cities. The culture of the Vietnamese is an old, but emerging, culture, with great cities of stone, brick, and mortar left as reminders of past empires. Early inhabitants followed the Red River from China to its fertile delta in the north, or migrated over the southern mountain ranges from India. The land was a crossroads of the two cultures and was long known by Westerners as Indo-China. The city of Hué, in the center of the country, is an ancient religious center that is still held sacred by the Vietnamese. Hindu and Buddhist shrines stood side by side in many parts of the great peninsula, which includes Cambodia, Laos, and Vietnam. Cambodia, Laos, and southern Vietnam bear evidence of the Indian settlements, but most of Vietnam was settled by the steady southward migration of Chinese people known as Vietnamese. The Vietnamese make up nearly ninety percent of the people of this country and are the people described here as Vietnamese.

The present capital city of Hanoi houses more than a million people; Ho Chi Minh City (Saigon), a comparatively new city in the south, is a city of more than three million. There is an even older

A Vietnamese tribeswoman wears her wealth in jewelry. *Courtesy of the Smithsonian Institution.*

city in the center of the elongated country, Hué, a city of nearly one-half million, that was the religious center centuries ago.

Communism and tradition. Before the 1950s, most Vietnamese were rice farmers. The most important social unit was an extended family, which lived together and worked together to raise subsistence crops in a land that supported heavy rice crops. In this family, the eldest men were dominant, women subservient, and religion—whether Buddhist, Christian, or other—was liberally sprinkled with older beliefs in ancestor veneration. Next in order of importance as a social structure was the village—often made up of related families who also supported each other.

When Ho Chi Minh and his Viet Minh political party took control of the north in 1956, he began a program to eliminate the old class structures. In the end, the upper class of city-dwellers that he sought to eliminate were replaced by a new elite of Communist party officials. Land reform was initiated and the government began to take over some of the duties previously performed by fathers and village leaders. The structure of Vietnamese life began a slow change that has continued to the 1990s.

The resistance by the United States that resulted in dividing the country led to nearly twenty years of war. Young men were uprooted from families to serve in the armies of both north and south. Also, families fled from the agricultural war area to the larger cities, seeking protection and employment in the war industries. This move to the urban centers and the absence of the young males disrupted the Vietnamese dependence on family and village.

With Communist victory in the 1970s, Ho Chi Minh undertook to bring south Vietnam into the Communist fold. A major obstacle was the more than 3,000,000 people who had now settled in Saigon (now Ho Chi Minh City). To encourage change, many of the people of the city were relocated to areas chosen by the government for agricultural development. However, the Communist government did not have resources to hasten the development of this land. In addition, a number of leaders in Saigon, variously reported to have been between 40,000 and 150,000, were sent to Communist reeducation camps.

A number of five-year plans setting out agricultural objectives and industrial goals followed. Carrying out these plans sometimes tended to break up families and to redistribute land. Gradually, the government sought to take over roles traditionally held by family leaders. The Vietnamese desire to hold on to traditional values has, however, been strong. In the late 1980s, some government leaders of Vietnam projected that the change from tradition to the new order, in which national government dominates daily actions, would move ahead slowly through the rest of this century.

Economy. The Vietnamese have for centuries been wetland rice farmers in the Red River Valley and the Mekong delta areas. In this region, where rugged mountains alternate with fertile river lowlands, eighty-five percent of the people live in villages on the lowland coastal plains. While once they farmed for themselves and their families, under Communism individual families or small production teams raise crops to meet quotas assigned by the state. Excesses beyond the quotas may be sold by the Vietnamese farmers for individual profit. At first organized into the typical Communist communal farm system, land use changed in the 1980s. Farmers in some communes were permitted to lease the land they worked, thus becoming independent farmers under contract to and with quotas set by the government. Then in 1988 the government agreed that these leases could be transferred to a farmer's children. Thus landownership became virtually private.

As part of the European colonial system, the Vietnamese were not encouraged to participate in the worldwide industrialization. However, some agricultural land was converted from food production to large plantations producing rubber and jute for export. Following independence, Vietnam began to try to counter the sporadic droughts by encouraging the farming of crops not requiring as much water as rice. Maize and sweet potatoes have begun to emerge as major crops. With little aid, except from Japan and Scandinavia, industrialization was slowed for many years due largely to lack of machinery and petroleum. Construction of electric plants was costly and, therefore, slow. Despite this growth, Vietnam industries, such as cement plants and lumber mills have contributed to an industrial growth rate in recent years of nearly ten percent a year. Still, 20,000,000 of the 27,000,000 workers in Vietnam labor in agriculture. The progress in mechanization is reflected in this industry: in 1959 there were ten farm tractors in the entire country, and in 1989, 50,000. However, Vietnamese in the early 1990s remain among the poorest people of the world.

In 1987, the government of the Vietnamese began a program to encourage foreign investment in a developing industry. The hilly and mountainous land is potentially rich in natural resources of which coal and lumber is a primary trade commodity. It is in this area, particularly in the less populated north, that major relocations of Vietnamese are being encouraged by the government, and new industries directed toward exports and cash crops are being developed. Before its change in the 1980s, most trade was carried out with the Union of Soviet Socialist Republics and with China. Economic progress, however, was hampered by a United States trade embargo that resulted in reluctance by neighboring states to do business with Vietnam. This slowdown has perpetuated a poor economy in which sixty percent of the Vietnamese are engaged in agriculture and only twenty-seven percent of the income of the country comes from industry.

Much of the Vietnam upland was forested. Even though war resulted in much forest destruction, and deforestation for agriculture further eroded the forests, rich forest land remains one of Vietnam's major resources. Vietnamese are struggling to control the use of this resource so as not to further erode the land.

Religion. The first people to move into the area were animists, worshipping a number of deities who controlled earth and sky. A growing number became followers of Confucius, a renowned philosopher of ancient China. By the first century A.D., Confucianism was the dominant religion, but it was replaced between the second and sixth century by Buddhism imported from Ceylon. It is this religion that holds sway in most homes today even under the control of an anti-religious Communist government. A holdover from the time of French control, is a strong Catholic influence, with as many as 2,000,000 Vietnamese practicing this religion.

Food, clothing, and shelter. Forced by the changing waters into a semi-nomadic existence, many Vietnamese built lightweight houses of reeds and stone with just three fixed sides. The fourth side remained open during the day and was closed by grass curtains at night. Inside each house there was a worship alter, at which the head of the household presided over worship rituals for the family. He was guided in such rituals by the *Vietnamese Book of Rites*, a record of his people's traditional practices.

Today, most Vietnamese live in villages of 1,500 to 10,000 people and support themselves by planting rice or by fishing. However, most Vietnamese have traditionally lived in the lowlands nearest the coast, leaving a portion of inland hill regions undeveloped. Rice is the major food for these villagers and is eaten in many dishes, sometimes flavored with small bits of meat or chicken. A growing number of Vietnamese have moved toward the hills to establish new cities and a growing economy. Still, the greatest population density is in the Red River Valley in the south and the least is in the northern hill country. Fish, manioc, sweet potatoes, and other vegetables are included in the Vietnamese diet, and are incorporated into delicious soups for which the people of this country are known.

Nearly three million people live in the major cities of the north and south, Hanoi and Ho Chi Minh City. These people live in a variety of homes, from small houses on the outskirts of the cities to multistoried apartments over shops in the center of town. However, the gathering of people in the large cities has created a large unemployment problem and resulted in a movement to relocate citizens into other, less densely populated parts of the country. More than three million people have been shifted from such cities as Hanoi and Ho Chi Minh City to new towns and villages.

In the villages, men and women alike once wore baggy pants and a dark colored coat tied at the waist with a cord or sash. However, the long war exposed the city-dwellers, particularly in the south, to Western clothing. Both Western suits and the country styles are seen in the major cities.

Village life. Groups of related families once formed a village that was surrounded by a bamboo wall. The extended family was the basic working unit of the agricultural system, and the village leaders dealt with community property disputes. Today, Vietnamese citizens are gathering in new and more substantial towns and villages, sometimes living in government-built concrete apartments and homes. The relocation of many citizens has tended to break down the traditional family-based village structure.

Vietnam today, while holding to its union as a nation, is still divided by historic economics and contrasts between Indian and Chinese influences. The south remains densely populated, poor, and oriented to international trade as well as rice cultivation. The north, more hilly and rugged, is even poorer in farm and industrial products, but because of its less dense population has perhaps more potential for development. There remains a strong potential for off-shore petroleum production in the South China Sea, but that potential is clouded by territorial disputes with China, Taiwan, and the Philippines.

Vietnamese villagers. *Courtesy of the Smithsonian Institution.*

For More Information

Cima, Ronald J., ed. *Vietnam: A Country Study*. Washington, DC: Federal Research Division, Library of Congress, 1989.

Rutledge, Paul. *The Vietnamese in America.* Minneapolis: Lerner Publication Co., 1987.

Tedwell, Colin E. and Kimball, Linda Amy. *Introduction to the Peoples and Cultures of Asia.* Englewood Cliffs: Prentice-Hall, 1985.

COUNTRIES TODAY

AUSTRALIA

Commonwealth of Australia

Population: 17,200,000 (1991 estimate).
Location: An island continent in the southern hemisphere, bounded by the Timor Sea, Arafura Sea, Coral Sea, South Pacific Ocean, and Indian Ocean.
Language: English.
Principal cities: Sydney*, 3,431,000; Melbourne*, 2,932,000; Brisbane*, 1,171,000; Perth*, 1,025,000; Adelaide*, 1,004,000; Newcastle, 429,000; Canberra (capital), 286,000.
(* indicates state capitals.)

Political Background

Before the twentieth century, Australia was already a nation of city and town dwellers. In 1891 more than two-thirds of the people lived in large cities and towns. They were at the time centers for regional divisions that later became states and territories within a federation. The boom and bust nineteenth century saw a gold rush, beginning industrialization, and a financial crash in the worldwide depression of the 1890s. Then came Australia's official change of status into a Commonwealth of the British Empire in 1901. Australia became a moderate international power in the 1900s, participating in both World Wars along with her British partners. Following the wars, Australia experienced a long period of peace, stability, and prosperity under the leadership of Sir Robert Menzies. However, labor forces were gaining strength during this period, and in 1972 the Labour Party became the dominant political factor in the country. Afterwards Australia continued to grow, developing a strong social welfare system and exerting national government control over vital industries such as air transportation. Growth

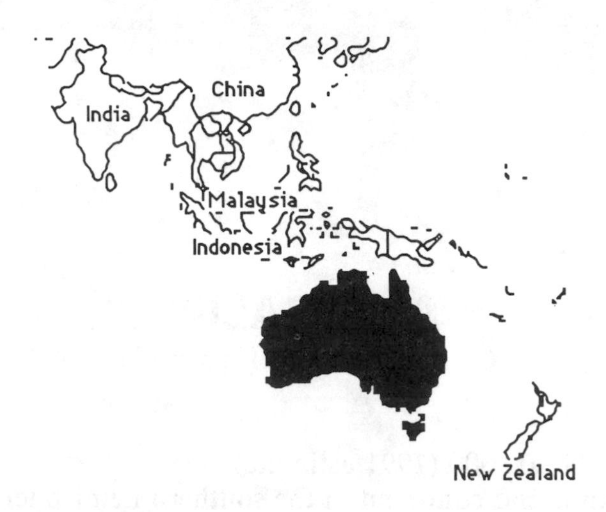

was tempered in the 1980s by a slowdown in the Australian economy. In recent years, this slowdown has, in turn, been tempered by large foreign investments in the country.

Government Today

Most Australians feel that they have the right to a secure, healthy standard of living and expect a strong national government to provide that. At the same time, the people of the various states still value local independence. There is, therefore, a two-tiered government. Nine million of the 17,000,000 Australians live in five large cities that are state capitals. Each of these states is ruled by an elected premier (prime minister) and a governor appointed by the representative of the Crown of Great Britain. This organization continues in each state. Each state's executive shares in government with a cabinet of ministers and a legislature. A state selects its legislature according to its own constitution.

The representative of the Crown for all of Australia is a governor-general. With the approval of a national legislature, the governor-general appoints a prime minister and a Federal Executive Council to manage the government. The prime minister and the council govern by advising the governor-general and by forming a cabinet to carry on the daily activities of government. At the federal level, the legislature consists of two groups: a House of Representatives and a Senate. Representatives are apportioned according to population;

European and Asian Australians along with Australian Aborigines make up the population of Australia.

senators are chosen by the states (at least six per state and two from the two territories).

A runaway economy in the early 1980s became a major issue of Australian politics. It resulted in an unpopular wage control by the federal government in 1988 and a decision to make private some of the industries that had been held by the government. Nuclear power has also presented the Australian government with challenges. Australia has voiced its dislike of French atomic testing in the Mururoa Islands, and the United States, Australia, and New Zealand have been drawn into conflict over nuclear-powered naval craft. The United States mans these ships and desires port privileges in return for protection of the area, but New Zealand has refused to allow its ports to be used by nuclear-powered ships. The issue has been cause for debate between New Zealand and Australia.

Ethnic Makeup

As in other Western nations, recent years have brought increased awareness of its minorities. The plight and the rights of the Australian

Aborigines are another subject of legislative debate and, also, of court challenges. As one result, Australians are divided on the celebration of the anniversary of European colonization, Australia Day (January 26). The Aborigines do not recognize this holiday at all, while other Australians observe the holiday but have begun to ignore the basis for it.

When English penal colonies were first founded in Australia, there were more than 300,000 Australian Aborigines living in small bands throughout the continent. European diseases and dispossession of their land reduced this number to about 40,000. While most Australians are transplanted Europeans or their descendants, the Aboriginal Australians descend from the land's original inhabitants. Today's Australian Aborigines still occupy land in the interior, and some find work in the lowest-paying jobs on the great sheep and cattle ranches.

BANGLADESH

People's Republic of Bangladesh

Population: 107,992,140 (1991 census).
Location: An independent nation surrounded on three sides by eastern India and on the south by the Bay of Bengal. There is a short southeastern border with Myanmar.
Languages: Bengali (Bangla); English. Ten percent of the population speak other ethnic dialects.
Principal cities: Dhaka (capital), 3,500,000; Chittagong, 1,400,000 Seven other cities of more than 100,000 population: Khulna, Rajshahi, Comilla, Barisal, Sylhet, Rangpur, Jessore, Saidpur.

Political Background

In the 1940s some predominantly Muslim sectors of India broke off and formed the country of Pakistan. This country was divided into two parts by hundreds of miles of India. Although the eastern section had the greater population, Pakistan was governed and policed from the western sector. The imbalance of power flared in 1952 when the government in West Pakistan decreed that Urdu, the language used there, would be the official language for East Pakistan as well. The language and political differences led to open rebellion. In 1971 East Pakistan became an independent nation, with the rebels naming their country Bangladesh (Bengali speakers). By 1972, Bangladesh had proclaimed itself a parliamentary and constitutional democracy. The new country was directed by a parliament called the Jatiya Sanqsad.

In 1975, a military officer, Sheikh Mujib, took control of government and abolished the constitutional form. He was soon replaced by Major General Ziaur Rahman who became known as General Zia. Zia installed a new constitution that declared Islam to be the basic

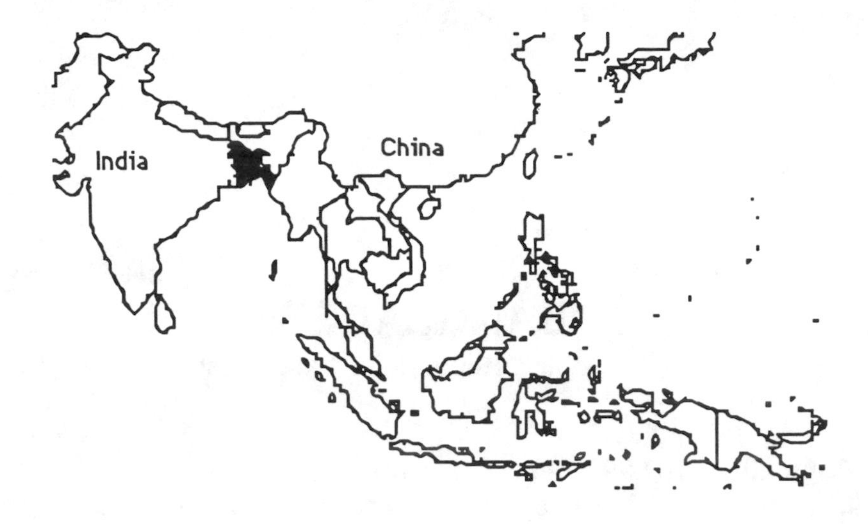

governing principle of Bangladesh. Since that time, Bangladesh has been an on-again, off-again democracy governed by military officers who have sometimes been elected by popular vote. From 1982 to 1986 the constitution was abandoned, and the military ruled. In 1986 an army general resigned to run for office as a civilian. He was elected president.

Government Today

The Bangladesh constitution was written in 1972 and has been rewritten eight times since then. Under its present form a president is elected for a five-year term. Three hundred members of a single-house legislature are also elected to serve for five years unless instability in the government results in the disbanding of the current legislature. The president chooses members of this legislature to be his advisers, the cabinet. Ruled under Muslim law, the country, even with a constitutional guarantee of equality, features a parliament of which most members are males. To ensure women's rights, the 300 elected parliament members choose 30 women to add to the number in the legislature. The country is divided into *upazilla* (counties) of about 260,000 people each.

Bangladesh is a country plagued with natural disasters such as floods and earthquakes. This places increased pressure on leaders to develop a sound national government capable of providing help in

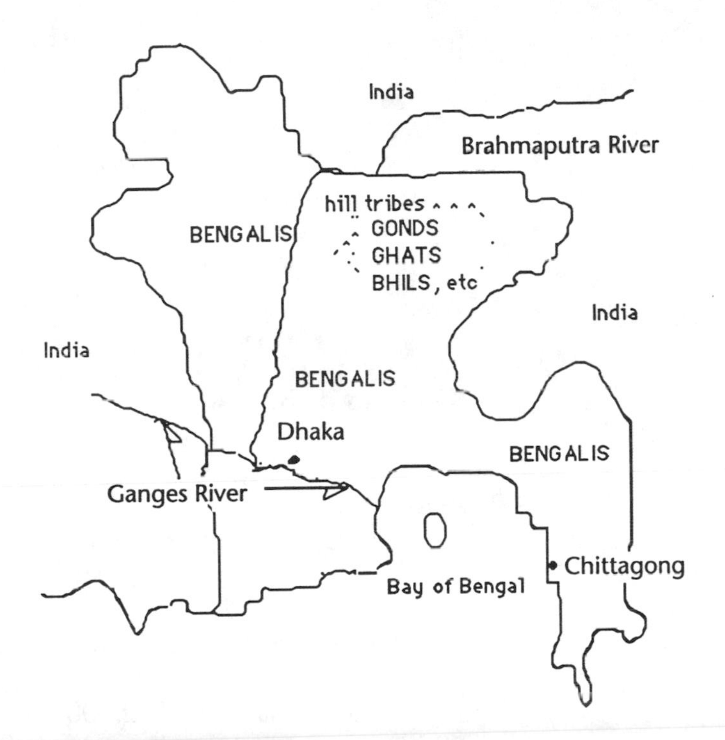

Some of the peoples of Bangladesh.

times of distress. Forming and maintaining a stable government is one of Bangladesh's greatest challenges.

Another issue is poverty. With an average income of 170 dollars per person per year, Bangladesh is one of the poorest countries of Asia. The country struggles to be self-sufficient in food for its dense population. Controlling the rapid population growth is a necessary step toward improving Bangladesh economics.

In addition to its internal strife, Bangladesh and Indian people along the common border have been subjected in recent years to terrorist raids across the boundary.

Ethnic Makeup

Most of the people of Bangladesh are Bengalis. In the hilly areas known as the Chittagong Hills live about a dozen separate tribes of mixed and ill-defined origin.

BHUTAN

Kingdom of Bhutan

Population: 1,300,000 (1990 estimate).
Location: North of Bangladesh in the Himalaya Mountains, bordered on the north and northwest by China (the Xizang Autonomous Region, once Tibet) and on the south by India.
Languages: Dzongkha, a language written in Tibetan script; Nepalese.
Principal cities: Tashigang, 177,000; Samchi, 172,000; Gaylegphug, 110,000; Chirang, 108,000. The capital city, Thimphu has a population of 59,000.

Political Background

Around 1616 a lama (religious leader) from Tibet moved to Bhutan and established himself as both a spiritual and temporal ruler called the Shabdrung (meaning "at whose feet one submits"). He set up a government run by an elected spiritual guide, the Je Khenpo, and a civil guide, the Desi, who dealt with stately matters. Overall authority was held by the Shabdrung. For close to 300 years the area was governed by rulers who claimed mental reincarnation from the first Shabdrung. Under these rulers, men with the title *penlop* governed lesser territories. Over the years, the penlops came to compete with one another. By 1900 the central government had weakened and the penlops' powers increased.

The last Shadrung died in 1903 and the last Desi in 1904, leaving two strong penlops in control of what is now Bhutan. One of these sided with the British who wanted to establish themselves in nearby Tibet to ward off the Russian interests there. Eventually this penlop, Ugyen Wangebuck, was knighted by the British and, as a result,

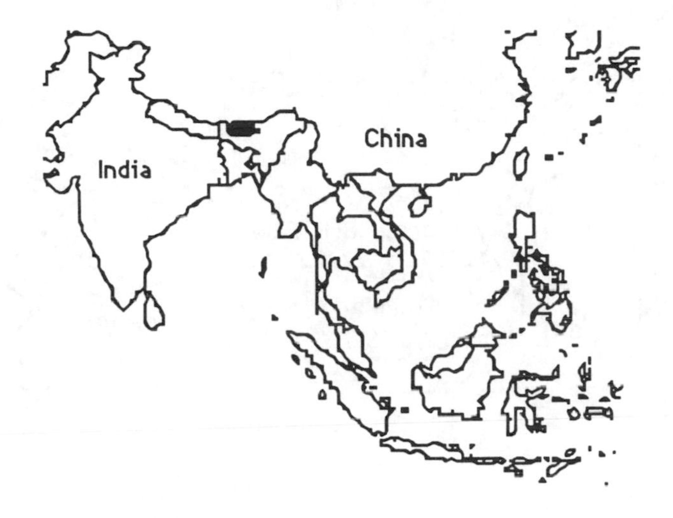

gained great status in Bhutan. In 1907, Sir Ugyen Wangebuck was elected the first king of Bhutan in what was to be a hereditary monarchy. His great grandson is the present king of Bhutan.

Bhutan has been greatly aided by India, that country having seen the value of a buffer between itself and China. One result has been a migration into the south of the country by people from India and Nepal followed by ethnic tensions in the country.

Government Today

Bhutan has no written constitution. Rather the people are governed under a growing and changing body of laws and procedures. These laws lay down the rules for electing a royal advisory council (Lodoi Tsokde) and a legislature (Tshogdu). The king, in addition, surrounds himself with a council of ministers (Lhengye Shungtsog). Both the advisory council and the council of ministers are responsible to the legislature. There are 18 districts under this central government, each administered by a Dzongda. Another leader, called a Thrimpon, is in charge of judicial affairs. However, in Bhutan, the king is the real decision maker and ruler.

The present king, in power since 1974, early decided that Bhutan should strive to become a modern Asian country. With India at first paying all the bills for development, Bhutan began to build power plants, to increase the agricultural land used for export products, and to establish small manufacturers of export goods. A major concern

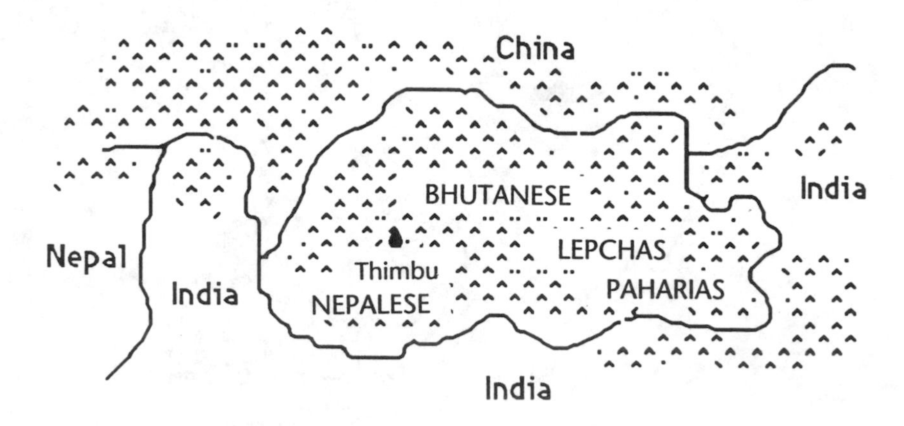

Major groups in Bhutan.

of the Bhutanese is their dependence on India. The present king has declared it necessary for Bhutan to become more self-supporting.

A second issue to be faced by the Bhutan government is the control of immigrants. Early in Tibet's takeover by China, 6,000 Tibetans fled to refuge in Bhutan. They have been joined, mostly in the south, by immigrants from Nepal and India.

Provision of health services is another concern of the Bhutanese. In the entire country there are only about 140 doctors (for a population of close to 1.3 million) and only enough hospital beds for one in every 1,480 Bhutanese.

Ethnic Makeup

The majority of people of Bhutan are Bhutanese or Bhotias. Related to Tibetans, they share a common border with that people. The Nepalese of southern Bhutan comprise about one-fifth of the population in the country. Other ethnic groups, the Lepchas and Paharias, live in the southeastern foothills.

CAMBODIA

Population: 8,055,000 (1989 estimate).
Location: Southeast Asia, bordered by Vietnam, Laos, Thailand, and the Gulf of Thailand.
Languages: Khmer; Vietnamese; Chinese.
Principal cities: Phnom-Penh (capital), 800,000 (only city of more than 100,000 population).

Political Background

Cambodia (Kampuchea) was once a part of a greater kingdom of the Khmer. As this old kingdom aged and decayed, the Cambodians found themselves more and more at the mercy of their neighbors. First the Vietnamese had ambitions to incorporate the Khmer land

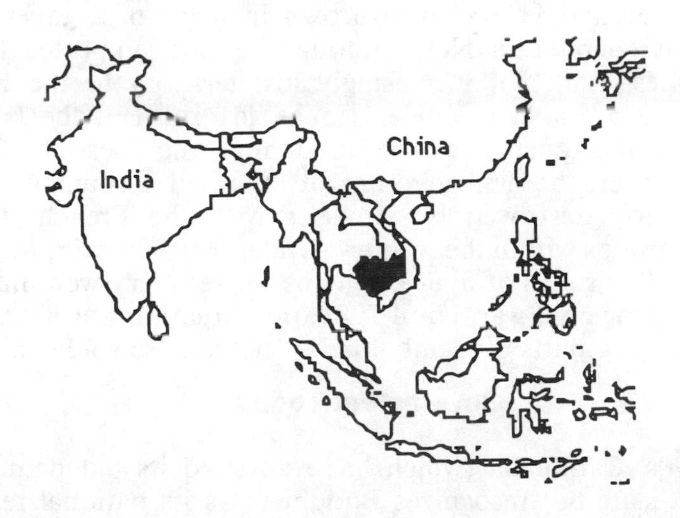

into their own rule. The Khmer responded by appealing to Thailand for help, only to find themselves in danger of being absorbed into that kingdom. Finally, in 1863, the Cambodians asked the French, who were establishing themselves in Indochina, for protection. The result was nearly a century of colonialism under a mostly indifferent French government.

Then in World War II the puppet French government sided with the Japanese who presided over the separation of some Cambodian land and its absorption by Thailand. In this turmoil Cambodia's aged king died and 18-year-old Nordrom Sihanouk took the throne. In his zeal to rid the country of its colonial yoke, Sihanouk first sought international aid from the West, then sided with the Communists centered in North Vietnam. France attempted to regain control after the war and later was replaced by the United States in its attempt to influence the whole of Indochina. However, by 1954 Cambodia had gained independence and embarked on the road to a new Khmer republic.

Interested in control of the country and in what he believed to be the welfare of Cambodians, Prince Sihanouk first sided with Communists as the only viable alternative. He then formed a government-in-exile, emerging from time to time as the power in Cambodian government. On one occasion, he joined forces with the Khmer Communists, the Khmer Rouge. The prince worked with them in a re-education of Cambodians that resulted in a great purge and relocation of townspeople to the country. Later, he withdrew from the Khmer Rouge and again went into exile to protest against the violent methods being taken to control the people. Finally the power of Prince Sihanouk waned and he was overthrown in favor of a government headed by General Lon Nol. Although he was supported by the United States, Lon Nol increasingly lost territory to the Khmer Rouge. In 1975, under a Khmer Rouge government, the People's Republic of Kampuchea was formed after the Russian-Chinese model. However, the new government inherited a country of devastation—nearly destroyed by struggles with the French, United States, and groups within the country. Under Heng Samrin, who took office in 1979, a series of five-year plans for recovery were initiated amid continuing civil war. Until 1989, this situation was aggravated by occupation of parts of Cambodia by Vietnamese soldiers.

Government Today

In the 1990s, Cambodia (which has reinstated its old name) is a communist state but recognizes Buddhism as its national religion.

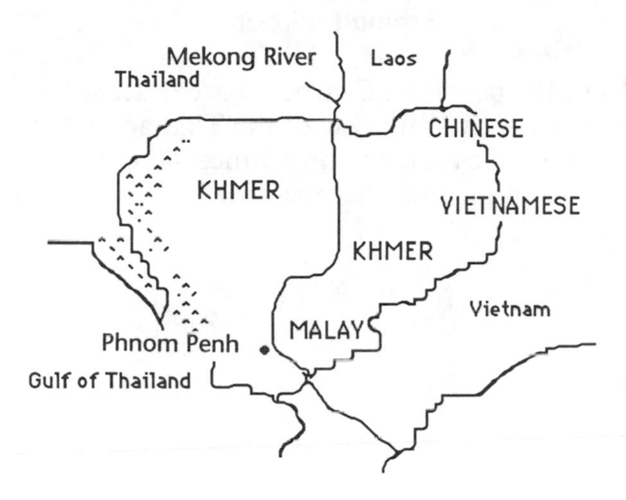

Some of the peoples of Cambodia.

The government is directed by a Council of Ministers, which is chosen by and responsible to an elected National Assembly. Throughout the provinces and towns, people's committees make local policy and provide for public security. In 1986 national control of land and manufacturing was relaxed to allow for some private enterprise.

Prince Sihanouk, working in exile, had formed a Democratic Kampuchean government and then had changed the name to the National Government of Cambodia, a move to place some distance between his government and the Khmer Rouge. With four different factions fighting for power within the country, both Prince Sihanouk and Hun Sen, who was president of the council of ministers, sought United Nations aid. Given that aid, along with a peace proposal developed by Australia, Cambodia faces its most important issue: the reconciliation of all contending parties and formation of a strong government.

With relative peace in the land, Cambodians can turn to other pressing problems—the need to increase productivity, particularly in food products, and to expand its foreign trade base. Some 90 percent of Cambodia's foreign trade has been with the former Soviet Union. The aim in solving these problems is to meet the long-term goal, a rise in the standard of living throughout the country. The average income in Cambodia is 78 dollars per person per year.

Ethnic Makeup

Seven-eighths of the people in Cambodia are descendants of the old Khmer dynasty who have mixed with the Thai and Chinese to form the present Khmer. Vietnamese and Chinese live in the north; Malayan descendants of the old Champa kingdom live in the south.

FIJI

Population: 727,104 (1989 estimate).
Location: Four main islands and more than 800 smaller ones in the Pacific Ocean, lying north of New Zealand and northeast of Sydney, Australia.
Languages: English; Fijian.
Principal cities: Suva (capital), 150,000; Lautoka, 37,000.

Political Background

In 1874, at the request of Chief Thakombau, the Fijian islands became a British possesion. Various ethnic groups peopled the islands. A decline in the numbers of ethnic Fijians and an increase in immigrants from India was a serious threat to Fijian unity and peace in

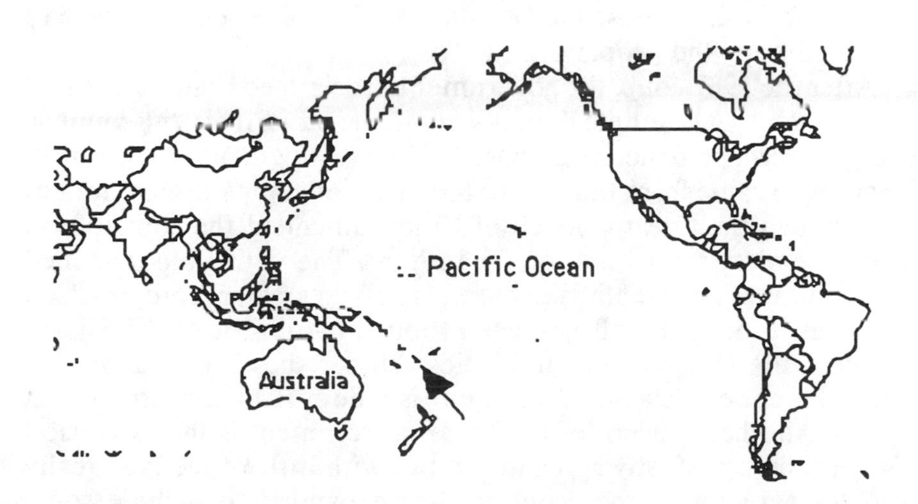

the 1980s. This concern lies at the center of recent political maneuvering. When the elections of 1987 resulted in a Cabinet that had a majority of Indian members, a military coup followed. More than 7,000 Indian Fijians fled the country, including two-thirds of the lawyers, half the doctors, and a large proportion of the country's teachers.

After some manipulation by the military, the former British governor-general of Fiji became its prime minister. He immediately began attempts to separate the government from military influence, which prompted the leader of the military coup to resign his commission so that he could take a civilian post in the cabinet. However, ethnic Fijians are divided into a great number of clans led by hereditary chiefs. Some 70 of these chiefs form the Great Council of Chiefs, without whose approval nothing of consequence can be done by Fiji's government. This council met in 1990 and 1991 to approve a new constitution.

Government Today

The Great Council of Chiefs appoints a president of the republic, who must be an ethnic Fijian, and also recommends 24 members of the Senate. Appointed by the president, the members of the Senate (34) must include 24 ethnic Fijians. The main work of this chamber of the legislature is to protect the interests of ethnic Fijians. In the House of Representatives are 70 members plus a speaker and deputy speaker appointed by elected members. The method of defining representation in this House has been the subject of much difference of opinion among the people of Fiji.

After the 1987 coup, the government proclaimed that, for the first time in many years, ethnic Fijians were in the majority in the country. The government structure is based on that judgment. As a result, Fijians who came from India have felt abandoned by the government even though the Great Council of Chiefs amended the constitution to include more representation for Indians. The voting blocs defined for selection of representatives have also given greater representation to Fijians in outlying villages, even though two-thirds of the Fijians live near the larger towns and cities. Under these conditions, the establishment of a stable government is a dominant concern among Fijians. Another concern of the Fijian government is the expansion of the economy. Mostly agricultural, but with little of the land really used for agriculture, the economy has expanded to include some

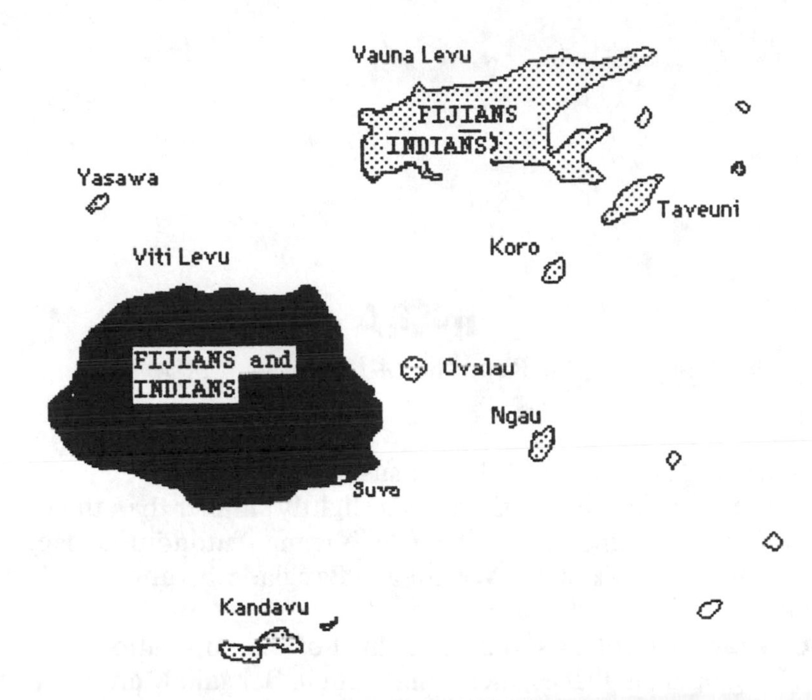

The original Fijians share the island nation almost equally with Indians who were imported to work the plantations.

industry (largely sugar processing), mining, and manufacturing (mostly clothing). Growth in the economy was steady until the 1987 coup. In that year production fell by one-fifth and the government has been seeking to restore economic growth ever since.

Ethnic Makeup

The people of Fiji are nearly equally split between the various clans of ethnic Fijians and Indian immigrants.

INDIA

Republic of India

Population: 843,930,161 (1991 census).
Location: A country in Southern Asia slightly smaller than the United States. India is bounded by Tibet (the Xizang Autonomous Region), Nepal, Bhutan, Pakistan, Myanmar, Bangladesh, and the Indian Ocean.
Languages: Hindi (spoken by one-third of the population); English; and 16 regional languages, including Telugu, Bengali, Marathi, Tamil, and Urdu.
Principal cities: Bombay, 8,250,000; Delhi, 4,900,000; Calcutta, 3,300,000; Madras, 3,300,000; Bangalore, 2,600,000; Hyderabad, 2,200,000; Ahmedabad, 2,200,000; Kanpur, 1,500,000; Nagpur, 1,200,000; Pune, 1,200,000. Fifty other cities with greater than 300,000 population and New Delhi (capital) with 274,000 people.

Political Background

Empires rose and fell in India before the advent of the British, who gained more and more control after 1750. The British ruled partly by direct government and partly through alliances with local maharajas. In 1947, after 200 years of such rule, India became a dominion within the British Commonwealth of Nations and then a republic in 1950. A longtime leader of the struggle for independence, Jawahar Lal Nehru took office as the first prime minister. He was immediately faced with internal strife among the various states; they were contending with the newly formed Pakistan over borders and with China over jurisdiction in the northern state of Kashmir. Nehru died in 1964 and was succeeded for two years by Lal Bahadur Shastri. Shastri managed to resolve the conflict with China before his death.

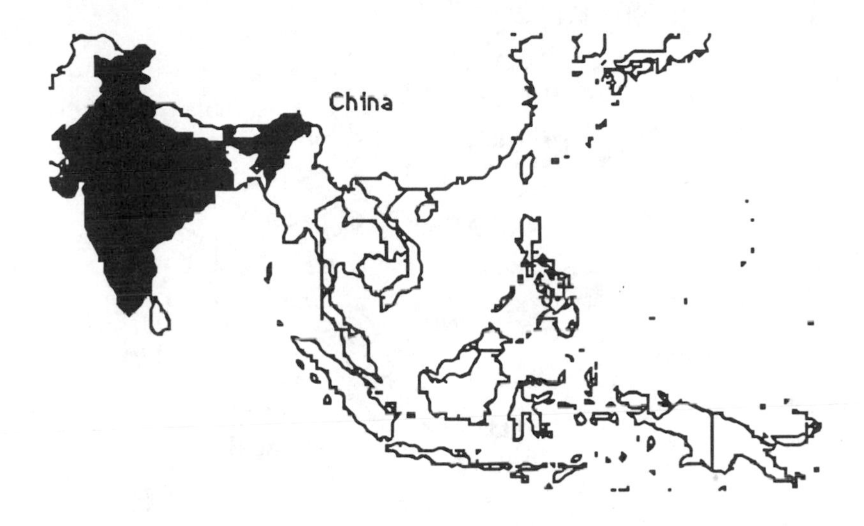

He was replaced as prime minister by Nehru's daughter Indira Gandhi. Prime Minister Gandhi ruled until 1977 and resumed office from 1980 until her assassination in 1984. Her son, Rajiv Gandhi, ruled from 1985 to 1989. Throughout and prior to the rule of the Gandhis, India was forced to concentrate much of its attention on the settling of regional disputes. Kashmir remained at odds with the central government, as did the Sikhs of Punjab and the citizens of Assam. Along with these conflicts the government was periodically hampered by accusations of corruption. Both Indira Gandhi and her son Rajiv were so accused and later declared innocent. Widespread distrust of government has since continued, as has the struggle to unite the 25 self-governing states and seven territories of India.

Government Today

The government of India is a complex interaction between the central government and the governments of the various states and territories. India is a federation of independent states. It is ruled by a president and a two-house legislature: the Rajya Sabha (Council of States) and the Lok Sabha (House of the People). Two hundred forty-five members of the Rajya Sabha are elected by the state assemblies to represent the individual states. Five hundred forty-two members of the Lok Sabha are elected by universal suffrage and represent districts and precincts much like those represented by congress members in the United States. The president is chosen for a five-year term by an

A few of the peoples of India.

electoral college drawn from the two houses of parliament and the legislatures of the various states. The president appoints a prime minister and works with that minister to select a cabinet to direct the functions of government. The president also appoints a governor for each of the 25 states and a council of ministers for each state. Legislatures in the states are popularly elected and vary; some of them are divided into two houses, some have only one house of legislation.

Internal strife has plagued India since its inception. In the 1980s the people of Punjab and Assam rebelled. The Punjab rebellion was put down with the destruction of one of the Sikh's most holy temples. The Muslims of Kashmir sought independence or alliance with Pakistan in the 1990s. Also in the 1990s, additional disputes erupted between Nepal and Pakistan, involving parts of India, and the Sikh-Hindu differences continued in Punjab. Hindus and Muslims continue to battle wherever the two religious groups share the same government.

The rigidity of the states and lack of cooperation with the federal government has resulted in great economic imbalances among Indians. Overall the citizenry is poor; annual per capita income is 340 dollars. Another effect has been the generally poor quality of public services from the different governments. An example is the sporadic enforcement of compulsory education, which is a state function. Though the national government encourages education to be free and compulsory to age 14, only 12 states have made schooling free beyond age 11, and the compulsory aspect is widely neglected. About half of all Indian citizens are illiterate.

Ethnic Makeup

India's history of settlement is long and the merging of peoples has eliminated many of the ethnic differences in the country. Still Indians are sometimes placed in broad groupings based on past history and location. Dravidians inhabit the south, Indo-Aryans the southwest, and various groups occupy the north. Distinctions are also made on language, but the most operative differences among Indians are religious. The predominant Hindu followers are often in dispute with Muslims and Sikhs.

INDONESIA

Republic of Indonesia

Population: 179,321,641 (1990 census).
Location: 13,700 islands between mainland Southeast Asia and Australia. Principal islands: Java, Sumatra, Kalimantan (a section of Borneo), Sulawesi (Celebes), the Moluccas, and Timor.
Language: Bahasa Indonesian.
Principal cities: Jakarta (capital), 7,350,000; Surabaya, 2,225,000; Medan, 1,800,000; Bandung, 1,570,000; Semarang, 1,000,000. Nine other cities with populations greater than 300,000.

Political Background

The people who settled in Indonesia before the 1400s brought with them the Hindu religion. Hindu empires held sway at first. However, Muslim missionaries arrived by the 1400s and between that time and 1900, Indonesians became predominantly Muslim.

The Dutch had meanwhile appeared to exploit the islands' resources. In the early 1800s the British temporarily claimed Indonesia. Then Dutch governors ruled the country under a system that required landowners to give a portion of their crops to the Dutch government.

The area was not organized as a single nation until independence was proclaimed in 1945 and Dr. Sukarno, who had led the fight for self-rule since 1920, became president. In reaction, the Dutch did not recognize this declaration of independence but tried instead to maintain their control of the area while organizing a federation of cooperating but independent states. After four years of negotiating and fighting, the Dutch finally yielded to Indonesian independence; they had at the same time successfully promoted their idea of federation. The various island states formed a United States of Indonesia. Su-

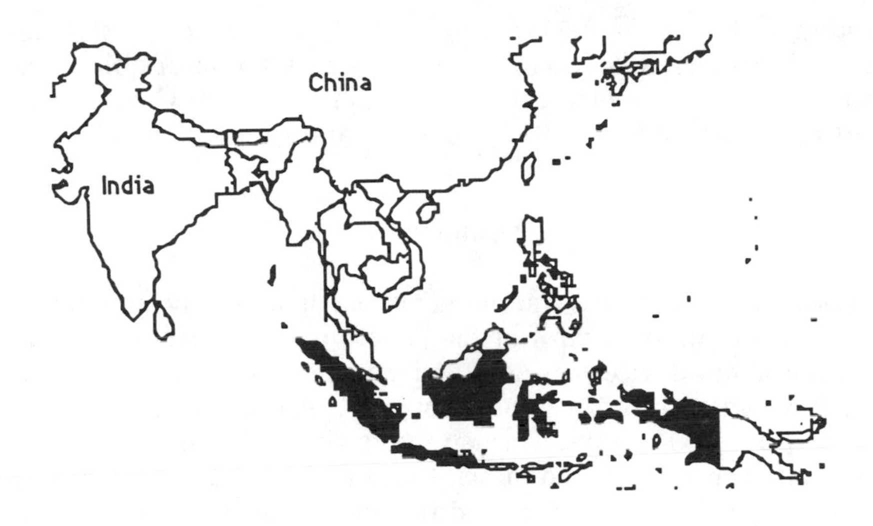

matra was a wary member of this federation, fearing that the greater productivity in Sumatra would yield products that would be used mostly to improve conditions in Java. Under Dr. Sukarno's fierce advocacy of unity, the federation soon gave way to a single nation, the Republic of Indonesia. The constitution, written under Dr. Sukarno's direction, established five principles on which the government was to be based: (1) belief in one supreme God (Islam as the state religion); (2) a just and civilized humanity; (3) unity of all Indonesia; (4) democracy led by wisdom of deliberations among representatives; and (5) social justice for all people of Indonesia.

From 1949 to 1957, the new country was a parliamentary democracy. However, progress was slow and in 1957 Dr. Sukarno abandoned parliament in favor of a dictatorial "guided democracy." Sukarno pressed for national unity while establishing sound relations with China and appearing to be anti-Western. He also kept a careful balance between the two strongest forces in Indonesia—the communist party and the army. By 1965, Dr. Sukarno had sufficient standing to transfer the power of parliamentary government to a three-person Supreme Operational Command. Indonesia moved toward a complete dictatorship.

In 1966 Dr. Sukarno yielded governmental power to the army chief-of-staff General Suharto. General Suharto immediately declared a "new order" in which the communists would play no part. In the years that followed, hundreds of communists who resisted Suharto would be destroyed. General Suharto has been re-elected to head

Indonesia five times, the last time in 1988, despite incidents of unrest by Indonesians. Since 1976 there has been a union of citizens dedicated to fighting Javanese dominance in the country. Other, student-led protests erupted in 1977 and 1978, and riots against Chinese in Indonesia occurred in 1984.

Government Today

President Suharto rules Indonesia almost dictatorially, and has tried to ensure military control of the government by installing General Sudharmono as vice-president and several other military figures in positions in the ruling cabinet. There is a People's Consultative Assembly of 1,000 members, structured to give voice in government to the various peoples of Indonesia. Five hundred of these members are elected by universal suffrage and the remaining 500 by various local and regional schemes. In choosing these 500 members, village assemblies play important roles. The National Assembly meets at least once every five years to elect the president. From the National Assembly, a smaller People's Representation Council is chosen to handle ongoing legislative concerns.

Rich in minerals and petroleum, the nation has been led by Dr. Sukarno and General Suharto toward unity and toward industrialization at a fairly steady pace. In 1985 industries such as tire man-

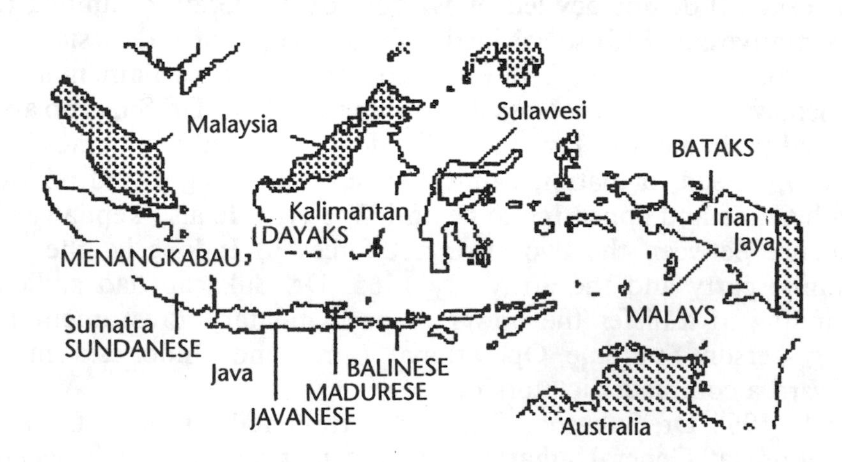

There are many groups of people on the islands that make up Indonesia.

ufacture, fuel production, and electronic assembly accounted for about one-fifth of the Indonesian income and occupied only about nine percent of the workers. More than half the working population was still engaged in fishing and farming. The average annual per capital income in 1990 was 535 dollars. Making full use of its resources and moving toward an industrialization that provides greater employment for the people are major challenges for the Indonesian government. Equally challenging is the need to do away with internal suppression of opinions voiced by students and by citizens who feel that their efforts are not returned in services to their own people, but are diverted to enhance the well-being of others. This feeling is most often displayed in anti-Javanese attitudes on Sumatra and some other islands.

Ethnic Makeup

A minority of the people of Indonesia are Chinese and these residents often work as merchants in the port cities. Almost all other residents are known as Indonesians even though they might belong to smaller, distinct ethnic groups such as the Menangkabau, Dayaks, Balinese, Madurese, and Bataks.

JAPAN

Population: 123,611,541 (1990).
Location: Several islands of a chain in the west Pacific Ocean off the coast of Asia.
Language: Japanese.
Principal cities: Tokyo (capital), 8,000,000; Yokohama, 3,000,000; Osaka, 2,500,000; Nagoya, 2,100,000. Seven cities of more than 1,000,000 population: Sapporo, Kobe, Kyoto, Fukuoka, Kawasaki, Hiroshima, Kitakyushu.

Political Background

Long ruled by emperors and warriors, Japan's government underwent pivotal changes in the twentieth century. The current government of

Japan dates from 1945, or the end of World War II, when the emperor was forced to renounce his claim to divinity. Two years later, a constitution patterned after that of the United States, but specifically renouncing war, was enacted.

Government Today

Under the constitution of Japan, the emperor remains head of state, but is without specific governmental authority. The government of the country is in the hands of the Diet, a two-house legislature of Representatives and Councillors. This Diet appoints a prime minister (usually the leader of the majority political party) and the prime minister selects a cabinet with the approval of the Diet. The prime minister is the actual leader of government. There are also local political leaders. Japan is divided into 47 districts, or prefectures, each with its own governmental structure operating under the national government.

Once appointed, the prime minister operates under a budget approved by the Diet. From 1976–1987 this budget limited the amount spent on defense to one percent of the national income. The limit has since been abandoned and mild increases made in defense spending, which pleases the United States. Since World War II, Japan has

Japanese and a very few Ainu form the majority of the population in Japan.

largely depended for its defense on the United States and has invested much of its income in international business.

The small amount spent on defense has been an issue between Japan and the United States. Japan's investment in manufacturing and trade has created a second important issue between Japan and its trading neighbors. In short, Japan's income from foreign trade exceeds its spending in foreign countries by more than 70 percent. The United States and Japan are in frequent discussions over this imbalance. Meanwhile, to support its manufacturing effort, Japan has signed trade agreements with China, even though the countries are traditional foes and are in dispute over some territory.

Both Japan and China claim five Senkaku Islands that lie in the East China Sea about 200 miles from Japan. The two countries from time to time discuss the ownership of these uninhabited islands. Similarly, Japan claims the right to four nearby islands that were occupied by the Soviet Union after World War II and have not yet been returned to Japan.

Rapid economic development has demanded cooperation between business and government in Japan. This cooperation has sometimes tempted government officials to act illegally. In the 1980s, scandals at top government levels included accusations and trials of some officials for accepting bribes, soliciting illegal support from industrialists, and taking advantage of government information to perform illegal share trading on the stock market.

Ethnic Makeup

The exact origins of most Japanese today are uncertain, but their ancestors are thought to have emigrated from mainland Asia. They may have migrated from Mongolia in waves that were organized by one of the last migrating groups, the Tenno clan. Arriving in Japan in the second and third centuries A.D., these migrants found an earlier group living on the islands, the Ainu. In the twentieth century, the Ainu are nearly all integrated into Japanese society.

LAOS

Lao People's Democratic Republic

Population: 4,167,000 (1991 estimate).
Location: Southeast Asia, in rugged upland cut by narrow river valleys and bordered by China, Vietnam, Cambodia, Thailand and Myanmar.
Languages: Lao, spoken by two-thirds of the population; various tribal languages; French.
Principal cities: Vientiane, or Viangchan (capital) 377,000; Savannakhet 51,000; Peksé, 45,000; Luang Prabang, 44,000.

Political Background

Before Europeans appeared, Laos was divided among two or, more often, three smaller kingdoms. Vientiane in the center of the country and Luang Prebang were ancient headquarters for some of these kingdoms. The present country of Laos was created through French intervention between 1883 and 1886. In early 1945 Japanese took control of the French holdings in Southeast Asia. Later that same year Laotians declared independence under King Suavang Vong at Luang Prabang and under Prince Phetsarath at Vientiane. While these two monarchs struggled for dominance, the French re-entered Laos from the south and by 1947 were in enough control to establish a constitutional monarchy based at Vientiane. The old ruler Prince Phetsarath fled with his allies, princes Souvana Phouma and Souphanouvong, to Thailand and established a government-in-exile. Within two years, Prince Souphanouvong had dissociated himself from this government-in-exile. Believing that alliance with the Viet Minh, a Chinese-supported Communist group organized to free Vietnam from the French, was the best hope for ridding Laos of colonialism,

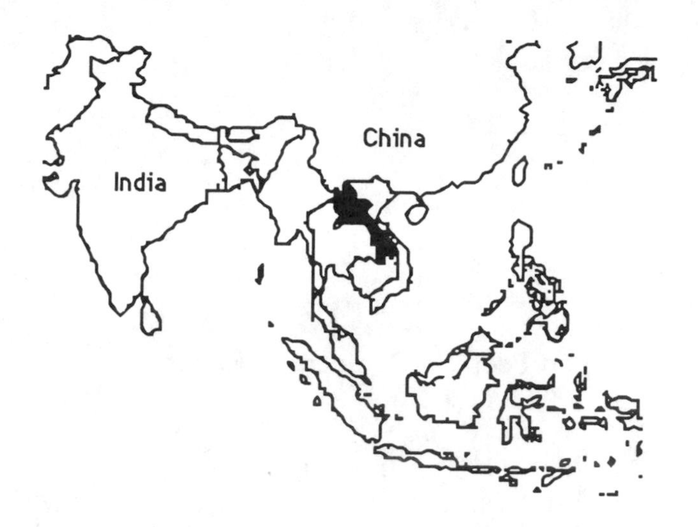

Prince Souphanouvong joined with the Viet Minh and established a Laotian counterpart, the Pathet Lao.

Thereafter, the history of Laos was one of internal strife and civil war, with both sides aided by outside forces. In 1955, the Western supported king of Laos reorganized the Laotian government and began to work for unity among the contending groups. A coalition government that included the Pathet Lao took effect by 1958 but was abandoned at the urgings of the United States. By 1961, the country was engaged in a war between the government at Vientiane and the Pathet Lao, who controlled the north. This civil war continued through the early 1970s and eventually was won by the communist forces. In 1975, after nearly 30 years of unrest, a government patterned after that of China and the Soviet Union was installed. It embarked on a long struggle to reconstruct a country devastated by civil war and foreign intervention. This struggle began with land reform and government ownership of much of the economy, but this organization would change. By 1991 there was a new constitution that allowed for some private ownership of land and industry.

Government Today

Laos is controlled by the Lao People's Revolutionary Party. From the members of this party a National Assembly is elected to serve for five years. This group meets infrequently but elects a president and standing committee to conduct government. The standing com-

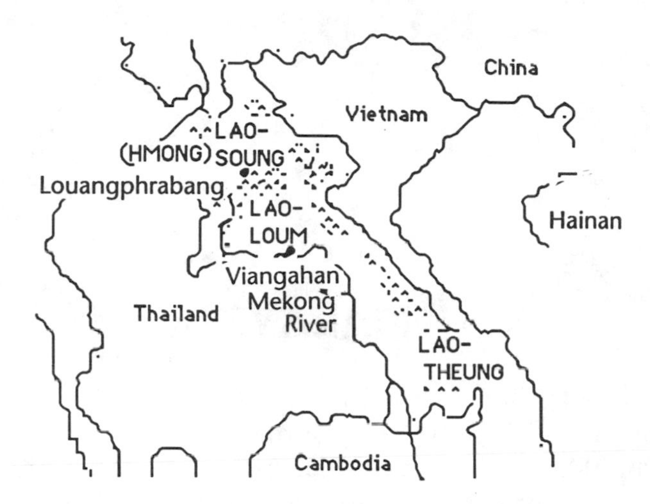

The Tai people of Laos are sometimes divided according to the part of the country in which they live.

mittee selects a prime minster and a council of ministers who transact the daily business of government.

A major issue in Laos is reconstruction of the agriculture and industrial bases for the country, a reconstruction that includes economic reform. This rebuilding is slowed by the reluctance of other world powers to come to the aid of Laos. As part of its effort to recover, Laos in 1990 began a program to divest the national government of businesses and industries, and to encourage some private ownership of land and business.

Another issue is strengthening relations with Thailand, a country that once controlled much of Laos. In its civil war, in which the United States took an active role, some Laotians (for example, the Hmong) sided with the United States against the Pathet Lao. When the Pathet Lao emerged victorious, many of these people fled to Thailand. The flood of refugees strained the already tender relations between Laos and Thailand.

Ethnic Makeup

Two-thirds of the people of Laos are Tai people related to the Thai of Thailand and live in the lowlands of the country. Various tribal groups less related to the Thai live in the north and are collectively known as Lao-theung. In the far north, the region of the famous Ho Chi Minh Trail of the Vietnam War, live a few thousand Vietnamese.

MALAYSIA

Population: 17,755,900 (1990 estimate).
Location: The Malay Peninsula, extending south from Southeast Asia, and islands extending to the two states Sarawak and Sabah in northern Kalimantan (Borneo). Bordered by Thailand, the Gulf of Thailand in the South China Sea, the Straits of Malacca, and the Bay of Bengal.
Languages: Behara Malaysian; English; Chinese; Tamil; and Iban.
Principal cities: Kuala Lumpur (capital), 920,000; Ipoh, 300,000; Pentaling Jaya, 210,000; Kelang, 192,000; Kuala Trengganu, 180,000, Kota Bahru, 170,000; Taiping, 146,000, Seremban, 133,000, Kuantan, 132,000; and Kota Kinabalu, 110,000.

Political Background

Modern history in Malayasia begins with the appearance of the first sultanate around A.D. 1400. A half-century later, in 1896, Britain acquired four of the nine original sultanates that make up mainland Malaysia. The British formed them into the Federated Malay States with a capital at Kuala Lumpur. In 1909, Britain was ceded four more states by Siam, and these became unfederated states. The total was increased by the addition of Jahore in 1914, when a British adviser was appointed to that sultanate. Under British leadership, the traditional rulers began to allow development of tin mining and rubber. These industries required workers who were imported by conscription from China and India. Eventually the Chinese population grew to be nearly one-third the population of Malaysia.

Rule through the old sultanates continued without interruption until World War II. In that war, Japanese troops claimed Malaysia and encouraged unification of the various segments of the country.

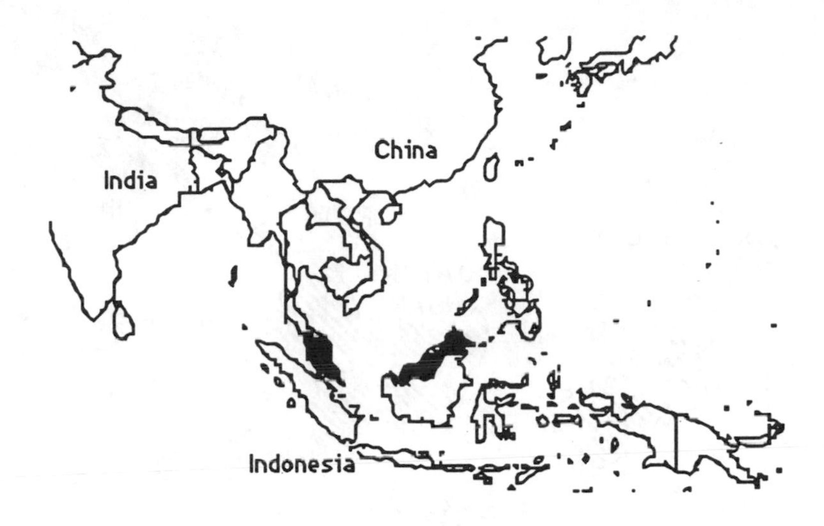

The British meanwhile planned to rid the country of the sultans and to establish a democratic form of government. Sultans and citizens alike opposed this intrusion from a foreign agent. In 1946 they succeeded in establishing the Federation of Malaysia. Communism appeared and was accepted as one of the ways Malaysia could rid itself of its colonial status. Finally, in 1957 Malaysia formally won independence and Tunku Abdul Rahman was installed as prime minister. Sarawak and Sabah on the island of Borneo were added to the nation in 1963.

Under a federal plan for economic growth, ultimately called the National Development Plan, Malaysia has undergone a fairly steady build-up of industries backed by rubber production, tin mining, and the development of the country's petroleum resources. This NDP has also changed the direction of the Malay economy from one dependent on international trade with the United States and Europe to a commitment to leadership in improving economic conditions in all of Southeast Asia. Malay is one of the wealthier of the Southeast Asian nations with a per capita production of 6,600 dollars in 1991.

Government Today

The nine hereditary rulers are still very powerful in Malaysia. With heads of other regions, they form a Conference of Rulers. This conference elects a Yang di Pertuang Agong (Supreme Head of State) who must come from the nine hereditary rulers, and who serves for

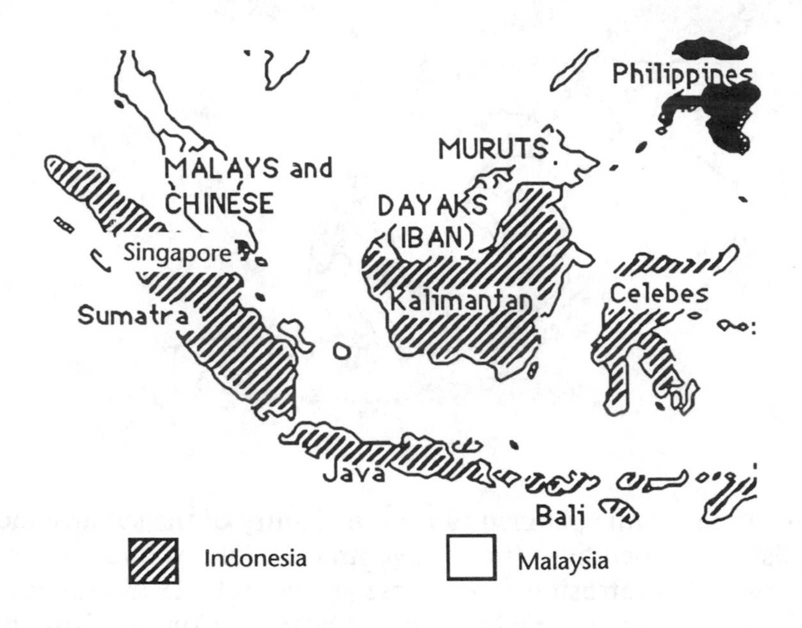

The major peoples of Malaysia.

five years. The Yang di Pertuan Agong rules the country with the advice of a cabinet chosen by him and a parliament of 70 members, of which 30 are elected and 40 appointed by the Conference of Rulers.

While development continues, the government is continually pressed to defend Malaysian rights in the wake of strong immigration and entry into Malaysian businesses of Chinese and Indians. Added to this tension is the dissension of the Malays of Sabah who feel that they are underrepresented in the federation. Sabah has become such a troublesome element that for a while it was suspended from participation in the federal government on the grounds of corruption among its leadership.

Ethnic Makeup

About half the people of Malaysia are Malays born in Indonesia, Singapore, and Malaysia. About one-third of the people of Western Malaysia are Chinese and one-tenth are Tamils from southern India. Eastern Malaysia (Sarawak and Sabah) is inhabited by many tribal groups. Among them are the Iban (Sea Dayaks and Land Dayaks), Malays, and Melanau of Sarawak, and the Bajaus, Bruneis, Dusuns, Kedayans, and Muruts of Sabah.

MONGOLIA

Mongolian People's Republic

Population: 2,102,000 (1991 estimate).
Location: East Central Asia, bordered by Russia and the People's Republic of China.
Languages: Mongol (written in a vertical script or more recently using a Cyrillic alphabet); Kazakh.
Principal cities: Ulan Bator (capital), 575,000; Darhan, 90,000; Erdene, 57,000.

Political Background

The history of modern-day Mongolia begins with the fall of the Manchus of China in 1911. This allowed leading nobles among the no-

mads of the rugged mountain and Gobi desert country to declare their independence—with support from Russia. These nobles agreed to form a monarchy under the Living Buddha. When they tried to include Inner Mongolia in the new monarchy, China and Russia objected. A Mongolia-Chinese war ensued that lasted until Russia, China, and the Mongol nobles agreed to a form of independent government under Chinese suzerainty, or rule in world affairs. In the process, parts of the land claimed by the Mongolians were instead recognized as areas under the control of China or Russia.

In 1920, Chinese General Xu Shuzeng invaded Mongolia and it was again forced to submit to Chinese rule. In the same year, Mongolians formed a Mongol People's Party that aligned itself with the Soviet Union. When the Mongolian king died in 1924, this party changed its name to the Mongolian People's Revolutionary Party and proclaimed a new republic after the Soviet pattern. This form of government clashed with the Mongolian Lamaist religion and tensions grew as the new Mongolia tried to emulate the Soviets. A 1929 attempt to collectivize the nomadic herdsmen and their cattle resulted in economic collapse as one-third of the country's cattle died.

In 1936 Marshal Choybalsan took power in Mongolia, he proceeded to outlaw religion and kill many of the old leaders as traitors who were allegedly aiding the Japanese. Choybalsan also instituted a program of industrialization, but aid from the Soviet Union declined as World War II progressed. Following the war, Mongolia again claimed independence and was recognized by the Soviet Union and China, both of whom felt a need for a buffer zone between them.

Some industrialization continued despite the lessening of Soviet aid and the fleeing of Mongols and their herds (cattle, horse, sheep, goats, and camels are raised in the country) to other lands. In 1990 the government attempted to revitalize a declining economy by changing the form of government and by allowing some private ownership of industry and livestock.

Government Today

The second nation in the world to espouse the Soviet form of communism, Mongolia was directed by a Mongolian People's Revolutionary Party through an assembly called the People's Great Hural. A 1990 amendment to the 1960 constitution removed the description of the People's Revolutionary Party as the "guiding force" of the nation. However, the People's Great Hural of 430 representatives

Kazakhs and Mongols make up most of the population of Mongolia.

elected for five-year terms continued to be the major governing body. It meets four times in five years to approve policy and to elect a president and vice-president. The People's Great Hural selects a State Great Hural, or standing committee, and a State Little Hural to manage government. The standing committee elects a cabinet that, with the president and vice president, conducts the business of government. As in the model set by the former Soviet Union, other assemblies direct matters at provincial and town levels.

Major issues for Mongolians are adjusting to reduced support from Russia and continuing to develop an industrial economic base.

Ethnic Makeup

Eighty percent of the people of Mongolia are Mongols, although they represent several distinct groups of different tribal origins. Kazakhs, a Turkish people, live in the west.

MYANMAR

Union of Myanmar

Population: 39,350,000 (1988 estimate).
Location: Southeast Asia, bounded by India, China, Laos, Thailand, Bangladesh, and the Bay of Bengal.
Languages: Burmese (spoken by 80 percent of the people); English; several less-commonly used languages.
Principal cities: Yangon (formerly Rangoon, capital) 2,513,000; Mandalay, 533,000; Mawlamyine (Moulmein), 220,000; Bago (Pegu), 151,000.

Political Background

Myanmar (formerly Burma) has long been the homeland for Pyus, Mons, Burmans, Shan, Karen, Kachin, and other hill-dwelling groups. Burmans (or Bamars) arrived in the area and settled in the Irrawaddy River valley by the tenth century. Soon they outnumbered the other groups who lived mostly in the northern hill country. In the 1200s, 1500s, and 1700s, the Burmans briefly established kingdoms that included most of the people of present-day Myanmar. Between 1824 and 1885, the British in India exerted more and more influence on Myanmar. Eventually, the land then known as Burma was incorporated into India and ruled by the British under a system in which the tribal village headmen were supported by and reported to the central government.

However, the Burmans and hill peoples of Burma desired independence. In 1930, influential citizens of Burma formed an unofficial government called Thakin (masters' government) to press for a free Burma. In 1937, they succeeded in separating Burma from India while still under British control. Then in World War II Japanese forces

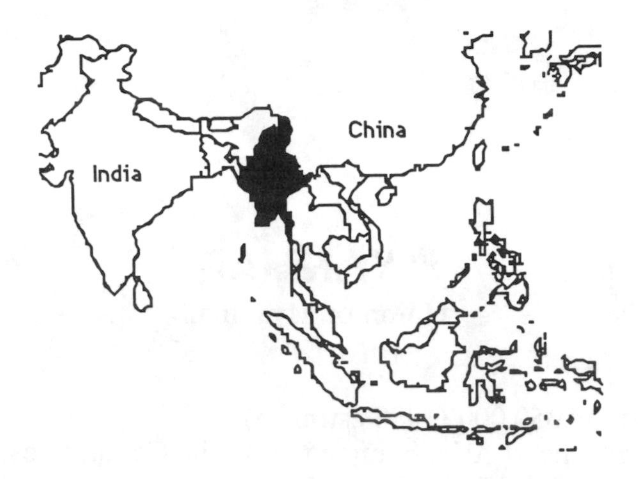

replaced the British and encouraged Burma's independence. Dr. Ba Maw was named to head a Burmese government.

Immediately the Burma people divided. Some supported the Japanese while others organized an Anti-Fascist People's Freedom League led by Aung San. By war's end this league was supporting the Allied forces.

The war ended and the British returned. Now there were two armies in Burma: British forces mostly recruited from the hill tribes, and a Burma Army, mostly of Burmans. Aung San and his League pressed for independence from Britain and succeeded in uniting a 10,000 troop army, which was organized by divisions of the various ethnic groups. However, before independence was fully negotiated, Aung San was assassinated, and U Nu came to power. Under him, Burma became an independent nation in 1948.

For 14 years the government, a constitutional democracy, balanced pressures from the army powers, from a growing communist group, and from skeptical ethnic factions. Part of the difficulties during these years lay in the organization of the army, an organization that tended to emphasize ethnic differences. By 1962 differences between the Bamar army leaders and communist forces had grown. The Anti-Fascist People's Freedom League, formed during World War II, continued to dominate politics in the country, but by 1962 had split into two factions. General Ne Win declared military rule and then proceeded to reorganize the army so that Bamar officers and enlisted men would be spread throughout the divisions. General Ne Win

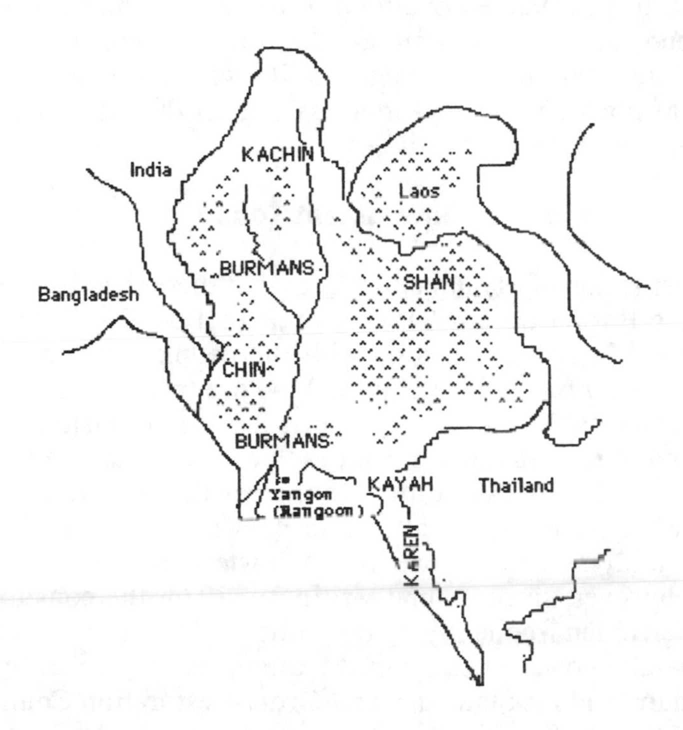

A few of the peoples of Myanmar.

became U Ne Win and led the country toward socialism. The "Burmese Way to Socialism"—calling for national unity, free expression of religion, and government ownership of all property—became the guiding document for Burmese government. A Council of Ministers drawn from the socialist party, Lanzin, set the policy for the country. U Ne Win became prime minister and directed the country with the aid of a cabinet of nine retired and three active army officers. The former president, U Nu, in exile in Thailand, formed a National League for Democracy and challenged the U Ne Win government. However, the military has continued to rule over Burma, with General Saw Maung taking charge and establishing a council of 19 army officers, which he called the State Law and Order Restoration Council.

General Saw Maung brought sufficient order for elections to be held for a national assembly in 1990 under the old constitution. This election saw 93 active political parties vying for places in the assembly, reflecting the variety of ethnic groups and opinions in Myanmar. In the end, General Saw Maung refused to recognize the new assembly, claiming that its sole responsibility was to shape a new constitution. Military rule in Myanmar, as well as the distrust of the Burmans by other groups, continues.

Government Today

The constitution of Myanmar declares that there shall be one political party, the Burma Socialist Programme Party. Also, it declares that the power of government rests with the people as expressed by the People's Assembly (Pyithu Hluttaw), whose members are elected for four-year terms. The Assembly selects a prime minister. This prime minister and representatives from each of the 14 states and divisions form a State Council. According to the constitution, this council can convene the Assembly. It also submits a list of names from which the Assembly selects a Council of Ministers to operate the government. However, since its first writing in 1974, the constitution has been overridden frequently by the military. September 1988 saw the military take power once again. Myanmar is now ruled by General Saw Maung and his State Law and Order Restoration Council, made up of 19 army officers.

Ethnic Makeup

Burmans make up 75 percent of the population of Myanmar. However, there are large groups of the various "hill people" in the country. These include Shan, Karen, Kachin, Chin, Nagas, and Kayahs. There are also large populations of Indians, Pakistanis, and Chinese in Myanmar.

NEPAL

Kingdom of Nepal

Population: 18,916,000 (1990 estimate).
Location: The Himalayan Mountains and the plain of the Ganges River between India and the Xizang Autonomous Region of China (formerly Tibet).
Languages: Nepali; Munda; various Tibeto-Burman dialects; Hindi.
Principal cities: Katmandu (capital), 235,160 (1991 census).

Political Background

Nepal claims to be the birthplace of Buddha, about 560 B.C. in a small town (Lumbini) near Nepal's border with India. The country's official beginning can be attributed to the invasion of Gurkha warriors

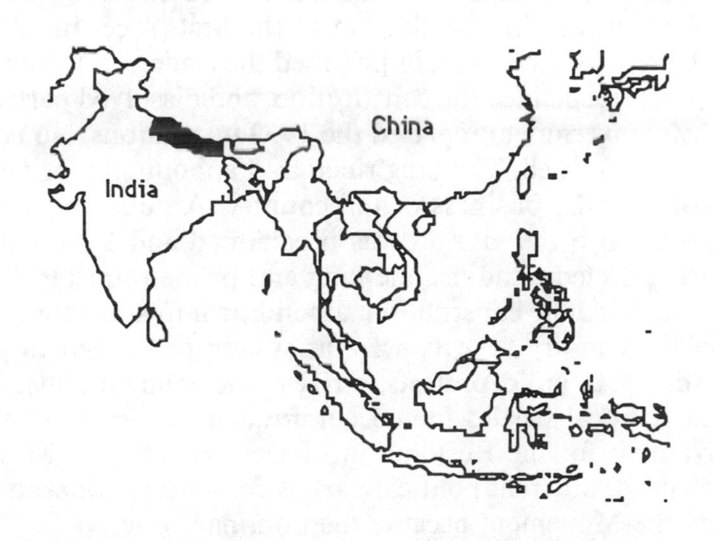

who were expelled from India in 1303. From that time, Nepal has been ruled by various royal families.

A Gurkha leader of the 1700s, Prithvanarayan Shah, is considered to be the founder of modern Nepal. For more than a hundred years after his rule, however, Nepal's leaders governed under the direction of British "residents." A war with British forces over the rights of British tradesmen to enter Nepal was fought between 1814 and 1816. When the Nepal ruler, Bhim Sam Thopa, sued for peace, the response was that he was to accept a British supervisor (resident) or continue the war. A British resident guided affairs of Nepal until 1926.

Meanwhile, the royal family continued as figureheads in Nepal. In 1837 Jung Bahadur Rana succeeded in wresting control of the government from the king. The Rana family was to direct the Nepal government until 1950. A member of the Rana family became Maharaja of Nepal (prime minister) under the British.

Following freedom from the British in 1926, India took an active role in Nepal. All trade from Nepal flowed through India. Indian Prime Minister Nehru succeeded in toppling the Rana system and establishing King Tribhuvan as the leader of a democratic monarchy. By 1959, King Mahendra Bu Bikren Shah Dev had developed a constitution for the country that provided for two houses of parliament. A Senate consisted of 36 people, half of whom were elected by a House of Representatives and half by the king. A 109-member House of Representatives was to be elected by the people. Political parties formed under this constitution and threatened the king, who had reluctantly prepared the constitution in the first place. In 1960, the king conducted his own coup, imprisoned the leaders of the principal political party, suspended the constitution, and dissolved parliament. A Panchayat government replaced the 1959 institutions. No political parties were permitted. The king ruled and appointed a prime minister to conduct the business of the country. A policy of returning the government to the villages was proclaimed and a National Assembly was selected to advise the king and prime minister. In 1980 the king reinstated the constitution, amending it to allow for political parties in the country. The Panchayat system continued to govern Nepal until 1990, amid protests, strikes, and student riots. Meanwhile, old political parties joined communist advocates to form a new Movement for the Restoration of Democracy. The May 1991 elections saw 20 different political parties contending for seats in the Assembly; the Movement became the dominant one.

Government Today

Through government changes the king has remained as a symbol of Nepalese nationalism. He now exercises limited control; his actions in government are subject to the approval of a Council of Ministers. This Council is selected from members of parliament, as is the Prime Minister, leader of the dominant political party in the parliament. The Prime Minister and Council conduct daily government business. They are responsible to the lower house of parliament, the House of Representatives, which has 205 members elected by the people. There is also an upper house, the National Council. Heads of local committees form an electoral college to select 15 members of the National Council; 10 members are chosen by the king; 35 are elected by the House of Representatives.

Economic conditions, especially of the poor in outlying villages, are a primary concern for the government. The annual income of the people of Nepal averages about 300 dollars. Ninety percent of the workers are in agriculture. There are a few small manufacturing concerns mostly producing carpets (which account for more than half of Nepal's exports) and cotton clothing. Progress in diversifying this economy has been slow. First, Nepal has been bound by trade agreements that have made India the exclusive agent of Nepal. Then, there is a large group of civil service workers demanding higher pay and sometimes striking for increases. These demands, the government

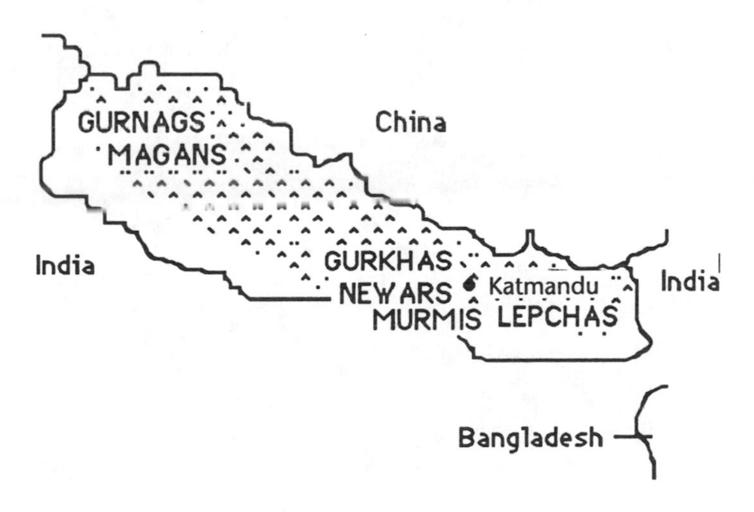

There are many tribes living in Nepal.

feels, cannot be met in view of the poor economy and an inflation rate that reaches 20 percent. Along with these issues are frequent accusations of corruption in government.

Ethnic Makeup

The original Indian Gurkhas merged with Mongolian peoples, who lived in the mountain areas to form the present-day Nepalese. (The name *Gurkha* is used variously to mean all Nepalese, those living in the region of the capital of the old kingdom, and a subgroup of Nepalese who have come to depend on service in the Indian and British armies for part of their livelihood. For a description of this last population, see GURKHAS.) The Nepalese have been long divided into groups according to their place of residence. Newars and Murmis live in the central valley, Gurungs and Magars live in the west, and Kiratis and Lepchas in the east.

NEW ZEALAND

Population: 3,435,000 (1991 estimate).
Location: Two large islands and several smaller ones, lying 1,200 miles southeast of Sydney, Australia, and separated from Australia by the Tasman Sea.
Languages: English; Maori.
Principal cities: Auckland, 865,000; Wellington (capital) 326,000; Christchurch, 303,000.

Political Background

Officially New Zealand became part of the British Empire in 1840, although European whalers and missionaries had previously settled in the islands. At first these settlers depended on the cooperation of

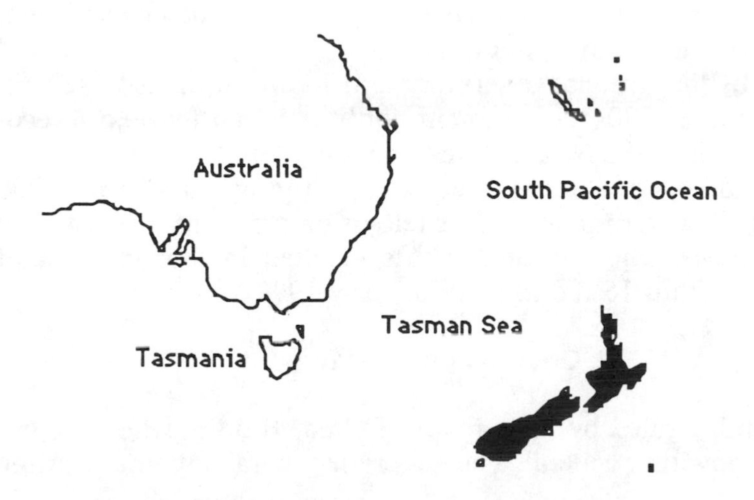

the Maori people who already inhabited the islands. The Maoris agreed to British sovereignty over the area in the 1840 Treaty of Waitangi, which was written in the interest of setting up a British Crown Colony.

In 1852 the British in fact established a Crown Colony, which included six British settlement areas as provinces. The Maoris were pushed into the mountainous interior. As more settlers came in the mid 1800s and especially after the discovery of gold in 1860, the Maoris demonstrated concern over their land rights. There were incidents of conflict that mushroomed into a series of Anglo-Maori land wars in the 1860s and 1870s, the rebellious Maoris losing to superior Anglo firepower. In the course of these wars, the provinces united under a single government at Wellington.

Independence as a nation within the British Commonwealth came in 1947. But even before that, the history of New Zealand was being shaped by a political division into two dominant parties: a Labour Party advocating government control of New Zealand's resources and a National Party advocating more free enterprise. The liberal-conservative debates resulted in early recognition of minorities and women in government (the first Maori woman member of parliament was seated in 1949) and some movement to privatize industry (New Zealand's state-operated coal mines were sold to private parties in 1949). Distant from other European settlements except those in Australia (with which New Zealanders had no interest in uniting), the European New Zealanders felt a strong need to be protected by their government against individual economic downturns. The result has been almost total dominance by the Labour Party, the development of a strong social welfare system, and strong control of New Zealand economics by the national government, including at times wage controls. In the late 1980s, government controls began to yield to economic demands as the New Zealand economy fell. For the first time, New Zealand college students were charged an annual fee of 1,200 dollars and the government sold its television company, Telecom, to private interests. The economic shifts resulted in four changes of government within 15 months in the early 1990s.

Government Today

New Zealand is ruled by the Crown of Great Britain, who is represented by a governor general. The governor general appoints a prime

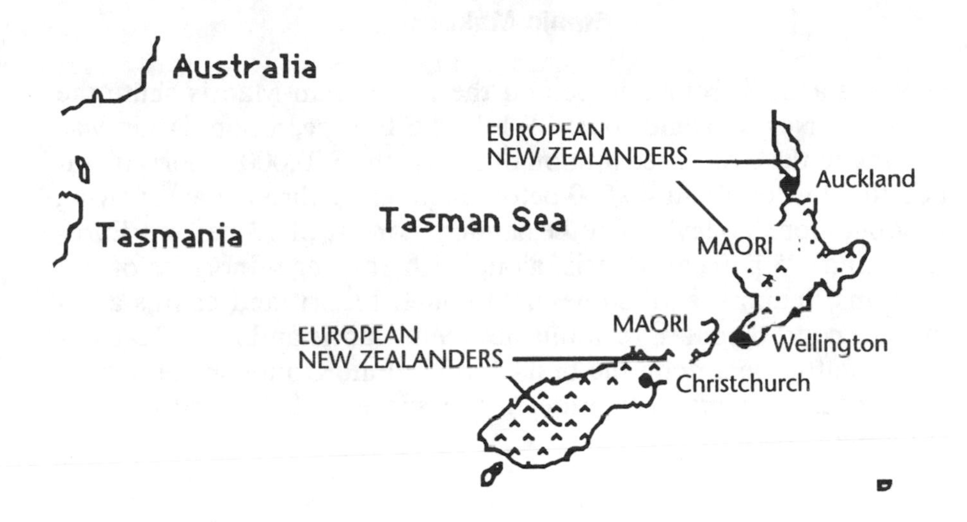

The Maori and New Zealanders who later came to the islands from Europe and Asia make up the population of New Zealand.

minister and works with that person to select ministers for an executive council. Laws are enacted by a single House of Representatives with 97 members, including four Maoris. A supreme court of New Zealand reviews Maori claims for New Zealand land, and this has created one of the major issues for the government.

Maoris claim 70 percent of the land of New Zealand although British New Zealanders control most of it. The potential number of court cases that might result from these claims is a major concern to New Zealanders. New Zealand also faces two international issues. Having joined Australia and the United States in a mutual defense pact, New Zealand then banned nuclear-powered ships from its ports. This problem has created problems for United States ships in the area.

In 1985, a ship operated by the environmentalist group Greenpeace, the Rainbow Warrior, docked at Auckland preparing to join in a protest against French atomic bomb tests in nearby islands. While in port in New Zealand this ship was blown up. Subsequently, two French nationals were accused of the bombing and convicted. Over French protests, New Zealand imprisoned the two bombers and have refused to return them to the French. This has resulted in some tension between the two countries.

Ethnic Makeup

New Zealanders from Europe and the Polynesian Maoris share the islands of New Zealand today. While the European population was growing to the over three million of today, the 350,000 Maoris dwindled to a low of about 40,000 before recovering through an upswing in population. Today's New Zealanders consist of 73 percent Europeans and 9.5 percent Maoris, along with smaller minorities of Polynesians, Indians, and Chinese. Although Maori land claims are a point of court disputes, relations between Maoris and New Zealanders are felt to be among the best of any ethnic groups in the world. All New Zealanders take pride in the success of their citizens regardless of race.

NORTH KOREA

Democratic People's Republic of Korea

Population: 21,902,000 (1989 estimate).
Location: The Korean Peninsula, situated southeast of China, bordered by China, the Sea of Japan, South Korea, and the Yellow Sea.
Language: Korean.
Principal cities: Pyongyang (capital), 2,000,000; Hamhung, 670,000; Chongin, 530,000; Sinuiju, 330,000; Kaesong, 310,000.

Political Background

Before 1905 North and South Korea were united as a single monarchy. The Japanese invaded this monarchy in 1905 and finally annexed Korea in 1910. All of the Korean Peninsula was part of Japan from that time until the end of World War II. After the war, Korea was divided arbitrarily along the thirty-eighth parallel, with the north falling under the influence of the Soviet Union. In 1946, a Korean Communist Party organized and by 1948 succeeded in electing Kim Il Sung as premier. War broke out between the two Koreas, supported in the north by the USSR and in the south by the United States. Lasting from 1950–1953, the war ended with an armistice and a strip of land that was designated as a demilitarized buffer zone between the two Koreas.

President Kim Il Sung has controlled North Korea's government from various governmental and party positions since its beginning. In recent years he has begun to turn over much of the control to his son Kim Jong Il, who has become one of the three-member Presidium that governs the single political party.

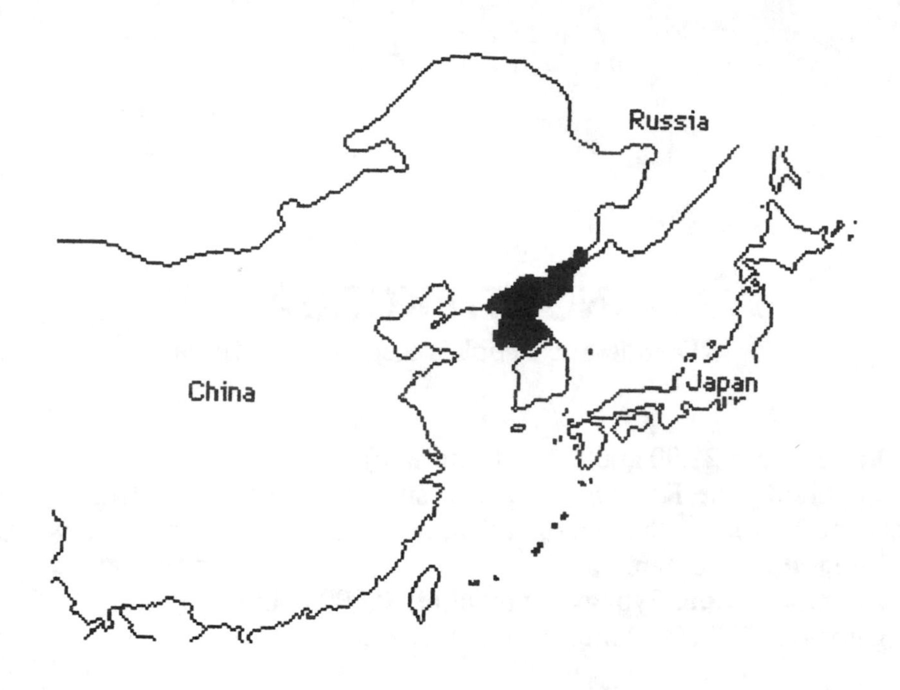

Government Today

The government of North Korea is organized on the Soviet pattern. From the single political party, a Supreme People's Assembly of 687 members is elected to serve for four years. This Assembly elects a president and a Central People's Committee, a standing committee that meets regularly to review the actions of government. The Supreme People's Assembly also appoints a premier (prime minister) while the Central People's Committee selects a group of ministers to form a cabinet. The Prime Minister and cabinet form an Administrative Council to carry out the duties of government.

Less rapidly than in the South, North Korea has initiated a series of seven-year plans to advance the country through increased industry and production. More than one-third of the North Koreans still work in agriculture (the nation is struggling to become self-sufficient in food production). Another third of the workers now serve in industry, principally in the manufacture of machinery and in textile works. North Korea's chief natural resource is magnesite of which the country controls 50 percent of the world's known resource. In its indus-

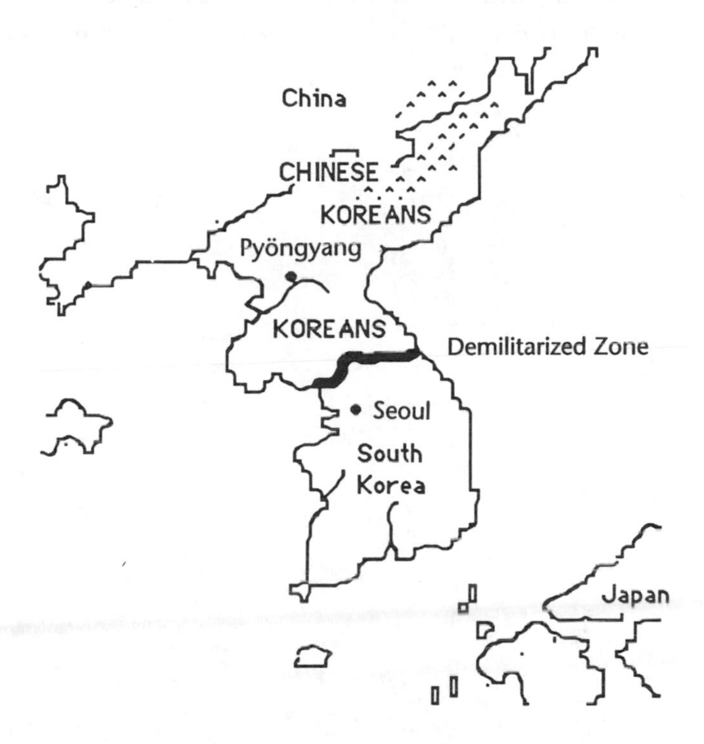

Except for a few Chinese, Korea is populated by Koreans.

trialization process, North Korea now faces the problem of replacing a major trading partner, the former Soviet Union; this nation once consumed 50 percent of North Korean production.

North Korea, at least as strongly as South Korea, has from its beginning advocated unification into a new single Korea. When that idea waned after discussions in 1971, 1972, and 1984, North Korea sought the intervention of the United Nations. In 1988 North Korea asked that organization to aid in uniting the two Koreas into a Federation of independent states. They proposed to call this federation after the ancient name of the old empire, Koryo.

Ethnic Makeup

Though there is a minority of Chinese, most inhabitants of North Korea are Koreans, a people believed to have Mongol ancestry.

PAKISTAN

Islamic Republic of Pakistan

Population: 112,000,000 (1990 estimate).
Location: Southern Asia bounded by India, Afghanistan, Iran, and China.
Languages: Punjabi; Pushto; Sindhi; Saraiki; Urdu; English. (Urdu, the official language of Pakistan is used by less than 8 percent of the people.)
Principal cities: Karachi, 5,200.000; Lahore, 3,000,000; Faisalabad, 1,000,000; Rawalpindi, 800,000; Hyderabad, 750,000; Multan, 735,000; Guijranwela, 660,000; Peshawar, 510,000, Islamabad (capital), 220,000.

Political Background

Pakistan was created in 1947 when Muslim people in what was then India demanded an independent state. At first, the new country was in two parts, separated by 1,000 miles of India. In this arrangement, most of the population of the new country was in an eastern section but the government and military was based in the west. When, in 1971, the resentment over this arrangement grew in the east, causing the government to send troops into eastern Pakistan, a civil war erupted. The war, with the east supported by India, resulted in a division into two nations. Eastern Pakistan became Bangladesh while western Pakistan became the Islamic Republic of Pakistan. The Muslim people of old India are now split between these two countries and a northern section claimed by both India and Pakistan–Jammu and Kashmir.

Established as a democracy with a national assembly and an executive branch of government defined by a constitution, Pakistan

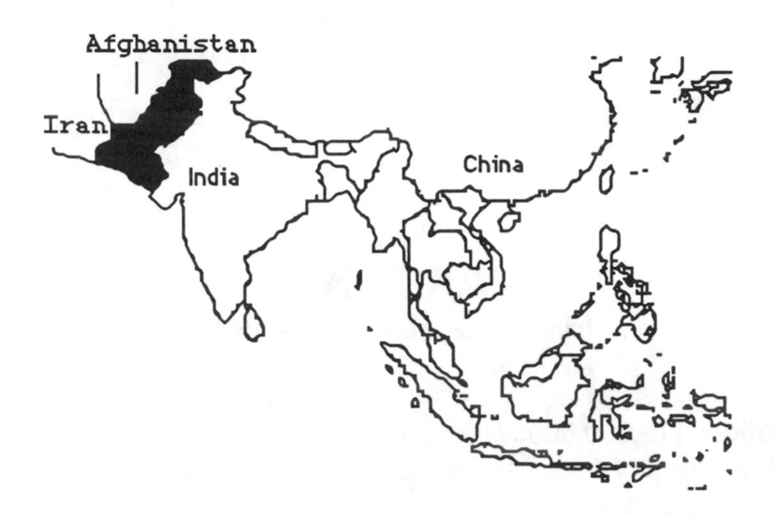

has, from its beginning, been plagued by political unrest. A large part of its brief history has found the Pakistanis under martial law, and almost always the military has played an important role in government. Even before the breakaway of Bangladesh, Pakistan was governed by the military. A list of the leaders of the country indicates the power of the armed forces.

Under Prime Minister Sherif, Pakistan has struggled to take a place among the world's nations, sending 11,000 troops to participate in the Gulf War and petitioning to be readmitted into the British Commonwealth—a membership opposed by India.

Government Today

Only since 1986 has Pakistan made significant advances toward a democratic government. It is currently directed by a prime minister and a cabinet. Legislation is enacted through a National Assembly of 237 members elected for five-year terms and 87 senators elected for six years. However, much of the control of government is delegated to four provinces, the capital district, and a number of regions called tribal areas.

Throughout its history, Pakistan has set goals through a number of five-year plans. A little more than one-fourth of the country's wealth is produced in agriculture by about 57 percent of the workers. The principal crop has been cotton. The five-year plans have aimed at developing industry—primarily in textile production and food pro-

1958	President Ishander Muza dismissed the legislature and established martial law with General Muhammad Ayub Khan as administrator.
1960	General Khan became president.
1971	With the separation of Bangladesh, President Khan resigned and Zulfiqar Ali Bhutto, a civilian, became president then prime minister under a new constitution.
1975	Following a rebellion in northwestern Pakistan, martial law was again established under General Mohammad Zia al-Haq and a 4-man military commission.
1977	A coup replaced Bhutto with General Zia.
1978	General Zia attempted to relieve martial law by appointing a 16-member advisory council. At the same time, opposition leader Bhutto was convicted of corruption during his presidency and hanged.
1980	President Zia reinforced martial law.
1981	Nine political parties called for a return to parliamentary government and a new cabinet of 21 members was formed.
1983	The daughter of Bhutto, Benazir, an opposition leader was imprisoned.
1984	To strengthen the country's commitment as a Muslim nation, prayer wardens in each town were appointed by the military government.
1985	Pakistan returned to parliamentary government with the establishment of a National Assembly and a Senate and the lifting of martial law by President Zia.
1988	General Zia was killed in an air crash. Benazir Bhutto became prime minister of Pakistan, but immediately was denounced by Muslim leaders who demanded that the position be filled by a man.
1990	Bhutto was charged with corruption and ousted, to be replaced as prime minister by Mian Nawez Sherif with Ghullam Ishaq Khan as president.

cessing. The seventh five-year plan covering 1988 to 1993 reemphasized the need for industrial growth. To accelerate this growth, in 1991 Pakistan began to privatize many industries that were formerly controlled by the government.

Ethnic Makeup

The west of Pakistan is mostly populated by Baluchi people who are themselves divided into more than ten groups. These people are probably of Arab origin. In the southeast are Sindhi tribes. Centrally, Punjabis extend their territory across Pakistan and into India and

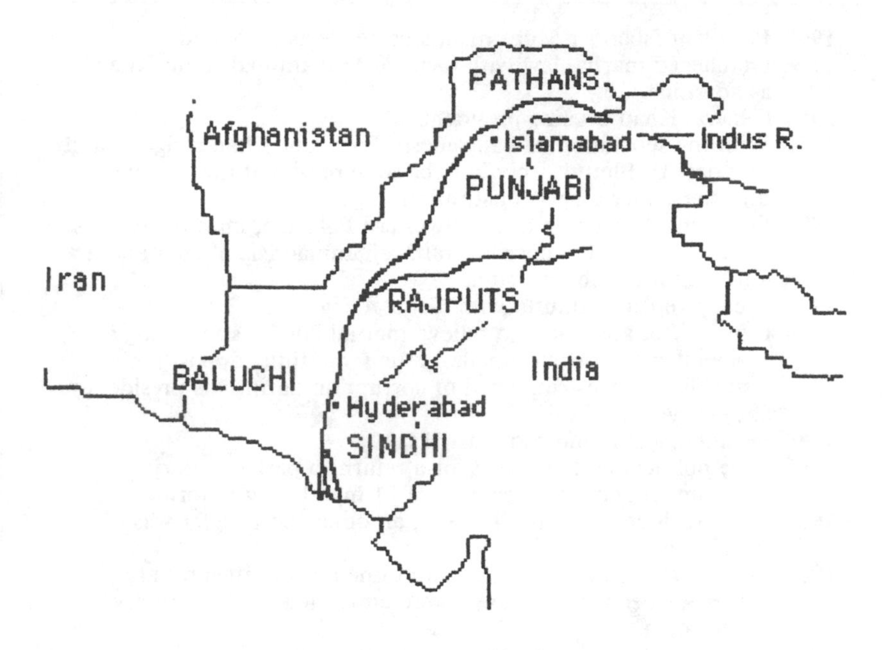

A few of the peoples of Pakistan who are bound together by a single religion.

the disputed territory of Kashmir. The north nomadic Pathan people spread across Pakistan and Afghanistan.

PAPUA NEW GUINEA

Independent State of Papua New Guinea

Population: 3,699,000 (1990 estimate).
Location: The eastern portion of island of New Guinea, second-largest of the world's islands, located east of Indonesia and northeast of Australia.
Languages: Pidgin, English, and Motu are official languages. There are about 740 native languages.
Principal cities: Port Moresby (capital), 150,000.

Political Background

Late in the 19th century, European nations began to take an interest in the island of New Guinea. In 1884 Germany claimed the north-

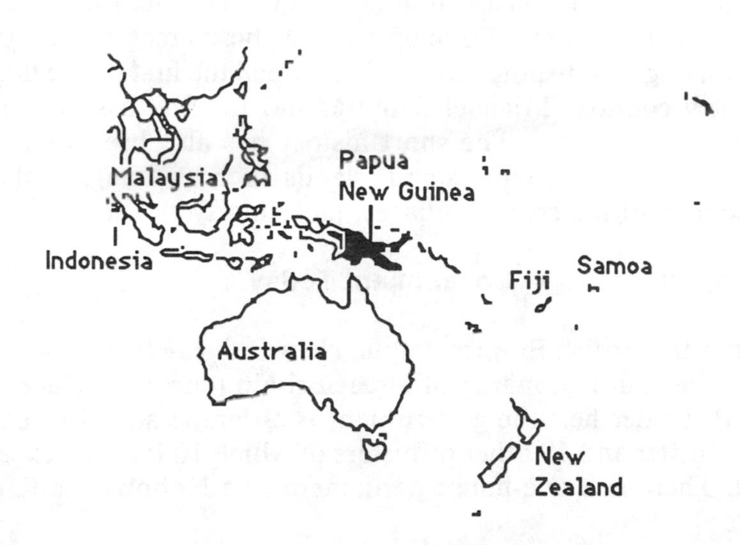

eastern section of the island (called New Guinea) and in 1886 Great Britain claimed the southeastern portion (called Papua). When Germany was defeated in World War I it was stripped of its claim to New Guinea and that territory then was administered by Australia a few hundred miles to the south. Australia supervised both New Guinea and Papua until 1942 when, in World War II, Japan took control of the island. Reclaimed by Australia after the war (1945), Papua and New Guinea were again governed as separate British claims until the Australian government united the two under one government in 1949. In 1973 the area officially became the self-governing Territory of Papua New Guinea. This state became an independent member of the British Commonwealth in 1975. Meanwhile, the western section of the island remained that part of Indonesia called Irian Jaya.

At first, the new country attempted a democratic government concentrated at Port Moresby. However, road transportation through the interior jungles of the island had never been developed and communication from the seat of government was difficult. In 1976, the national government decentralized, giving much of the power of government to 20 provincial governments and 160 local governing bodies.

The economic history of Papua New Guinea since it became independent has been a steady, if not spectacular, growth in income. The Independent State of Papua New Guinea is rich in minerals—gold, silver, copper, chromite, and petroleum. It has abundant forests, and the coastline provides farmland for growing roots and tubers, coffee, cocoa, coconuts, rubber, and tea. High mountain ridges provide run-off water for fast-running streams that could be harnessed for hydroelectric energy. Development in these areas has continued despite an ongoing dispute until 1987 between the first prime minister of the new country, Michael Somare, and his first assistant prime minister, Paias Wingti. The short history has also been marked by rebellion with the outlying small islands such as Bougainville and with sections of the coastal villages, particularly at Lae.

Government Today

As part of the British Empire, Papua New Guinea claims, as its head of state, the ruling monarch of Great Britain (currently Queen Elizabeth II). Under her, the government is a democracy directed by a prime minister and 19 other ministers of which 10 form an executive cabinet. There is a one-house parliament, the National Parliament,

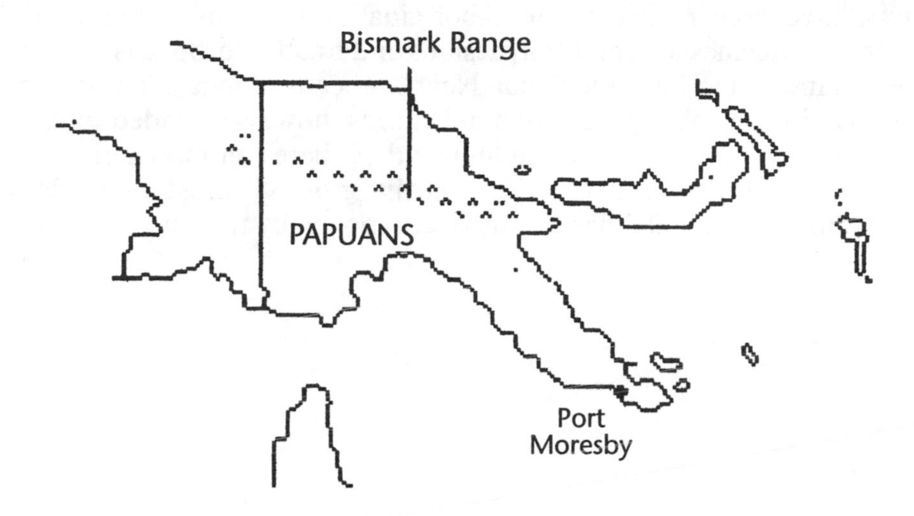

There are many small tribes living in Papua New Guinea. They are collectively called Papuans.

of 109 members that are elected for five-year terms. The National Parliament recommends a person to be prime minister and that person is then appointed by the Head of State (the queen). The same procedure is followed to select a governor-general to act for the queen (although in 1992 none was selected).

Under this government, Papua New Guinea has since the 1980s been working toward increased productivity and foreign trade. Two-thirds of the workers are still employed in agriculture but there is a growing industry producing fabrics and fibers, copper, and wood products. In the northwest of the country there is a rich gold field but, because of the lack of roads, it is only accessible by air. (Because of this transportation problem, it is claimed that few places on earth are as little known as the interior of Papua New Guinea.)

The fledgling government has been supported by Australia in its efforts to industrialize. That country contributed 45 percent of the money spent for development in Papua New Guinea in 1991. Part of this money has been spent on the island country's first hydroelectric project on the Ramu River. Papua New Guinea trades mostly with Australia and Japan.

Ethnic Makeup

Papua New Guinea has been populated for more than 25,000 years by a mixture of peoples from other places. The earliest inhabitants may have been related to the Aboriginal Australians. Then came negritos, Melanesians, and Polynesians and finally Europeans. These people merged to form the Papua New Guineans of today. The dense tropical jungle and rugged mountain ranges, however, tended to isolate various groups so that, even though they share common heritages, the wide range of Papua New Guinea tribal groups is illustrated today in the more than 740 different languages spoken by the island people.

PEOPLE'S REPUBLIC OF CHINA

Population: 1,133,682,501 (July 1990 census).
Location: A country in Asia slightly larger than the United States. China is bounded by Russia, Mongolia, Korea, the Pacific Ocean (China seas), Vietnam, Laos, Burma, India, Bhutan, Nepal, Pakistan, and Afghanistan.
Languages: Chinese; minority languages (Uighur, Mongol, Tibetan).
Principal cities: Shanghai, 7,300,000; Beijing (capital), 6,800,000; Tianjin, 5,600,000; Shenyang, 4,400,000; Wuhan, 3,650,000; Guangzhou, 3,500,000. Eleven other cities of more than 2,000,000 population and 22 cities of more than 1,000,000 people.

Political Background

China's long history has seen the rule of monarchs, dynasties, and, in the twentieth century, national leaders. Beginning in 1911, a few stormy decades ended with the supremacy of communism in government. The history of the People's Republic of China begins in 1949 when the old government was overthrown by a communist party headed by Mao Tse-tung. Mao was chairman of the communist party and head of state. He was a strong advocate of Marxist policies, so staunch in his beliefs that he broke with the Soviet Union in the 1950s because he thought that country was turning toward capitalism. To make China an independent communist power, Mao initiated a move toward industrialism in the middle 1950s. Seventy million farmers were recruited to work in poorly equipped factories, making materials such as steel. China is a mountainous land with large fertile basins carved by three great rivers. Still, less than ten percent of the land grows the crops that must feed one-fifth of the world's population. The loss of 70,000,000 farmers to industry resulted in widespread famine and the deaths of more than 30,000,000 Chinese.

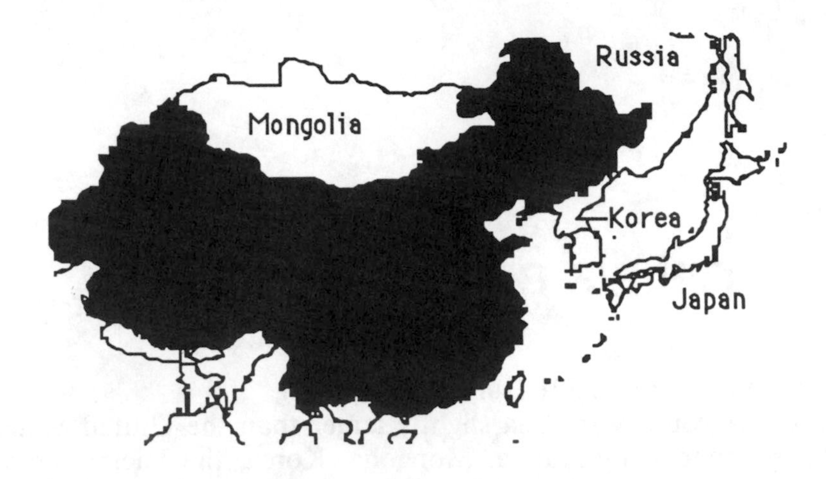

In 1975, the office of head of state was abolished and replaced by a head of government. Mao remained in control as party chairman and Zhou Enlai became head of government (prime minister). Since its formation, the Chinese Communist Party has had virtually the same leadership. The aging party members of today are led by Jiang Zemin, who has moderated the Chinese communist stance in order to participate in the world economy.

Government Today

China's constitution declares that the ultimate power lies with the people and is actualized through local people's congresses (about 30 of them) and a National People's Congress. The Chinese citizens elect members of the local congresses, who in turn elect 3,000 members of the national congress. The national congress meets irregularly but elects about 155 members to a standing committee that directs daily government. Also the national congress elects a president and vice-president. This president appoints the state council—a premier, councillors, ministers, and the secretary—which forms the ruling body of The People's Republic of China. A president's appointees must be approved by the national congress and the standing committee. Moreover, all these groups are subject to the will of the Communist Party and its General Secretary, since it is the only political party recognized in the country.

Minority groups around the borders of China make up a small part of the population.

A major issue in China is population. In a mountainous land with less than ten percent suitable for growing crops, the yield must supply food for an overcrowded, growing population. Struggles to accomplish this and still develop an industrial base have met with slow success. Accusations of corruption in government have been frequent, and economic problems have continued to plague the country. Competing for work and food in an overflowing population, the average Chinese person earns about 300 dollars a year.

In 1989, issues of corruption and a declining economy prompted widespread student protests. These eventually centered in protests at Tiananmen Square. Negotiations between the government and the students failed, and the army was called in to suppress the students. More than 500 protesters were killed or arrested for treasonable acts. The reaction around the world has slowed international economic support for development within China. Still, the Chinese economy grows by 10.5 percent each year—nearly two-thirds of this growth in agriculture as the government's five-year plans improve farm methods.

Hong Kong, which has been a British-controlled capitalist center on the edge of China, will be restored to China in 1997. Preparing for this event while attempting to establish trade agreements with Japan and the United States is a challenge for a Chinese government that is apparently more moderate than in the past.

With a standing army of 3,030,000, the government of China maintains control of its territory, claims other territory (as it has successfully done with Tibet), and controls its great mass of people. The constitution defines rights and also duties of the people. One duty is to stand by for a selective conscription through which the army recruits soldiers to serve for a three-year period.

Ethnic Makeup

The more than one billion people of China are predominantly Han Chinese. Only about eight percent of the citizens are of other origins. These include the Chuang in the south, a people related to the Thais; the Tibetans in the east; the Uigurs, a Muslim people of the northwest; the Yi and Miao living in the southwest, and the Mongols of Inner Mongolia in the north. About 1,000,000 Koreans live in China near its border with Korea.

PHILIPPINES

Republic of the Philippines

Population: 60,684,887 (1990 census).
Location: 7,100 islands in the Pacific Ocean along the Asian coast south of the islands of Japan; 880 of them are inhabited. One in 17 of these islands is larger than one square mile; two islands, Luzon and Mindanao, make up two-thirds of the total area.
Languages: Pilipino (a form of Tagalog); English; various native languages.
Principal cities: Quezon City, 1,667,000; Manila (capital), 1,600,000; Caloocan, 761,000; Cebu City, 610,000.

Political Background

Under Spanish control from 1571 to 1887 and then United States rule from 1898 to 1946, the Philippines became independent after World War II while still maintaining strong military ties with the United States. In 1965, Ferdinand Marcos took control of the government as a virtual dictator in what was intended to be a democracy. Marcos remained in power until 1986, when discoveries of governmental corruption resulted in his defeat. Marcos at first refused to accept the vote that replaced him with Corazon Aquino, widow of a Marcos opponent who had been earlier assassinated. Both people had themselves sworn in as the 1986 president. However, the Philippine army supported Aquino, and Marcos soon was pressured by his old ally, the United States, to withdraw. He fled to Hawaii. Corazon Aquino was elected to serve for six years. A 1987 constitution disallowed re-election, and Corazon Aquino declared that she would not contend for another term. In February 1991, Fidel Ramos replaced Corzaon Aquino as president of the Phillipines.

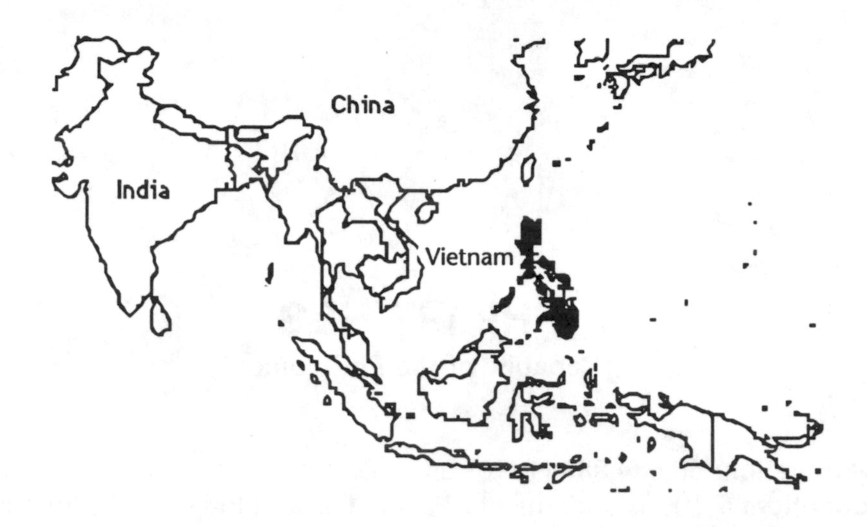

Government Today

The government of the Philippines is directed by a president who is head of state and commander-in-chief of the armed forces. Elected to serve one six-year term, the president is joined by a legislature of two houses: the Senate of 24 persons, and the House of Representatives (about 250 people, of which 200 are elected and 50 appointed by the president to represent ethnic minorities). Local citizens' assemblies play important roles in selecting these representatives. Twelve members of the Senate and 12 from the House of Representatives are chosen to form a Commission on Appointments. The president submits selections for a cabinet to this commission for approval. Otherwise, the duties of Senate and House are patterned after the United States legislature.

Happy in the 1800s to rid itself of a Spanish rule that governed by ignoring the Philippines, the people of this nation became equally determined to rid the islands of the colonialism of the United States. Early in the period of intervention by the United States, the American military built large naval and air bases in the islands. These bases contributed a great deal to an economy that depended mostly on agriculture and was struggling to support its people. A series of agreements permitted the United States to maintain Subic Bay as a navy base and Clark Field as an air base. Meanwhile, Filipino resistance to this presence grew, and the government vacillated between demanding complete removal of the bases and demanding very high

The Philippines is a country of many islands.

sums to continue the leases. In 1983, the agreements were extended until 1989, then until 1991. Filipino senators opposed any further extentions. By the close of 1992, the United States presence on bases had been eliminated.

Meanwhile, Corazon Aquino's government was plagued by rebels within the difficult-to-manage, physically fractured country. These rebels sometimes vented their anger on the Aquino government and sometimes directly on Americans. Between 1987 and 1990, ten American servicemen were killed by Filipino rebels. The difficulty was further aggravated when the United States decided to actively support the defense of Corazon Aquino during a coup attempt. Many Filipinos felt that this was intervention in the internal affairs of the

These are just a few of the language groups of the Philippines.

country. The trials of Aquino were brought to a close in 1991 in compliance with the Philippine constitutional limit of a single six-year term for any president. Fidel Ramos replaced Aquino in February 1991 and continued the dismantling of United States bases and the attempts to expand the economy to compensate for the loss of revenue from Subic Bay and Clark Field.

Since 1987 the economy has expanded from its agriculture base. While 45 percent of the workers are still employed in agriculture, 15 percent now work in industries, and ten percent work in manufacturing.

Ethnic Makeup

People of Malayan and Indonesian ancestry constitute almost all the inhabitants of the Philippines. However, the earlier settlers from Malaysia and Indonesia lived in relative isolation from one another on the various islands, developing distinct cultures. There are more than 200 ethnic groups that have been identified in the Philippines. In addition, Filipinos are divided by religion with a substantial representation of Muslims and some animists dwelling among the predominant Christian population.

SOUTH KOREA

Republic of Korea

Population: 42,380,000 (1989 estimate).
Location: The Korean peninsula, situated southeast of China, bordered by North Korea, the Yellow Sea, the East China Sea, and the Sea of Japan.
Language: Korean.
Principal cities: Seoul (capital), 9,700,000; Pusan, 3,500,000; Taegu, 2,000,000; Inchon, 1,400,000. Eleven other cities with populations greater than 200,000.

Political Background

Once claimed by Japan and long united with North Korea into a single kingdom, South Korea began with an election supervised by the United Nations to organize a national assembly in 1945. Dr. Syngman Rhee became the first president of the new country. In 1960 Dr. Syngman Rhee resigned the presidency and in 1961 a military coup installed General Park Chung-Hee as ruler of the country. General Park abolished the national assembly in favor of a Supreme Council for National Reconstruction. Under a new constitution and supported by a new political party, Park was elected president in 1963. South Korea's history since then has been one of strong military intervention in government and of rapid economic growth. In 1972 President Park declared martial law and organized a National Conference for Unification of the two Koreas. General Park was assassinated in 1979 and since that time Korea has seen several military coups and has been troubled by frequent student riots over corruption in government. Despite government instability, Korea has established itself as a major industrial country. The average income of the Koreans has grown to about 4,400 dollars per person per year.

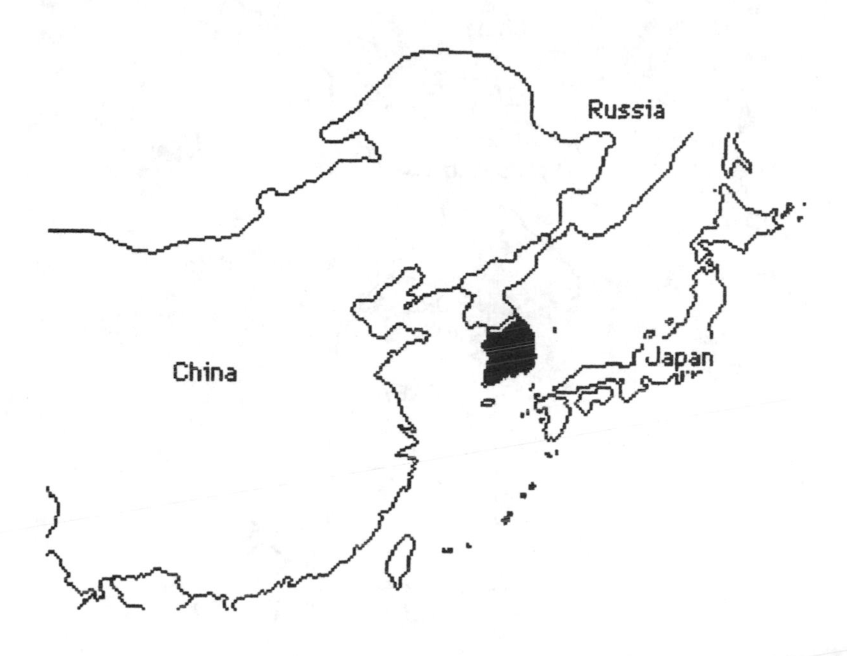

Government Today

Elected by the people of South Korea, a president holds office for five years when the military is not in power. The president is aided by a National Assembly of 299 members, who are chosen to govern for four years. Two hundred twenty-four of these assembly people are elected by popular vote, 38 are selected by the ruling political party, and 37 are chosen to represent other political parties and interests. A major role of the Assembly is to approve the president's selections of a prime minister and a State Council charged with day-to-day management of the country.

Korea is a flourishing nation with but two major issues. Frequent discovery of corruption among high government officials has prompted student-led protests. At the same time, this state of affairs has accentuated a second problem: defining the role of the military in government. Both Koreas have declared unification into one nation, Koryo, to be a primary objective, and the two countries agreed in the 1970s to annual meetings to implement this unification. There have been intermittent meetings, though, due to many differences between the the two Koreas—most notably, the imagined threat of

Almost all the people of South Korea are Koreans, a group that migrated earlier from China.

invasion of South Korea by the North, as suggested by discovery of tunnels under a demilitarized zone between the two countries; perceived affronts, such as the refusal of South Korea to allow North Korea to share in the production of the 1988 Olympic Games in Seoul; and North Korea's displeasure in the annual show of United States military support of South Korea.

Ethnic Makeup

Since Japanese colonists were ousted from Korea following World War II, nearly all the people of South Korea are Koreans, a people believed to have been of Mongol ancestry. Less than one percent of the population is Chinese.

SRI LANKA

Democratic Socialist Republic of Sri Lanka

Population: 16,993,060 (1990 estimate).
Location: An island in the Indian Ocean, separated from the southern tip of India by the 70-mile-wide Palk Strait.
Languages: Sinhala; Tamil.
Principal cities: Colombo (capital), 615,000; Dehiwala-Mount Lavina, 196,000; Maratuwa, 170,000; Jaffna, 129,000; Katle, 109,000; Kandy, 104,000.

Political Background

Before the twelfth century, Indo-Aryans from India had migrated to the island long known as Ceylon and had established a kingdom in

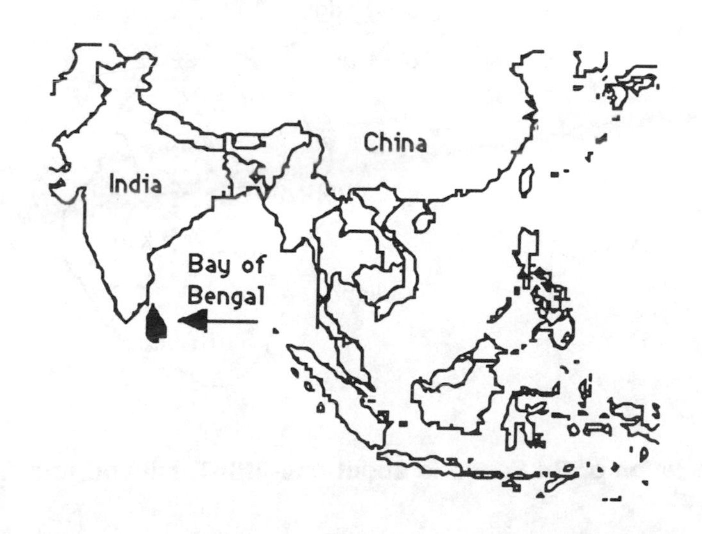

the dry northern plains. There these immigrants, who were ancestors of the Sinhalese, had established irrigation and built a great empire. Perhaps pushed by other newcomers, the Indo-Aryan immigrants ultimately abandoned their irrigation systems and empire in the north and moved to the wet hill country of the southwest in the 1200s. Dravidian (southern Indian) Tamils replaced them in the north. Since that time, Sri Lanka's (Ceylon's) history has been one of conflict between the larger Buddhist Sinhalese population and the Hindu Tamils.

The island also attracted European interests. Portuguese traders arrived in the 1500s, followed by the Dutch in 1660 and the British in 1796. The island was divided not only between Tamils and Sinhalese, but between Dutch and British along the coasts and Kandyan kingdoms that controlled the central highlands until 1810. By that time, the British had established a firm hold that grew into control of the entire island. They brought a plantation system to Sri Lanka and began to produce coffee, tea, rubber, and coconuts, largely using Sinhalese labor. As in other parts of Asia, the people of Ceylon long

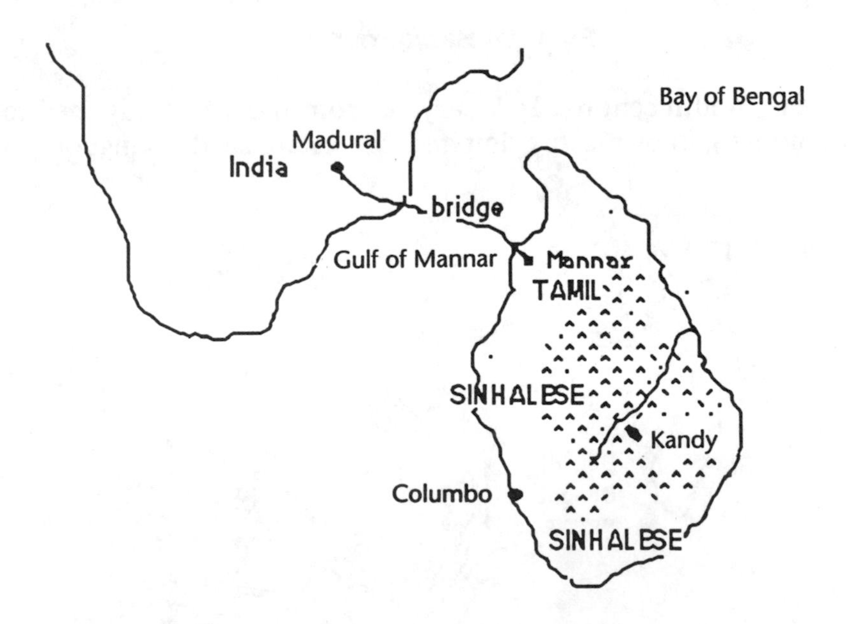

The population of Sri Lanka is about one-fifth Tamil and four-fifths Sinhalese.

struggled to rid themselves of this colonial yoke. Buddhist religious figures had stimulated a strong nationalism movement by 1875, and by 1919 a Ceylon National Congress had organized for independence. Fearing domination by the Sinhalese, Tamils rose in rebellion in 1920. However, progress toward self-government continued. Constitutional reforms for more native voice in government were instituted in 1931. By 1944, the British were prepared to grant self-government, albeit with restrictions to protect the British enterprises, and in 1948, Ceylon became independent. Independence brought some economic collapse until the country revived under strong Sinhalese/Buddhist leadership. This leadership attempted to promote nationalism by advancing Sinhala as the state language. In 1957, this movement reached a peak under Sirimava Bendaraneike, wife of an earlier leader. Tamils felt increasingly attacked as she strove to make Sinhala the national language and also to put all the schools under state control in order to advance this universal language idea. Resistance was so strong that by 1970 Sirimava Bendaraneike had to join forces with a growing communist group to hold onto power in government. The communist victory was temporary, though. By 1977, the combined leftist parties had lost their hold on government and a presidential form of democracy came into being.

This did not appease the Tamils, who were gaining strength through immigrations from southern India. From 1983 to 1988, Tamil riots, often supported by India, disrupted the land. The Sinhalese government responded with powerful security forces. By 1990 it was estimated that these forces had killed between 25,000 and 50,000 rebels. Meanwhile, international powers encouraged discussions between the governments of Sri Lanka and India with the objective of removing Indian troops from the island. Steps toward this goal have progressed as scheduled, but Tamil-Sinhalese tensions still shake the Sri Lankan government.

Government Today

At the head of government in Sri Lanka is a president elected by popular vote for a six-year term. The president selects a cabinet and a prime minister to manage the government. Laws are introduced by a parliament of one house elected by direct vote of the people. Despite the direct elections, there has been controversy since independence over who has a voice in government.

One of Sri Lanka's greatest problems, since the 1960s, has been unemployment. Agriculture continues to occupy about half the workers, with about half of these in subsistence agriculture and half in plantation labor.

Ethnic Makeup

Nearly three-fourths of the people of Sri Lanka are Sinhalese. About thirteen percent are Tamils born in Sri Lanka; about seven percent of the population that are Tamils from India. Indian Tamils nearly equal in number another divergent group, Muslim Sinhalese.

TAIWAN

Population: 20,360,000 (1990 estimate).
Location: One island and smaller ones in the China Sea, midway between Japan and the Philippines, separated from The People's Republic of China by the 90-mile-wide Taiwan Strait.
Language: Mandarin Chinese.
Principal cities: Taipei (capital), 2,700,000; Kaohsiung, 1,400,000; Taichung, 750,000; Tainan, 675,000; Panchiao 530,000. Thirteen other cities with populations greater than 200,000.

Political Background

From 1928 until 1949, mainland China was a republic dominated by the Guomindang (a Nationalist Party) with General Chaing Kai-

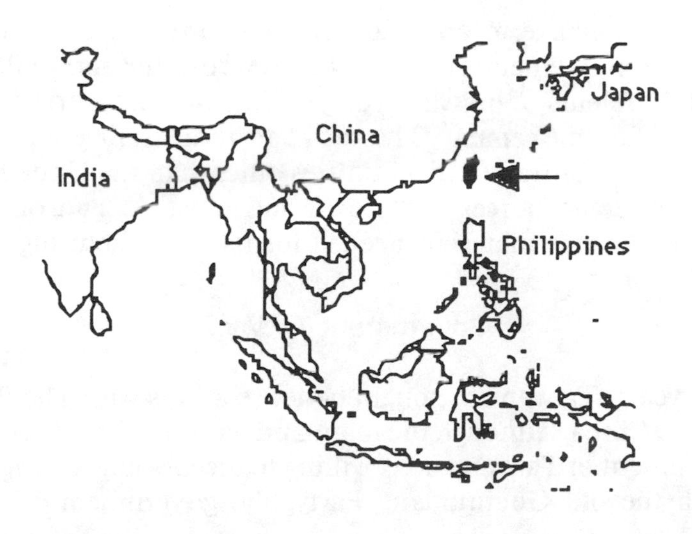

shek as its president. When the Communist Party prevailed in 1949, this government fled to an offshore island then known as Formosa. This island had early been inhabited by Malays, then in the fifteenth century by Chinese, followed by the Dutch, Portuguese, and again the Chinese. In the last part of the nineteenth century, the island was heavily populated by immigrants from mainland China. Given to Japan in 1895, it was returned to China after World War II.

In 1954, the United States signed an agreement with The Republic of China on Taiwan to protect that country. This agreement protected the island nation from continuing claims to the island by the mainland Chinese. (Between 1945 and 1949, Taiwan had been a province of the larger China.)

Chaing Kai-shek ruled through a military government from 1949 to 1952. During this time a National Assembly of more than 1,300 lifetime members served as a stamp of approval for the army leaders.

In 1972, President Chaing Kai-shek agreed to an open election for 53 new members of the National Assembly who would serve for six years. The country began to shift from an agricultural economy to an industrial one. In 1979, the United States withdrew from its protective treaty position, but continued as a strong trading partner with Taiwan. Taiwan continued to grow as an industrial nation. Although the Goumindang remained in power, there was a growing pressure to open the government to other parties. This finally occurred in 1986. In keeping with the new political openness, Taiwan has begun to seek friendly trade relationships with other Asian countries.

The rapid change to an industrial economy has resulted in an equally rapid movement of the Taiwanese from the rural villages to the cities. Problems of housing, congestion, and transportation have grown with this movement. The move to industrialize has also resulted in a need for trade with countries other than the United States. Taiwan has few resources of its own and must depend on foreign trade to get the raw materials needed for its manufacturing.

Government Today

In recent years, Taiwan has sought better relations with The People's Republic of China. Although the mainland nation refuses to recognize the government of Taiwan and is willing to discuss new arrangements only with the old Goumindang Party, the government of Taiwan

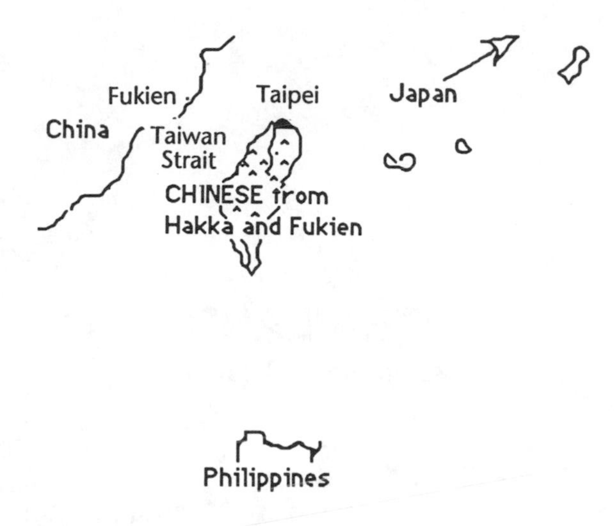

The people of Taiwan are Chinese.

continues to press for recognition by mainland China and for some diplomatic relations between them.

The National Assembly of Taiwan consists of 691 (1990 number) popularly elected delegates, who meet to vote for the president and to vote on constitutional amendments. Elected for six years, the president serves as head of state and commander of military forces and receives assistance from the Executive Yuan Executive Branch Council Cabinet), the highest administrative body. The highest lawmaking body is the Legislative Yuan (Li-fe Yuan) which, in 1990, consisted of 267 members. Elected by local councils, there is also a Control Yuan that investigates the work of government executives.

Ethnic Makeup

Almost all people of Taiwan are Chinese who have migrated from mainland China or are descendants of these immigrants. They are sometimes divided according to the part of the mainland they originally came from and the time of their migration: Hakka who came to Taiwan before the nineteenth century from Kwangtang, and Fukiens, who followed in the eighteenth and nineteenth century from Fukien Province.

THAILAND

Kingdom of Thailand

Population: 56,340,000 (1990 estimate).
Location: Southeast Asia bordered by Myanmar, Laos, Cambodia, and Malaysia.
Languages: Thai; Chinese; several tribal languages.
Principal cities: Bangkok, 5,800,000; Songkhla, 172,000; Chon Buri, 115,000; Nakhon Si Thammarat, 102,000; Chiang Mai, 101,000.

Political Background

Once the Thai inhabited the kingdom of Nan-Chao in what is now south China. The inhabitants of this kingdom fled from the Chinese, the Tibetans, and the Mongol forces of Kublai Khan to settle on the

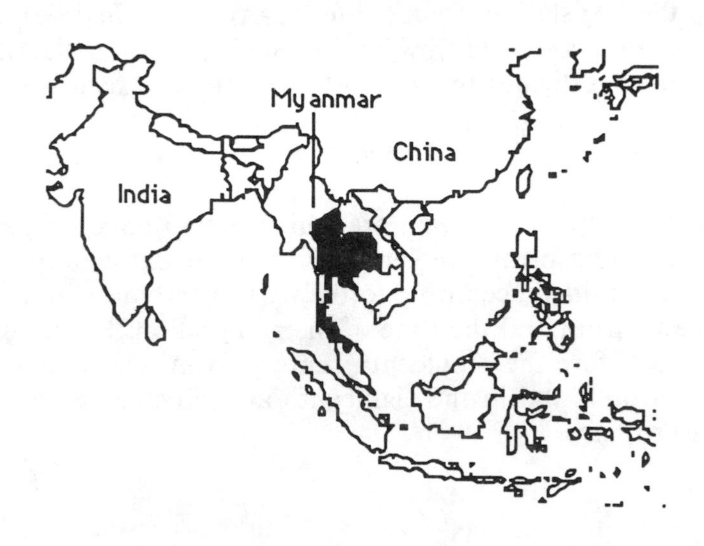

flood plains of the Chao Phraya and Mekong rivers of southeast Asia. Thailand remained a feudal state, expanding its territory at the expense of Lao, Burmese, and Cambodian societies and enriching its own government through trade agreements with Great Britain and France. Under the reign of King Mongkut (1851–1868), the feudal state ended. This king and his successor, Chulalongkorn, abolished slavery and established a form of government that included an advisory cabinet to the king.

Despite the economic and social progress begun by these two rulers, the monarchy was overthrown in 1932. Since that time Thailand (once Siam) has been under military rule except for short breaks in recent years, during which efforts have been made to form a constitution and to govern by it.

In the last half of the twentieth century Thailand has been moving toward an industrial economy. Still, nearly two-thirds of the people perform agricultural labor. These people provide one-sixth of the country's wealth, while the newer industries employ less than ten percent of the workers and produce nearly one-fourth of the wealth. As in other areas moving toward industrialization, Thailand has been experiencing mass movement of its people to the cities. The capital Bangkok, for example, grew nearly 25 percent in population from 1980 to 1989. City workers in Thailand produce textiles, automobile tires, cement, electronics parts (for example, computer chips), and products based on agriculture.

A major difficulty in industrial development in Thailand is a shortage of energy sources. To operate their industries, the Thais have depended on petroleum for energy. The country has some petroleum production of its own, but petroleum is still among Thailand's most costly imports.

Government Today

In the late 1980s and early 1990s, Thailand's government was weakened by accusations of corruption. One outcome of these accusations, and student and worker rebellions that followed, was a bloodless revolution in which the military ruler, General Chatichai, who had governed only since 1988, was replaced by General Sunthorn Kongsompong in 1991. These military leaders have been hampered in advancing the Thai economy by border disagreements with Laos and Cambodia and by trade union uprisings against the state-operated industries. An added burden since 1975 has been the Vietnam ref-

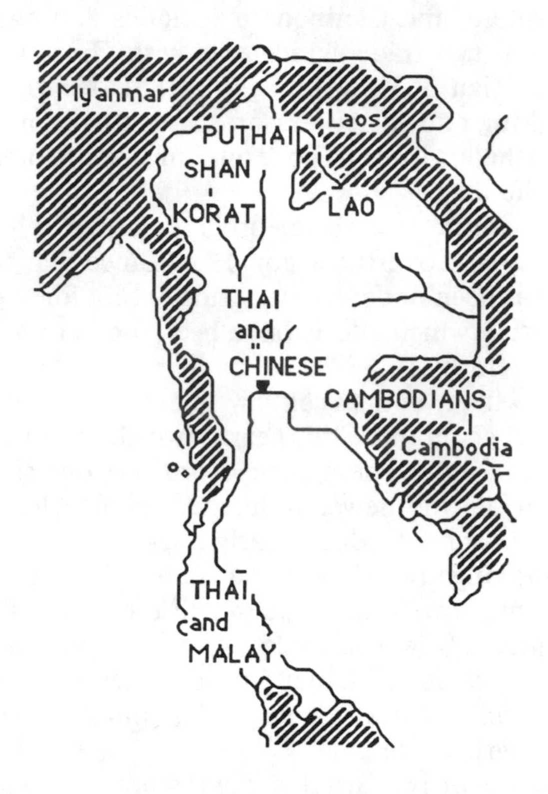

The dominant people of Thailand are Thais, people who changed their name to distinguish them from the Tai people of Laos and Vietnam.

ugees who fled communist rulers in that country and, in many cases, found a first asylum in Thailand.

Thailand is a constitutional monarchy. Officially, a king functions as head of state and of the armed forces. The king appoints a prime minister and Council of Ministers, who hold executive power. Legislative power is vested in a two-house National Assembly, a Senate (237 appointed members) and House of Representatives (357 popularly elected members).

Ethnic Makeup

The large cities and the rich agricultural land of the central Chao Phraya Valley are the homes of Thai and Chinese people. However,

Thailand is pot-shaped with a long "handle" extending down the Malay Peninsula. Malays join Thais in populating this panhandle. In the southeast Laos and Cambodians live near the borders of their countries, and in the north smaller groups of Puthai, Khorat, and Shan share the upper reaches of the river system.

VIETNAM

Socialist Republic of Vietnam

Population: 64,411,700 (1989 estimate).
Location: Southeast Asia, bordered by the South China Sea, China, Laos, and Cambodia.
Language: Vietnamese, an Asian language written using Roman script.
Principal cities: Ho Chi Minh City (Saigon), 3,169,195; Hanoi (capital), 1,088,862; Haiphong, 457,000; Da Nang, 371,000. Eleven other cities with populations greater than 100,000.

Political Background

Until the 1800s, the area that is now Vietnam was divided. The Trinh family controlled the north while the Nguyen family ruled the south. In 1802 the last Nguyen ruler conquered the north and reconquered the central region of the country, uniting the land into one kingdom. By 1820, this kingdom had gained in territory and strength. In that year, Minh Meng became ruler and under his leadership much of Cambodia fell to Vietnamese government.

European interests gained a solid foothold in 1862 when the French were able to command three provinces in the country. By 1882 French troops had conquered Tongking and declared their intention to "protect" Vietnam. By 1885, this intention had grown to complete French control. Eventually, Vietnam was included along with Cambodia in a greater French colony, French Indochina. French control of Vietnam continued through World War II in spite of resistance that prompted the French to imprison many Vietnamese leaders in the 1920s. In the midst of World War II, following some support by the United States, a Vietnamese leader, Ho Chi Minh,

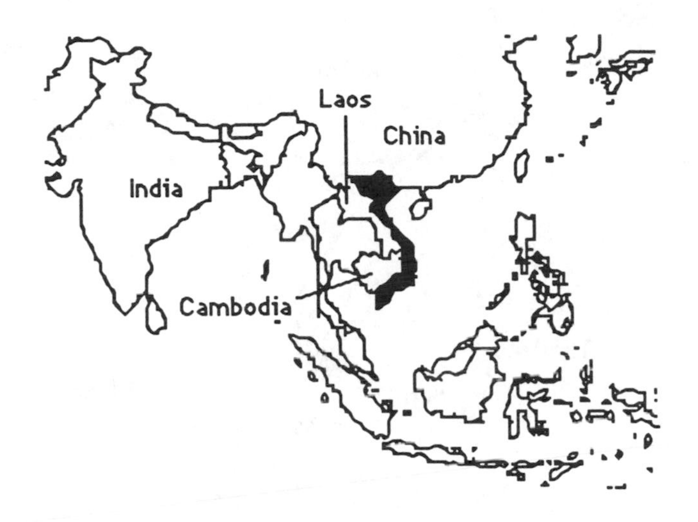

joined the Communist Party of China and formed its counterpart in his own country, the Viet Minh, to seek Vietnam's freedom from colonialism. At the end of the war this group was sufficiently strong to declare Vietnam's independence following the 1945 resignation of the king. The terms for ending the World War divided Vietnam. In the north the Chinese were chosen to take charge of the surrender of the Japanese, while British forces would do the same in the south. Ho Chi Minh remained in control in the north and the French were allowed to return to the south. From 1946 to 1954 these two forces were at war over control of the country. In 1954 an international conference officially divided Vietnam. Then, in 1956, French forces withdrew from the country. The United States chose to support the Vietnamese government in the south and, with the Chinese supporting the north, the civil war continued. There was afterwards great destruction of the country until 1973. In that year, the United States agreed to withdraw from Vietnam. By 1975, the government of the south collapsed and Vietnam was reunited under a communist government, organized after the Soviet pattern.

Government Today

Local People's Councils participate in the election of a National Assembly with only one political party allowed to participate. The National Assembly then selects from among its members a Council of State that, with the head of the communist party as chairman, acts

The several mountain tribes of central Vietnam are collectively known as Montagnards.

as a collective presidency to direct the country's affairs. There is also a Council of Ministers, named by the National Assembly, to draft law and budgets.

Following Vietnam's unification, relations between the government of Kampuchea (now renamed Cambodia) and the communist government at Hanoi deteriorated rapidly. The United States, South Vietnam, and North Vietnam had long held portions of Cambodia—the north to provide an avenue for transporting military goods, the south to thwart this movement. In 1977, Vietnamese troops made full-scale attacks on Cambodia, remaining there until 1989. Negotiations between these two countries has been a major concern. In 1989 international pressure convinced the Vietnamese to agree they would withdraw their troops from Cambodia. Meanwhile, the Vietnamese government has worked to collectivize the agriculture that provides work for 70 percent of the people and is 50 percent of the nation's wealth. Some Vietnamese, particularly in the south, have been uprooted from the towns and cities and moved to remote areas to clear land and expand the agricultural base of the country. Meanwhile, state-owned industry has also expanded so that it now makes up 27 percent of the national income. The rapid governmental changes in agriculture resulted in a drop in productivity in 1988, which led to a severe famine, felt most strongly in the north. Today's Vietnamese are still recovering from that disaster.

Ethnic Makeup

In the north of Vietnam 85 percent of the people are Chinese-Tai (Vietnamese) people who moved into the area long ago from northern China. They are joined by mountain tribes that include Tai, Chinese, Khmer, Tay, Muong, and Nung. The descendants of Chinese-Tai Vietnamese are also the majority in the south, where they share the land with Cambodians, mountain peoples of nearly 100 tribes (collectively called Montagnards), and a few Malays.

WESTERN SAMOA

Independent State of Western Samoa

Population: 164,000 (1990 estimate).
Location: Two large volcanic islands (Savai'i and Upolu) and seven smaller ones (five are uninhabited). The islands lie in the South Pacific 1,500 miles north and slightly east of New Zealand.
Languages: Samoan, the oldest existing Polynesian speech; English.
Principal city: Apia (capital), 33,170.

Political Background

Western Samoa is part of a cluster of islands inhabited by a Polynesian people who developed a distinctive culture in the isolated area and became known as Samoans (suh' moh ans). An eastern group of

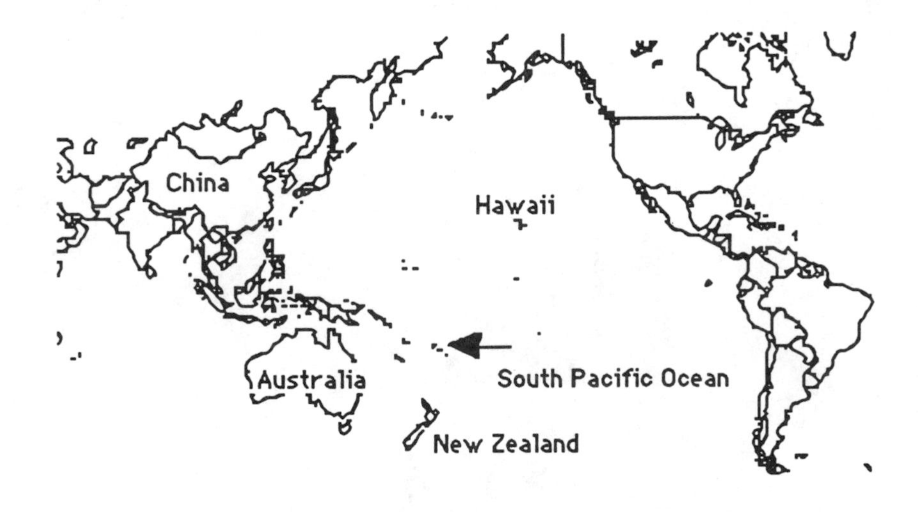

islands is governed by the United States and is called American Samoa. The western islands were for many years a German colony. They were occupied by New Zealanders in World War I and given to that country as a protectorate by the League of Nations in 1920. In 1946, following World War II, this protectorate was placed in trusteeship with New Zealand by the United Nations. The intent was for the western islands to develop the capability of self-government. Steady progress was made toward this objective until, in 1961, Western Samoa became an independent constitutional democracy.

However, this democracy presided over the traditional Samoan clan structure. The many clan chiefs are collectively called *Matai.* From among the Matai the first government of the new country drew two paramount chiefs to share the new title of head of state. Slowly, the new government has addressed the problem of unifying the country and of breaking down the traditional dominance of a ruling class that included only men. In 1990, Western Samoans adopted universal suffrage, the right of all adult citizens to vote. In 1991, the government appointed its first woman cabinet member. Also in these two years, the government felt sufficiently strong to return some rights of government to the many village councils. This action did, however, result in a split among members of the ruling cabinet.

Government Today

The power of the old clan system is seen in modern Western Samoa's government. Forty-seven members are elected to a national assembly, the Fono. Forty-five of these are elected from the Matai and two from among people who are not Samoan clan members. Political power has become so popular in recent years that a large number of new Matai titles have arisen to make more Samoans eligible for political positions. The Fono selects the Head of State. While the constitution calls for this selection every five years, the Head of State in the 1990s has been appointed for life. This Head appoints a prime minister, a person backed by the Fono. Also, a cabinet of eight ministers is selected from the Fono.

Western Samoans have close economic and political ties with New Zealand. Until recently, a Western Samoa citizen moving to New Zealand automatically became a full New Zealand citizen. New Zealand supported a weak Western Samoan economy in which two-thirds of the workers were in agriculture. In recent years, the government of Western Samoa has begun to build an industrial base for

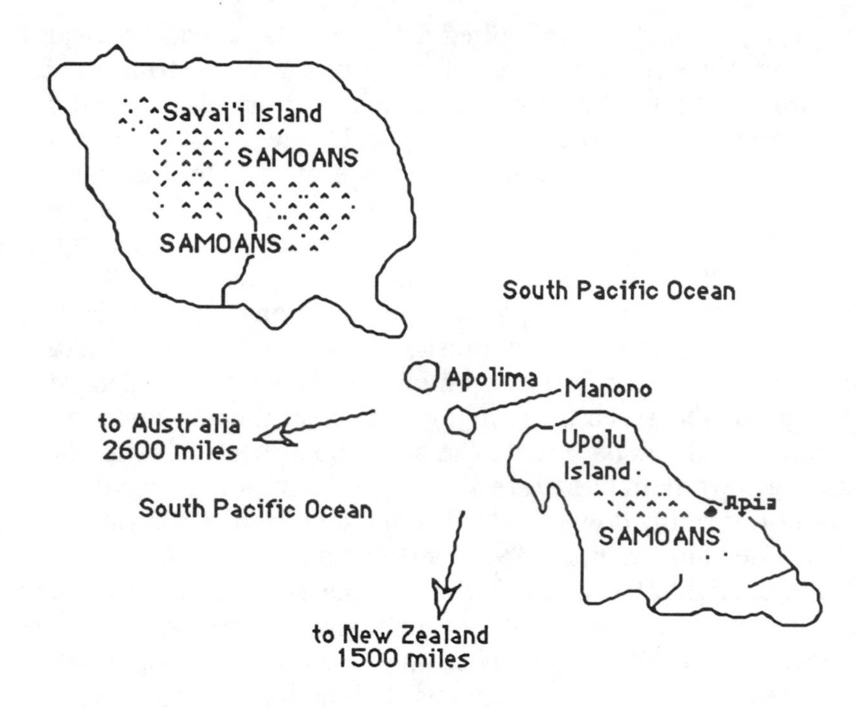

Most of the people of both Western Samoa and American Samoa are Samoans.

the economy that includes processing plants for coconut oil, copra, and such trade products as paints and concrete.

Ethnic Makeup

Occupied primarily by Polynesians, these Samoan islands are thought to have been the original home of various peoples who now inhabit islands further east. Most Samoans today are Christians.

Glossary

akam Tamil poems of love.

amera Iban stories.

amor proprio In the Philippines, "self-esteem."

ayan goren Javanese fried chicken.

balintawak A two-piece costume worn by Filipino women.

banjar A village cooperative society in Bali.

barang tagalong A long-tailed shirt worn frequently by men in the Philippines.

barangay A Filipino village.

bhakti A religious movement initiated by Tamils and centered around worship of the god Shiva.

bilik The family apartment in an Iban longhouse.

biraderi A Punjab group of households whose members descend from a single common ancestor.

Brahman A universal soul.

Brahmans A priest class seeking to become one with Brahman through self-sacrifice.

buramumin The lowest class among Japanese.

burga Head-to-foot gown worn by Punjabi Muslims.

chappati In Punjabi, "bread."

chappetis A round flat-bread eaten by Bengalis.

chownk A cup-shaped hat worn by a woman.

Cochin China The largely India-influenced southern section of Vietnam.

dagaba A dome-shaped structure used to house Buddhist relics of the past.

dalang Javanese puppeteer.

dhoti A long cotton cloth used as leg coverings by Hindu men.

godo-godo Javanese vegetable salad with a peanut oil sauce.

gopuram An identifying gateway to a Tamil temple.

Goumindang The government of Chiang Kai Shek on Taiwan.

Goyigama The Sinhalese class of landholders.

gulai kambing Mutton curry.

Gunung Agung The Balinese "great mountain," a religious site.

guru Teacher.

hiya Fear of bringing disgrace to the family.

hse Shirt extending below the knees worn by Karen women.

Hua ch'iai Chinese people who have migrated overseas to such countries as Malaysia.

jamdani Silk cloth woven or dyed in geometric patterns.

jatra A Bengalese folk opera.

Khalsa Ritual comparable to Christian baptism or confirmation that binds Sikh men to the five K's of their religion.

kamben Among Javanese, a male-female costume made of handwoven cloth wrapped around the waist or used as a headdress.

Kampuchea Cambodia.

kantha A Bengalese quilt depicting scenes of village life.

kesh, kangha, kara, kach, kirpan The five K's required of Sikh men who are khalsa (pure), meaning uncut hair, a comb, a steel bangle, knee-length shorts, and a dagger.

khaing An association of Shan villages.

Lapita A Samoan society and pottery style popular between 1500 and 1000 B.C.

lungi A Muslim male costume consisting of a length of colored cloth wrapped around the waist and extending to the ankle.

maharajah A king or prince of one of the native states of India, Bangladesh, or Pakistan.

Mahayana Buddhism The form of Buddhism found in China, Korea, Japan, and Vietnam that emphasizes that the way of salvation is for all people, not just for monks.

manipuvi The ballet-like dance of the Bengalis.

mantou Chinese dumplings.

martabak Javanese stuffed pancakes.

maskapan Balinese wedding festival.

molhalla A block of houses around a central courtyard in an older Punjab village.

Mons Early inhabitants of Myanmar who developed a great society in the south of the present country.

mufakat The outcome of musyawarah, a consensus opinion.

muong A Laotian political unit similar to a state.

musyawarah Literally "discussion"—the method of settlement of Javanese family or village disputes.

myothugy Ruler of a khaing.

Pathet Lao The political group formed originally to fight for liberation of Laos from colonialism.

poutu Iban songs.

puram Tamil poems of kings, warriors, and social behavior.

pwess Burmese plays based on ancient stories.

Pyo An ancient language of the Burmese.

raja A prince or chief in India and the Malay peninsula.

rudi A commons in an Iban longhouse.

saca Balinesian calandar based on the movements of the moon.

Sanskrit An ancient Indo-Aryan language that is the basis of many modern dialects.

sari The costume of Indian, Pakistani, or Bengali women consisting of a single long cloth wrapped around the waist to form a skirt and draped over the shoulders.

satrias Balinese ruling royalty claiming divine right to rule.

shade Dravidian term for human spirit.

sheik The leader of a Muslim family, village, or tribe.

Sikh A religious follower of Nassah Deo; many residing in the state of Punjab, India.

sing-sing Papuan celebration. For example, the three days of dancing and singing that commemorated the tenth anniversary of the founding of the country of Papua New Guinea.

sitio A Filipino cluster of homes of interdependent families.

stupa Dome-shaped Buddhist shrine.

Sufism A branch of Islam emphasizing self-knowledge and meditation.

tanju An open porch, part of the Iban longhouse.

Theravada Buddhism The "Way of the Elders." A form of Buddhism found largely in Sri Lanka, Myanmar, Thailand, Cambodia, and Laos emphasizing salvation through renunciation of worldly ways and made visible by monks who shave their heads and wear saffron robes.

tiwala In the Philippines, "trust."

Vailala Madness The name given to a Samoan cult arising in 1919 believing that ancestral spirits would return and bring with them "cargo" similar to the wealth brought to the islands by white men.

varnas Hindu castes.

Viet Minh The political group formed originally to fight for liberation of Vietnam from colonialism.

Wat A Buddhist place of worship, a pagoda.

wayang kulit Javanese theater featuring flat shadow puppets.

wayang topeng Javanese masked dance.

wesias Balinese military class.

wuku Balinese calendar based on temple festivals.

Yang di Pertuan Agong The supreme ruler of Malaysia.

Bibliography

Ayábe, Tsuneo, editor. *Education and Culture in a Thai Rural Community.* Fukuoka, Japan: Research Institute of Comparative Education and Culture, 1973.

Baglin, Douglass and David Moore. *People of the Dreamtime.* New York: Weatherhill, 1970.

Banavia, David. *The Chinese.* New York: Lippencott and Crowell, 1980.

Baxter, Craig. *Bangladesh: New Nation in an Old Setting.* Boulder: Westview Press, 1984.

Belo, Jane. *Traditional Balinese Culture.* New York: Columbia University Press, 1970.

Bernatzik, Hugo Adolph. *Akha and Miao.* New Haven: Human Relations Area Files, 1970.

Berndt, Ronald M. and Catherine H. *The Aboriginal Australians.* Sydney: Pitman Publishing Pty. Ltd., 1983.

Berndt, Ronald M. and Catherine H. *The World of the First Australians.* Sydney: Rigby Publishers, 1985.

Bixler, Norma. *Burma Profile.* New York: Praeger Publications, 1971.

Cameron, Nigel. *Hong Kong: The Cultured Pearl.* Hong Kong: Oxford University Press, 1978.

Cockcroft, John. *Isles of the South Pacific: Papua and New Guinea, New Britain, New Ireland, Bougainville.* Sydney: Angus & Robertson, 1968.

Covarrubias, Miguel. *Island of Bali.* New York: Alfred A. Knopf, 1956.

Cox, Harry. *The Australians: A Candid View from Down Under.* New York: Chilton Books, 1966.

Cummings, Joe et al. *China: A Travel Survival Kit.* Hawthorn, Australia: Lonely Planet Publications, Ltd., 1991.

Curth, Hank. *Papua New Guinea.* Brisbane, Australia: Jacaranda Press Pty. Ltd., 1968.

de Beauclair, Inez. *Tribal Cultures of Southwest China.* Taipei, Taiwan: Orient Culture Service, 1974.

Dreyer, June Teufel. *China's Forty Millions.* Cambridge: Harvard University Press, 1976.

Elkin, A. P. *The Australian Aboriginal Australians.* Sydney: Angus & Robertson Publishers, 1979.

Endacott, G. B. *Fragrant Harbor: A Short History of Hong Kong.* Hong Kong: Oxford University Press, 1968.

Fisk, E. K. and H. Osman-Rani, editors. *The Political Economy of Malaysia.* Kuala Lumpur: Oxford University Press, 1982.

Fisk, E. K., editor. *New Guinea on the Threshold.* Pittsburgh: University of Pittsburgh Press, 1968.

Geertz, Clifford. *The Religion of Java.* London: The Free Press of Glencoe, 1960.

Haas, David F. *Interaction in the Thai Bureaucracy: Structure, Culture, and Social Exchange.* Boulder: Western Press, 1979.

Holt, Claire. *Art in Indonesia: Continuities and Change.* New York: Cornell University Press, 1967.

Imber, W. and K. B. Cumberland. *Pacific Land Down Under.* London: Reed, 1973.

Israel, Samuel, ed. *Insight Guides: India.* Singapore: APA Publications, 1990.

Latourette, Kenneth Scott. *A Short History of the Far East*, fourth edition. New York: Macmillan, 1964.

Lyons, Elizabeth. *Thai Traditional Painting*. Bangkok: Siva Phorn Ltd. Partnership, 1963.

Macciocchi, Maria Antonietta. *Daily Life in Revolutionary China*. New York: Monthly Review Press, 1972.

McGregor, Craig. *Profiles of Australia*. London: Hodder and Stoughton, 1966.

Metge, Joan. *The Maori of New Zealand*. London: Routledge & Kegan Paul, 1967.

Mi Mi Khaing. *Burmese Family*. Bloomington: Indiana University Press, 1962.

Mitchell, A. *The Half-Gallon, Quarter-Acre, Pavlova Paradise*. Wellington, New Zealand: Whitcombe and Tombs, 1972.

Moser, Leo J. *The Chinese Mosaic: The Peoples and Provinces of China*. Boulder: Westview, 1985.

Mulder, Niels. *Everyday Life in Thailand*. Bangkok: Drang Kamol, 1979.

Palmier, L. H. *Indonesia*. New York: Walker and Company, 1965.

Percival Spear, editor. *The Oxford History of India*. London: Oxford University Press, 1958.

Raghavan, C. Vira. *Tamil Nadu*. New Delhi, India: Publications Division, Ministry of Information, Government of India, 1973.

Rajadhon, Phya Anuman. *Introducing Cultural Thailand in Outline*. Thai Cultural New Series No. 1. Bangkok: The Fine Arts Department, 1960.

S. Husin Ali, *The Malays: Their Problems and Future*. Kuala Lumpur: Heinemann Asia, 1982.

Sandhu, Ranbir Singh. "The Sikh Problem," an article written for the Sikh Religious and Educational Trust, 1988. (Dr. Ranbir Singh Sandhu is a professor of engineering at Ohio State University.)

Sastri, K. A. Nilakanta. *A History of South India.* Madras: Oxford University Press, 1955.

Schell, Orville. *To Get Rich Is Glorious: China in the 80s.* New York: Pantheon Books, 1984.

Sih, Paul E. T. *Taiwan in Modern Times.* New York: St. John's University Press, 1973.

Sinclair, Keith. *A History of New Zealand.* New York: Penguin, 1969.

Storey, Robert. *Taiwan: A Travel Survival Kit.* Hawthorne, Australia: Lonely Planet Publications, 1990.

Tandon, Prakash. *Punjabi Century 1857–1947.* Berkeley and Los Angeles: University of California Press, 1968.

Taylor, John G. and Andrew Turton, editors. *Sociology of "Developing Societies": Southeast Asia.* Houndmills, England: Macmillan Education, 1988.

Trager, Frank N. and William J. Koenig. *Burmese Sit-Tans, 1764–1826.* Tucson: University of Arizona Press, 1979.

Trager, Helen G. *We the Burmese, Voices from Burma.* New York, Frederick A. Praeger, 1969.

Tully, Mark and Jacob Satish. *Amritsar: Mrs. Gandhi's Last Battle.* London: Jonathan Cape, Ltd., 1985.

Wingstedt, Richard et al. *Malay Proverbs.* London: Murray, 1950.

Winstedt, Richard. *The Malays: A Cultural History.* London: Routledge and Kegan Paul Ltd., 1961.

Zainu'ddin, Ailsa. *A Short History of Indonesia.* Melbourne: Cassell Australia, 1968.

Index